Independent Music in Russia

This book explores Russian independent music – *nezavisimaia muzyka* – in a time of profound transformations in Russian society, looking especially at the mutual influence between music and the socio-political context in which it was created. Contrary to what is commonly believed, the book argues that *nezavisimaia muzyka*, as a widespread form of non-state-sponsored culture, was not necessarily oppositional to the Russian state; instead, it was rooted in identity quests that could overlap with some aspects of the official narrative as they could mock, disrupt and refashion others.

The book demonstrates that Russian independent music is considerably more than the creation, appreciation and dissemination of sounds. For the practitioners, to get involved in the scene is to participate in the construction of cultural legitimacy, imagined communities and national identity, involving values that can be cosmopolitan, "Western", conservative, supposedly "Russian" and often a mixture of all these. In addition, the book examines Russian independent music's interaction with Western and global trends and assesses its successes and failures in conquering a niche in foreign markets.

This book will be of interest to scholars of Russian culture, media and politics, as well as to scholars of popular music, sociology, national identity and Russia–West relations.

Marco Biasioli is a Lecturer in Russian and East European Studies at the University of Manchester, UK. His interests include Soviet, Russian, Ukrainian and Belarusian popular music, culture-power interactions, Russian literature and nationhood.

BASEES/Routledge Series on Russian and East European Studies
Series editors:
Sociology and anthropology: Judith Pallot (Chair), *University of Oxford*
Economics and business: Richard Connolly, *University of Birmingham*
Media and cultural studies: Birgit Beumers, *University of Aberystwyth*
Politics and international relations: Andrew Wilson, *School of Slavonic and East European Studies, University College London*
History: Matt Rendle, *University of Exeter*

This series is published on behalf of BASEES (the British Association for Slavonic and East European Studies). The series comprises original, high-quality, research-level work by both new and established scholars on all aspects of Russian, Soviet, post-Soviet and East European Studies in humanities and social science subjects.

152. **The Economics of Growth in Russia**
Overcoming the Poverty Trap
Ararat L.Osipian

153. **Religious Life in the Late Soviet Union**
From Survival to Revival (1960s-1980s)
Edited by Barbara Martin and Nadezhda Beliakova

154. **Putinism – Post-Soviet Russian Regime Ideology**
Mikhail Suslov

156. **The Political Economy of Hungarian Authoritarian Populism**
Capitalists without the right kind of capital
Samuel Rogers

157. **The Russian Revolution of 1917 – Memory and Legacy**
Edited by Carol S. Leonard, Daniel Orlovsky, and Jurej Petrov

158. **Modern Russian Cinema as a Battleground in Russia's Information War**
Edited by Alexander Rojavin and Helen Haft

159. **Independent Music in Russia**
Escapism, Patriotism and Protest (2008–2022)
Marco Biasioli

For a full list of available titles please visit: https://www.routledge.com/BASEES-Routledge-Series-on-Russian-and-East-European-Studies/book-series/BASEES

Independent Music in Russia
Escapism, Patriotism and Protest (2008–2022)

Marco Biasioli

LONDON AND NEW YORK

First published 2025
by Routledge
4 Park Square, Milton Park, Abingdon, Oxon OX14 4RN

and by Routledge
605 Third Avenue, New York, NY 10158

Routledge is an imprint of the Taylor & Francis Group, an informa business

© 2025 Marco Biasioli

The right of Marco Biasioli to be identified as author of this work has been asserted in accordance with sections 77 and 78 of the Copyright, Designs and Patents Act 1988.

All rights reserved. No part of this book may be reprinted or reproduced or utilised in any form or by any electronic, mechanical, or other means, now known or hereafter invented, including photocopying and recording, or in any information storage or retrieval system, without permission in writing from the publishers.

Trademark notice: Product or corporate names may be trademarks or registered trademarks, and are used only for identification and explanation without intent to infringe.

British Library Cataloguing-in-Publication Data
A catalogue record for this book is available from the British Library

Library of Congress Cataloging-in-Publication Data
Names: Biasioli, Marco, author.
Title: Independent music in Russia : escapism, patriotism and protest (2008-2022) / Marco Biasioli.
Description: Abingdon, Oxon ; New York : Routledge, 2025. | Series: BASEES/Routledge series on Russian and East European studies | Includes bibliographical references and index.
Identifiers: LCCN 2024062060 (print) | LCCN 2024062061 (ebook) | ISBN 9781032164700 (hardback) | ISBN 9781032164717 (paperback) | ISBN 9781003248699 (ebook)
Subjects: LCSH: Alternative rock music--Political aspects--Russia (Federation)--History--21st century. | Alternative rock music--Social aspects--Russia (Federation)--History--21st century. | Music and state--Russia (Federation)--History--21st century.
Classification: LCC ML3917.R8 B53 2025 (print) | LCC ML3917.R8 (ebook) | DDC 306.4/84260947--dc23/eng/20250114
LC record available at https://lccn.loc.gov/2024062060
LC ebook record available at https://lccn.loc.gov/2024062061

ISBN: 978-1-032-16470-0 (hbk)
ISBN: 978-1-032-16471-7 (pbk)
ISBN: 978-1-003-24869-9 (ebk)

DOI: 10.4324/9781003248699

Typeset in Times New Roman
by KnowledgeWorks Global Ltd.

To Ivan.

Contents

Acknowledgements	*viii*
Note on transliteration	*ix*
Note on translation	*x*
Previously published material	*xi*
Introduction	1
1 The history, structures and politics of *nezavisimaia muzyka*	27
2 "We also can. We're not worse": The Anglophone Wave (2008–2012)	69
3 "I live in Russia and I'm not scared": Russia's conservative turn, the new Russian Wave and metamodernism (2012–2018)	103
4 *Patrioprotest*: The ambiguous resistance of *nezavisimaia muzyka* (2018–2022)	153
5 From the margins and back?: The transnational spread of *nezavisimaia muzyka*	213
Conclusions	261
Index	*268*

Acknowledgements

I would like to thank my wife Emily, my family and my close friends for providing the emotive foundation on which my professional life is built.

I am profoundly indebted to a lot of people, but specifically: the MHRA for their generous funding for the writing of this book; Vera Tolz for her expertise, pastoral care and unwavering faith that this book could be completed; Stephen Hutchings for his insightful comments and suggestions; all the staff at REES, Manchester for their support; Polly McMichael for her mentorship during my postdoc; my PhD supervisors Rachel Platonov and Barbara Lebrun for their guidance; my MA supervisor Barbara Ronchetti and all the staff at the Department of Slavonic Studies at Sapienza University of Rome for infusing me with passion and curiosity about Russia and its culture when I was a student. I also want to thank Katerina Pavlidi and Isa Jacobs for reading and commenting on some of the chapters of the book.

I owe an immense deal to all the Russian music practitioners I met during my fieldwork – their voices have built this work. I also want to thank Sergio, Julia, Maria, Egor, Anton, Ded, Serezha, Masha, Nikita and Slava for their openness, friendship and encouragement during my research in Russia. Credits go to Aleksandr Gorbachev for his expertise, which has informed a section of Chapter 4.

Steve Smith deserves special mention for the countless conversations about culture, often conducted in lockdown-induced spaces – without him, this book would not exist.

The writing of this book was funded by the Modern Humanities Research Association's Postdoctoral Scholarship in Modern Languages.

Note on transliteration

The book follows the Library of Congress Romanisation for Russian in its simplified version (e.g., й = i; э = e). As an exception, Russian band names have been transliterated according to how the individuals/bands themselves write them in Latin script (e.g., Pompeya, not Pompeia; Ploho, not Plokho). The same criteria have been applied to those names of Russian personalities transliterated in the Anglophone world in a different, now "traditional", way (e.g., Artemy Troitsky, not Artemii Troitskii).

Note on translation

All song lyrics are translated from Russian by the author, except Pompeya's song lyrics and Coockoo's song lyrics, which were written directly in English.

Previously published material

Some of the published material below has been reused or reworked in the book:

Biasioli, M. 2020. '"We Also Can. We're Not Worse": The Anglophone Wave in Russian Indie Music (Indi), 2008–2012'. *Popular Music*, 39, 2, pp. 294–311.

Biasioli, M. 2021. 'Russophone or Anglophone? The Politics of Identity in Contemporary Russian Indie Music'. *Europe-Asia Studies*, 73, 4, pp. 673–90.

Biasioli, M. 2022. 'Between the Global and the Intimate: Russian Popular Music and Language Choice'. *Modern Language Review*, 117, 2, pp. 164–90.

Biasioli, M. 2023. 'Songwashing: Russian Popular Music, Distraction, and Putin's Fourth Term'. *The Russian Review*, 82, 4, pp. 682–704.

Introduction

"We've fucked up everything" wrote a Russian music critic in a Telegram post a few days after Russia's full-scale invasion of Ukraine. They referred to the independent music community, of which they had been part all their adult life. "Imagine that you built a sandcastle on the beach, for fun", they explained, "and the castle turned out to be so beautiful that other vacationers come to take selfies with it. [...] And then comes the guardian of the beach, says 'it is not allowed' and smashes the castle with one kick". The metaphors could be interpreted based on the context: the beautiful castle stood for the world that independent practitioners created in the 2010s; the other vacationers referred to the listeners, both domestic and foreign; the guardian of the beach represented the Russian state. The post was immediately shared by music professionals across their media channels. It became the requiem to the independent music community of the 2010s, a world that had been shattered by political events beyond its control and was lost forever.

This book is the story of that world. It is the story of a community that thought it could exist within, and parallel to, an increasingly authoritarian and repressive state, until the state tore it apart. In the aftermath of the full-scale invasion, among declarations of guilt and despair, many industry workers emigrated. According to the newspaper *Kommersant*, 30% of performers left the country or interrupted their activities between February and September 2022 (Lebedeva 2022). Out of the 42 practitioners I interviewed between 2016 and 2019, only half remained in Russia after the full-scale invasion. The independent community underwent a tectonic shift, and the analysis of the specificities of such reconfiguration will be no doubt the task of future studies.

Since the start of Putin's third term in 2012, musicians had indeed been affected by a sense of civil powerlessness reminiscent of Soviet times, but such dramatic turn of events was not accounted for. Powerlessness had until 2022 concerned only the political, in the sense of state institutions and the possibility of their transformation. Such political incapacity had, like in the late Soviet period, the effect of enhancing independent creative activity as a major locus of sociability, enthusiasm and excitement. Unlike the late Soviet period, however, independent practitioners were also able to perform their activities in the open, in venues as well as on the internet. Treading the interiorised line between critically commenting on their present and avoiding clashes with power, independent creators were relatively free to

DOI: 10.4324/9781003248699-1

2   Independent Music in Russia

operate within, and shape, their own art world. The majority of them did not turn a blind eye to the elephant in the room – in fact, through sound, they increasingly reflected on and commented on the authoritarian derive of Russian politics across the 2010s – but the danger it represented for the independent industry was underestimated. Hardly any practitioner expected it to end the way it did.

The changes in the zeitgeist were clearly visible in and through independent music production. In early 2012, Pompeya, an Anglophone band from Moscow and undoubtedly the trendiest group in the Russian indie soundscape of that time, released the video for "Slow", a single later included in the second edition of their debut album *Tropical*. The video was set in sunny Los Angeles, and featured the band members engaging in carefree banter, relaxing on the beach, walking by the seafront and observing skaters. The airy synthesiser, the funky rhythm of the guitar and the catchy groove of bass and drums created an atmosphere of cheerfulness, which was complemented by lyrics expressing a forthcoming change in a relationship: "We're more than good friends/Come and sew my heart/Find a child in me/Let's have a good time". In late 2019 Shortparis, a post-punk band from St. Petersburg and arguably the most influential band in the independent panorama of the late 2010s, produced the video for "Tak Zakalialas Stal" (Thus the Steel Was Tempered), the third single from their eponymous 2019 album.[1] The video was set in a military camp, and featured a young trainee committing a series of brutal and senseless murders. In an escalation of violence, the soldier kills several people with his bare hands before performing hara-kiri. Heavy and obsessive drumming patterns, dissonant guitars and distorted synthesisers accompanied the images, while singer Nikolai Komiagin wailed in an erratic and overdramatic falsetto: "Thus eternity is built/Thus the table is set/Thus the doctor looks at the enemy/While giving an injection/Thus the steel was tempered".

The aesthetic differences between the two videos were profound: the English language made way for Russian; bright melodies and arrangements were replaced by minor and gloomy progressions; relaxed ambiances were substituted by a sense of impending menace; palms and beaches were supplanted by military camps and Soviet panel-houses; the sentient "I" turned into a subjectless and cold narration of facts, the love song into a sinister tale, the heart into steel, the "good time" into an eternity of enemies. The dissimilarities between Pompeya and Shortparis did not simply pinpoint these two bands' artistic choices but rather epitomised a change in values and meanings in Russian independent music (henceforth, also: *nezavisimaia muzyka*).[2] This change, in turn, evidenced deeper and wider political and cultural transformations in the way Russian musicians perceived their country: from cosmopolitan and outward-looking to a militarising state. Even though only seven years elapsed between the two videos, their different aesthetics talked of different socio-political milieux. Entwined with their times, the songs reflected and responded to the evolution of Russia as a whole in the 2010s.

This book presents three central arguments. Firstly, for the participants involved in the scene, *nezavisimaia muzyka* was considerably more than the creation, appreciation and dissemination of sounds: to participate in the scene was to construct cultural legitimacy, autonomy, (imagined) communities and philosophical

Introduction   3

values, be these cosmopolitan, "Western", conservative or supposedly "Russian". Because *nezavisimaia muzyka* was entangled with, rather than merely opposed to, Russia's ever-changing quest for national identity, it was also usually interactive – rather than just embattled – with official narratives of nationhood. The values it proposed were not entirely in conflict with the state, as they were to some degree influenced by top-down processes of nation-building at any given point across the period studied.

Secondly, the ways in which participants perceived their roles and aims in the music industry, and more broadly in society, interacted not only with the internal political milieu, but also with the evolution of Russia-West power relations. As we will see in the course of the book, important cultural occurrences in Russian music culture and society such as the "Anglophone Wave" (2008–2012), the Pussy Riot affair (2012) and the "New Russian Wave" (2014–2022) emerged at the intersection of local and international political developments. These comprised Dmitrii Medvedev's illusory liberalism (2008–2012), Putin's shift towards neo-traditionalism and nationalism (2012–2018), the crisis with Ukraine, the annexation of Crimea and the escalation in international tensions thereafter (2014–2022). In any phase, Russia's Other – "the West" – participated in shaping the official discourses of Russia's nationhood. The consequences of such political interactions (e.g., Western sanctions and Russia's increased isolation from, and confrontation with, "the West" after 2014) trickled down to independent practitioners in ways beyond their control but that nonetheless influenced musical fashions. In other words, practitioners applied their agency and creativity within the framework set by these new challenges, at the nexus between the changing global (as well as domestic) realities and the intimate.

Thirdly, if placed in a broader historical perspective, the discourses of *nezavisimaia muzyka* were largely inherited discourses around the idea of the nation. The debates over bands like Pompeya or Shortparis in the music community of the 2010s, for instance, showed comparable patterns to those between Westernisers and Slavophiles that animated Russia's intellectual history in the nineteenth century, which centred around following or not the path of Western Europe, pursuing or undoing Peter the Great's Westernising reforms and finding a distinctive way for Russia's development. Boiled down to their core, then and now, these discussions were about imagining and projecting notions of what Russia is or could be, vis-à-vis "the West" on one side and the repressive state on the other. Then and now, of course, there was no single vision of "Russianness": ideas of the country were multifaceted, contested, nebulous, malleable, imbued with a good degree of essentialism and imbricated in the context of – and as a response to – imperial, nationalist, post-colonial or decolonial agendas (Tolz 2020). In short, *nezavisimaia muzyka* replicated, on a smaller scale but with stunning similarity, the long-standing discursive fluctuations about Russia's relationship with the West and with its own national identity.

The exploration of these key themes extends well beyond the immediate realm of music and should be, I believe, of interest to scholars working on post-Soviet history, politics, society, culture and their interactions, as well as on resistance,

4   *Independent Music in Russia*

identity, fan communities and art worlds. Countless studies have of course analysed the political, societal and cultural evolutions in recent Russian history, be these concerning official cultural policies, globalisation, nationalism, imperialism, political protest, media strategies and relationship with the West.[3] Crucial emphasis has been placed on Russia's shift, from a quasi-democratic country tentatively self-identifying as Western in the 2000s, to a conservative, autocratic and imperial reality in the 2010s. As studies of contemporary Russian culture have explained,[4] this reconfiguration affected cultural producers – including independent ones – in the ways in which they positioned themselves within the new political climate and in the aesthetics they constructed. Protest against the regime tended to be vocalised subtly and indirectly, in contrast with the frontal confrontation performed by the art collective Voina or Pussy Riot in the early 2010s (though explicit forms of dissent also continued) or became entangled with patriotic sentiments that eventually had more than one point in common with Kremlin-endorsed values. In the context of Russian popular music, pioneering works like Cushman (1995), Pilkington et al. (2002), Urban and Evdokimov (2004) and Beumers (2005), which investigated Soviet/Russian rock, music taste among post-Soviet youth, Russian blues and pop (music) culture respectively, though extremely valuable in opening the field, dealt with pre-Putin contexts. Studies on the relationship between rock and the state (Steinholt 2005; Steinholt and Wickström 2009; Rogatchevski and Steinholt 2016, McMichael 2019) have complicated earlier binary approaches to Soviet and Russian music of the 1980s and 1990s (Troitsky 1988; Ryback 1990) by showing high levels of political ambivalence among the participants, though they have mostly analysed *russkii rok* or the evolution of Soviet rock in the post-Soviet era.[5] Contemporary literature on local independent music scenes worldwide has often placed the accent on the character of resistance – political as well as commercial – that independent and do-it-yourself (DIY) music allegedly possesses.[6] This, as I will try to demonstrate in this book, may not be a fitting template for the study of the Russian case. In this regard, recent scholarship on Russian punk (McMichael 2013; Steinholt 2012a, 2012b; Gololobov et al. 2014) and St. Petersburg's alternative scene (Wickström 2014) has provided a significant entry point into Russian independent music communities, showing their internal nuances in terms of political (dis)affiliation, authenticity, national identity and relationship with *russkii rok* and Western music. However, these studies have examined events up to 2012, leaving uncovered most of the last decade and how its radical cultural and political transformations influenced independent music production. This book, therefore, seeks to advance existing scholarship by looking at the period 2008–2022, in order to study the interrelationship between *nezavisimaia muzyka* and the changes in Russian society, unveiling how the two informed each other in this crucial period, as well as framing such changes in a wider transnational context.

To explore the abovementioned issues, this book asks the following questions: (1) How did Russian independent music interact with official discourse? (2) How did it react to the changes in the political zeitgeist? (3) How did it interrogate ideas of national identity? (4) What happened when it spread beyond Russia's borders? By investigating these questions, the book has the following four aims: (a) To offer,

Introduction 5

for the first time, a comprehensive analysis of the aspirations, thoughts, actions, utterances and tensions of the communities involved in Russia's independent music scene between 2008 and 2022, and to frame the evolution of such discourses chronologically. (b) To provide an account of the interplay between top-down and bottom-up narratives in Russia's recent past, using as examples communities that professed to be autonomous from the state. (c) To complicate notions of language choice, independence and resistance in independent music. (d) To embed *nezavisimaia muzyka* in a global framework.

Despite the commonality of intent in creating an autonomous and culturally significant space, the independent music community was by no means a homogeneous entity. Of course, for a scene to gather a critical mass of participants and emerge as a noticeable, sizeable phenomenon, cooperation among practitioners from different subgenres is needed. If that is lacking, practitioners may end up building self-contained, "clustered solidarities" (Gololobov et al. 2014, 198–203) not in communication with each other even if they are in the same city (in Gololobov et al.'s case, punk micro-scenes in St. Petersburg). But together with cooperation, conflict was often also at play, particularly in relation to how this cultural space should sound. The struggle for cultural legitimacy in *nezavisimaia muzyka* represented not only the struggle between groups of participants with different ideas but also reflected a linguistic clash between English and Russian. In turn, these two languages came to be seen as embodiments of two different sets of values: the former of openness, modernity and global participation; the latter of tradition, distinctiveness and cultural pride. However dichotomous or reductive this opposition, it was strongly felt – and actively constructed – by the participants of the scene.

The case studies analysed in the following chapters are all crucial works from popular independent artists, invested with significance and authority by the community of tastemakers and audiences around them, and contributing decisively to the evolution of the *nezavisimaia muzyka* scene in the timeframe selected. For instance: Pompeya were the main exponents of the Anglophone Wave; Buerak and Pasosh represented the pinnacle of the 'New Russian Wave' (*novaia russkaia volna*); Shortparis and Monetochka were very successful artists both commercially and critically, featuring in independent webzines and liberal media outlets as well as on the state-controlled TV channel Pervyi Kanal (Channel One); Khaski was one of the main rappers of the 2010s, and his legal troubles garnered nationwide attention; Ic3peak were one of the sensations of Russian popular music in 2018; Manizha was Russia's Eurovision representative in 2021.

I have chosen the timeframe 2008–2022 for cultural and political reasons. In independent music, 2008 signalled the beginning of an unprecedentedly successful trajectory for a consistent community of individuals united by the intent to westernise the soundscape of Moscow and, broadly, Russia. In the course of the 2010s, the priorities of such community veered towards reaffirmation of ideas of Russianness and projections of locally identifiable cultural codes, but the community itself expanded in size as well as in cultural and commercial capital. February 2022, on the contrary, marked a huge blow to the community, prompting a downsizing of activities and a mass relocation of practitioners, as well as casting uncertainty upon

6 *Independent Music in Russia*

the future of *nezavisimaia muzyka*, both domestically and in exile. Politically, this period is contained within Medvedev's election as president in 2008 and the start of the full-scale war in Ukraine in 2022. The significance of Medvedev's presidency is now downplayed in scholarly literature as nothing more than a liberal façade, but for the protagonists of the Muscovite cultural scene in the thick of the events, Medvedev represented a period of positive transformation, flourishing, anticipation. Such perceptions and hopes were thwarted by Putin's third election in 2012, with all that this entailed: the violent suppression of protest, the Pussy Riot affair and the drift from unstable democracy into autocracy. Due to the contrast with what came after, the Medvedev's era would be remembered, perhaps for some time to come, as the last window of opportunity for Russia to follow a path of democratisation and rapprochement with Europe. On the other end of the timeframe, 2022 represented the conclusion of what was initiated in 2012 and particularly enhanced in 2014: the confrontation with the West, the efforts at the multipolar world, the renewed imperial claims, the internal tightening of control, censorship and repression. The state system turned into an invasive organism of fear and violent self-legitimation after being a "spin dictatorship" for most of the 2010s (Guriev and Treisman 2022), characterised by staged pluralism, democracy simulation and selective punishment of dissent.

Here I should clarify what I mean by "state" (in Russian: *gosudarstvo*). Following the work of Stephen Hutchings and Mark Galeotti among others, I do not identify the "Russian state" before February 2022 as a homogeneous and strictly vertical governing unit, but as a vast and complex entity characterised also by confusion and inconsistency (Hutchings 2022, 21–24). Despite the country's authoritarian chain of command, state actors from the Kremlin on down through regional representatives, municipal authorities, the state-controlled media, as well as state-aligned institutions such as the Orthodox Church, did not always speak or act in unison (Galeotti 2017, 3). As far as independent music goes, of course, the Kremlin did not have the resources to directly survey, index, and control every practitioner and their activities at the grassroots level. Similarly, the various components of the state apparatus rarely engineered control through lengthy machinations; rather, they adapted and improvised according to the circumstances at play. This necessarily involved collaborating with, or co-opting, non-governmental cultural actors from below. These relationships were, on the part of state organs, often cynical and "parasitic", but they were nonetheless fundamental in shaping, reinforcing, or projecting narratives of nationhood, and in managing the "chaos" of internal multi-voicedness (Strukov 2016; Galeotti 2017). After 2012, grassroots narratives did not necessarily conform to what was often taken to be the neo-traditionalist, "official" line of Russia "the state"; rather, they inflected Russia "the country" (its history, traditions, cultures, language, etc.) in multiple ways, including resistance to the status quo, creating a "layering of performance upon performance and the need for each new performance layer to bracket, respond to, and assert ownership over, prior layers" (Hutchings 2022, 173). Subversive bottom-up narratives of nationhood, like in the case of Manizha described in Chapter 4, were also appropriated by state institutions, commodified for international liberal audiences and refashioned

Introduction 7

as patriotic for domestic ones. Thus, rather than strictly top-down and monolithic, a plastic, "multidirectional, ambiguous, and often contradictory" system of state influence was in operation (Strukov 2016, 33).

Lastly, I should explain what is meant in this book by "nation" and the process of its articulation – "national identity", or "nationhood" (I use the latter two interchangeably). Russia is a complicated case from the onset. It is the largest country in the world, populated by a myriad of ethnicities, languages, religions, cultures. Russians have two words for referring to themselves: *russkii* (more narrowly ethnic) and *rossiiskii* (citizen of Russia, regardless of ethnicity). The Russian, as a language, is *russkii iazyk*. Over the eras (Imperial, Soviet and post-Soviet), Russian cultural figures have thought of their nation in multiple ways (Tolz 2001; 2020), from purely ethnic to civilisational, from civic to imperial, and this has caused a high degree of "historical indeterminacy" (Byford et al. 2020, 16) in today's conceptions of identity. Together with this, intellectuals have often refused to see Russia as an empire, or have seen the empire as a nation-state (Tolz 2001), in different (in their view, more humane) terms in comparison to Western powers, against which they have moved accusations of colonial exploitation and violence (while ignoring theirs).[7] What we might understand today as post-colonial or decolonial discourses against West-centrism were strongly articulated in Russia already in the mid-nineteenth century (Tolz 2020). Such discourses resurfaced again in the post-Soviet era, and were finally appropriated in the 2010s by the political elite to conceal Russia's own imperial and colonial actions, including the full-scale invasion of Ukraine (Ivakhiv 2022; Engström 2022; Tolz and Hutchings 2023; Durdiyeva 2023). All the above ingredients – national, linguistic, supranational, multinational, civilisational, imperial and so on – have contributed to shape a "deliberate confusion [for the Russians] of Russia's national and state boundaries" (Tolz 2001, 164), a confusion reiterated by president Putin himself, who called Russia both a "civilisation-state" (*gosudarstvo-tsivilizatsiia*) and a "civilisation [that] has no borders", based, rather than on territory, on "people" (Putin 2023). This confusion, however, provides fertile ground for state institutions to constantly switch between definitional criteria according to the circumstances at play. The commonplace idea that the empire impeded the formation of a strong national identity in Russia (Hosking 1998) is true only insofar as we do not consider the flexibility, multiplicity and often overlap of understandings of Russian nationhood.[8]

In her historical analysis of Russian national identity, Tolz (2001, 237–238) summarised five criteria of Russians' self-identification, which she saw as influential in the post-Soviet intellectual debates: (1) the *union identity*, defined by an imperial mission or by the task of creating a supranational state within the borders of the former USSR; (2) the *Slavic identity*, which sees Russians as a nation of all Eastern Slavs, including Belarus and Ukraine; (3) the *linguistic identity*, whereby Russians are a community of Russian-speakers, irrespective of their ethnicity; (4) the *racial identity*, through which Russians are defined by blood ties and physical features (the radical, exclusive *russkii* aspect); and (5) the *civic identity*, which comprises all the citizens of the Russian Federation, regardless of their ethnic or cultural background (the *rossiiskii* factor), united by loyalty to the political institutions. To this,

8 *Independent Music in Russia*

we can add: (6) the *ethnic identity*, that is Russians as defined narrowly as a nation (the *russkii* factor) united by a common cultural and psychological make-up; and (7) the *civilisational identity*, based on the idea of Russia as a standalone, unique cultural and political reality formed by the historical intermingling of different people, which demands and expects a sphere of influence in the geopolitical game.

The identity that most of the independent musicians interviewed in this book would refer to when they talked about Russia is *civic* minus the loyalty to state institutions. On the one hand, independent practitioners often referred to Russia as a country (*strana*), as a nation in the broader sense, consisting of multiple cultures, religions and peoples united by common layers of past and present and by equal rights.[9] Since practitioners viewed ethnicity as a blurred, ephemeral category (many of them, indeed, have mixed backgrounds), they tended not to think of the nation on narrow (*russkii*) ethnic terms, but on broader *rossiiskii* ones, as "participating citizenry" (Hosking 1998, xx). On the other hand, one of the common features of this participating citizenry was a negative attitude towards the institutions governing the country, meaning the state. While the state partly relies on popular disapproving outlooks for its survival, as they provide basis for social venting and bonding (Herzfeld 2004), the *rossiiskii* civic identity projected by musicians sought shelter from the state, rather than willingness to work with it. Such creative citizenry was involved in culture-making processes about the *strana* but often in a problematic relationship with the *gosudarstvo*, including with its internal legitimation as well as global projection. Independent practitioners, to borrow Byford et al.'s (2020, 18) formulation, "may still be fundamentally patriotic, but their patriotism is that typical of a Russian intelligentsia traditionally wary of state power". Their products tend to avoid "direct association with the state and envisage Russian culture […] not as a cultural projection of Russian statehood but, quite the contrary, as […] actively freeing itself from the state" (Byford et al. 2020). This was applicable for independent music aimed both domestically and internationally.[10]

Music (in the sense of folk music) has always been an important ingredient of Russian national identity, and one of the key elements which classical composers sought to capture in their work.[11] One only has to think about Igor Stravinsky's transcriptions of peasant songs for his oeuvres, or the *kuchkists'* anxieties over finding an "authentic" Russian sound, bound in the soil and as a true expression of the people (Figes 2002, 179; 282–87). There are of course parallels between the construction of national identity through classical music in the nineteenth century and what occurred in the 2010s through popular music. In both instances practitioners held dear the idea that a Russian song had to be sad and melancholic, and that melancholy was the primary expression of the national character and the true Russia soul. As Marina Frolova-Walker (2007, 38–40) elucidates, Pushkin, in a half-mocking, half-joking way in *Onegin*, viewed "pain" as the great unifier of all Russian people: "From the coachman to the greatest poet, /we all sing our gloom". She continues by describing how the intellectual Alexander Radishchev, already at the end of the eighteenth century, thought that Russian folk songs epitomised the grief of the Russian soul, and that the song was best suited to express the national character (Frolova-Walker 2007, 40). There are connections with the present here:

Introduction 9

as we will see in Chapter 3, the main musical event of the Russian independent scene of the 2010s took the name of *Festival' Bol'* (Pain Festival), and "gloomy" (*mrachnyi*) became the adjective used by participants to describe it as well as a synonym for the "authentic" sound of Russia.

In addition to grief as a national pillar, in the early twentieth century another set of attributes became entangled with Russian music: eccentricity, strangeness, exoticism (Frolova-Walker 2007, 47–50). The music (or better, audio-visual performance) of Diaghilev's *ballets russes*, for example, emphasised its difference from the "Western" canon: excess and exaggeration became the trademark of the *saisons russes* in Paris and a highly marketable strategy in Western Europe. As we will see in Chapter 5, excess and self-exoticisation constituted also the strategy of Little Big, Russia's main popular music export, to navigate the global, Anglo-American–dominated market.

Not every musical output is a direct response to geopolitical, political or social events, of course. Important dynamics are also at play within the community itself, the so-called "art world" (Becker 1982), characterised by people in disparate roles cooperating in the creation and dissemination of art (e.g., musicians, festival organisers, venue promoters, studio technicians, music journalists, etc.). To build a career, these practitioners often have to move according to (or constrained by) the conventions of that world, its rules, styles, networks of informal and formal connections, as well as inequalities of various nature (gender, class, etc.). Hands-on, everyday professional preoccupations shape the ways in which practitioners do things, including creating, disseminating and promoting music, in ways that are perhaps more significant than political engagement. The activity of music is also imbued in emotions, pleasure, entertainment, leisure, in doing things together, in enjoyable "communities of practice" (Patsiaoura 2013) – all of which tend to throw politics (in the sense of the relationship of the individual with state institutions, state narratives and state interpellations) on a secondary plane.

Nevertheless, music does react to socio-political developments with considerable speed and "freedom" (perhaps more so than any other cultural medium). In an epoque in which information is disseminated in an endless and instantaneous stream that surpasses any cultural attempts to pin it down, and in a local reality (Russia) where censorship is implemented to a significant degree, the fact that songs can be produced quickly (quicker, indeed, than feature films, documentaries, books, etc.), that they do not rely on external funding for publication (unlike many other art forms) and that they spread through online channels of distribution largely outside the state remit (e.g., YouTube), is one of the reasons why studying Russian independent music can be particularly illuminating to understand the cultural and sociopolitical milieux of the country.

Moreover, "doing" music is both making it and listening to it: music is multimodal, multimedia and multisensory participation involving mind and body simultaneously. Especially when experienced collectively (e.g., at a concert) (Frith 1996, 128; Finnegan 2004, 191), music shapes communities of belonging in a way that is as powerful and extended as hardly any other art form. And while notions of collective identity "emanate from a common stock of understandings concerning music's

10   *Independent Music in Russia*

relationship to the local", through which individuals "author space" (Bennett 2004, 3), the disputed character of "local" space today means that localities and local musics are always in dialogue with global trends, ideas, flows. Indeed, the formal hybridity of the song "opens the way to an understanding of its national, geographical, and linguistic hybridity too" (Bullock 2019, 310). This signifies that Russian popular music is at the same time Russian and transnational, local and global, for the "song is at once the most intimately national and also the most portable unit of cultural life" (Bullock 2019, 291). The very fact that Russian music (in the sense of being produced by Russian individuals in Russia) can be sung and marketed in English for a domestic audience (see, e.g., Chapter 2) testifies to this great plasticity, which may be difficult to achieve for other cultural forms (e.g., literature) more anchored in the specificities of the domestic language. For all the reasons above, looking at sociopolitical events and transformations through the prism of independent music is extremely valuable, as it can better inform our understandings of Russia and the culture-power interactions happening within the country.

The colonial question

The full-scale invasion of Ukraine sharpened issues concerning the "colonial character" of Russian culture and popular culture (Bekbulatova 2022; Kuvshinova 2022; Yermolenko 2022). This included music too: after the start of the war, for example, the Ukrainian government banned the dissemination of songs by Russian artists released after 1991, unless these artists spoke out against the war (Rzheutska 2023). For several commentators, Russia's renewed imperialist vision was expressed not only in how culture was appropriated or mediated by the state, but also across grassroots production. According to this view, colonialism and imperialism were "intrinsic" to Russian culture and historically upheld from the top down as much as from the bottom up. In some cases, these commentators did have a point: one does not have to look further than Alexander Pushkin's *Prisoner of the Caucasus*, entries from Fedor Dostoevsky's *Diary of A Writer*, Joseph Brodsky's "On the Independence of Ukraine" (Bertelsen 2015), or Aleksei Balabanov's dilogy *Brat* and *Brat 2* (Brother; Brother 2) (Condee 2009). In recent musical activities, one can consider: the Z-music marathons in support of the government's decision to invade Ukraine (Churmanova 2022); the project "Ia ostaius" (I Will Remain) (Sukhachëv 2022), a patriotic call to stay in Russia no matter what; the rise of pop singer Shaman (Gorbachev 2022) and his ethnonationalist anthem "Ia russkii" (I am Russian); or the works of Tatiana Chicherina before and after the start of the full-scale war in Ukraine – see, for example, the song "Russkie maiaki" (Russian Lighthouses) (Leps et al. 2023), in which Russian history and culture end up as ill-digested and ahistorical name-dropping with the aim of sustaining Russia's imperial greatness (see also Saprykin 2023).

It is crucial to remember, though, that swearing allegiance to power was and is only one of the strategies of artistic positioning in relation to the country's imperialist actions, and by far not the most common one. In culture as well as in music, practitioners responded to political events differently: some conformed, some remained silent, others challenged and contested (e.g., by migrating somewhere else precisely because they disagreed with their government and wanted to disaffiliate with it). To reduce Russian popular music production – let alone Russian culture as a whole (Shishkin 2022) – to instances of passive, tacit or active compliance with power would be as wrong as assuming or expecting unanimous resistance to it. Given Russia's history of a self-colonised and colonising superpower (Moore 2001; Etkind 2011), its peripheral imperial character (Martinez 2013), its anti-Western "decolonial" stance but West-European "colonial" consciousness (Tolz 2020), its inferiority complex towards European powers and its expansionism at the expenses of weaker colonial subjects (Tlostanova 2018), or, as Viatcheslav Morozov (2015) formulated, its condition as a "subaltern empire" in a Eurocentric world, studying how musical practitioners confronted and interacted with questions of imperialism and colonialism does not lend itself to easy, straightforward answers.

To start with, the tendency towards maximising the expression of the national character in independent music was hardly a colonial or imperial one. As we will see in Chapter 3, the marginalisation of internal otherness concerned a combination of sound, style and English language, not ethnicity or nationality. Indeed, many ethnically non-Russian or mixed performers were central to Russian popular music in the late 2010s (not to mention the omnipresent posthumous legacy of Kino's singer Viktor Tsoi, who was of Korean descent). Between famous ethnically non-Russian performers living and working in Russia in the late 2010s we could cite: the pop star Filipp Kirkorov (Bulgaria), the rapper Timati (half Jewish, half Tatar), the pop singer Manizha (Tajikistan), Aigel (Tatarstan) and the rapper Morgenshtern (Jewish and Bashkir). Again, these performers positioned themselves in various ways in relation to power (e.g., Timati became one of Putin's "trusted figures" and supporters of the war, while Morgenshtern left the country before the full-scale invasion and was labelled as a "foreign agent" by the government). Moreover, decolonising and decentring practices in Russian music started before the war in Ukraine, prompting new and urgent discussions around how to redefine Russian culture outside of imperialist structures of thinking (Sibgatullina 2022).

As far as the domestic music scene was concerned, the imbalance between the "centres" (Moscow and St. Petersburg) and the so-called Russian "provinces" was more economic than epistemic. The same cannot be said in terms of Russian cultural production more broadly, where the provinces have historically been portrayed as the repository of national tradition but also as the loci of scarcity, dejection and dispossession (Parts 2015). Many of my respondents were aware that the centres' commercial magnetism caused to some extent a "talent depopulation" in the provincial scenes, with local practitioners moving to Moscow or St. Petersburg to enhance their opportunities. But the disadvantaged musical position of the provinces was underpinned by the enduring lack of resources and investment at political and administrative levels rather than by culturally arrogant attitudes of practitioners in the centre.[12]

To tackle the problem, bottom-up initiatives took place through books, showcases, festivals and the creation of a database of resources aimed at developing

12 *Independent Music in Russia*

regional scenes (*IMI* 2020; Kashapov 2020; Grunin 2021; Khomiakova 2021a; Boiarinov 2022). Even if the organisation of these initiatives often involved practitioners from Moscow or St. Petersburg, it was not informed by assimilationist, centripetal ways of thinking, but was rather devoted to mapping out musical diversity with the view of fostering infrastructural and intraregional connections, as well as decreasing local practitioners' heavy reliance on Russia's "two capitals" for career advancement. Prime examples of this attitude across the period studied were: the Colisium International Music Forums taking place in Ekaterinburg, Kazan, Krasnoyarsk, Novosibirsk, Sochi, Ulan-Ude and Ufa, (in addition to Moscow and St. Petersburg), which served as music conferences as well as networking opportunities; the festival Indiushata, a contest gathering indie bands from all over Russia to display their talent in front of Moscow's music industry professionals; and Moscow Music Week, a hybrid event whose showcases included acts grouped according to their regional provenance.

However, since Russian independent music is a world that has generally pursued autonomy from the state and retreated from state politics, questions concerning Russia's renewed imperialism were also overlooked, with the risk of feeding the imperial subconscious. Primarily due to the role of Russian as the dominant language, practitioners tended in some instances to conflate the post-Soviet space into a pan-Russian space with Moscow at its centre. In 2011, for example, the reputable entertainment and lifestyle magazine *Afisha* selected the most representative post-Soviet pop songs of the last two decades. The collection was titled "99 Russian hits" [*99 russkikh khitov*] (*Afisha*, 2011), even if several of the performers on the list were ethnically non-Russians or not Russian nationals at all. Key here is the adjective *russkii*: in Russia, as mentioned before, "citizen of Russia" (*rossiiskii*) and "ethnic Russian" (*russkii*) are perceived as distinct entities, and "these two terms make visible the coexistence of geo-political and ethno-cultural criteria of self-description" (Franklin and Widdis 2004, 5). This coexistence is by no means stable, as the *rossiiskii* criteria have at times been glossed over (also at state level) by nationalist narratives aimed at shaping a homogeneous, *russkii* image of Russia (Hutchings and Tolz 2015, 249–253; Blakkisrud 2016). This has created an "unresolved tension within the Kremlin's entire nation-building discourse: between the vision of Russia as a multi-ethnic, multi-confessional society of equal citizens and that of Russia as a national state in which Russian culture, language and Orthodoxy have primacy" (Hutchings and Tolz 2015, 2). Moreover, *russkii* also refers to Russian as a language (*russkii iazyk*), and therefore points at another criterion of self-description, whereby a *rossiiskii* person is a *russkii* speaker. Nevertheless, *Afisha*'s compilation featured also a song not in Russian ("Lasha Tumbai" by Ukrainian drag performer Verka Serduchka).

When journalist Aleksandr Gorbachev (2022) looked back at his work as the compilation curator, he admitted that the *russkii* in the title had more than an unfortunate tinge of cultural imperialism, precisely because several of the musicians in the collection were not Russian, but came from all over the post-Soviet space (so, they were not even *rossiiskii*). The fact that at the time no objections were raised in naming the collection in that way (also by the non-*russkie*) was also indicative

Introduction 13

of a certain carelessness and unawareness in relation to colonial outlooks. Yet, as the decade progressed and the Russian regime bolstered its imperialist policies, several music practitioners became more conscious of the challenge. In the updated version of the compilation, released in 2021, the term *russkii* was replaced by "post-Soviet" (*postsovetskii*).[13] The main title was: *Don't Be Shy: A History of post-Soviet Pop Music in 169 Songs*. "Don't be shy" (*ne nado stesniat'sia*) was a line taken from the 2011 song "Stytsamen", a homage to Ukrainian singer Ivan Dorn, who was heralded as the gamechanger in the conception and production of pop across the whole area. Dorn was not alone in the Olympus of foreign Russophone performers: although the majority of songs were produced by artists living and working in Russia, a significant part of musicians hailed from outside of it, and the compilation recognised the major influence of non-*rossiiskie* Russophone artists over the Russian ones. In music journalism, Ukraine was generally heralded as a leading and most original scene with a massive impact on the Russian one (Trabun 2012; Ovchinnikov 2022), perhaps partially due to its closer proximity to Western Europe. Therefore, Russophone artists from neighbouring countries were seen as part of a shared cultural space that spanned from Central Asia to Moldova and from the Far East to Belarus, and were crowned as innovators and chief figures in it.

Does this mean that Russian music practitioners viewed Ukraine or other post-Soviet countries as "theirs", unaware of cultural and national differences? Was there an unequal relationship of prestige and power between Russian musicians and the rest, or a condescending attitude on the part of Russian musicians towards their foreign colleagues? In my view, the answer is "no" in most cases. Just like its European or Anglophone equivalents, the Russophone music market shared a common space which, for historical and linguistic reasons, largely coincided with the territory of the former Soviet Union. But this territorial overlap with the past empire did not necessarily make the emerging musical discourses imperial. Artists from Ukraine, Kazakhstan, Belarus and so on, toured in Russia and vice versa, while practitioners (e.g., producers, sound engineers, festival organisers, promoters, etc.) from one country worked with musicians of another, creating a transnational network across the former Soviet republics. The intensity of musical exchange upheld the continuation in the post-Soviet era of the common musical market that formed in the late Soviet period. This extended music industry comprised Russian practitioners who worked with or promoted music projects not only from Russia, but from across the post-Soviet space, which at times was also featured on domestic mainstream or state-controlled radio, TV and press (e.g., Ukrainian musicians who performed on the popular late-night show *Vechernii Urgant*, such as Ivan Dorn in 2019 and 2021, the singer Luna (Moon) in 2017, or the band Poshlaia Molli (Vulgar Molly) in 2018. Even though the main language that facilitated this musical communication was Russian, and the largest market was within Russian borders, this was no colonial relationship between centres and peripheries.

While several performers living in the former Eastern European Soviet bloc also looked to the West (e.g., the Belarusian post-punk group Molchat Doma, or Ukrainian neo-folk band Dakha Brakha), Russia remained for many Russophone performers a most lucrative market in which to sell records, perform and tour,

14 *Independent Music in Russia*

because of the linguistic and geographic proximity and simply because of the number of potential audience members (around 140 million people). True, Crimea had an impact on the musical relationships between Russia and Ukraine: Russian musicians who performed in the peninsula after 2014 were barred from entering Ukraine (see Kazakov and Hutchings 2019, on how these tensions played out in the Eurovision song context), and the conflict in the Donbas found in songs one of its articulations (Hansen et al. 2019), but many independent artists from Ukraine, Belarus, Russia, Kazakhstan and other former Soviet republics continued to shape and work in a common musical market up until February 2022.

The existence of this common musical industry has now been challenged by the war in Ukraine. For some pundits this shared space has been erased outright (Gorbachev 2022; Ovchinnikov 2022). After February 24, several Ukrainian artists, including Ivan Dorn, withdrew their songs from Russian streaming services. Other Belarusian or Kazakh performers cancelled their concerts in Russia, which found itself cut off, musically, from their neighbours. The idea that music culture could continue to bridge people from different countries in spite of political strains declined as the scale of violence of the Russian army increased. Needless to say, this outcome was the opposite of what the independent practitioners wanted, including the ones with a Russian passport.

Structure of the book

Chapter 1 offers an historical account of *nezavisimaia muzyka*, examining the ways in which its development – very different from that of independent music in the West – has influenced the ways in which practitioners think about their practice today. Particular stress is placed on the relationship between independent community and the authoritarian system, commerce, national identity and Western musical traditions.

Chapter 2 investigates the Anglophone Wave in *nezavisimaia muzyka* (2008–2012), specifically how Russian Anglophone bands came about in the late 2000s and what they signified for Russian culture. I suggest that, while Russian groups had previously sung in English with scarce public recognition, the conjunction of a series of socio-political circumstances encouraged the appearance of a conspicuous Russian Anglophone community in the Medvedev years. These were: perceived political relaxation (internally and in Russia-West relations), Russia's economic growth, Moscow's urban renovation, and the increase in connectivity across the indie community. Linked to this, the chapter investigates how ideas of cosmopolitanism and Europeanness during the late 2000s were an agenda shared by politicians, Moscow's administration, businessmen, indie trendsetters and hipsters, with local Anglophone indie becoming the "soundtrack" of Russia's modernisation. Lastly, the chapter contends that escapism was a fundamental component of this cultural movement. This does not carry a negative meaning; on the contrary, escapism in music can construct a new sense of self shared by an alternative community (Walser 1993) and bring about spatial, social and cultural change. For Moscow indie musicians, it entailed the creation of a movement towards an "Imaginary West" (Yurchak 2006), and then the local enactment of this West until it became real.

Introduction 15

Chapter 3 deals with the changes in *nezavisimaia muzyka* vis-à-vis the conservative turn that took place in political, societal and cultural spheres after Putin's comeback in 2012 and the outbreak of the Russo-Ukrainian conflict in 2014 (up until 2018). This redefinition of music trends led to the New Russian Wave, that is, to a Russophone music movement heavily influenced by post-punk, infused with subtle political critique and irony and preoccupied with problems of national authenticity and cultural sovereignty. The chapter evidences how both the Anglophone Wave and the New Russian Wave were instances of, and stages in, Russia's processes of self-identification. The latter was in part a reaction to the former, instigated, on top of geopolitical trends, by Russian practitioners' inquiries into ideas of derivativeness and authenticity which had, as object of comparison, the Western (particularly Anglo-American) popular music tradition. Some of the independent music generated after the conservative political shift displayed characteristics of metamodernism (Vermeulen and Van den Akker 2010; Engström 2018; Khrushchëva 2020), a condition characterised by a fluctuation between modern grand narratives and postmodern disillusion. The chapter shows how metamodernism became common currency in independent music as a means to express both Russia's isolation and its cultural ferment, and as an aesthetic and civil choice simultaneously. In contrast to the direct political contestation of Pussy Riot, the artists of the New Russian Wave chose a lack of clear political messages as a survival strategy to allude to politics while avoiding potential clashes with power.

Chapter 4 explores the relationship that *nezavisimaia muzyka* had with political resistance during Putin's fourth term up until the full-scale war in Ukraine (2018–2022). By analysing manifestations of protest in independent music during this time, the chapter contends that resistance was voiced across a continuum rather than from an unambiguously oppositional site. One of these tactics (a spin-off of the metamodernist trend) entailed ambiguity: together with criticism of the state, practitioners injected some degree of "state-friendly" messages in their songs, eventually spinning dissent and support into a yarn which was impossible to untangle. I term this occurrence *patrioprotest* (patriotism plus protest) precisely to acknowledge the fusion of backing and contestation of the status quo, recognising how similar tactics have historically existed in Russia before the period studied and beyond the musical field. I show how the musical works that I see as *patrioprotest* did not seek to explicitly hold the government accountable for its actions but, instead, remained deliberately ambivalent, refusing to delineate a definitive meaning between reinforcing and subverting official narratives. Picking a side was ultimately the task of the beholder, and the variety of reactions across different camps testified to the vitality of such musicians' tactics.

Chapter 5 examines the export of Russian independent music, as well as its successes and failures in conquering a niche in foreign markets. The chapter introduces the idea of "sonic capital" – understood as the international recognition and authority of a country's music – discussing how differences in sonic capital contribute to command different outcomes in the transnational spread of this or that country's music. At the same time the concept of "subflow" is presented to identify a transnational flow that occurs between two countries considered to be at

16 *Independent Music in Russia*

the fringes of a particular cultural discourse. Subflows, however, may not attempt to subvert hierarchical structures of centre/periphery, but may actually replicate hierarchies within the periphery. Following the adventures abroad of several Russian bands, the chapter also overviews the different strategies that Russian bands adopted in packaging their product for non-Russian audiences.

A note on methodology

This book was born, on the one hand, out of my desire as an independent musician to understand how other musicians in a different national context thought about their practice. On the other, it stemmed from my specialism on Russian culture and the numerous visits I conducted there since I first became acquainted with the country in 2006. It seemed therefore quite natural to merge the two. When I started collecting the material for this book in 2016, I had been a practicing musician for about 15 years, having played in Italy, where I am from, and the UK, where I had moved. My prior experience, I think, helped me gain the trust of the interviewees and an immediate understanding of the issues discussed. For example, all bands I was part of in Italy sang in English; in Italy, Anglophone performers garnered similar reactions in music discourse; a revival of national/regional markers of belonging, particularly in Rome, was visible; Italian music had also been traversed by ideas of imitation and peripherality in comparison to the Anglophone centres. Nevertheless, there were some themes, above all the importance of the idea of the country, the invasive state, the history of the development of the independent scenes, and so on, that were locally specific to Russia.

Richard Stites (1992, 7), one of the finest cultural historians of Russia, once observed that "part of comprehending a people's culture is knowing what they know". As the first step, therefore, I accessed (and tried to blend in) the scene. By following "who" and "what" was discussed on Russia's influential music outlets such as *Afisha, Look at Me, Colta, The Village, The Flow,* and so on, and by attending gigs, I identified potential interviewees and made contact with them. Although the professionals I selected were widely known in Russia and in some cases beyond, I was usually welcomed to a chat. Sociologist Thomas Cushman (1995, 342), who researched the Leningrad rock community at the end of the 1980s, similarly noted that Russian music practitioners are more accessible than their Western counterparts.

I carried out fieldwork in Moscow and St. Petersburg between 2016 and 2019, for a total of 14 months (June – July 2016; July 2017 – March 2018; November 2018; August – September 2019), collecting 42 in-depth conversations with musicians, critics and other industry professionals, more than 100 open-ended interviews with audience members, and data from participant observation at music-related events (concerts, festivals, showcases and conferences). Parallel to this, I conducted a web survey of 300 bands active in the Moscow territory in July 2017 to determine the various linguistic and stylistic preferences among Muscovite musicians. Lastly, I conducted another set of 42 interviews with practitioners outside of Russia (Tbilisi, Yerevan, Belgrade) between May and

Introduction   17

June 2023. Practitioners were aged between 22 and 62. All interviews were conducted in Russian, recorded and transcribed; interviewees have been anonymised in the case of practitioners and pseudonymised in the case of audience members for reasons of safety.

The face-to-face interviews with practitioners occurred in agreed-upon public places and informal settings (restaurants, cafes, bars), while interviews with the audience were conducted at gigs and festivals, and with no previous notice. For the practitioners, I used semi-structured questionnaires: the set of fixed questions was complemented by other questions tailored in accordance with the interviewee's role (e.g., whether they were a musician, venue promoter or festival organiser) and biography (e.g., questions about a specific album, event or professional endeavour). Such interviews were open-ended and invited more narrative and articulated responses. In regard to the concert attendees, I had a set of fixed questions, some of which required a one-word answer, and other ones open-ended. Social media, especially Facebook and Telegram, were of great use in terms of participant observation during and after the fieldwork. The web represented a forum where practitioners generated content daily by debating topical issues and new releases. As I befriended many of the people involved in the business, I followed their discussions and gained further useful information.

Even though I conducted two weeks of fieldwork in St. Petersburg, my data collection was primarily in Moscow. The reason why I chose Moscow is simply that, between 2008 and 2022, it was the main place for music production (bands, studios, labels) and consumption (venues, concerts, facilities), and had long since outweighed St. Petersburg, which was the core of independent music culture in the 1970s–1990s. Moscow was also the chief place of convergence of many musicians from disparate parts of Russia, attracted by the career opportunities of a metropolis.

Out of the practitioners interviewed, only fifteen were women (18%). This number reflected the minority of female performers and professionals in the *nezavisimaia muzyka* world. It was a testimony to a male-dominated industry (statistics on female/male percentages in the Russian music sector are, however, not available), but also to the fact that men were the majority among the émigré practitioners interviewed, owing to the risk of conscription in Russia after September 2022.[14] However, the immediate pre-COVID period suggested a growth of female presence in the business structure. For instance, at the Moscow Music Week conference and showcase in 2019, 24 delegates out of 70 were female (32%). The growing presence of women in the *nezavisimaia muzyka* industry and among performers was observed by Foster (2019a) at the same event in 2018. The rise of performers such as Monetochka or Manizha (Russia's 2021 Eurovision entry with the feminist song "Russian Woman"), was an important step in the direction of fairer participation. Also, the DIY charity event and music festival "Ne Vinovata" ("Not Her Fault"), organised in support of victims of domestic violence, functioned as a platform for several activists to articulate ideas of gender equality (*Calvert Journal* 2021). That said, much work still needs to be done on gender-based issues in the industry, as reported in a survey (Khomiakova 2021b), conducted after the independent sector

18   *Independent Music in Russia*

was shaken by allegations of domestic violence with male musicians as perpetrators (Danilov 2021; Zav'ialov 2021). At the same time, women in the Russian music industry have long moved beyond their role of "enablers" or "organisers" of male musicians, which, as Steinholt (2005, 3) has noted, they held across the independent scene in the late Soviet period.

Interviews and sources were analysed through discourse analysis, that is, the description, interpretation, explanation and critique of collective epistemological and psychological patterns (observable in the individual's language) that shape the ways in which people speak, think, act and perform. Discourse analysis continuously requires "a movement from context to language and from language to context" (Gee 2010, 20) on the basis that words are not only constative, but also performative, something through which people do things that have practical consequences for their lives and the lives of others (Austin 1999). Such analysis enabled the assessment of the outcomes, issues and possibilities created by different discourses (Potter and Wetherell 1987) and the struggle for power between them (Foucault 1972). Participants' opinions, which at times ended up conflicting with one another, were compared and contrasted with articles from established newspapers, magazines and webzines, with quantitative data from my own survey and public polls, with personally conducted participant observation and with theoretical academic literature on similar topics inside and outside Russia. Interviews were also complemented by lyrics, video and performance analysis (Chapters 2–5), as well as an examination of fan communities (Chapter 5). Informants may change their behaviour, and consequently their utterances, when knowing they are being watched, studied or scrutinised (Carnevale et al. 2008). Lying, exaggerating, diminishing and mythicising are not rare interviewing issues, as there might be a gap between what respondents say and what they actually think and do (Hammersley and Gomm 2008). Cross-examination, therefore, informed the overall adjustment of analysis and conclusion.

The problem with studying the contemporary is that the context may change in rapid and dramatic ways which profoundly impact the activities of the practitioners, like in the case of Russia's full-scale invasion of Ukraine. I entered the field when the New Russian Wave was in full swing, and I complete this work as several participants are trying to reconfigure their careers in the context of emigration. I originally accessed a music world that was growing internally and internationally, building infrastructure and acquiring confidence in exporting its products. I finish this book at a time when the indie industry, in terms of economics and workforce, is in tatters. A considerable degree of "elasticity" helped integrating these changes in the course of work. At the same time, though, the chain of events also calls for the structuring of this study as a historical journey. Therefore, the chapters have been organised both chronologically and thematically: each one of them describes a particular set of concepts and problems that were acutely present in a particular period. Since narratives within independent music in Russia changed over the 2010s, analysing the salient issues and reporting the plurality of voices of its protagonists through a chronological lens became the most useful strategy in order to untangle the richness of Russian independent music culture.

Introduction 19

Notes

1 The screenplay for the video was written by the band themselves in the summer of 2019 (Logacheva 2019), when the band had not yet signed with a major (Universal Russia). The title is a reference both to the socialist realist novel *How the Steel Was Tempered* by Nikolai Ostrovsky (1904–1936) and to the 1988 album of the same name by the punk band Grazhdanskaia Oborona (Civil Defence).

2 As explained in the next chapter, the term *"nezavisimaia muzyka"* at times overlaps with "indi", though the former is less sound-specific and refers to a broader set of musicians without affiliation to a major label. The adjective *nezavisimyi* stems from the verb *viset'* (to hang), declined in the participle form. *Za-* is in Russian a prefix that indicates something external, while *ne-* is a negation. In short, the adjective denotes "something that does not hang from something else".

3 See for example: Blum (2008), Laruelle (2015), Hutchings and Tolz (2015), Neumann (2016), Kolstø and Blakkisrud (2016), Bassin and Pozo (2017), Strukov and Hudspith (2019), Byford et al. (2020) and Yaffa (2021).

4 See for example: Jonson and Erofeev (2018); Laruelle and Engström (2018); Engström (2018); Semenenko (2021); Hutchings (2022).

5 *Russkii rok* is the type of "underground" rock, made in the Russian language, that developed in the Soviet Union during the 1970s and 1980s, whose main representatives were bands such as Mashina Vremeni (Time Machine), Akvarium (Aquarium), DDT and Zoopark (Zoo). As discussed in Chapter 1, it is a genre founded upon a strong literary legacy and preoccupied with the adaptation of Western rock music into Soviet cultural codes.

6 See, for example: Mitchell (2001), Connell and Gibson (2003), Berger and Carroll (2003), Turino (2003), O'Connor (2004), Pennycook (2007), Wallach (2008; 2014), Greene (2012), Luvaas (2013), Garland (2014), Epstein (2015), Arriagada (2016), Parkinson (2018) and Kim (2019).

7 Traditionally, the idea of a nation refers to a group of people united by common history, language, culture and ways of thinking and doing things, who usually inhabit a particular territory (there are also exceptions, such as diasporic communities scattered across multiple places). A nation may or may not be organised around a state, that is, around a recognised political entity with borders and a system of governance. However, the nationalist movements that emerged in the eighteenth and nineteenth centuries envisioned nations and states as congruent and led to the demise of most of the large multinational polities, the empires. Russia was one of these empires and, like the Austro-Hungarian and Ottoman Empires, collapsed, albeit not completely. Springing from the chaos of the revolution and the tragedy of the civil war, the Soviet Union reassembled, often through violence, the shards of the Tsarist state, keeping most of its territories. The Soviet Union was the first socialist, self-proclaimed anti-imperialist state in the world, and the question of nationality was crucial to its transformative project. The Soviets drew borders between republics and regions precisely based on the idea of a "nation" as envisaged by Lenin and Stalin, that is, as "a historically constituted, stable community of people, formed on the basis of a common language, territory, economic life, and psychological make-up manifested in a common culture" (Stalin 1913). These partitions aimed at fostering local national cultures and languages, which, in the Bolsheviks' plan, would then coalesce into a supranational Soviet identity, similarly to what Marx predicted in his vision of socialism. Indeed, by spreading the socialist message, national cultures would engineer the new Soviet person and national differences would eventually wither away. The contradictory policies that followed during the 70 years of Soviet rule did and undid nations: on the one hand the Communist Party promoted ethnic particularism; on the other, it cruelly squashed instances of nationalism and desires for more autonomy in the republics, deeming them as "bourgeois" or "counterrevolutionary". As Terry Martin (2001) put it, the Soviet Union was "an affirmative action empire", a highly centralised,

20   *Independent Music in Russia*

controlling and authoritarian entity that coercively dictated its own version of national development to the constituent republics. Russia, as the largest heir of the Soviet Union, inherited many of the problems of its predecessor (see next note).

8   Today's Russia is of course not a nation-state, in which ethnic and state borders coincide. Formally, it is a federation (*Rossiiskaia federatsiia*) of 83 constituents with various levels of autonomy, populated by a myriad of different nationalities, ethnicities, cultures, religions and languages with nominally the same rights. In practice, it is a country still caught up between the inclusion of its diverse population into a common supranational fabric and the upholding of Russian language, Orthodoxy and Imperial culture as its foundational features. Political (and to a degree cultural) discourse has also projected the Soviet past, particularly through the intensification of the myth of WWII, as a nationwide, extra-linguistic and extra-religious social glue. Together with this, neo-Eurasianist ideas of Russia as a "civilisation" with a distinctive historical evolution, cultural make-up and geopolitical destiny, which were in the 1990s the subject of investigation of conservative circles at the margins of intellectual life, found their way into the political mainstream as the 2010s progressed (Laruelle 2015; Engström 2022). Both the myth of WWII and the civilisational discourse have served to justify the political elite's neo-imperialist policies in the "near abroad", including the invasion of Ukraine.

9   Words like *natsiia* or *imperiia* (nation, empire) were not used by respondents in the interviews conducted before 2022.

10   Nonetheless, as we will see in the course of this book, the participants' idea of nationhood, as constructed through music, varied significantly. Initially, it encompassed a vision of Russian global identity, in which Russian musicians could "absorb" and at the same time "contribute" to "global culture" (Interviewee 10). Out of this interchange, they believed, a "new form of Russian culture" could also emerge (Interviewee 10). This impression was based on the premise of a transnational music community shaped by globalisation and interconnected with local realities. During the 2010s, this discourse morphed at times into more patriotic or even civilisational discourses based on the idea of Russian music as a unique and treasured cultural phenomenon, though, in my view, never acquiring the revanchist or imperial tones typical of official discourse.

11   Russia's excellence in literature and classical music became recognised across Europe in the second half of the nineteenth century, particularly due to the "promotional" work of the writer Ivan Turgenev (then living mostly in Paris) and his companion, the mezzo-soprano Pauline Viardot (Figes 2020). By the start of WWI, Russian writers and composers were undoubtedly major contributors to the forging of a cosmopolitan European culture and the strengthening of Russia's European cultural identity (Figes 2020).

12   Some local scenes, such as Vorkuta in the north and Krasnodar in the south have been explored in Gololobov et al. (2014). The study evidenced the scenes' peculiarities and differences in comparison with music foci of Moscow or St. Petersburg, showing how the dynamics, meanings and values of domestic independent music present variations in relation to the place in which participants live and create.

13   In cultural and academic discourse, some commentators have taken issues with the word "post-Soviet", proposing instead the term "New East" to describe a diverse space that is coming to terms and at the same time distancing itself from the Soviet colonial past. The term "New East" was discussed at length in the *Calvert Journal*, a media outlet that dealt with culture from the former Eastern Bloc, now discontinued. Indeed, while scholars generally agree on the necessity of a new term to describe the territories of the former Soviet Union in light of their different developments, it is very difficult to come up with an unproblematic one (see, e.g., Urbinati 2021). First of all, words like "post-communist" or "post-socialist" may be as dated as "post-Soviet" and may denote the same traumatic past. Secondly, some of the shared tropes and objects among the countries in question are indeed rooted in the common Soviet past (e.g., Soviet blocs, now hugely fashionable in the West, or informality, as the ability to bypass institutions to

Introduction 21

gain something, or popular distrust in the state and its institutions). Thirdly, because "ignoring this past contained in the prefix '-post' is ignoring historical reality", including the overcoming of this past and the differences between past and present (MacFadyen in Riabov 2022).

14 This number was not proportionate to the actual Russian population at the end of the 2010s, in which women were 60%, but it was comparable to the situation in America, where women made up 21.7% of artists, 12.3% of songwriters and 2.1% of producers (Kelley 2019). A similar number was found in Europe, where women accounted for 16.8% of the musical sector (*Soundreef* 2019). Globally, a recent study (Wang and Horvàt 2019) found that female artists have, on average, fewer collaborators or are more frequently on the periphery of the collaborative network, which may signal structural barriers female artists face in the advancement of their careers. The study also discovered that men release more songs than women, and that out of the nearly 5,000 record labels in the study's data set, only one third have ever signed at least one female artist.

References

Afisha. 2011. '"Afisha" sostavila spisok samykh iarkikh i zapomnivshikhsia russkikh pop-khitov za poslednie 20 let i vyiasnila istoriiu kazhdoi iz nikh u sozdatelei'. URL: https://daily.afisha.ru/archive/volna/archive/pop/ (accessed 4 March 2025).

Arriagada, A. 2016. 'Unpacking the 'Digital Habitus' of Music Fans in Santiago's Indie Music Scene'. In Hracs, B., Seman, M., Virani, T. (eds.) *The Production and Consumption of Music in the Digital Age*. New York and London: Routledge, pp. 223–36.

Austin, J. 1999. *How to Do Things With Words*. Oxford: Clarendon Press.

Bassin, M., Pozo, G. (eds.). 2017. *The Politics of Eurasianism: Identity, Popular Culture and Russia's Foreign Policy*. London and New York: Rowman & Littlefield International.

Becker, H. 1982. *Art Worlds*. Berkeley, CA: University of California Press.

Bekbulatova, T. 2022. 'Posle Buchi nel'zia bol'she govorit' o rossiiskoi kul'ture'. *Kholod*, 4 April. URL: https://holod.media/2022/04/04/rodnyansky/ (Accessed 16 October 2023).

Bennett, A. 2004. 'Music, Space and Place'. In Whiteley, S., Bennett, A., Hawkins, S. (eds.) *Music, Space and Place: Popular Music and Cultural Identity*. Farnham: Ashgate, pp. 2–7.

Berger, H., Carroll, M. (eds.). 2003. *Global Pop, Local Language*. Jackson: University of Mississippi Press.

Bertelsen, O. 2015. 'Joseph Brodsky's Imperial Consciousness'. *Scripta Historica*, 21, pp. 263–89.

Beumers, B. 2005. *Pop Culture Russia! Media, Arts and Lifestyle*. Santa Barbara: ABC-CLIO.

Blakkisrud, H., 2016. 'Blurring the Boundary between Civic and Ethnic: The Kremlin's New Approach to National Identity Under Putin's Third Term'. In Kølsto, P., Blakkisrud, H. (eds.) *The New Russian Nationalism: Imperialism, Ethnicity and Authoritarianism 2000–2015*. Edinburgh: Edinburgh University Press, pp. 249–74.

Blum, D. (ed.) 2008. *Russia and Globalization: Identity, Security and Society in an Era of Change*. Washington: Woodrow Wilson Center Press.

Boiarinov, D. (ed.) 2022. *Po Rossii: muzykal'nye stseny i iavleniia*. Moskva: IMI.

Bullock, P.R. 2019. 'Song in a Strange Land the Russian Musical Lyric beyond the Nation'. In Platt, K. (ed.) *Global Russian Studies*. Madison: University of Wisconsin Press, pp. 290–311.

Byford, A., Doak, C., Hutchings, S. (eds.). 2020. *Transnational Russian Studies*. Liverpool: Liverpool University Press.

Calvert Journal. 2021. 'Russian and Feminist: How a New Generation of Activists are Fighting for Their Rights'. URL: https://www.calvertjournal.com/features/show/11551/new-russian-feminism-movement-russia-z (accessed 7 October 2021).

22   *Independent Music in Russia*

Carnevale, F.A., Macdonald, M.E., Bluebond-Langner, M., McKeever, P. 2008. 'Using Participant Observation in Pediatric Health Care Settings: Ethical Challenges and solutions'. *Journal of Child Health Care*, 12, 1, pp. 18–32.

Churmanova, K. 2022. 'Gastroli patriotov: Kak kremlevskie eksperty i shou-biznes zarabatyvaiut na koncertakh 'Za Rossiiu''. *BBC Russia*, 11 May. https://www.bbc.com/russian/features-61401033 (accessed 3 June 2022).

Condee, N. 2009. *The Imperial Trace: Recent Russian Cinema*. Oxford: Oxford University Press.

Connell, J., Gibson, C. 2003. *Sound Tracks: Popular Music, Identity and Place*. London: Routledge.

Cushman, T. 1995. *Notes from the Underground: Rock Music Counterculture in Russia*. New York: State University of New York Press.

Danilov, A. 2021. "On govoril, chto, esli nadavit sil'nee, ia slomaius': Anna Zosimova ob otnosheniiakh s Petarom Martichem". *Wonderzine*, 18 March. URL: https://www.wonderzine.com/wonderzine/life/experience/255589-zosimova (accessed 7 October 2021).

Durdiyeva, S. 2023. "Not in Our Name:' Why Russia is Not a Decolonial Ally or the Dark Side of Civilizational Communism and Imperialism'. *The SAIS Review*, 29 May. URL: https://saisreview.sais.jhu.edu/not-in-our-name-why-russia-is-not-a-decolonial-ally-or-the-dark-side-of-civilizational-communism-and-imperialism/ (accessed 2 March 2024).

Engström, M. 2018. 'Monetochka: The Manifesto of Metamodernism'. *Riddle*, 26 June 2018 https://www.ridl.io/en/monetochka-the-manifesto-of-metamodernism/ (last accessed 7 May 2020).

Engström, M. 2022. 'We Are Not Supporting the 'Special Operation': We're Carrying it Out'. *Russia.Post*, 3 May. URL: https://russiapost.info/politics/special_operation_carrying_it_out (accessed 5 July 2022).

Epstein, S. 2015. 'Us and Them: Korean Indie Rock in a K-Pop World'. *The Asia-Pacific Journal*, 48, 1, pp. 1–19.

Etkind, A. 2011. *Internal Colonization: Russia's Imperial Experience*. Cambridge: Polity Press.

Figes, O. 2002. *Natasha's Dance: A Cultural History of Russia*. London: Penguin.

Figes, O. 2020. *The Europeans: Three Lives and the Making of a Cosmopolitan Culture*. London: Penguin.

Finnegan, R. 2004. 'Music, Experience, and the Anthropology of Emotion'. In Clayton, M., Herbert, T., Middleton, R. (eds.) *The Cultural Study of Music*. New York: Routledge, pp. 181–92.

Foucault, M. 1972. *The Archeology of Knowledge and the Discourse of Language*. New York: Pantheon Books.

Franklin, S., Widdis, E. 2004. 'All the Russias'. In Franklin, S., Widdis, E. (eds.) *National Identity in Russian Culture*. New York: Cambridge University Press, pp. 1–8.

Frith, S. 1996. *Performing Rites: Evaluating Popular Music*. Oxford: OUP.

Frolova-Walker, M. 2007. *Russian Music and Nationalism. From Glinka to Stalin*. London: Yale University Press.

Galeotti, M. 2017. 'Controlling Chaos: How Russia Manages Its Political War in Europe'. *European Council on Foreign Relations*, pp. 1–18.

Garland, S. 2014. Music, Affect, Labor, and Value: Late Capitalism and the (Mis)Productions of Indie Music in Chile and Brazil. PhD thesis, Columbia University.

Gee, J. 2010. *An Introduction to Discourse Analysis Theory and Method*. Hoboken: Taylor and Francis.

Gololobov, I., Pilkington, H., Steinholt, Y. 2014. *Punk in Russia: Cultural Mutation from the 'Useless' to the 'Moronic*. Oxon: Routledge.

Gorbachev, A. 2022. 'Postsovetskaia Estrada unichtozhena. Na rossiiskoi teper' poiut pro krov''. *Kholod*, 14 September. URL: https://holod.media/2022/09/14/gorbachev_pop/?fbclid=IwAR0QE3uwJQg_cogekA6jvodvRQcoR_UwlO9KXIJFwlfYx1xFspesh8UH0Go (accessed 15 September 2022).

Greene, S. 2012. 'The Problem of Peru's Punk Underground: An Approach to Under-Fuck the System'. *Journal of Popular Music Studies*, 24, 4, pp. 578–89.

Grunin, N. 2021. '"Dat' pinok lokal'noi stsene": Stepan Kazarian o festivale Awaz'. URL: https://i-m-i.ru/post/awaz-interview (accessed 16 October 2023).

Guriev, S., Treisman, D. 2022. *Spin Dictators: The Changing Face of Tyranny in the 21st Century*. Princeton and Oxford: Princeton University Press.

Hammersley, M., Gomm, R. 2008. 'Assessing the Radical Critiques of Interviews'. In Hammersley, M. (ed.) *Questioning Qualitative Inquiry: Critical Essays*. London: Sage, pp. 89–100.

Hansen, A., Rogatchevski, A., Steinholt, Y., Wickström, D.E. 2019. *A War of Songs – Popular Music and Recent Russia-Ukraine Relations*. Stuttgart: Ibidem-Verlag.

Herzfeld, M. 2004. *Cultural Intimacy: Social Poetics in the Nation-State*. New York and London: Routledge.

Hosking, G. 1998. *Russia: People and Empire, 1552–1917*. London: Fontana.

Hutchings, S. 2022. *Projecting Russia in a Mediatized World Recursive Nationhood*. London: Routledge.

Hutchings, S., Tolz, V. 2015. *Nation, Ethnicity and Race on Russian Television: Mediating Post-Soviet Difference*. Abingdon: Routledge.

IMI. 2020. 'Regiony' (database). URL: https://i-m-i.ru/themes/nemoskva (accessed 16 October 2023).

Ivakhiv, A. 2022. 'Decolonialism and the Invasion of Ukraine'. *E-flux*, 23 March. URL: https://www.e-flux.com/notes/457576/decolonialism-and-the-invasion-of-ukraine (accessed 29 March 2022).

Jonson, L., Erofeev, A. (eds.). 2018. *Russia – Art Resistance and the Conservative-Authoritarian Zeitgeist*. London: Routledge.

Kashapov, R. 2020. 'Tatarskaia Estrada: baian, den'gi, korporat'. *IMI*, 28 December. URL: https://i-m-i.ru/post/tatarskaya-estrada-bayan-dengi-korporat (accessed 16 October 2023).

Kazakov, V., Hutchings, S. 2019. 'Challenging the 'Information War' Paradigm: Russophones and Russophobes in Online Eurovision Communities'. In Wijermars, M., Lehtisaari, K. (eds.) *Freedom of Expression in Russia's New Mediasphere*. London: Routledge, pp. 135–58.

Kelley, K. 2019. 'The Music Industry Still Has a Long Way to Go for Gender Equality'. *Forbes*, 6 February. URL: https://www.forbes.com/sites/caitlinkelley/2019/02/06/music-industry-study-annenberg-gender-equality/#6f0471fa5f81 (accessed 12 August 2020).

Khomiakova, N. 2021a. 'Kogo slushat' na festivale Awaz'. *IMI*, 30 April. URL: https://i-m-i.ru/post/awaz-musicians (accessed 26 October 2023).

Khomiakova, N. 2021b. '"K nam otnosiatsia kak k chemu-to ekzoticheskomu': opyt zhenshchin v muzykal'noi industrii'. *IMI*, 19 august. URL: https://i-m-i.ru/post/women-in-music?fbclid=IwAR1fIDP4xPYD5vHFURUP34GD7jbnGOY-UHzVX3nWXh-HXQ8LjNcAFxiPH0M4 (accessed 7 October 2021).

Khrushcheva, N. 2020. *Metamodern v muzyke i vokrug neë*. Moskva: Ripol Klassik.

Kim, S. 2019. '"Now It's Indie': The Creative Turn of the Cultural Policy in the Korean Indie Music Scene'. *The International Communication Gazette*, 81, 2, pp. 193–208.

Kolstø, P., Blakkisrud, H. (eds.). 2016. *The New Russian Nationalism: Imperialism, Ethnicity and Authoritarianism 2000–15*. Edinburgh: Edinburgh University Press.

Kuvshinova, M. 2022. 'Poka imperskii zariad ne budet obezvrezhen, rossiiskaia kul'tura ostaetsia opasnoi dlia sosedei'. *Kholod*, 24 March. https://holod.media/2022/03/24/kuvshinova_balabanov/ (accessed 25 March 2022).

Laruelle, M. 2015. 'The Paradoxical Legacy of Eurasianism in Contemporary Eurasia'. In Bassin, M., Glebov, S., Laruelle, M. (eds.) *Between Europe and Asia: The Origins, Theories, and Legacies of Russian Eurasianism*. Pittsburgh: University of Pittsburgh Press, pp. 187–94.

24 *Independent Music in Russia*

Laruelle, M., Engström, M. 2018. 'Vizualnaia kultura i ideologiia'. *Kontrapunkt*, 12, pp. 1–17.

Lebedeva, V. 2022. 'A klouny ostalis'. *Kommersant*, 2 September. URL: https://www.kommersant.ru/doc/5538114 (accessed 1 October 2022).

Leps, G., Chicherina, T., Malenko, V. 'Russkie maiaki'. 30 September 2023. URL: https://www.youtube.com/watch?v=aakBEYKb_vA (accessed 30 October 2023).

Logacheva, A. 2019. 'Klip Shortparis 'Tak zakalialas' stal'', posviashennyi nasiliiu'. *The Village*, 7 November 2019. URL: https://www.the-village.ru/village/weekend/wknd-news/366549-shortparis (last accessed 30 May 2020).

Luvaas, B. 2013. 'Exemplary Centers and Musical Elsewheres: On Authenticity and Autonomy in Indonesian Indie Music'. *Asian Music*, 44, 2, pp. 95–114.

Martinez, F. 2013. 'On the Peripheral Character of Russia'. *e-cadernos CES*, 19, pp. 54–84.

McMichael, P. 2013. 'Defining Pussy Riot Musically: Performance and Authenticity in New Media'. *Digital Icons: Studies in Russian, Eurasian and Central European New Media*, 9, pp. 99–113.

McMichael, P. 2019. '"That's Ours. Don't Touch'. Nashe Radio and the Consolations of the Domestic Mainstream'. In Strukov, V., Hudspith, S. (eds.) *Russian Culture in the Age of Globalization*. London: Routledge, pp. 68–98.

Mitchell, T. (ed.) 2001. *Global Noise. Rap and Hip-Hop Outside the USA*. Middletown, CT: Wesleyan University Press.

Moore, D.C. 2001. 'Is the Post- in Postcolonial the Post- in Post-Soviet? Toward a Global Postcolonial Critique'. *PMLA*, 116, 1, pp. 111–28.

Morozov, V. 2015. *Russia's Post-Colonial Identity. A Subaltern Empire in a Eurocentric World*. Basingstoke: Palgrave Macmillan.

Neumann, I.B. 2016. 'Russia's Europe 1991–2016: Inferiority to Superiority'. *International Affairs*, 92, 6, pp. 1381–99.

O'Connor, A. 2004. 'Punk and Globalisation: Spain and Mexico'. *International Journal of Cultural Studies*, 7, 2, pp. 175–95.

Ovchinnikov, N. 2022. 'Postsovetskoi muzyki bol'she net'. *Telegra.ph*, 6 September. URL: https://telegra.ph/Postsovetskoj-muzyki-bolshe-net-09-06?fbclid=IwAR3twX2gxqjj6ml UC2tKYDVU5CfoJManTVD3fIcd6y9fW7NA6btMVsIOLUQ (accessed 20 September 2022).

Parkinson, T. 2018. 'Indiestanbul: Counter-Hegemonic Music and Third Republicanism in Turkey'. *Popular Music*, 37, 1, pp. 40–62.

Parts, L. 2015. 'Topography of Post-Soviet Nationalism: The Provinces—the Capital—the West'. *Slavic Review*, 74, 3, pp. 508–28.

Patsiaoura, E. 2013. 'Musicking, Participating, and Identifying Selves Through Musical Communities of Practice: A Cosmopolitan Band in Greece'. In Russell, I., Ingram, C. (eds.) *Taking Part in Music: Case Studies in Ethnomusicology*. Aberdeen: Aberdeen University Press, pp. 216–34.

Pennycook, A. 2007. *Global Englishes and Transcultural Flows*. London: Routledge.

Pilkington, H., Omelchenko, E., Flynn, M., Bluidina, U., Starkova, E. 2002. *Looking West? Cultural Globalization and Russian Youth Cultures*. Philadelphia: Pennsylvania State University Press.

Potter, J., Wetherell, M. 1987. *Discourse and Social Psychology. Beyond Attitudes and Behaviour*. London: Sage.

Putin, V. 2023. 'Zasedanie diskussionnogo kluba Valdai'. *Kremlin.ru*, 5 October 2023. URL: http://kremlin.ru/events/president/news/72444 (accessed 18 July 2024).

Riabov, I. 2022. 'Issledovatel' Devid Makfad'en – o tekushem vospriiatie rossiiskoi muzyki na zapade'. *IMI*, 29 August. URL: https://i-m-i.ru/post/david-macfadyen-interview?utm_source=telegram&utm_medium=imi_social (accessed 5 September 2022).

Rogatchevski, A., Steinholt, Y. 2016. 'Pussy Riot's Musical Precursors? The National Bolshevik Party Bands, 1994–2007'. *Popular Music and Society*, 39, 4, pp. 448–64.

Introduction 25

Ryback, T. 1990. *Rock around the Bloc: A History of Rock Music in Eastern Europe and the Soviet Union, 1954–1988*. Oxford: Oxford University Press.

Rzheutska, L. 2023. 'Kyiv Imposes Ban on Russian-Language Culture'. *DW*, 20 July. https://dw.com/en/kyiv-imposes-ban-on-russian-language-culture/a-66301913#:~:text=In%20June%202022%2C%20the%20Ukrainian,and%20distribution%20of%20Russian%20books (accessed 13 October 2023).

Saprykin, Y. 2023. 'Balalaika i Ko'. *Kommersant*, 27 October. URL: https://www.kommersant.ru/doc/6283696 (accessed 30 October 2023).

Semenenko, A. (ed.) 2021. *Satire and Protest in Putin's Russia*. New York: Palgrave.

Shishkin, M. 2022. 'Don't Blame Dostoevsky'. *The Atlantic*, 24 July. URL: https://www.theatlantic.com/ideas/archive/2022/07/russian-literature-books-ukraine-war-dostoyevsky-nabokov/670928/ (accessed 30 October 2023).

Sibgatullina, G. 2022. 'Changing the tune: Can Russia's Ethnic Minority Musicians Challenge Imperialist Connotations of Russianness?' *Russia.Post*, 9 May. URL: https://russiapost.info/regions/changing_tune (accessed 23 September 2022).

Soundreef. 2019. 'More Women In Music: nel settore musicale solo il 16,8% di donne. Guardiamo i numeri con le autrici Soundreef'. 2 March. URL: https://www.soundreef.com/blog/more-women-in-music-nel-settore-musicale-solo-il-168-di-donne-guardiamo-i-numeri-con-le-autrici-soundreef/ (accessed 6 October 2021).

Stalin, J. 1913. Marxism and the National Question. URL: https://www.marxists.org/reference/archive/stalin/works/1913/03a.htm.

Steinholt, Y. 2005. *Rock in the Reservation: Songs from the Leningrad Rock Club 1981–1986*. Bergen – New York: The Mass Media Music Scholar's Press.

Steinholt, Y. 2012a. 'Punk Is Punk but by No Means Punk: Definition, Genre Evasion and the Quest for an Authentic Voice in Contemporary Russia'. *Punk and Post-Punk*, 1, 3, pp. 267–84.

Steinholt, Y. 2012b. 'Siberian Punk Shall Emerge Here: Egor Letov and Grazhdanskaia Oborona'. *Popular Music*, 31, 3, pp. 401–15.

Steinholt, Y., Wickström, D.E. 2009. 'Visions of the (Holy) Motherland in Contemporary Russian Popular Music: Nostalgia, Patriotism and Ruskii Rok'. *Popular Music and Society*, 32, 3, pp. 313–30.

Stites, R. 1992. *Russian Popular Culture. Entertainment and Society Since 1900*. Cambridge: Cambridge University Press.

Strukov, V. 2016. 'Russian 'Manipulative Smart Power': Zviagintsev's Oscar Nomination, (non)Government Agency and Contradictions of the Globalize. *New Cinemas: Journal of Contemporary Film*, 14, 1, pp. 31–49.

Strukov, V., Hudspith, S. (eds.). 2019. *Russian Culture in the Age of Globalization*. London: Routledge.

Sukhachëv, G. 2022. 'Ia ostaius''. 11 July 2022. URL: https://www.youtube.com/watch?v=Zn4sk-OdlWM (accessed 30 October 2022).

Tlostanova, M. 2018. *What Does It Mean to Be Post-Soviet? Decolonial Art from the Ruins of the Soviet Empire*. Durham and London: Duke University Press.

Tolz, V. 2001. *Russia: Inventing the Nation*. London: Arnold.

Tolz, V. 2020. 'Transnational, Multinational, or Imperial? The Paradoxes of Russian (Post) Coloniality'. In Byford, A., Doak, C., Hutchings, S. (eds.) *Transnational Russian Studies*. Liverpool: Liverpool University Press, pp. 37–49.

Tolz, V., Hutchings, S. 2023. 'Truth With a Z: Disinformation, War in Ukraine, and Russia's Contradictory Discourse of Imperial Identity'. *Post-Soviet Affairs*, 39, 5, pp. 347–65.

Trabun, D. 2012. 'Evolutsiia Dorna: Kak ukrainskaia pop-muzyka pobedila rossiiskuiu estradu'. *Look At Me*, 16 October. URL: http://www.lookatme.ru/mag/archive/experience-other/182512-ukr-pop (accessed 16 October 2023).

Troitsky, A. 1988. *Back in the USSR: The True Story of Rock in Russia*. London: Faber & Faber.

26 *Independent Music in Russia*

Turino, T. 2003. 'Are We Global Yet? Globalist Discourse, Cultural Formations and the Study of Zimbabwean Popular Music'. *British Journal of Ethnomusicology*, 12, 2, pp. 51–79.

Urban, M., Evdokimov, A. 2004. *Russia Gets the Blues. Music, Culture and Community in Unsettled Times*. Ithaca, NY: Cornell University.

Urbinati, M. 2021. 'Enough of Hammers and Sickles: Towards a Post-Post-Soviet Aesthetics'. *Jordan Center*, 5 March. URL: https://jordanrussiacenter.org/news/enough-of-hammers-and-sickles-towards-a-post-post-soviet-aesthetic/ (accessed 15 October 2023).

Vermeulen, T., Van den Akker, R. 2010. 'Notes on Metamodernism'. *Journal of Aesthetics & Culture*, 2, 1, pp. 1–14.

Wallach, J. 2008. 'Living the Punk Lifestyle in Jakarta'. *Ethnomusicology*, 52, 1, pp. 98–116.

Wallach, J. 2014. 'Indieglobalization and the Triumph of Punk in Indonesia'. In Lashua, B., Spracklen, K., Wagg, S. (eds.) *Sounds and the City: Popular Music, Place and Globalization*. Basingstoke: Palgrave Macmillan, pp. 148–61.

Walser, R. 1993. *Running With the Devil: Power, Gender, and Madness in Heavy Metal Music*. Hanover: Wesleyan University Press.

Wang, Y., Horvàt, E.A. 2019. 'Gender Differences in the Global Music Industry: Evidence from MusicBrainz and the Echo Nest'. *Proceedings of the Thirteenth International AAAI Conference on Web and Social Media* (ICWSM 2019).

Wickström, D.E. 2014. *Rocking St. Petersburg – Transcultural Flows and Identity Politics in Post-Soviet Popular Music*. Stuttgart: Ibidem.

Yaffa, J. 2021. *Between Two Fires. Truth, Ambition and Compromise in Putin's Russia*. New York: Penguin.

Yermolenko, V. 2022. 'From Pushkin to Putin: Russian Literature's Imperial Ideology'. *Foreign Policy*, 25 June. URL: https://foreignpolicy.com/2022/06/25/russia-ukraine-war-literature-classics-imperialism-ideology-nationalism-putin-pushkin-tolstoy-dostoevsky-caucasus/ (accessed 30 January 2024).

Yurchak, A. 2006. *Everything Was Forever, Until It Was No More: The Last Soviet Generation*. Princeton, NJ: Princeton University Press.

Zav'ialov, V. 2021. 'Petara Marticha i Bahh Tee obviniali v nasilii. Pochemu u pokhozhikh keisov – raznye posledstviia'. *Afisha*, 25 March. URL: https://daily.afisha.ru/music/19239-petara-marticha-i-bahh-tee-obvinyali-v-nasilii-pochemu-u-pohozhih-keysov-raznye-posledstviya/ (accessed 7 October 2021).

1 The history, structures and politics of *nezavisimaia muzyka*

Introduction

Russian independent music (*nezavisimaia muzyka*) is a sonically diverse cultural movement centred on alternative channels of production and distribution through which its networked participants strive to carve a space of possibilities for their ideas, careers and lives.[1] Crucially, since its inception in the 1960s, this space has usually been confronted by a heavily ideological political milieu. More than a response to the market, as in the case of several Western countries, independent music in Soviet and post-Soviet Russia has been the story of an endless negotiation with political power, whose various attitudes towards independent culture have shifted, at times arbitrarily and suddenly, between hostility, censorship, surveillance, indifference and even support, and whose agendas have ranged between cosmopolitanism, nationalism, imperialism and pro- and anti-Westernism. This negotiation has shaped Russian independent music's peculiar oscillations between retreat and engagement, aestheticism and politicisation, support and critique of the status quo, irony and seriousness.[2] These dynamics, which make "culture politically relevant and power culturally productive" (Etkind 2011, 3), take sharp forms throughout modern Russian history. Like other cultural formations in Russia, domestic independent music has always emerged *parallel to*, *despite*, but also *thanks to* the erratic and often repressive system that enclosed it.

With perhaps more intensity than in other independent music scenes, particularly in the Anglophone world, *nezavisimaia muzyka*'s object of enquiry has been the country and its history, questions and problems. In its demarcated national referentiality, independent music has been consistent with other forms of culture in Russia, synchronically and diachronically. As in the past, the interrogation of the country (*strana*) stemmed from feelings of devotion to it, as well as dissatisfaction with, and alienation from, the state (*gosudarstvo*) that ruled over it. Like many previous Russian writers, artists and intellectuals, independent practitioners were animated by visions of Russia (the *strana*) whose composite elements often diverged from the official narrative (the *gosudarstvo*) but at times also overlapped with it. At any rate, the authoritarian state constituted an unpleasant hurdle, but strategies differed among practitioners as to how to relate to it: attack, ignore, ingratiate, comply, circumvent or anything in between.

DOI: 10.4324/9781003248699-2

28 *Independent Music in Russia*

It is not an overstretch to say that Russian independent musicians inherited the sceptre of moral leadership that once was the prerogative of poets and novelists. The written word made way to the recorded audio-visual product; the discussion evolved from the salons and thick journals (or, later, the Soviet kitchens) to music venues and social media platforms. The same cannot be said of other cultural figures in the 2010s. Mainstream performers, for instance, while articulating their own version of defiance (particularly in relation to official discourses concerning LGBTQ+ communities),[3] had more privileges to lose and less willingness to criticise the system that rewarded them. The same issues concerned film directors, who were to a considerable extent reliant on state funding for their work, or visual artists, whose exhibiting spaces (e.g., museums) were "intercepted" by and subsumed to state capital and, eventually, narratives (Chukhrov 2023). The burden (or privilege) of the country's moral consciousness was thus seized by independent musicians, to a lesser degree exposed to the mechanisms of compromise typical of the pre-2022 Putin era (Yaffa 2020), but equally capable of reaching large audiences, particularly young ones.

It is extremely difficult to define past and contemporary *nezavisimaia muzyka* as a particular "sound", because this music has comprised a broad range of styles: rock (including indie, punk, post-punk, hardcore, new wave and psychedelia), but also rap, pop, noise, witch-house and ambient, to name a few. As cross-pollination between styles, pastiche and experimentation expanded in the digital era, contemporary Russian independent music has not possessed – nor has it wanted to possess – any clear sonic underpinnings. It makes sense, therefore, to look for what united the different practitioners working within these styles, that is, the idea of musical community (in Russian: *muzykal'noe soobshchestvo* or *muzykal'naia tusovka*). The community was the locus of musical activity and network connection, coordination, solidarity and expansion. Through its horizontal structures, artists emerged, developed and gained listeners, resources were shared and values were shaped. The internet, in itself an alternative to old media (radio and TV), functioned as a digital spin-off of such a community and stood in a complementary relationship with it, as a territory of experimentation and intellectual freedom, which seemed for most of the 2010s beyond the eye of the state.

In what follows, I pinpoint some overarching themes that inform this book throughout. Firstly, I outline some of the features of independent music in "the West", particularly in the Anglophone sphere, and then investigate how *nezavisimaia muzyka* took shape and what special characteristics it displays in comparison with its Western neighbour. Secondly, borrowing from Crossley's (2015) conceptualisation of "music world", I define *nezavisimaia muzyka* as the result of a collective effort and particular historical conditions, delineating how this music world generates a shared sense of identity for their participants that feeds back into the cultural practices of society, and, at the same time, how it is influenced and shaped by the political realities in which it operates. Thirdly, this chapter frames *nezavisimaia muzyka* as an "imagined community". As nationalism scholar Benedict Anderson (1983) maintained, "imagined communities" are large groups of individuals unknown to each other but united by a similar vision of the nation.

The History, Structures and Politics of Nezavisimaia Muzyka   29

However, incessant disputes around "where" this community was located (if in the world, or specifically in Russia) divided the *nezavisimaia muzyka* participants into mainly two camps, influencing the debate on "how" domestic music culture should look and sound: between a Westernised cosmopolitanism and a localised difference. Of course, this division was not always neat, but it was nonetheless actively constructed by participants in their discourses.

Connected to the last point, I examine the notion of the Other (Hall 1996b) and its application to *nezavisimaia muzyka*, where practitioners almost infallibly understood it as "the West" (*zapad*) – particularly Western Europe and North America. Based on the participants' own understanding of geopolitical events, Russia and "the West" were projected as two different entities – at times reconcilable, at times not – depending also on the period analysed. Of course, "the West" is more than a geographical category: it is cultural and developmental, "defined through common cultural, social and political traits and patterns of development" (Tolz 2010, 197). It could converge with, but also diverge from, imaginings of Europe (*Evropa*), in line with modern Russian intellectual history since the nineteenth century, where the values negatively associated with "the West" (e.g., liberalism, capitalism, individualism, lack of spirituality, etc.) have at times differed from more positive and familiar ideas about "Europe", which mainly centred upon the legacy of the Enlightenment, scientific advancement, preservation of national traditions, promotion of collective national spirit and Christianity (though the latter could also be seen in antagonistic terms). In recent official discourse, the idea that (Western) "Europe" forgot its true values, which Russia now protected (Neumann 2017), involved a split, and "'the West' became defined as liberal multiculturalism, in which Europe's Christian foundations are suppressed" (Engström 2020b, 142). At the cusp of the 2020s, and particularly after February 2022, this ideology was flanked, if not overwhelmed, by the resurgence of the idea of "Russia as a civilisation" and its clash with "the West" (Mjør and Turoma 2020; Engström 2022). Nevertheless, in all these phases, modern, recent and contemporary, the Other – be this Europe, "the West" or a coalescence of both – has always been the "main ingredient of Russian identity" (Tolz 2010, 197). I therefore review the important implications that this Other has had for Russia's musical production, and how *nezavisimaia muzyka* practitioners positioned themselves in relation to it.

All in all, by presenting these frameworks and how they interplay in the Russian independent music context, the chapter aims to reveal the complexities of a cultural world that may at first seem small, independent or alternative, but that has reflected, elaborated on and projected the preoccupations, philosophies and dynamics of Russian society at a broader level.

Independent music in "the West"

It is traditionally assumed that "independent" music emerged in Britain in the late 1970s.[4] In the British context, the abbreviation of "independent" ("indie") gained popularity in the early 1980s to describe a particular mode of production and distribution of guitar-based music that relied on do-it-yourself (DIY) principles, constituted an alternative to vertical corporate structures, centred on equitable relationship between labels and musicians and self-proclaimed a certain superiority in relation to the mainstream (Hesmondhalgh 1996, 111–113; Hesmondhalgh 1999, 35; Hibbett 2005).

Over time this characterisation has mutated, with "indie" becoming a term that now challenges a coherent and all-encompassing definition (Galuszka and Wyrzykowska 2018). Firstly, as experimentation constituted one of the early practitioners' priorities, the genre expanded and diversified sonically: "indie pop", "indie hip-hop", "indietronica" and "indie-folk" are examples of combinations that have blurred the genre lines. Nonetheless, the appearance and enduring global success of bands like the Strokes, Interpol and Arctic Monkeys in the 2000s have contributed to maintain the strong ties between indie and rock, along with the immediate emergence of a plethora of less popular or ephemeral similar collectives – some of whom became known in music journalism as "landfill indie" (Rafaeli 2016; Power 2019). Indie has continued to this day to be perceived by most audiences primarily as a guitar-driven sound.

Secondly, indie in the West has long been a highly successful commercial genre. On the one hand, by the late 1980s and early 1990s, indie bands like the Smiths, R.E.M. and Nirvana conquered the top charts worldwide. On the other, the alternative indie model was progressively integrated into the capitalist system. In 2017, around 70% of the global market share was controlled by only three majors: Warner, Sony and Universal (Mulligan 2017). These majors had incorporated many independent labels under their umbrella, with varying degrees of effectiveness in concealing verticality of structure to maintain an image of purity for the listener (Wikström 2014; Wikström and DeFilippi 2016). Notwithstanding the shifts brought about by music streaming in terms of distribution, decentralisation and releasing opportunities, this proportion has not changed very much in the early 2020s. Again, industry analyst Mark Mulligan (2021) reports that even though the portion of recorded music controlled by majors in 2020 decreased to 65%, indie labels still owned around 30% of the market. The remaining 5% was occupied by musicians without affiliation. On the one hand, musicians without label affiliation represented the large majority of the creators (around five million), but, on the other, they earned a meagre pro capita revenue of around £180 a year. Mulligan calls them "artists direct"; journalist Tom Ingham (2019) terms them "DIY artists"; Qu et al. (2021) define them as "self-releasing". These musicians can be also identified as "independent" (they de facto are), but usually their access to resources and outreach is way more limited than that of artists with an independent label behind them. In the Russian context, however, it makes more sense to also see "self-releasing" artists as "independent", not only because this category includes several musicians of national relevance, but primarily because there is not much difference between these musicians and artists affiliated with an indie label in terms of access to resources, outreach and modus operandi (see the next section for more detail).

The integration of the leftist, democratising and anti-corporate economics of independent music into corporate structures has also impacted, and in many cases disarmed, its political potential as an alternative to capitalism. Mark Fisher (2009, 9)

The History, Structures and Politics of Nezavisimaia Muzyka   31

provokingly claimed that "alternative" and "independent" "don't designate something outside mainstream culture; rather, they are styles, in fact *the* dominant styles, within the mainstream". Under neoliberalism, Fisher argued, critical and subversive viewpoints are sought after and pre-incorporated: "nothing runs better on MTV than a protest against MTV" (Fisher, (2009, 9). For journalist Rhian Jones (2013), this process goes two ways: capitalist thinking has been interiorised by indie performers, who now play "by the rules of the game" as if it was something taken for granted, common sense. The result, she argues, is insipid music, stereotypification of the working class and homogenised political disengagement aimed at pursuing individual careerism. However, Jones talks about widely known independent musicians, overlooking that the all-encompassing, expansionist and absorptive character of the neoliberal market affecting sizeable indie labels has pushed micro-indie labels to seek and occupy niches which corporations or other big indie labels are unaware of or uninterested in (Hesmondhalgh and Meier 2015, 94). In these marginal settings, like before, economic and political alternatives can still be sought, though without any ambition to enter into real challenge with the dominant order. Thus, on the one hand, the meaning of "indie" as alternative production, distribution and values has become contested; on the other, the work of myriad micro-indies has retained a good degree of the genre's original political and ideological alternativeness. As a result, instead of two fixed categories we can recognise a plurality of subcultures and mainstreams that interact in the fluid sphere of popular music culture, often overlapping with one another (Baker et al. 2013).

Interconnected with structure is an important value in independent music: autonomy, in particular creative autonomy. Traditionally, creative autonomy has been considered to matter more to independent artists than mainstream ones (Hesmondhalgh 1999), yet even this terrain has become unstable. As Luvaas (2013, 96) observes, autonomy is measured by its perceived distance from mainstream musical practice, but as the distinctions between mainstream and indie have become elusive, autonomy is "perpetually undefined, deeply contextual, and decidedly more performative than objective". Indie labels usually operate on a smaller scale, common vision with the artists and fairer terms, but, as Klein et al. (2017, 232) note, "major labels can fit comfortably with values associated with independence" as well, offering tailored support to musicians and leaving them space for autonomous creative decisions.[5] In Russia, bands like Little Big or Shortparis, which "upstreamed" to majors in 2018 and 2019 respectively, continued to have great autonomy over their product after their deal, including scripting and filming their own music videos. Signing to a major, for them, did not equate to "selling out" or renouncing control, but signified more opportunities for outreach and the streamlining of organisational matters, such as tour schedules. Autonomy is thus negotiated within the system (Holt and Lapenta 2010, 224) and is a constant work in progress that depends not on the artist alone, but also on ever-changing interrelationships involving the internal rationales of the art world, the dynamics of commerce and other external social demands (Banks 2010, 265).

In this process of negotiation of autonomy, audience perception still matters considerably. Fans of independent music attribute values of "alternativeness" or

32   *Independent Music in Russia*

"authenticity", usually by contrasting independent music against what is felt to be "manufactured", conformist or subordinated to profit. On the one hand, this subjective and collective construction that fans make, whereby "authenticity is ascribed to, rather than inscribed in [the music, artist or performance]" (Moore 2002, 220), implies that for each indie fan regarding indie as the most "authentic" genre of popular music, there is a fan of corporate pop regarding this genre as equally meaningful and authentic (consider, for instance, the rise of K-pop). On the other hand, acknowledging that "every music, and every example, can conceivably be found authentic by a particular group of consumers" (Moore 2002, 220), does not discard audience perception, but merely categorises it: indie becomes indie when fans contrast it to an implicit and imaginary non-indie world. As Barbara Lebrun (2009, 159) notes, even though "there is nothing inherently 'authentic' about this mode of engagement with popular music, however sincerely felt this opposition may be", it creates meaning for its participants.

At least in the beginning of their career, indie acts tend to be tightly connected to their local musical identity (e.g., Manchester, New York, etc.), in a relationship of mutual exchange and support between the musicians and other scene participants. Even in the digitalised era, physical, circumscribed spaces and communities continue to provide the infrastructure of music scenes and promote the idea of local sounds. As Holly Kruse (2010, 625) explains: "the decentralisation and globalisation of music production and dissemination have not resulted in the disappearance of local identities, local scene histories or the perception that there are local sounds". Similarly, Connell and Gibson (2003, 107) maintain that even if the internet attempts to de-link scenes from localities, "scenes continue to rely on fixed infrastructures within localities for their survival". The ties of the community to places, clubs, neighbourhoods and cities as gathering foci are felt and constructed by indie participants with more intensity than in mainstream environments that make extensive use of corporate, geographically dispersed support (Epstein 2015, 6–7). The smaller scale of the phenomenon allows for more horizontal informal systems based on mutual sympathy over profit maximisation (though profit of some sort must be made to continue musical activities). Since independent scenes are constructed by participants tightly connected with one another, we can therefore conceive of indie as "a term of membership rather than simply a declaration of independence" (Luvaas 2013, 97) and as a landscape communally validated rather than a particular or "authentic" style of music.

Because the conditions of this "membership" are partially defined by locality, the values of each independent scene varies in accordance with the scene's geography and history: "indie" in the UK differs from independent music in Russia, Korea or Indonesia, in terms of the Other against which it is defined (e.g., "pop" or "classic rock", K-Pop, Soviet rock or Indonesian rock), sound peculiarities, number of participants, extension and strength of networks, commercial success and political priorities. Within a country, regional and urban scenes will differ too. Thus, even if common aesthetic elements can be found in musical movements across the globe (Regev 2013), these movements do happen locally (Pennycook 2007, 2010) and present diverse characteristics and preoccupations. For what concerns politics,

The History, Structures and Politics of Nezavisimaia Muzyka   33

for example, not all scene participants construct their relationship with state power in the oppositional way Western literature on the topic often describes them doing. As the incorporation of Western indie's alternative values into neoliberal structures progressed, Western scholarship nostalgically resurrected indie's subversive character elsewhere. Especially in non-Western countries of unstable democracy or autocracy, studies have tended to emphasise the politically nonconformist and resistant nature of indie (Way 2016; Parkinson 2018; Webb-Gannon and Webb 2019). This approach has been criticised in other studies as West-centric and reductionist (Nooshin 2017; Sprengel 2020). Resistance may well be primary in the case of *some* artists, but pitting a unified oppressive state against a homogeneous Westward-facing youth may also reinforce Orientalist views, ignore the multi-directionality of state-culture relations and overlook that in non-Western milieus music scenes can function differently from the West.

Nezavisimaia muzyka: a historical account

Nezavisimaia muzyka centres on a DIY ethos and relies on independent networks and small-sized companies for production, promotion and distribution in a similar way to how Western indie operated during its early days. As in the West, *nezavisimaia muzyka* develops in local hubs and through horizontal webs of people who are connected to each other not only by business, but also by passion, and not only as professionals, but also as acquaintances and friends. Similarly to the West, independent practitioners in Russia regard creative autonomy as essential to making music, and being part of a local scene is extremely important for the development of their careers. However, as a cultural phenomenon that originated from a particular social structure and ideological system,[6] *nezavisimaia muzyka* presents several differences in comparison with its Western namesake, such as a strong path dependence from the late Soviet period, an underdeveloped verticalisation and an ingrained and normalised economic precarity. A historical contextualisation is needed in order to explain these peculiarities, crucially bearing in mind that, throughout its evolution, this musical movement had to coexist with a political system that did not favour its existence, and to which practitioners responded with defiance, more than antagonism.

Soviet "independent" music

Soviet unofficial music emerged and developed within the gaps of a totalitarian system and not within a free market, which endowed the music with demarcated traits of literariness (the primacy of lyrics over sound), irony, marginality and abstraction. Traditionally, this style of music has been known as "*russkii rok*" (Russian rock), primarily because the language of the music's lyrics was Russian and because the epicentre of this movement was in Leningrad.

   "Soviet rock" and "*russkii rok*" have often been used as synonyms by critics as well as participants – a conceptualisation which may echo the centre's advantaged epistemic position in relation to the other Soviet republics, even in the context of

34   *Independent Music in Russia*

unofficial, underground cultures. In Soviet Ukraine, for example, the local adaptation of Western rock, including manifestations of fandom and attempts of the KGB to contrast or accommodate it, resulted on the one hand in the further Russification of Soviet (Eastern) Ukrainian popular music and, on the other, in resentment towards the centre for its privileges, in "provincial envy of Moscow" (Zhuk 2010, 308–310). Moreover, by no means was all unofficial rock in the Soviet Union sung in Russian (Ward 2014). But aside from hierarchies of language and knowledge production within unofficial culture, several Soviet Russophone rock bands would not identify with the "*russkii rok*" label either, or they would be in open opposition to it, simply in terms of sound and style – for example, several Soviet new wave or post-punk bands of the 1980s (Steinholt 2003, 93; Petrova and Kurakin 2016).

Therefore, even though "*russkii rok*" and "Soviet rock" are often used interchangeably, "Soviet rock" refers to rock created in the Soviet Union, while "*russkii rok*" is one of its strands – the most studied – which formed in Leningrad in the 1970s and achieved nation-wide popularity in the 1980s. An influential Soviet and Russian rock critic (Interview 13), describes *russkii rok* as: "A literary song with the accompaniment of an electric guitar. […] A rock of little energy, essentially devoid of sexual elements and very difficult to dance to, but [with] deep philosophical content and beautiful poetry". Similarly, Andrei Tropillo, who worked as a sound engineer and producer on many seminal Soviet unofficial rock albums in the 1980s, viewed *russkii rok* as "derivative" (*vtorichnyi*) in relation to Anglo-American music, but not in terms of lyrics (Tropillo in Gorbachev and Zinin 2014, 207). As the quotations illustrate, *russkii rok* proceeded through negotiations with its source (Western rock) and its place (the Soviet milieu), out of which its distinctiveness formed.

Scholars have conceptualised this broad and heterogenous rock movement vis-à-vis the political environment as countercultural, underground, unofficial, nonconformist and so on,[7] but these musicians could have not been more "independent" in their modes of production and channels of distribution. In order to create an alternative space in which to operate, Soviet "independent" practitioners constructed autonomy not from the "mainstream" market (that was already taken for granted) but from the state system that controlled this market.

In the stagnation years (1964–1985), Soviet state control over the phonographic industry (in the form of the monopolistic label Melodiya, established in 1964) extensively filtered out Western rock as corruptive, capitalistic and individualistic music. The ideological filtering, however, generated a large black market of Western records, circulated and consumed particularly by the youth. When consumption of Western rock soon informed and inspired local "unofficial" production, authorities responded with the creation of the VIAs (*vokal'no-instrumental'nye ansambli* – vocal-instrumental ensembles, established in 1966) in the attempt to guide, Sovietise and accommodate the spread of domestic rock culture. VIAs were trained, salaried musicians with sanctioned repertoires who provided the Soviet public with an ideologically acceptable version of Western rock. However, as Thomas Cushman (1995, 79) notes, Soviet official rock was rarely mentioned as "rock" in public discourse because of the negative associations of the word with

The History, Structures and Politics of Nezavisimaia Muzyka   35

its capitalist birthplace, and, among informal communities, "the term rock music came to be synonymous with independent music".

Nonetheless, the social recognition of being a rock musician (and making a living out of it), rather than in the form of the market, occurred through state investiture. The state-regulated professionalisation of musicians caused a separation within the field between paid professionals and unrecognised amateurs, with the latter being confined (because of style, musical education or ideological nonconformity) to the underground (*podpol'e*) and the unofficial. Points of crossover were extremely rare but not impossible: Mashina vremeni (Time Machine), one of the most influential "amateur" Soviet rock groups, acquired official status in 1980. Moreover, while most musicians were comfortable maintaining autonomy at the cost of official recognition and access to good equipment, others did not want to stay outside the market permanently, as they "had ambitions in the direction of professionalisation" McMichael (2005, 684). In any case, the separation implied that unrecognised musicians had scarce access to resources (studios, equipment, good quality instruments, etc.), performed for small audiences and relied on informal self-release methods as the primary way to disseminate their music. These informal practice of recording and releasing came to be known as *magnitizdat*,[8] and it was of fundamental importance for Soviet rock. Unofficial concerts in apartments, university rooms and small clubs were taped, then copied and distributed across the black market and personal networks (Kan 2017). These recordings converged at the cusp of creativity and fragility (McMichael 2009), and their quality – often far from ideal to start with – decreased with each re-taping (McMichael 2009, 335; Interview 31).[9] *Magnitizdat* can be therefore regarded as a DIY, lo-fi practice involving alternative modes of production and distribution, which in turn speaks of the long history of discourses of independence in Russian popular music.

There follows that part of the Soviet recording industry that subscribed to the rules of an informal economy (unregulated, unmonitored and untaxed by the state), with elements of a gift economy, as services and goods could be also offered without any expectation of remuneration, on the basis of participant solidarity. Musicians were rarely paid for their records, which were instead pirated across social networks. As a consequence of this, the correspondence between stardom and wealth, taken for granted in Western popular music (including for indie musicians), was unknown to many Soviet musicians, who could become widely acknowledged cultural icons without earning any substantial income due to the unofficial dimension of their work.[10] Indeed, regardless of their widespread popularity, Soviet amateur musicians were officially employed outside of the music sector (usually in humble occupations, such as cleaners, porters or boiler room attendants). This also means that ideas of multi-jobbing, which are increasingly discussed in Western scholarship on the cultural industries as a source of precarity (Gill 2014; Tarassi 2018; Strong and Canizzo 2021), were long embedded and normalised in the Soviet context.

In terms of values, while early studies on Soviet rock emphasised its rebellious, subversive or countercultural character (Troitsky 1988; Ryback 1990; Cushman 1995), more recent scholarship has complicated this binary picture, positioning

36 *Independent Music in Russia*

Soviet rock as a parallel but not oppositional entity (McMichael 2005; Steinholt 2005, Yurchak 2006). The definition of *vnye*[11] offered by Aleksei Yurchak is useful here to understand this ambivalence. For Yurchak, "being *vnye*" in the late Soviet era meant living in a condition of outsideness but at the same time inside the system: "being within a context while remaining oblivious of it, imagining yourself elsewhere, or being inside your own mind" (128). Rather than outright dissidence, being vnye implied *defiance* of some parameters of official rhetoric, as well as a dialogical dimension between the subject and the system. As Yurchak maintains, Soviet people could "reject a certain meaning, norm, or value, be apathetic about another, continue actively subscribing to a third, creatively reinterpret a fourth, and so on" (28–29). Agency did not equate to political resistance, but to the invention of meaningful realities that in many ways turned their back to state politics. This form of escapism, enabled by the system's multiple gray areas and its ossified but omnipresent ideology, represented for Yurchak the dominant style of living of the last Soviet generation, as well as the main condition in which informal culture was created. It meant a retreat into – and the construction of – lifeworlds in which participants could bond and interact with like-minded friends and acquaintances (*svoi*) who showed neither support of nor dissent from Soviet authoritative discourse, but to whom this discourse was merely uninteresting. The Soviet rock *tusovka* (community, scene) was one of these lifeworlds. As Yngvar Steinholt argues, Soviet rock "did not simply talk back at the Soviet authorities and their ideology. Not only did it insist on changing the subject, it also spoke another language" (Steinholt 2005, 113). The marginality of this alternative subset of people, tastes and beliefs implied a "lack of participation" in the official discourse, which was at the same time caused by the system but also wilfully taken on by the subject (Platonov 2012, 42). It was, as Steinholt (2005, 113) noted, a cynical non-involvement with an ideology that had ceased to inform reality. Of course, this defiance of the political was in itself political, in the sense that it created alternative practices and meanings which groups of people considered worth pursuing. A similar situation is described by Toomistu (2018, 24) in Soviet Estonia, where "the affective engagements along the practices and experiences of rock music became the politics of the unpolitical" fostering the nonconformist youth's "sensorial divergence". As we will see, a similar condition of "apolitical engagement" with, or "political disengagement" from, an uninspiring system survived the fall of the Soviet Union and informed contemporary independent music practitioners as well.

Irony constituted a fundamental expression of the inside-outside state. Indeed, even if these milieus were "deterritorialised", the cultural production that emerged from them was grounded in Soviet reality and commented on it. A particular and ambiguous form of irony, called *stëb* (from the verb *stebat'*, "to mock"), became popular across musical production. *Stëb* centres on an excessive or inappropriate psychological identification (what Yurchak calls "overidentification") of the subject with the object discussed, and proceeds through decontextualisation and recontextualisation of such object in an unexpected terrain or form, ultimately engendering ambivalent reception and laughter. Yurchak maintains that *stëb*'s endgame is in itself ambivalent, as it presents the reader/viewer with the impossibility

The History, Structures and Politics of Nezavisimaia Muzyka   37

to tell appreciation from denigration, support from derision, admiration from scorn and so on (Yurchak 2006).[12] Since the recipient of *stëb* is usually a sacred, mythical, official or authoritative object, the doublevoicedness or even triplevoicedness of *stëb* (Hutchings 2017, 154) may be at the same time a profanation and a reaffirmation of the object profaned. *Stëb* is decoded differently by different audiences: "those 'in the know' who presume that [*stëb*'s] utterances, aside from signifying the obvious, also signify [...] the opposite of what is being stated straightforwardly" (Yoffe 2013, 209) may interpret in one way, and those 'outside the know' may understand it literally or as an absurd and tasteless joke (Yurchak 2011). Yoffe (2013) and Yurchak (2006) give examples such as the bands Zvuki mu (Sounds of Moo) and AVIA in the USSR, as well as Laibach in Slovenia, but *stëb* significantly informed the production of Soviet groups like Auktsyon (Auction) and Tsenter (Centre) (see also Saprykin 2023).

However, Yoffe (2013) has complicated Yurchak's approach, showing how *stëb*'s endgame *is* to make fun of the object addressed, "rendering it absurd or exposing its false and hypocritical nature" (Yoffe 2013, 209). When, in a now legendary programme aired on national TV in 1991, musician Sergei Kurëkhin explained in all seriousness and citing scientific scholarship that Lenin was a mushroom (Yurchak 2011), it became evident where he, as the author, stood in the discussion and in the assessment of the object in question. It became clear that he was *not* half-endorsing and half-mocking at the same time, but that he was masking irony as sincerity. Because Yurchak cites this joke as the epitome of *stëb*, there follows that *stëb* is a form of irony where the author's intentionality eventually gleams through for those who are prepared to capture it.

Stëb is of great importance for the understanding of recent Russian independent music too, as it provided the basis for the development of other forms of irony. As discussed in later chapters, in the post-actionist aesthetics that formed after 2012 (Engström 2018), particularly in music, *stëb* morphed into what Khrushchëva (2020, 29–30) calls "post-irony". Here, rather than being "turned over once", the utterance is "turned over twice" and "endlessly returns" to the initial meaning after having incorporated its opposite. Instead of irony masked as sincerity (as in the case of *stëb*), we see an oscillation between mockery and sincere endorsement that becomes unintelligible *also* for those in the know. Instead of postmodern, deconstructive and nihilistic, post-irony is meta-modern, constructive and positively charged. For instance, the discourse of "pain" as national myth and integral part of the Russian life (Chapter 3) was not only parodied in the musical production of the 2010s, but also affectively embraced. Practitioners were uninterested in actively making a decision about its value. In a typically meta-modern oscillation that refused dichotomies by incorporating both poles, the author's positionality was suspended and their judgement removed from the multiple layers that compose the text. Post-irony informed the production of independent acts such as Buerak, Pasosh, Monetochka, Khaski, Shortparis, Little Big and so forth. As we will see, the main ingredient that turned *stëb* into post-irony in the 2010s was patriotism, the devotion for Russia as a country. Such element was overall absent from the alternative cultural discourse of late Soviet society.

38   *Independent Music in Russia*

Irony animated another distinctive value of Soviet rock: logocentricity. Rock critics (and to a degree, musicians) from Russia have constructed the idea that in domestic rock the word is primary over the sound; this, they believe, is the most important and authentic feature of local rock in comparison to Western rock, where lyrics are secondary or even unimportant (Troitsky 1988; Zhitinskii 2007a, 2007b).[13] Paired with this is the admission that, sound-wise, Soviet (and then post-Soviet Russian) rock is derivative and its musicians cannot "outplay" Western ones. As Steinholt (2003) demonstrates, this idea is questionable: firstly, it taps into essentialist and immutable categories; secondly, many Soviet musicians have dedicated considerable attention to sound and many Western musicians have dedicated considerable attention to lyrics. Nonetheless, these hierarchies (word/sound, Soviet music/Western music) have been produced and perpetuated by Soviet music practitioners with so much intensity that they have become common knowledge among post-Soviet Russian music critics and, crucially, audiences too. Consequently, what holds a good degree of empiric demonstration is that Russian music (including independent music) often functions in society in a lyric-focused way,[14] meaning that audiences are usually very active in looking for immediacy and connection in the lyrics, and domestic music "speaks to them" with urgency at this level.

Finally, for what concerns creative autonomy, Soviet unofficial rock implied a constant negotiation with Soviet authorities and an ambition – actively constructed by its participants – to be regarded as high, serious culture (Steinholt 2003). The conditions to include this culture into the system materialised with the establishment in 1981 of the first official rock club – the Leningrad Rock Club. Steinholt (2005) has suggested that the founding of the club was the result of a deal between unofficial rock musicians (who finally obtained a venue to perform in and catalyse audiences with) and the KGB (which could finally monitor scene participants in one place). This step towards integration in the system, which would then culminate in the mainstream popularity of Soviet rock during perestroika and beyond, would have not been possible without the agency of the members of the *tusovka*. Soviet independent music was thus animated by a strong, dense and sympathetic community that carved alternative spaces for itself within an undemocratic system; instead of direct opposition to power, the *tusovka* preferred ironic non-involvement and, at some point, negotiation. These practices re-emerged with intensity across the independent music community in the 2010s, as illiberal and restrictive political conditions similar to those in the late Soviet period increasingly returned. To sum up, the Soviet ideological system profoundly impacted the forming of the structures, dynamics, conventions and values of the independent music scene, some of which carried over in the post-Soviet period, and, in turn, influenced the way in which today's independent musicians think about their activity and their industry.

From the 1990s to the mid-2010s

Continuity with, more than rupture from, the precarious conditions of the socialist system constituted the axis of Russian independent music in the 1990s and early 2000s. True, musicians were able to publish their songs without worrying about

The History, Structures and Politics of Nezavisimaia Muzyka   39

censorship. Moreover, the state lost its monopoly over the music industry and a myriad of small labels mushroomed. Both musicians and labels, however, were often precarious and temporary ventures that struggled in a field where the old social structures had collapsed but new stable ones were yet to appear.

One of the practices to emerge from the Soviet world and outlive its fall was piracy. In theory, the Soviet Union joined the Geneva Universal Copyright Convention in 1973, and its regulations carried over in the Russian Federation after 1991 (Elst 2004, 485–487). In practice, most citizens disregarded them completely. As music critic Artemy Troitsky summarises: "No one ever asked themselves whether there was any copyright, and whether they were infringing this copyright. No one ever even thought about it" (Troitsky in Biasioli 2021, 44). Like unofficial music, piracy grew as a by-product of the ideological conditions of the Soviet market and represented one of the means through which Soviet people "got by" in the interstices of the system, satisfying through illicit practices a demand for products that were not available in the state-controlled marketplace. This concerned not only foreign, but also domestic music, as piracy – in the sense of illicit copying and distribution without remuneration to the author – became the preferred means (in fact, often the only one) through which unrecognised performers could popularise their music.

Piracy is one of the prime factors in explaining the precariousness of the post-Soviet Russian music industry. From the 1960s to the mid-2010s, and from physical piracy havens such as Gorbushka to digital ones like VKontakte, piracy was so institutionalised as a practice (performed, at times, even by Melodiya) that it flanked and at times superseded the legal music business (Sezneva and Karaganis 2011; Kiriya 2012; Sezneva 2013; Kiriya and Sherstoboeva 2015; Biasioli 2021). For instance, Gorbushka, a gigantic open-air pirate market in the 1990s in West Moscow, stood not only as one of the symbols of Russia's "lawless" 1990s, but was also deeply influential in the Muscovite music scene. As Interviewee 18, a veteran music journalist, promoter and manager, recalls: "[Gorbushka's] stall vendors became the real trendsetters in Russian music in the 1990s", while its charts replaced those of radio stations (*Moskva 24*, 2016). In the digital sphere, VKontakte (literally: "in touch"), launched in 2006, has been the largest and most popular social network in Russia even before the state ban on Facebook in 2022, with more than 500 million subscribers around the world at the end of the 2010s, and most of its monthly active users from the ex-Soviet republics or Russophone diasporas. Until 2017 VKontakte (hereafter VK) functioned almost like Facebook, except that its users could publicly upload, share and download large files on it. Thanks also to the scant control exercised by its admins in terms of copyright protection, and the anti-corporate anarchism of its founder Pavel Durov,[15] VK rapidly turned into one of the most exhaustive audio and video libraries in the world, in which it was possible to find nearly every artefact and usually in simultaneity with its official release.

While piracy significantly delayed the growth of capitalist vertical structures, it also made independent networks unstable, preventing the emergence of a strong musicians' union, a functioning royalty collecting agency or the formation of a conspicuous "middle class" of practitioners, all of which occurred in the West

40 *Independent Music in Russia*

(De Beukelaer 2014). As prominent independent musicians remarked even in the mid-2010s, in Russia, "apart from the enthusiasm of the participants, there is nothing" (Interview 8), referring to the underdevelopment of industry infrastructures (see also Tolstad 2021). Another practitioner observed: "copyright? No one knows how it works" (Interview 6). Questions around musicians' unions or the Russian royalty collecting agency RAO (*Rossiiskoe avtorskoe obshchestvo* – Russian Author's Society) elicited laughs in several cases (Interview 42, 47, 53, 75). As a prominent Russian journalist remarked (Interview 11), "Russian musicians have never really counted on making money from their [recorded] music", relying instead on live activity as a primary source of income. The fact that many 2010's professionals started off from the "pirate underground" in the 1990s–2000s (Voronin 2022) not only highlights the fluidity between illicit and licit cultural practices in post-Soviet Russia, but also evidence that ideas of copyright do not have the same value in comparison with Western Europe. As Artemy Troitsky, one of the main Soviet and post-Soviet Russian music critic, discerned: "What the human intellect creates should belong to all humanity, so I'm definitely against copyright" (Troitsky in Biasioli 2021, 52).

The deep-seated uncertainty surrounding musical labour conditioned the development of structures, spheres of agency and discourses in the Russian music industry. Unlike in the West, for example, there is not much difference between DIY (or self-releasing) artists and artists affiliated to an independent label. As Jones (2021, 67) explains in the context of the UK, local indie and DIY scenes, once considered the same, started to separate in the early 1980s, when indie labels tried to reach a mass audience and "the difference in cost and method between the two became greater". This drift did not occur in Russia, where indie and DIY scenes have overlapped consistently. Both have remained what Toynbee (2000) would classify as "proto-markets", that is, scenes and networks bringing about actors in arenas that are not fully commodified, and in which economic factors alone cannot explain the intense levels of activity. Moreover, self-releasing musicians have often acted as independent labels themselves, gathering around them a small team of collaborators who dealt with touring, distribution, press and licensing. In the 2010s, some of these musicians achieved nationwide popularity with such arrangements, for example, Therr Maitz, Little Big, Shortparis and Manizha, who obtained millions of views and listens and toured domestically in large arenas without affiliation to a label, relying only on a close circle of collaborators. In this study, therefore, musicians signed to indie labels, DIY labels, micro-labels or self-releasing are considered all as "independent" creators within *nezavisimaia muzyka*. Even if this merging may be problematic when analysing Western music industries, it seems more appropriate for what concerns Russia as a less structured, more volatile and enthusiasm-based music industry.

Secondly, the agenda of alternativeness of independent musicians and labels to capitalist market structures, which initially informed Western independent music (Jones 2021; Qu et al. 2021), did not materialise in Russia after the fall of the Soviet Union, as there was no fully formed capitalist industry in the first place. This weakness included the mainstream scene, traditionally seen as one of the constitutive

The History, Structures and Politics of Nezavisimaia Muzyka   41

others against which the independent scene defines itself. Of course, Russia's painful transition from state-controlled to free-market economy in the 1990s gave rise to strictly profit-driven pop projects, but, again, this cannot be considered the result of the activity of organised, "vertically integrated, well financed and *big*" corporations (Hesmondhalgh and Meier 2015, 94) in the same scale as it has been in the West. The socio-political chaos that enveloped Russia in the first post-Soviet decade, of which endemic music piracy and state disinvestment in the cultural industries were manifestations,[16] cast precariousness across the economy of the music industry, generated a fragmented landscape, deterred major labels from investing in Russia and contributed to maintaining it as a proto-market. Because of this disorganisation, fleetingness and randomness, independent musicians did not take an interest in challenging the inchoate structures of the mainstream industry with the same intensity with which, for instance, post-punk musicians in late-1970's UK sought to undermine the centralisation of the Western majors. Moreover, mainstream genres such as *blatnaia pesnia/shanson*,[17] *estrada*[18] and *popsa* (pop)[19] seemed to be far-away, separate worlds not worth of any attention, including oppositional attention.

Instead, antagonism was directed at another alternative and independent movement that had ossified and deteriorated – *russkii rok*. In 1991, for example, Vsevolod Gakkel', ex-cellist of Akvarium and founder of the seminal independent club TamTam (1991–1997), announced that "every style of music could be played in his club except *russkii rok*" (Gakkel' in Bortnikov 2017). Gakkel' argued that the absorption of *russkii rok* into the mainstream deprived it of its sense of independence and autonomy, and that the long-craved acceptance of musicians in the system withdrew "life" from their music (Gakkel' 2007). New independent acts framed themselves in opposition to *russkii rok* by declaring the West as their main source of influence. For example, Evgenii Fedorov, leader of one of the most influential indie bands of the 1990s, Tequilajazzz, claimed: "we don't play *russkii rok*. I mean, I hope we don't. We have nothing to do with the Russians, in terms of lyrics and in terms of style. Our background is American" (Tequilajazzz 2007). This antithesis – paradoxical if we consider that the formation of *russkii rok* musicians was also indebted to Anglo-American influences – epitomises the construction of discourses of transformation within independent cultures: what is perceived as subversive, underground, authentic or "hip" is subject to change (Thornton 1995). As alternative cultures become perceived as conventional or mainstream (Hebdige 1979), they leave room for the birth of new alternative ones.

Thus, industry precarity furthered horizontal structures, strong ties between practitioners, small remuneration and indifference to copyright. It translated into independent and DIY projects being not far from the norm in the post-Soviet music scene, to the point in which these may have in fact constituted the majority of the market share (see also: McMichael 2019, 73). Even though labels' revenue statistics are in Russia a "carefully kept secret" (Galuszka 2021)[20] and there is no such thing as an authoritative Russian music chart (Zav'ialov 2020; Tolstad 2021), majors operating in Russia until 2022 did not remotely have a similar monopoly as in other countries, with the music business being more partitioned and leaving significant space for independent labels and self-releasing artists.[21]

42 *Independent Music in Russia*

From the mid-2010s to the full-scale war

The ingrained precariousness of the post-Soviet Russian music industry started to change around 2016–2017, when the implementation of copyright laws by VK and the rise of licensed streaming platforms prompted a development of musical infrastructure and a strengthening of coordination among practitioners. This resulted in more professionalisation and specialisation of musical labour, in contrast to the enthusiastic multi-tasking that characterised practitioners before (Goldenzwaig 2006). Indeed, the advent of streaming music services signalled a new era for independent musicians, who were finally able to monetise – albeit a little – on their recordings. On a rough calculation (Prokof'ev 2019; Sadkov 2020), Russia's main streaming services Yandex Music and VK paid right holders 6 kopeks and 1 kopek per stream, respectively (£0.0006 and £0.0001). This was significantly less than Spotify, which was launched on Russian territory only in July 2020 and withdrew in April 2022 (21 kopeks, £0.0021). Nonetheless, in the second half of the 2010s Russia went from constituting a weak market to seeing itself as an alternative music centre and a prospective global player (Galuszka 2021, 11). In 2018, Russia sat 23rd in the global ranking of music industries (IFPI 2019). In 2019, the Russian phonographic industry grew to a revenue of £510 million (out of which £92 million came from streaming services), with a rise of 16.4% from the year before (*PwC.ru* 2020), which already was twice the increase of 8.2% of the global market in the same period (IFPI 2020).

Encouraged by these developments, major labels started to buy off independent labels and reconfigure the industry. Warner, for example, bought Zhara Music, one of the main indies for rap, and rearranged it as the Russian subdivision of Atlantic Records (*IMI* 2021a). In September 2021, five distributors, publishing companies and independent labels merged into Zvonko (Loudly),[22] which branded itself as the first homegrown Russian major (Gorbash 2021). Before February 2022, Zvonko already controlled around 20% of the domestic music market (Gorbash 2021). The increase in professionalisation and sectorisation, therefore, was paired with international and domestic majors taking over large portions of the music market.

Despite signs of a process of verticalisation that did not differ much from what Western music industries experienced in the previous decades, the *nezavisimaia muzyka* scene thrived in the 2010s, particularly in its second half. Apart from the aforementioned regulation of streaming services, which furnished *nezavisimaia muzyka* labels and artists with modest but stable sums to reinvest in career growth (e.g., equipment, recording studios, promos, tours, etc.), the number of festivals increased exponentially, not only in Moscow and St. Petersburg, but across Russia. A new array of practitioners started to see independent music not just as a vocation or a cultural mission, but also as an interesting job opportunity. New mid-sized clubs appeared, which soon became centres for independent communities and experimental, unconventional music (for instance, Ionoteka in St. Petersburg and Powerhouse in Moscow, both established in 2013). Festival Bol' (Pain Festival), which ran in Moscow 2015–2019, also acted as a catalyst for *nezavisimaia muzyka* practitioners and for the expansion of the scene. The event grew from five bands and a few hundred spectators in its first year to 90 acts and 17,000 attendees in its last reiteration. The 2020 Bol' promised to double that number, but it was first postponed to 2021 due to COVID and then cancelled in 2022 when its organisers relocated abroad after the start of the Ukraine war. Moscow Music Week, an event dedicated to the development of ties and infrastructure within the domestic independent industry and with international partners, was launched in 2017 on the model of other similar events, such as Tallinn Music Week or Ljubljana's Ment. Moscow Music Week consisted of showcases of emerging acts and conferences with national and international industry practitioners. Among its priorities were to connect artists with industry professionals who could support them, and to display music from regions of Russia outside the centres of Moscow and St. Petersburg. In addition, IMI (Institut muzykal'nykh initsiativ – Institute of Music Initiatives) was established in 2019 at the crossroads of music journalism and industry development as a pool of technical resources, statistics, manuals, job postings and webinars to help audiences discover new music, assist young musicians in navigating the domestic industry and support practitioners in strengthening networks and sharing knowledge. Music journalism speeded up the pace to keep up with new bands constantly emerging on the independent scene, while diversifying the channels on which the conversations evolved (e.g., social media platforms). This coincided with the rise of Telegram (the preferred messaging and social media app for Russians today, established by the founder of VK, Pavel Durov). Among its functions, Telegram allows users to post content and have subscribers, and many music journalists and industry practitioners in various capacities (artist managers, concert promoters, musicians, label workers) opened a channel there. In 2020, *IMI* listed around 50 Telegram channels dedicated to music and the music industry which people must follow to keep up to date with events, news, artists, styles and professional opportunities (*IMI* 2020).

Nezavisimaia muzyka established a consistent presence on national TV too. In 2017, Sergei Mudrik – until then working in advertising and journalism – started working as musical curator for the very popular Russian late-night show *Vechernii Urgant* (Urgant's Evening Show). The programme aired on Russia's state-controlled Channel One (*Pervyi kanal*) five times a week, before its interruption in 2022. As Mudrik reminisced, *Urgant* worked as a "unique PR instrument" and a "springboard" for independent and alternative musicians (Riabova 2022). Together with the presenter Ivan Urgant, who also played music in an indie project called Grisha Urgant, Mudrik granted unprecedented levels of exposure to independent and up-and-coming artists on a channel whose musical entertainment is usually associated with mainstream pop and *estrada*. If one looks back, Oxxxymiron, Face, Noize MC and Monetochka (artists who left Russia after the start of the war and were labelled by the Russian Ministry of Justice as "foreign agents") all played there during this time, as did bands with socially engaged lyrics, such as Shortparis, Manizha and Spasibo (Thanks).

According to Mudrik, the appearance of such artists on Channel One was nothing but the inevitable overflow of a culture that formed and expanded through new media platforms (VK, YouTube, Telegram) and that traditional media could

44 *Independent Music in Russia*

no longer ignore. In Russia, like in many parts of the technologically advanced world, the advent of the internet complemented and accelerated (not replaced) the processes of community networking, creation and distribution of content traditionally performed through physical interaction. The partial online shift of the Russian independent scene in terms of distribution meant the partial online shift of participant networking. These online discussions, in turn, continued at in-person events, concerts, conferences, "music weeks" or informal meetings, feeding back into an ever-evolving loop. Participant observation at showcases, festivals and conferences such as Colisium Music Week 2017, Pain Festival 2017 and Moscow Music Week 2019 confirmed that many of the cultural producers of the Muscovite music scene utilised these events professionally and informally, for building networks and making business while having fun. Thus, social media and physical spaces did not overwrite each other, but worked together towards the development of *nezavisimaia muzyka* as a *tusovka*. As one of the main promoters and festival organisers in Moscow during the 2010s maintained: "here talented people are in one community, interact, influence each other and give each other confidence to develop further" (Interview 37).

Music journalist Kolia Redkin (2022) also identified the internet as the main locus – and reason – for the blooming of what he called "homemade culture" (*samodel'naia kul'tura*). According to Redkin, beyond the radar of the state on one side and free of mainstream diktats on the other, independent artists activated their "do-it-yourself Internet mode" [*internet rezhim 'sdelai sam'*] and created the most notable things in 2010's Russian culture (Redkin, 2022). Interestingly, Redkin listed as DIY culture indie, rap and post-punk, as well as other cultural forms, such as street art and stand-up comedy, that were not directly related to music but nonetheless contributed to the creation of a large scene animated by the same principles of independence. In short, at the turn of the decade, *nezavisimaia muzyka* was at its peak, expanding and asserting its presence in areas of culture and society in which it would not usually be granted visibility.

Because of this quick expansion, the *nezavisimaia muzyka* industry maintained a high level of porosity for the entrance to the scene of new artists – or what the interviewees call, in jargon, "no-names" (*nouneimy*). In addition, the time elapsing from an act's formation to performance on a respectable festival stage was often quite short, sometimes less than a year. Participants observed that this inclusivity was due to the novelty and limited competition of the scene, which made it easier to occupy a spot (Interview 79); others noted that the fact that the door was open did not mean that artists were able to live on their music, as the fees they received for the concerts they played were often not enough to live on (Interview 28, 61). For this reason, around half of the musicians interviewed had a side job outside of music, despite many years of active careers in the industry. This arrangement helped to sustain the economic precarity of their artistic profession. Many of those who did not have a side job were forced to take it up when COVID hit. Some started teaching online (Interview 43, 61), one worked as translator (Interview 62) and one as driver (Interview 75). The scarcity of music-related work during the lockdown and restriction periods – which in Moscow and Russia were nonetheless shorter

The History, Structures and Politics of Nezavisimaia Muzyka   45

than in Western countries like Italy or the United Kingdom – channelled some practitioners to organise and play gigs illegally (Interview 77, 78). These events *dlia svoikh* (for one's own circle of trusted people) took place in closed clubs, or in apartments, by invitation, and were reminiscent of Soviet times, when the practice of the *kvartirnik* (apartment concerts, from the word "kvartira" – apartment) was a widespread practice among unofficial practitioners to avoid the authorities and gain some money from musical activities (McMichael 2014; Kan 2017). As in many other parts of the world, COVID in Russia especially affected music workers in the middle tier – mostly independent ones – for whom live gigs represented the main source of income. Only about 1500 concerts took place in the first half of 2021, 70% less than in 2019, while in 2020 the concert industry lost more than 90% of revenue, leading to mass layoffs within companies and services (*IMI* 2021b). But however powerful the blow, the independent music industry resumed full activity in late 2021 and was on its path to recover, with a dense schedule of concerts, tours and festivals the following year to make up for time lost.

The course of these developments, however, was abruptly altered by Russia's full-scale invasion of Ukraine in February 2022. Since then, participants have tried to comprehend the scope of the impact the war has had on the music industry. The picture concerning new music languages within Russia is still blurred, but in terms of structure the change is visible already: the Russian music market in 2022 shrank and became insulated. Payment methods like Mastercard, Visa and PayPal, as well as distributors like CD Baby and streaming services like Spotify and Apple Music stopped operating, making it more difficult for Russian musicians to obtain revenue from (and upload songs to) music platforms. Warner, Universal and Sony closed their Russian branches or halted their operations. Touring in Europe for Russian musicians became more difficult. Several practitioners migrated abroad: the newspaper *Kommersant* estimated that around 30% of music professionals left Russia or stopped performing between February and September 2022 (Lebedeva 2022). The precariousness which had accompanied Russian musical labour for most of its history was back once again. Like in the late Soviet period, this precarity directly resulted from the state, its policies and ideology, rather than the market (as has been the case in the West). It is to this relationship between power and independent music that we now turn.

The politics of *nezavisimaia muzyka*

The concerns of contemporary Russian independent music practitioners have more to do with political rather than commercial independence. As explained in the previous sections, the commercial independence has conventionally been regarded as a matter of fact, whereas practitioners have often needed to actively maintain their practice outside of the sphere of influence or interference of the state Such independence, however, exists only as an ideal, a perception, ambition and approximation: practitioners may strive towards it, but they are unable to successfully and completely cut themselves off from the political context they inhabit. Music is after all social life and participation, and in an increasingly ideologising milieu the

46 *Independent Music in Russia*

political confronts the practitioners at each step. This tension between music and politics informed the production of *nezavisimaia muzyka* throughout the period studied, and it was particularly visible during Putin's third and fourth terms, when state discourse became more omnipresent and aggressive.

The contours of the independent musicians' unstable and paradoxical position thus emerged: on the one hand, seeking independence from the state and its authoritative discourse; on the other, attempting to articulate ideas about the nation that may enter in competition with the official line.[23] The Pussy Riot affair in 2012, with the harsh punishment of two of the group's members, served as a warning and as a watershed moment: the independent musical production that took shape after that point increasingly displayed both a post-actionist avoidance of direct political statements and a development of ambiguity as aesthetic method. Russian cultural studies scholar Maria Engström (2018), following Dutch thinkers Vermeulen and Van der Akker (2010), termed this trend "metamodernism", a multi-layered and interpretatively defiant artistic approach which was aimed not at a synthesis, but at a wavering between opposite poles (modern and post-modern, earnestness and mockery, grand narratives and the sceptical unattainability of those).

Strictly connected to the metamodernist approach was the musicians' treatment of contestation and resistance, through the emergence of what I term *patrioprotest*: the injection, and ultimately inextricable mixture, of patriotism and protest in the same cultural output. In production of this type, the love, loyalty and devotion for the *strana*, the sense of pride in in the *strana*'s culture and history, intermingled with objections to aspects of the *gosudarstvo*'s policies and actions. Such a tendency emerged particularly with Putin's fourth term, when the state level of interference in independent music matters became tangible. Framing protest within the context of patriotism was another way to articulate resistance while avoiding backlashes from the authorities which could be detrimental to the musicians' activities (e.g., concert cancellations or worse).

As explained in the next chapters, *nezavisimaia muzyka* fluctuated in indirect synchronisation with the political mood set by the state. For example, the creation of the cosmopolitan image of *nezavisimaia muzyka* performed by musicians and trendsetters at the end of the 2000s (the Anglophone Wave) emerged at the intersection of interests that also involved politicians and business people, that is, participants traditionally outside of the independent scene per se. Much like "Cool Britannia", "Cool Russia" coincided with the country's economic growth and, among its music participants, presupposed optimism in connecting and integrating Russia into West-defined global culture.

This cognitive remapping linked indissolubly with language choice. Since its inception, the Russian independent scene has engaged deeply with the question of language, and it is in this sense a chronicle of linguistic turnovers. For instance, one of the characteristics of *russkii rok* was the rejection, towards the end of the 1970s, of English, which had been up until that point framed as the "authentic" language of rock by many of the participants in the unofficial Soviet scene (Steinholt 2005; Interview 7, 29, 31). Underground Soviet musicians such as Boris Grebenshchikov and Mikhail "Maik" Naumenko were fundamental in the adaptation of Western

The History, Structures and Politics of Nezavisimaia Muzyka 47

rock for a Soviet audience and with Soviet themes, and they believed that Russian, as a language, was integral to this process (McMichael 2005). Conversely, *nezavisimaia muzyka* in the context of late 2000s Russia was associated by participants with a modernised sound, in contrast with the mainstream and logocentric *russkii rok*. Modernising meant also participating in an international community and the global market, and the dismissal of the mother tongue in favour of English was functional to this.

Oscillations in the opposite direction occurred following Russia's conservative turn in 2012 and the start of the conflict with Ukraine in 2014. After that, *nezavisimaia muzyka* increasingly provided criticism of, and even resistance to, the *means* with which the state set its goals and implemented its politics, but a part of these political *goals* – Russianness, rejection of (or competition with) "the West" and rediscovery of history and traditional tropes – were shared and endorsed across the independent community as well. In its own way (uncoordinated with the state), the artefacts of the independent community promoted the image of an autonomous, Russophone and Russo-centric music that suited aspects of the patriotic vision of culture that the state strove to enact. Juxtaposed with the failure of "Cool Russia" brought about by geopolitical reconfigurations, "Uncool Russia" entailed taking pride in one's isolation and exploring – and exploiting – the country's rich assets of self-perceptions and cultural tropes, including stereotypes. The practitioners' actions were congruent with what Michael Herzfeld (2004, 3) terms "cultural intimacy", that is, "the recognition of those aspects of a cultural identity that are considered a source of external embarrassment but that nevertheless provide insiders with their assurance of common sociality". In other words, "yes, Russia may be a backward country, but it is *our* backward country", or, as Little Big sing on "Everyday I'm Drinking" (2013), "Our country in deep shit [sic], yo, but I love her, but I love her".

It is worth emphasising again that the abovementioned processes happened in an unforced and indirect way, primarily as a consequence of the overarching state political and ideological milieu within which cultural producers operated and with which they interacted. The Russian popular music industry was and remains for the most part a non-governmental and independent sector, unlike, for instance, the film industry, which is largely state-funded. Popular music is the only cultural industry in Russia which is not subject to ministerial regulation (Safronov et al. 2019, 8–9). While the state adopted a system of patronage with film, it espoused the neoliberal model in music, leaving it to the market to sort out production and distribution. True, in the run-up to the full-scale invasion of Ukraine, authorities increasingly interfered, in a random and uncoordinated fashion, with the activities of individual musicians, particularly in the name of the 2012 law on Children's Protection (see Chapters 3 and 4). But in general, the neoliberal model made musicians less subject to state diktats than, for example, film directors, and freer to use their art as a political platform. This did not mean, however, that all musicians performed political protest; rather, it meant diversification and ambiguity. Over the course of the 2010s, some musicians engaged with the political with varying degrees of directedness; others tended to keep their aesthetic and civic positions separate, preferring to

48 *Independent Music in Russia*

create music that sheltered from politics as both a corrupt world and an uninspiring subject; many chose an in-between position, open to interpretation and ultimately defying one, a mixture of survival strategy and interiorised convention to address the political while avoiding the political's counterattack. The internet provided the ideal space for these modes of engagement (political, apolitical and anything in between), as it was viewed by participants as a territory of freedom seemingly outside the control of the authorities, a medium for counter or parallel publics and one of the main reasons for the growth of independent music culture in Russia (Redkin 2022, see also Denisova and Herasimenka 2019). In other words, the internet constituted the decentralised cultural space where new, non-state actors emerged and constructed a partially alternative vision of the nation to the one held by the state, though never fully competing with it. This happened despite the state's attempts – evident already at the beginning of Putin's third term – to curtail freedom of speech on the Russian internet and establish digital surveillance (*Lenta.ru* 2012). In sum, the coexistence and at times coalescence of such factors suggests that the key characteristics of *nezavisimaia muzyka* reside in its transversal position across global and national issues, and in the musicians' agency in examining and performing Russia's present.

Nezavisimaia muzyka as a music world

The independent Russian musicians who achieved popularity in the domestic scene between 2008 and 2022 were tightly linked not only to the time and place in which they lived but also to a whole array of people, sometimes with very different backgrounds, involved in the construction of culture. Musicians are therefore better understood as "representatives" of the beliefs and tastes of larger groups of people united by similar intents. As British composer Ralph Vaughan Williams (1987, 50) reasoned, "art is not a solitary phenomenon, its great achievements are the crest of a wave; it is the crest which we delight to look on, but it is the driving force of the wave below that makes it possible". This collective dimension connects to musicologist Christopher Small's (1998) idea of "musicking". Rather than being just the work of the composer, music is "an activity, something that people do" (Small, 1998, 2). This activity, crucially, requires connection and organisation among participants to shape meaning. The concept of "musicking" shifts the core of music from the individual to the social and extends the involvement in such activity to a whole community of people. As Small (1998, 9) puts it:

> To music is to take part, in any capacity, in a musical performance, whether by performing, by listening, by rehearsing or practicing, by providing material for performance (what is called composing), or by dancing. We might at times even extend its meaning to what the person is doing who takes the tickets at the door or the hefty men who shift the piano and the drums or the roadies who set up the instruments and carry out the sound checks or the cleaners who clean up after everyone else has gone. They, too, are all contributing to the nature of the event that is a musical performance.

The History, Structures and Politics of Nezavisimaia Muzyka   49

Musicking's collective nature as an organised activity is not limited to live performance, but can be extended further to encompass the people working in recording studios, the promoters booking gigs for musicians, the club owners offering the musicians a stage to perform, the festival organisers, the radio DJs and the curators of music programmes on TV. This contribution can be in turn expanded to music journalists, critics, writers, YouTubers, TikTokers, administrators of music pages on social media and generally, to all gatekeepers, trendsetters and cultural intermediaries who participate in different ways in the creation of music meaning, in filtering cultural content and in "defining what counts as good taste and cool culture in [the] marketplace" (Smith-Maguire and Matthews 2014, 1). After all, the popularisation of a music world would not be possible without specific people with acquired authority, who decide what type of art, what genres and what artists to promote, and, conversely, what type of art, genres and artists to neglect. Thanks to its performativity, intermediaries' speech can "claim (with the greatest chances of success) to be effective" and have material consequences (Bourdieu 1991, 70).

Cooperation between the participants is key in fashioning cultural significance. For music to be heard, distributed and validated, musicians need many more people than just themselves, and they need these people to interact with one another. Any work of art, as sociologist Howard Becker (1982) asserted, always shows signs of cooperation. This is why music not only reflects the time in which it is created, but also the ideas of the disparate people that participate in creating it (e.g., the distributors, promoters, journalists and other intermediaries and facilitators). Becker (1982, xxiv) terms all these activities, actors and relations between them as "art world". As he explains: "the network of people whose cooperative activity, organised via their joint knowledge of conventional means of doing things, produces the kind of art works that art world is noted for".

Music sociologist Nick Crossley (2015), applying Small's and Becker's framework to his investigation of British punk and post-punk, calls musical networks "music worlds". A "music world" is a cooperative system of like-minded people who strive towards a common goal (usually, to make a living out of music, whether by playing it, writing about it organising gigs, managing artists, etc.). Crossley (2015, 80) argues that, in order to succeed, networks have to be as tightly connected as possible and their participants must share resources and be so numerous as to reach a critical mass. This enacts a shared creativity that overflows into collective action and, eventually, leads to the popularisation and success of a "music world" outside its initially limited sphere of influence. This, Crossley continues, is more likely to happen in cities with large populations, especially where university or college students congregate, as these often represent the driving force of the network.

Following Small, Becker and Crossley, I frame *nezavisimaia muzyka* as a "music world" in which styles and meanings are created, endorsed, preserved and transformed by collective action. In the period studied, this collective action had as its epicentre Russia's largest city, Moscow. As we will see in the next chapter, the capital's agglomeration of people, flow of wealth and architectural and lifestyle Westernisation had a profound impact on the cultural life of its middle-class

50   *Independent Music in Russia*

inhabitants. Out of the interplay between spatial and cognitive transformations, and between 2008 and 2012, there emerged the local Anglophone bands, heralding the city's image of progress and cosmopolitanism. We term these Western-inspired, modern and fashionable bands, as well as the music world they contributed to form, the "Anglophone Wave". These bands were part of a larger network of artists, designers, directors, journalists, other musicians and music fans that imagined Moscow in a different way: their common goal was to place their city and Russia on the same foot as global cultural centres. The term of membership they sought was cosmopolitan and Westernised. In a similar way, the badge of belonging changed into a more localised and patriotic one during the course of the 2010s, when the fashion in *nezavisimaia muzyka* swayed towards Russophone lyrics and "darker" sounds – the so-called "New Russian Wave". However, the infrastructure created by the Anglophone Wave community served as a basis for further development: more places, more events, more festivals, more studios, more labels, more people involved and more connectivity. Similarly, many of the participants of the Anglophone Wave shifted into the camp of the New Russian Wave at a time when this movement was incorporating other upcoming acts and gaining momentum among intermediaries and audiences. Anglophone Wave musicians who did not conflate into the now-dominant Russophone style in *nezavisimaia muzyka* continued to foster their internationalised style of music, becoming the "niche of the niche", or the "alternative to the alternative".

Changes in the aesthetic direction of music networks exemplify two important phenomena. Firstly, networks are dynamic, and the sense of collective identity fluctuates in relation to (not necessarily in unison with, or in opposition to) the fluctuation of the social system in which it is constructed. Secondly, when new networks emerge, they carry signs of the previous ones: "the social systems which produce art survive in all sorts of ways, though never exactly as they have in the past" (Becker 1982, 6). Practitioners evolve for all sorts of reasons (economic, moral, philosophical, aesthetic), and as they change, networks also change.

Such changes may be better explained by following the line proposed by ethnomusicologist Thomas Turino (2008, 94), who argues that variations in meaning, identity and taste in music are "simply one example of the ongoing dialectics through which individual dispositions are shaped by the social environment". Crucial to Turino's work is the distinction between *habit* and *identity*. Habit is what the self regularly thinks and does, "a tendency toward the repetition of [a] behaviour, thought, or [...] reaction to similar stimuli in the present and future based on such repetitions in the past (Turino, 2008, 95). Habits can be relatively consistent but also changeable, thus explaining the stable yet dynamic nature of individual tastes and cultural constructions. Habits, in addition, can be personal, shaping the individual, but also shared among groups. Further, Turino argues that *identity* comprises only a selected few such habits, the ones that the individual thinks relevant to define themselves according to the social context. Thus, *identity* is a "partial and variable selection of habits and attributes that we use to represent ourselves to ourselves and to others" (Turino, 2008, 102). When identities join to share a specific set of *habits* on a regular basis they construct *culture*, which is where collective identity resides.

The History, Structures and Politics of Nezavisimaia Muzyka   51

In this category of collective identity we can include taste, social meaning and sense of belonging. The repeated occurrences of shared cultural habits create *discourse*, the "relatively systematic constellation of habits of thought and expression which shape people's reality about a particular subject or realm of experience" (Turino, 2008, 102). Yet, as the concept of *habit* suggests, discourse is not fixed, but rather plastic. The sets of utterances and behaviours that constitute it are subject to variation across time. Moreover, they are not unified, but rather diverse and coexisting in the same society: some acquire more weight than others, shaping dominant and subordinate discourses within a certain cultural practice. Music worlds, then, are made of the music habits of their participants: they are, in effect, "habits worlds" which reflect the participants' cultural discourses. These discourses, in turn, are influenced by the socio-political milieu: as the zeitgeist changes, they change too.[24] Thus, we can frame *nezavisimaia muzyka* as a multi-layered music world comprising networks of participants with shared habits who strive towards a collective identity. The repetition of these shared habits creates culture, and cultural producers shape convention-based thoughts and modes of action about how that culture should be (discourses). These discourses vary across time; their variation signals a change in the dominant music style and reflects a broader transformation in local as well as global political phenomena.

Nezavisimaia muzyka as an imagined community

Different discourses create different senses of belonging. At the most fundamental level, discourses reveal a construction of meaning based on binary differences in affiliation between the global and the local. An overview of such tensions is important, as it sheds a light on part of the contention in the Russian independent music world across the period analysed.

In the early 1960s, Marshall McLuhan (2001 [1962], 2011 [1964]) coined the term "Global Village" to explain the acceleration and pervasiveness of information regardless of the place in which a particular event occurred. This, McLuhan argued, was caused by more connectivity among people, which was in turn enabled by technological advancement. This "Global Village" had multiple critical evaluations, based on different standpoints. Some scholars claimed unidirectionality and homogenisation in the guise of Americanisation and cultural imperialism, arguing that "the imagery and cultural perspectives of the ruling sector in the centre shape and structure consciousness throughout the system at large" (Schiller 1976, 17). Others, instead, maintained that dominant information and cultural manifestations are actively transformed and blended by receiving countries into new products, thus preserving multidirectionality and heterogeneity. This was the interpretation animating concepts of hybridisation (Appadurai 1996), third spaces (Bhabha 1994), agency (Hall 1996a, 1996b), glocalisation (Robertson 1995) and transculturation (Appiah 2006), to name a few.

These ideas, which see dominant global flows transformed in multiple ways in the receiving location, remain hard currency in academia, despite the fact that the disparity of cultural flows from the "Great North" to the "Global South" is

52 *Independent Music in Russia*

also widely acknowledged (as well as the rise, in the last fifteen years or so, of decolonial thought, which seeks a radical break from Euro-centric epistemologies). Studies on music and globalisation pointed out the commodified and "consumer-friendly" tokenistic nature of "difference", hybridisation and cosmopolitanism (Feld 2000; Taylor 2012, 2013; Stokes 2013). Writing about the contested (and west-defined) category of "world music",[25] Feld (2000, 153–154) argued that "narrative positions on anxiety and celebration seem increasingly more intertwined". Indeed, if globalisation has often become a synonym for displacement (Feld, 2000, 153), music that is generated under its impact, however local, is already partially alienated from its geographical birthplace. True, a "pure" form of music has never existed, but the intensity with which mixing occurs between established Western products and local realities has considerably increased though globalisation and digitisation. Nevertheless, more recent scholarship has questioned the separation of "West – Rest" in approaching the subject of music globalisation, while acknowledging the growing connections between peripheries and the multidirectionality of transnational flows (Marc 2015), especially with the economic rise of "the rest" (Thussu 2015) and the worldwide booming of non-Western music movements such as K-pop (Lie 2015).

Intrinsic tensions between global and local, between cosmopolitanism and nationalism, West and non-West, supposed traditions and loss thereof, featured consistently in the discourses of Russian indie music *nezavisimaia muzyka*'s intermediaries in the 2000s and 2010s, constantly swaying fans' opinions from one side to the other. If *nezavisimaia muzyka* pundits at the end of the 2000s imagined Russia as part of a transnational and unifying world culture, over the course of the 2010s participants increasingly argued for a music that could be distinctively Russian. Former promoter Sergey Poydo, one of the architects of the "Anglophone Wave" in the independent scene at the end of the 2000s, stated (citing McLuhan directly):

> We held [in 2006–2010] the idea that the world was becoming a global village, the 'McLuhan's theory'. A 25-year-old person in Berlin is absolutely the same as a Muscovite of the same age. And that we are now united at the level of ideas, thoughts and transmission of information, rather than by a geographical principle.
>
> (Poydo in Sheveleva, 2015)

Whereas one of Russia's main music journalists and a committed advocate of the New Russian Wave (Interview 5) maintained:

> You'll never guess that Pompeya[26] is Russian music. Before, on social media and in the press, there was this comment, which was meant as a compliment: 'I've just listened to Pompeya and I can't believe they're Russian!' It used to upset and pain me. I've always wondered: 'what's good about that?' For me music should speak about the space and time in which it exists. In that sense Pompeya speak first and foremost about their absence from space and time.

The History, Structures and Politics of Nezavisimaia Muzyka   53

If, on the one hand, in contemporary, liquid times (Bauman 2007) geographical distinctions may lose value and the concept of nation may be overwritten by a global community (Poydo's position), it is exactly the geographical principle, once seemingly lost, that Interviewee 5 reinstates with all that this entails (e.g., the existence of a quintessentially national music). These opinions epitomised those of many participants in the debates around *nezavisimaia muzyka*, raising questions as to where to locate cultural products and what the marker of such localisation could be.

In the global supermarket from which musicians borrow, adapt and mix styles, the main (perhaps the only) effective locator at the participants' disposal (apart from the extra-sonic, e.g., the video) seems to be language. Ridding a song of its lyrics, and therefore of its language, may transform it into a nation-less, suspended product (how can we locate instrumental groups that do not feature prominent folk themes or timbres?). Attaching English lyrics to a song (for a non-Anglophone band) may shift it towards another pool of belonging, another "imagined community" based on a transnational tradition. Choosing the national language, conversely, may bring the song back to its native ground, and turns it to confront a national tradition. As discussed in the Introduction of this book, in the case of Russia, this "national" is particularly multifarious, contested and connected with the problematic legacies of empire.

Of course all these three instances (instrumental, Anglophone, vernacular) can intersect, but the problem is that the concept of "imagined communities" devised by Anderson in 1983, according to which individuals feel part of a specific group without knowing all its members but based on perceived similarities, is valid for constructing both a common national idea and a shared international one. The implications of this binarism consist of tensions and fluctuations among intermediaries, audiences and musicians that are hardly resolvable, as they originate from the same framework but rely on the different interpretation that participants attribute to it. These tensions, in turn, create cultural narratives and musical identities that are caught up in a struggle for recognition, regardless of the size of the music movement analysed. Therefore, on the one hand Russian independent music in the 2010s exemplified such global dilemmas; on the other, it also merged them with unresolved and acutely Russian historical issues, to which I now turn.

Nezavisimaia muzyka and the Other

The process of identity-shaping entails the concept of *difference* as one of its key features. It is through contrasting ourselves against "other" realities that we rewire our sense of self:

> Identities are constructed through, not outside, difference. This entails the radically disturbing recognition that it is only through the relation to the Other, the relation to what is not, to precisely what it lacks, to what has been called its constitutive outside that the 'positive' meaning of any term – and thus its 'identity' – can be constructed.
>
> (Hall 1996b, 4)

54   *Independent Music in Russia*

Looking at a cultural entity as a dialectical mechanism enables us to understand the decisive role played by otherness in identity formation. Indeed, to define ourselves we need to recognise a term of comparison, a point of reference, an Other.

Without underestimating the role played by other Slavic people or Asia, the Other for Russia has primarily been the West since the two entities fully encountered each other in the eighteenth century through Peter the Great and his reforms. By "West" here is meant Western Europe and later the United States (nowadays, this has extended to the majority of what is called "The Global North"). For most Russians, "the West" is a construct that, as it simplifies differences, groups together capitalist countries which are imagined as having a common colonial past, a current globalising agenda and a primacy on the world's cultural, technological and economic matters. In Russian official discourse over the past decade (and with aggressive intensity after the start of the full-scale war in Ukraine), the West acquired a "collective" character as Russia's strawman (*kollektivnyi Zapad*), a united inimical front constantly plotting against Russia and its sphere of influence to preserve the world as "unipolar" (Putin 2021; *RIA Novosti* 2022). This value differs from the one that most of the independent music community attributed to the West – as we will see, practitioners relentlessly borrowed and adapted from Western musical trends, often with great admiration. Yet the process of constructing the West as a single Other appears to be persistent there too: "Western music" (*zapadnaia muzyka*) for independent participants holds the traits of a one-size-fits-all category that does not distinguish between popular music produced in Britain, the US, Australia, Canada, Ireland and other Anglophone countries, occasionally including other Western European ones like Germany and France.

The persistence of the Other in Russia's national, cultural and overall identitarian discourse has made Russia's quest for the national character oscillate across a spectrum of options for the past three centuries: Russia is part of Europe and the West, Russia is not part of the West, Russia is Asia, Russia is a standalone Eurasian civilisation and so on. Key in this "geo-schizophrenic" fluctuation (Bassin 2012, 66) is the fact that any phase of enthusiasm of self-identifying as the West is followed by rejection of the West as model and the reaffirmation of a supposed "Russianness" that differs from it. Such patterns have been consistent, as well as unresolved, since the eighteenth century.[27] Russian thinkers have agonised, to this day, over them: how should their country develop? What path should it follow? In the nineteenth century, intellectuals presented two solutions: the first group, the Westernisers, suggested that Russia had to "catch up" with the West through adoption of Western secularism, technology and the liberal system of governance; the second group, the Slavophiles, feared that the institutionalisation of the Western modus operandi would lead to a loss of the Russian modus vivendi, deemed the Westernising Petrine reforms a mistake that interrupted the natural evolution of Russia as a nation and presented the West as an unsuitable model for Russia (Greenfeld 1992, 232). Slavophilism was the answer to an identity crisis among Russian intellectuals (Rabow-Edling 2012, 2) that advocated for Russia's own path of development, but, like the Westernisers, Slavophiles were unable to analyse these supposedly Russian traditions outside of the context of a comparison with the

The History, Structures and Politics of Nezavisimaia Muzyka   55

West, and in this comparison, "they felt the urge to argue for Russia's superiority at all costs" (Tolz 2001, 66). Thus, the mirror with which Russia looked at itself returned an enigmatic image: on the one hand, it created a lack and the simultaneous impossibility to resolve this lack within a "Russian" framework; on the other hand, it engendered what Liah Greenfeld (1992, 15) identifies as *ressentiment*: "a psychological state resulting from suppressed feelings of envy and hatred [...] and the impossibility of satisfying these feelings".

Ressentiment is a recurrence in Russian history that follows repeated patterns. Usually, the identification of the Other as the cultural model produces hostility towards it, because its perceived "superiority" diminishes the culture outsourcing it. As a reaction, initial mimesis turns into an inferiority complex, excitement gives way to suspicion and acceptance to competition. Different societal values are (re)proposed, and cultural intermediaries place great emphasis on the past and the local as the bastions of national "authenticity". In the case of Russia, dynamics of ressentiment start with Russia's impetus to "catch up" with the West and end with the upsurge of anti-Western nationalism; the process first encompasses the idea that Russia is a Western country on its way to close a gap, then entails the realisation of an unbridgeable difference and eventually prods claims of uniqueness on the basis of Russia *not* being a Western civilisation.

The argument, following from the above, is that Russian popular music – including *nezavisimaia muzyka* – displays the patterns of the broader historical relationship between Russia and the West. As Pilkington et al. (2002, 181) noted, "the peculiar history of the development of popular music in Russia means that musical preferences and uses inevitably have expressed not only aesthetic tastes or social roots but also changing attitudes to the West". Regardless of the point in the cycle – be this imitation, absorption, acceptance, rejection, resentment, competition or anything else – Russian musicians and tastemakers have constantly positioned themselves in response to Western trends and defined Russian music culture vis-à-vis the music culture of the Other. This relationship, while being extremely productive for the development of Soviet and Russian music cultures, has also been traversed by the same "accursed" questions of identity which have populated the intellectual and political sphere since the Imperial period (see also Friedman and Weiner 1999). Contemporary Russian music – including independent music – cannot be studied without an awareness of Russia's recursive issues, because the same issues that have animated discourses of nation-building have played out in the field of popular music on a smaller scale, while mechanisms of sameness and difference, as they animated imperial intellectual salons, have also fuelled twenty-first-century music blogs, zines and public discussions. Interviewee 5, a former editor of two influential cultural media outlets in Russia, for example, claimed that:

There are bands-Westernisers and bands-Slavophiles. [*est' gruppy zapadnikov i gruppy slavianofilov*] [...] Pompeya, as well as On-The-Go and Tesla Boy were the main flagmen of the [Westernisers'] movement.[28] Those were people who said: 'we're going to picture the situation – we're going to play – so that actually Moscow and Russia aren't any different from Manchester,

56   *Independent Music in Russia*

New York, London, Paris, that we have *here* [*tut*] the same cultural space as *there* [*tam*], and *we* [*my*], of course, will fall into the same sonic trends as *they* [*oni*] have there'.

In framing the contemporary cultural context with reference to the nineteenth century's most famous philosophical dispute, Interviewee 5 shows the persistence, as well as the urgency and the unresolvedness, of such discourses around the imagining of the nation. The respondent constructs difference (*here/there*, *we/they*) in the same dialogical way: in this, the Other (the West, its musical traditions and trends) continues to play a pivotal role (we are here because we are *not* there, and we have our cultural space because we do *not* have theirs). Russian Anglophone bands, therefore, become an *internal Other*, a hybrid displaying elements of both one and the other culture (for example, being a Russian citizen and singing in a foreign language). This process of identity blending is not unprecedented: Soviet consumers, for example, through the influence of Western popular culture, consistently have created *internal Others* in society since the 1950s. *Stiliagi*, *bitniki*, *khippi* and *rokery* all represented the difference *inside* Soviet culture and lifestyle.

In addition, like in the case of some Westernisers, whose intellectual arc at times developed into Slavophilia (Tolz 2001, 93; Greenfeld 1992, 27), a significant level of fluidity of discourse animated recent *nezavisimaia muzyka* too. Many bands that sang in English at the beginning of the 2010s – Glintshake, Shortparis, Ic3peak, Tesla Boy, to name a few – sang in Russian at the end of it. Journalists and trendsetters changed direction: Stepan Kazaryan, the catalyst behind much of the taste transformations in domestic independent music across the 2010s, started the decade as the manager of the influential Anglophone band On-The-Go and became the mastermind of the New Russian Wave in the second half of it.

But the repeated comparison with Western music has also led to stark admissions of inferiority complexes and derivativeness. When commenting on the scarcity of Russophone songs presented in the contest *Golos* (The Voice), for example, pop star and judge Leonid Agutin traced this problem back to the supremacy of Anglo-American music (and therefore to the secondariness of Russian music): "What can we do? We are second, *we* [*my*] always come after. *They* [*oni*] invented this sort of music *there* [*tam*]" (Agutin in Gritsenko and Aleshinskaya 2015, 41, emphasis added). Speaking of "sound" and execution, Interviewee 13, one of Russia's major rock critics, bluntly admits: "I think there is an evident inferiority. […] You can't change that. It's like football. Russians were never able to play football. I think it will never change. […] It's not in Russian people's veins". This perceived inferiority seems, in the words of Interviewee 13, almost innate, hopeless and immutable. At times, this idea is reflected in the popular consensus: many Russian independent music fans interviewed have deemed Anglo-American music superior in terms of quality, originality, execution and sound.[29] Egor, 18, for example, claims that Anglo-American music is "better in mentality and performance". Andrey, 29, reasons that "Russian music offers a lower quality product than Western music". Natalia, 21, maintains that "the level of Western music is higher, and the music itself is better, even though lyrics are elementary".

The History, Structures and Politics of Nezavisimaia Muzyka   57

This deep-seated inferiority complex has included the language for the lyrics too. It is for this reason that musicians abandoned Russian for English, according to Interviewee 24, the former bassist of an internationally renowned post-punk band:

> Everything Western, everything foreign seems to be something cooler. This was the case in Russia and in the Soviet Union, and it is generally part of our cultural code. And I think back then [late 2000s] many people thought that way, that's how the whole movement started, really. It was like, if you sing in Russian you're some kind of loser.

Interviewee 24 argues that the Russian-language musical products appeared to be associated with a general and intrinsic cultural un-coolness, which is none other than an adaptation of the long-standing discourse (internally and externally constructed) of Russia's "backwardness". As echoed by Interviewee 5, the unappealing image of "dirty trousers, beards and Shevchuk"[30] corresponded partly to a "cultural trauma" derived by the degradation of *russkii rok* and the aesthetics of *Nashe Radio*[31] during the late 1990s and early 2000s, and partly to a resurgence of narratives of inferiority and secondariness that extended to the language as well. As we will see in the next chapter, musicians of the Anglophone Wave experimented with English in response to these cultural perceptions: since Russian was the language of a supposedly derivative music, they wanted to understand whether the gap could be levelled by singing directly in popular music's lingua franca, English. This process, however, seldom led to the desired outcomes, and many Russian Anglophone bands failed to achieve international notoriety or build a career abroad. For some of their colleagues, this was a demonstration that "no one was waiting for them" (Interview 13) or "no one was interested in Russian music in the West" (Interview 27), and that Russian groups "were useless there [*nikomu ne nuzhny*]" (Interview 27). This contributed to sharpening perceptions of a rift between the local and the global scenes.

Nonetheless, as the Slavophiles turned inferiority complexes into markers of superiority, in the course of the 2010s this idea of Russia as musically inferior was turned on its head and framed as a sign of authenticity, pride and Russianness. Critics and trendsetters performed such an inversion by emphasising the peculiarities of Russian music in contrast with the Western tradition (e.g., its literary character, its specific irony, its capacity to comment on the state of the nation). They argued for the impossibility of understanding Russian music in Western terms (Interview 13) and endorsed a path for Russian music outside of Western hegemony (Interview 5). In some cases, "the West" and "Europe" were conflated. In a pivotal article on the state of domestic popular – mostly independent – music, for example, journalist Aleksandr Gorbachev (2019) described the end of what he called the "European Project":

> What do I mean by 'European Project'? The general definition is this: Russia is part of the global world that the West has for the most part created. If it's like this, then it means that we can, and we must, behave like we live in that world [...] even if this doesn't correspond to the reality around us.

58 *Independent Music in Russia*

Despite the terminological blurriness, the article captured the changes in the domestic musical trends of the last decade. Gorbachev argued that by playing and behaving as if in the West, the musicians of the previous generation (2000s and early 2010s) espoused a narrative of Russia as integrated in the global culture, whereas, also because of the political events between 2011 and 2014 (the violent repression of anti-Putin protests, the start of the conflict with Ukraine, the sanctions, etc.), it became increasingly clear that "Russia [was] no longer a part of Western civilisation and it [wouldn't] be for some time to come".[32] Further, Gorbachev maintained that the latest generation of Russian musicians rediscovered their roots by substituting abstract, apolitical and sentimental images in their songs (somehow Western-inspired) with descriptions of the nitty-gritty of Russian everyday life and humble, ordinary, common situations (the so-called *byt*). This, for Gorbachev, was an act of intellectual honesty and aesthetic authenticity. This revival of local sources of inspiration came with the realisation that Russia was on its own: the new generation of musicians turned their gaze to their country, both *despite* and *thanks to* Russia's authoritarian turn, isolation, societal flaws and contradictions. Consequently, the sound turned gloomier and more unrefined, topics became more trivial and the mode more ironic, while the language switched from English to Russian. In this process, the Other was deemed unreachable and was therefore dismissed for a more "authentic" self, even if (*and* particularly if) the package came with imperfections.

Notes

1 In Russia, the term "*nezavisimaia muzyka*" at times overlaps with the term "*indi*" (in Cyrillic: 'инди', borrowing from the English "indie"). "*Indi*" seems to have entered the Russian music lexicon at the end of the 1980s. The Soviet unofficial bands that appeared on the scene in the 1980s, though identifiable as "indie" in terms of sound, described themselves as "new wave" or "post-punk". The word "independence" (used directly in English and to denote "indie music") appears in the music press in an interview with Egor Letov, the leader of the Omsk-based punk band Grazhdanskaya Oborona in 1990 (Grazhdanskaya Oborona 2020). *Indi* features with consistence in the name of the independent music festival *Indiuki*, a recurrent event which took place for the first time in Moscow in 1991 and displayed a dozen of independent bands from all over the country. The festival is now called *Indiushata* and continues to exist with the same ethos of showcasing talents from outside the established music foci of Moscow and St. Petersburg. Because the term "*indi*" is contained in the title of the festival, it stands to reason to infer that it had been already circulating in the music scene for some time, as it was supposed to be known also to the target audience. Thus, its appearance in the Russian music terminology can be tentatively located in the late 1980s, while its appearance as a practice could be situated in the 1960s. Despite their relative interchangeability, "*indi*" evokes more specific associations with a particular type of guitar-driven music; therefore, I have preferred to use "*nezavisimaia muzyka*" as a term to also incorporate the plurality of soundscapes in the independent scene in Russia.
2 It is from this contradictory state of inside-outside (*vnye*) that Russian independent music has developed its ambiguous metamodern condition and its original character of *patrioprotest* (see later).
3 See, for example, the work of mainstream artists such as Aleksandr Gudkov, Filipp Kirkorov, Valery Leontev (Engström 2020a, 2021; Brock and Miazhevich 2022)

The History, Structures and Politics of Nezavisimaia Muzyka   59

4 This approach may have a tinge of Eurocentrism, in the sense that it does not take into account practitioners who circumvented industry structures in non-Western places perhaps earlier than what occurred in the West.

5 This, however, seems to happen with artists who are already at the top of their game: Klein *et al.* quotes the case of Nine Inch Nails or Prince returning to majors after an independent period.

6 By "structure", I follow Crossley's (2022, 166) definition as "a network comprising social actors (human and corporate) and the relations connecting them. Defined thus, structure has measurable properties which generate both opportunities and constraints for actors and which shape processes [...] which affect and implicate them". Personal and collective agency stand inside the structure and interact with it. At the same time, since cultural creation is also based on imagination, cultural producers often act with the desire to go beyond existing systems and shape new ones.

7 For studies of *russkii rok* and Soviet rock see, among others: Steinholt (2005), McMichael (2005), Kan (2017), Cushman (1995). For studies in Russian, see the series *Russkaia rok-poeziia* by Domanskii et al. (published almost yearly since 1998). For a conceptualisation of Soviet rock as an informal lifeworld among many, see Lipovetsky et al. (2021).

8 *Magnitizdat*, a compound word of *magnitofon* (tape recorder) and *izdatel'stvo* (publishing) refers to both the process of copying music records and the unofficial culture that stemmed from it in the late Soviet period (1953–1991). The name echoes a phenomenon that is perhaps more familiar to the Western reader: the samizdat (*sam* + *izdatel'stvo*, self-publishing), that is, the clandestine (re)production and distribution of unauthorised texts in the Soviet Union and the Eastern Bloc. *Magnitizdat*, however, was more pervasive than samizdat and harder to control for Soviet authorities. Copying songs was usually easier and faster than carbon-copy lengthy texts, and, thanks to technological advancement, tape recorders became a very common feature of Soviet homes (Yurchak 2006).

9 This began to change in 1979, when the first "producer" of Soviet rock, Andrei Tropillo, started recording bands in his studio at a Young Pioneers club in Leningrad, which he equipped with machines of decent quality. Tropillo officially taught kids the basics of sound engineering but unofficially recorded amateur rock groups. As music writer Aleksandr Kushnir (1999) observes, the Young Pioneers club became the Soviet equivalent of Abbey Road: in the early 1980s, Tropillo recorded many of the unofficial Soviet rock bands which would acquire nationwide fame during perestroika: Akvarium (Aquarium), Kino (Cinema), Zoopark (Zoo), Alisa (Alice), Strannye Igry (Strange Games) and so on.

10 This changed with Gorbachev's economic reforms, when forms of private enterprise in the music sector were introduced, creating competition between state-owned organisations and the new cooperatives. For a comprehensive account of the transformations of the Soviet music market during perestroika, see Wojnowski (2020).

11 *Vnye* in English is translated as "outside', "out of", "off-" or "extra-". Yurchak borrows the term from Bakhtin's (1992) idea of *vnenakhodimost'* (literally, "the condition of being outside" or "outsideness"), which he, however, infuses with a dialogic connotation between outside and inside in relation to the literary author and his/her hero.

12 These ideas stem from Bakhtin's (1984) concept of carnivalisation. For Bakhtin, the carnival parody was already something deeply ambivalent, in which "ridicule was fused with rejoicing" (127).

13 Soviet rock, and particularly its *russkii rok* strand, enjoyed proximity with another logo-centric music tradition, that of guitar poetry (*avtorskaia pesnia*), which exerted influence on several Soviet songwriters (see Steinholt 2003, 100). With guitar poetry, *russkii rok* shared also marginality and hostility from the authorities.

14 For a discussion of different approaches to lyric writing and lyric-focused music in the Soviet/Russian context, see Steinholt (2003, 96), who follows a persuasive argument from Lindberg (1995) about the distinction between rock lyrics into *focused lyrics*

60   *Independent Music in Russia*

(driving the music's meaning), *musified lyrics* (shaped by the sound); and *freely shaped lyrics* (a mixture of the two).

15 VKontakte incarnated in many ways the dreams of early tech-utopians who advocated for a free, democratic and anti-hierarchical cyberspace. Pavel Durov, a controversial figure with anarchic-libertarian political beliefs, expressed his intentions in the first point of his "manifesto": "To rid society of the burden of old laws, licenses and limitations that feed corruption. The world mutates too fast for regulators to react accordingly. In the 21st century the best legal initiative is the absence of such initiative" (*Afisha* 2012).

16 As Moss (2007, pp. 144–145) reports, during the 1990s, the newly formed Russian state "withdrew" from supporting culture: "The state budget for culture fell by 40 per cent from 1991 to 1997. [...] Attempts to stabilize it by setting a minimum of 2 per cent of federal expenditure failed even at the budget-setting stage. In 1999 it stood at 0.58 per cent".

17 As Anastasia Gordienko (2023, 5–7) conceptualises it, the *blatnaia pesnia* is "folklore produced by criminals, outcasts, social misfits, or those living 'outside the law' and associated with [...] underworld culture", as well as "the music – some folklorized, some not – embraced by these populations as their own, and also identified by the general, law-abiding public as blatnie pieces". The *shanson*, instead, "ranges beyond the blatnaia pesnia" to incorporate songs with no visible connection to the criminal underworld (such as romantic *shanson*). The genre became increasingly mainstream in the 1990s and was gradually incorporated by power under Putin (*shanson* contests and events repeatedly took place in the Kremlin palace since the early 2000s, for instance).

18 Estrada, as David MacFadyen (2002, 3) has it, is Soviet (and post-Soviet) "light entertainment, [...] a wide-ranging term that includes pop music but also applies to modern dance, comedy, circus arts, and any other performance not on the 'big' classical stage".

19 *Popsa* is a widespread (derogatory) term for pop music in Russia. *Popsa* crosses over with *estrada*, but it also relies less on the charismatic persona of the performer and more on the ready-made character of the hit, irrespective of whom sings it. As Aleksandr Gorbachev (2021, 28) defines it, *popsa* is "radio hits. What plays from every corner and medium". As he points out, in the 2010s *popsa* acquired an increasingly positive meaning and was consistently incorporated as cultural heritage in alternative genres, while in the 2000s *popsa* would evoke negative or embarrassing connotations for several independent musicians.

20 As two of my informants within the industry reported (personal communication, 5 May 2020), Russian major labels unanimously refuse to share market data, including with other people in the industry (e.g., promoters, journalists, etc.). Labels usually analyse their data themselves, and the charts complied by streaming services often display contrasting data among themselves – a musician could be in the top 5 of the Apple Music Russia's chart, but outside Yandex Music's top 50. As Zav'ialov (2020) notes, the silence of the labels and the discrepancy in the data available make streaming charts unreliable and unworthy of accreditation.

21 Notwithstanding the conspicuous presence of indies in the industry, however, making money through a label was an extremely difficult endeavour: the founders and workers of various Russian indie labels (Interview 73, 74, 80) confirmed that the money coming from label activity was not enough, and that they had other forms of income from other areas in the industry (usually concert or festival organisation).

22 The companies are: Pervoe muzykal'noe izdatel'stvo (publishing), Natsional'noe muzykal'noe izdatel'stvo (publishing), Soiuz Music (label), Effective Records (label) and Natsional'nyii tsifrovoi agregator (digital distributor).

23 Similar mechanisms of "oblique" positioning of independent musicians in relation to state discourse have been observed in other authoritarian regimes, such as China (Baranovitch 2003; Jian 2018).

24 The importance of the zeitgeist in the emergence of a music style cannot be overstated. For example, the entrepreneurial abilities of Malcolm McLaren, the charismatic

The History, Structures and Politics of Nezavisimaia Muzyka 61

presence of Sex Pistols and the formation of punk networks across Britain played a fundamental role in the breakthrough of the genre, but this breakthrough was equally facilitated by the alienation of the youth and the economic stagnation of the UK in the late 1970s. Similarly, the changes in *nezavisimaia muzyka* are partly due to the enhancement of connectivity within the network, the amelioration of industry structures and the appearance of affordable technology and new spaces of production, but these developments alone would not explain why Russian *nezavisimaia muzyka* sounds the way it does, and why changes such as the abandonment of English for Russian, or the revival of Soviet post-punk, happened over the course of the 2010s. Music worlds are situational, they negotiate their existence with political contexts and these political contexts act on them to a considerable extent.

25 "World music" was originally born in the West as an umbrella term that encompassed ethnic, folk and indigenous music different – at the level of sound – from typically "Western" guitar genres like rock, pop, jazz and blues. Gradually, as its commodification went on (especially in the 1980s), "world music" became widely used as a category of music made in non-Western countries.

26 A Russian Anglophone band representing one of this work's case studies.

27 Convinced of Russia's backwardness, Peter travelled across Western Europe, where he studied and learned new technologies and local customs. On his return to Russia, the tsar imported knowledge and Western masters (who built St. Petersburg) and enforced new West-European traditions upon the nobility. These traditions were alien to Russians: it was a case of semi-forced, self-imposed colonisation which relied on the acknowledgment of Western superiority and consisted of mimesis of the West. The newly built St. Petersburg, Russia's new capital and "window to Europe", "in its entirety can be considered an example of cultural borrowing for the promotion of national consciousness" (Hart 1999, 89). After Peter, the prevalence among the intelligentsia of West European literary and philosophical trends (Enlightenment, Idealism and Romanticism especially) continued throughout the eighteenth and nineteenth centuries, while St. Petersburg became a cosmopolitan melting pot of nationalities (Cross 2004). However, the new, Westernised national consciousness created a rift in Russian society between Westernised elites and the large majority of the rural population, who continued to live in backward conditions of serfdom. The fact that these two Russias could not communicate to each other pressed intellectuals to mediate and commit to reconcile the ambivalence. To start with, the cosmopolitan enthusiasm that led important thinkers such as Nikolai Karamzin to declare that Russia had almost "caught up" with the West was questioned (Karamzin 1984, 254). For some, the attempt to gain a European identity was only superficial. Alexander Radishchev's (2020 [1790]) *Voyage from Petersburg to Moscow*, for instance, revealed a disjoined society that was still profoundly rooted in serfdom and abuse. The failure of the French-inspired Decembrist uprising in 1825 only sharpened this feeling. In his *Philosophical Letters* (1828–30, published in Russia in 1836), Russian intellectual Petr Chaadayev argued (in French) that Russia lacked a national identity completely, that it lagged behind other civilised European countries, that it imitated without absorbing, and that it unjustifiably and paradoxically felt entitled to a "mission". One of the outcomes of this juxtaposition with the West was the birth of an inferiority complex, that is, the acknowledgement among intellectuals that Russia was still "clearly, painfully, hopelessly inferior" (Greenfeld 1992, 227), which clashed with narratives of imperial grandeur that skyrocketed after Russia's victory over Napoleon in 1812.

28 All three bands sang in English and displayed a cosmopolitan vibe. They are all discussed in the next chapter as main representatives of the Anglophone Wave.

29 The following interviews with members of the audience (and throughout the book) were collected at Gorky Park in July 2016 and at *Stereoleto*, *Nashestvie* and *Bol* festivals in July 2017.

30 Iurii Shevchuk, singer of the band DDT, traditionally associated with high-quality lyrics but basic arrangements.

62 *Independent Music in Russia*

31 *Nashe Radio* (Our Radio), one of the leading radio stations in Russia, which airs nearly exclusively Russophone music belonging to the style of *russkii rok* or Soviet rock.
32 Aleksandr Gorbachev, speech at "Russian Culture after 2010" symposium, Manchester, 7 February 2020.

References

Afisha. 2012. 'Grazhdanskie manifesti. Pavel Durov, osnovatel' Vkontakte'. *Afisha*, 18 March.

Anderson, B. 1983. *Imagined Communities. Reflections on the Origin and Spread of Nationalism*. London: Verso.

Appadurai, A. 1996. *Modernity At Large: Cultural Dimensions of Globalization*. Minneapolis: University of Minnesota Press.

Appiah, K.A. 2006. *Cosmopolitanism: Ethics in a World of Strangers*. London: Penguin.

Baker, S., Bennett, A., Taylor, J. (eds.) 2013. *Redefining Mainstream Popular Music*. London: Routledge.

Bakhtin, M. 1984. *Problems of Dostoevsky's Poetics* (ed. by Caryl Emerson). London and Minneapolis: University of Minnesota Press.

Bakhtin, M.M. 1992. *Speech Genres & Other Late Essays*. Austin: University of Texas Press.

Banks, M. 2010. 'Autonomy Guaranteed? Cultural Work and the 'Art–Commerce Relation'. *Journal for Cultural Research*, 14, 3, pp. 251–269.

Baranovitch, N. 2003. *China's New Voices: Popular Music, Ethnicity, Gender, and Politics, 1978–1997*. Berkeley: University of California Press.

Bassin, M. 2012. 'Asia'. In Rzhevsky, N. (ed.) *The Cambridge Companion to Modern Russian Culture*. Cambridge University Press, pp. 65–93.

Bauman, Z. 2007. *Liquid Times. Living in an Age of Uncertainty*. Cambridge: Polity Press.

Becker, H. 1982. *Art Worlds*. Berkeley, CA: University of California Press.

Bennett, A. 2018. 'Conceptualising the Relationship between Youth, Music and DIY Careers: A Critical Overview'. *Cultural Sociology*, 12, 2, pp. 140–155.

Bhabha, H.K. 1994. *The Location of Culture*. London: Routledge.

Biasioli, M. 2021. 'Piracy as an Institutionalised Social Practice in Soviet and Post-Soviet Russia'. In Galuszka, P. (ed.) *Eastern European Music Industries and Policies after the Fall of Communism: From State Control to Free Market*. Abingdon and New York: Routledge, pp. 41–61.

Bourdieu, P. 1991. *Language and Symbolic Power*. Cambridge: Polity Press.

Brock, M., Miazhevich, G. 2022. 'From High Camp to Postmodern Camp: Queering Post-Soviet Pop Music'. *European Journal of Cultural Studies*, 25, 4, pp. 993–1009.

Chukhrov, K. 2023. 'Technologies of Interception of Art and Culture in Putin's Russia.' *E-flux*, 13 October, https://www.e-flux.com/notes/569926/technologies-of-interception-of-art-and-culture-in-putin-s-russia (Accessed 1 July 2024).

Connell, J., Gibson, C. 2003. *Sound Tracks: Popular Music, Identity and Place*. London: Routledge.

Cross, A. 2004. 'Them: Russians on Foreigners'. In Franklin, S., Widdis, E. (eds.) *National Identity in Russian Culture*. New York: Cambridge University Press, pp. 74–92.

Crossley, N. 2015. *Networks of Sound, Style and Subversion. The Punk and Post-Punk Worlds of Manchester, London, Liverpool and Sheffield, 1975–80*. Manchester: Manchester University Press.

Cushman, T. 1995. *Notes from the Underground: Rock Music Counterculture in Russia*. New York: State University of New York Press.

De Beukelaer, C. 2014. 'Creative Industries in "developing" Countries: Questioning Country Classifications in the UNCTAD Creative Economy Reports'. *Cultural Trends*, 23, 4, pp. 232–251.

The History, Structures and Politics of Nezavisimaia Muzyka 63

Elst, M. 2004. *Copyright, Freedom of Speech, and Cultural Policy in the Russian Federation*. Leiden: Brill.

Engström, M. 2018. 'Monetochka: the manifesto of metamodernism.' *Riddle*, 26 June. URL: https://ridl.io/monetochka-the-manifesto-of-metamodernism/ (accessed 1 July 2018).

Engström, M. 2020a. 'Alexander Gudkov and Russia's queer turn in the 2020s'. *Riddle*, 21 August. URL: https://ridl.io/alexander-gudkov-and-russia-s-queer-turn-in-the-2020s/ (accessed 2 April 2024).

Engström, M. 2020b. 'Re-Imagining Antiquity: The Conservative Discourse of "Russia as the True Europe" and the Kremlin's New Cultural Policy'. In Mjør, K.J., Turoma, S. (eds.) *Russia as Civilization: Ideological Discourses in Politics, Media, and Academia*. Abingdon: Routledge, pp. 142–163.

Engström, M. 2021. 'Transgressing the Mainstream: Camp, Queer and Populism in Russian Visual Culture'. In Semenenko, A. (ed.) *Satire and Protest in Putin's Russia*. Palgrave Macmillan (e-book), pp. 97–120.

Engström, M. 2022. 'We don't support the 'special operation', we're carrying it out'. *Russia. Post*, 3 May, https://russiapost.info/politics/special_operation_carrying_it_out (accessed 1 July 2024).

Epstein, S. 2015. 'Us and Them: Korean Indie Rock in a K-Pop World'. *The Asia-Pacific Journal*, 48, 1, pp. 1–19.

Etkind, A. 2011. *Internal Colonization: Russia's Imperial Experience*. Cambridge: Polity Press.

Feld, S. 2000. 'A Sweet Lullaby for World Music'. *Public Culture*, 12, 1, pp. 145–171.

Fisher, M. 2009. *Capitalist Realism: Is There No Alternative?* London: Zero Books.

Friedman, J., Weiner, A. 1999. 'Between a Rock and a Hard Place: Holy Rus' and Its Alternatives in Russian Rock Music'. In Barker, A.M. (ed.) *Consuming Russia: Popular Culture, Sex and Society since Gorbachev*. Durham: Duke University Press, pp. 110–137.

Gakkel', V. 2007. 'Esli bylo by net kluba?' *Muzykalnyi leksikon*, 26 February. URL: http://art.specialradio.ru/index.php?id=262 (last accessed 20 March 2017).

Galuszka, P. 2021. 'Contextualising Research on the Eastern European Music Industry'. In Galuszka, P. (ed.) *Eastern European Music Industries and Policies after the Fall of Communism: From State Control to Free Market*. Abingdon and New York: Routledge, pp. 3–21.

Galuszka, P., Wyrzykowska, K. 2018. 'Rethinking Independence: What Does 'Independent Record Label' Mean Today?. In Mazierska, E., Gillon, L., Rigg, T. (eds.) *Popular Music in the Post-Digital Age: Politics, Economy, Culture and Technology*. New York: Bloomsbury Publishing US, pp. 33–50.

Gill, R. 2014. 'Academics, Cultural Workers and Critical Labour Studies'. *Journal of Cultural Economy*, 7, 1, pp. 12–30.

Goldenzwaig, G. 2006. *EMO Export Handbook Russia*. European Music Office (online).

Gorbachev, A. 2019. 'Epokha Zemfiry i mumiy troll zakonchilas. Teper' vsyo inache'. *Meduza*, 2 January. URL: https://meduza.io/feature/2019/01/02/epoha-zemfiry-i-mumiy-trollya-zakonchilas-teper-vse-inache (accessed 12 March 2019).

Gorbachev, A., Zinin, I. 2014. *Pesni v pustotu*. Moskva: Corpus.

Gorbash, L. 2021. '"V Rossii est' svoi natsional'nyi maidzhor': chto takoe Zvonko Group. *IMI*, 9 September. URL: https://i-m-i.ru/post/chto-takoe-zvonko?fbclid=IwAR1WFSEJIllB16P336V4WpOvpCjE63iBJQIh5G3YKpgwdsBOYwBWAQf3dCo (accessed 8 October 2021).

Gordienko, A. 2023. *Outlaw Music in Russia: The Rise of an Unlikely Genre*. Madison: The University of Wisconsin Press.

Grazhdanskaya Oborona. 2020. 'Interview with Egor Letov'. URL: http://www.gr-oborona.ru/pub/anarhi/1056981372.html (accessed 10 June 2020).

Greenfeld, L. 1992. *Nationalism: Five Roads to Modernity*. Cambridge, MA: Harvard University Press.

Gritsenko, E.C., Aleshinskaya, E.V. 2015. 'Angliiskii iazyk v televizionnom muzykalnom shou 'Golos'. *The Humanities and Social Studies in the Far East*, 1, 45, pp. 37–43.

64   *Independent Music in Russia*

Hall, S. 1996a. 'The Question of Cultural Identity'. In Hall, S., Held, D., Hubert, D., Thompson, K. (eds.) *Modernity. An Introduction to Modern Societies*. Oxford: Blackwell, pp. 596–633.

Hall, S. 1996b. 'Who Needs 'Identity'? In Hall, S., du Gay, P. (eds.) *Questions of Cultural Identity*. London: SAGE, pp. 1–18.

Hart, P.R. 1999. 'The West'. In Rzhevsky, N. (ed.) *The Cambridge Companion to Modern Russian Culture*. Cambridge: Cambridge University Press, pp. 85–102.

Hebdige, D. 1979. *Subculture: The Meaning of Style*. London: Methuen & Co.

Hesmondhalgh, D. 1996. *Independent Record Companies and Democratisation in the Popular Music Industry*. PhD thesis, Goldsmiths College.

Hesmondhalgh, D. 1999. 'Indie: the Institutional Politics and Aesthetics of a Popular Music Genre'. *Cultural Studies*, 13, 1, pp. 34–61.

Hesmondhalgh, D., Meier, L. 2015. 'Popular Music, Independence and the Concept of the Alternative in Contemporary Capitalism'. In Bennett, A., Strange, N. (eds.) *Media Independence: Working with Freedom or Working for Free?* London: Routledge, pp. 94–116.

Hibbett, R. 2005. 'What Is Indie Rock?. *Popular Music and Society*, 28, 1, pp. 55–77.

Holt, F., Lapenta, F. 2010. 'Introduction: Autonomy and Creative Labour'. *Journal for Cultural Research*, 14, 3, pp. 223–229.

Hutchings, S. 2017. 'A Home from Home: Recursive Nationhood, the 2015 STS Television Serial, Londongrad, and Post-Soviet Stiob'. *Russian Journal of Communication*, 9, 2, pp. 142–157.

IFPI. 2019. *Global Music Report*. London: IFPI.

IFPI. 2020. *IFPI issues annual Global Music Report*. 4 May. URL: https://www.ifpi.org/ifpi-issues-annual-global-music-report/ (accessed 7 October 2021).

IMI. 2020. '46 Telegram-kanalov o muzyke i vokrug neë'. 21 May. URL: https://i-m-i.ru/post/telegram-chanels (accessed 23 June 2020).

IMI. 2021a. 'Warner Music Group kupil leibl Zhara Music i pereformatiruet kompaniiu v rossiiskoe podrazdelenie Atlantic Records. Ego vozglavit Bahh Tee'. 24 March. URL: https://i-m-i.ru/news/warner-music-group-bought-zhara-records?utm_source=email&utm_medium=imi_social (accessed 7 October 2021).

IMI. 2021b. 'Eksperty podschitali ubytki kontsertno industrii iz-za koronavirusnykh ogranichenii'. 10 September. URL: https://i-m-i.ru/news/covid-aftermath.

Ingham, T. 2019. 'DIY Artists Will Earn More Than $1 Billion This Year. No Wonder the Major Labels Want Their Business'. *Rolling Stone*, 6 May. URL: https://www.rollingstone.com/pro/features/diy-artists-will-earn-more-than-1-billion-this-year-no-wonder-the-major-labels-want-their-business-830863/ (accessed 26 June 2023).

Jian, M. 2018. 'The Survival Struggle and Resistant Politics of a DIY Music Career in East Asia: Case Studies of China and Taiwan'. *Cultural Sociology*, 12, 2, pp. 224–240.

Jones, E. 2021. 'DIY and Popular Music: Mapping an Ambivalent Relationship across Three Historical Case Studies'. *Popular Music and Society*, 44, 1, pp. 60–78.

Jones, R. 2013. *Clampdown: Pop-Cultural Wars on Class and Gender*. Winchester and Washington, DC: Zero Books.

Kan, A. 2017. 'Living in the Material World: Money in the Soviet Rock Underground'. In Fürst, J., McLellan, J. (eds.) *Dropping Out of Socialism: The Creation of Alternative Spheres in the Soviet Bloc*. London: Lexington Books, pp. 255–276.

Karamzin, N. 1984 (1790). *Pis'ma russkogo puteshestvennika*. Leningrad: Nauka.

Khrushchëva, N. 2020. *Metamodern v muzyke i vokrug nego*. Moskva: RIPOL klassik.

Kiriya, I. 2012. 'The Culture of Subversion and Russian Media Landscape'. *International Journal of Communication*, 6, pp. 446–466.

Kiriya, I., Sherstoboeva, E. 2015. 'Russian Media Piracy in the Context of Censoring Practices'. *International Journal of Communication*, 9, pp. 839–851.

Klein, B., Meier, L., Powers, D. 2017. 'Selling Out: Musicians, Autonomy, and Compromise in the Digital Age'. *Popular Music and Society*, 40, 2, pp. 222–238.

The History, Structures and Politics of Nezavisimaia Muzyka   65

Kruse, H. 2010. 'Local Identity and Independent Music Scenes, Online and Off'. *Popular Music and Society*, 33, 5, pp. 625–639.

Kushnir, A. 1999. *100 magnitoal'bomov sovetskogo roka 1977–1991: 15 let podpol'noi zvukozapisi*. Moscow: LEAN.

Lebedeva, V. 2022. 'A klouny ostalis', *Kommersant*, 2 September 2. URL: https://www.kommersant.ru/doc/5538114 (accessed 15 February 2023).

Lebrun, B. 2009. *Protest Music in France. Production, Identity and Audiences*. Farnham: Ashgate Publishing.

Lenta.ru. 2012. 'Podsudnyi den': v Rossii nachal deistvovat' reestr zapreshchënnykh saitov.' 6 November. URL: https://lenta.ru/articles/2012/11/01/reestr/ (accessed 11 January 2024).

Lie, J. 2015. *K-Pop. Popular Music, Cultural Amnesia, and Economic Innovation in South Korea*. Berkeley, CA: University of California Press.

Lindberg, U. 1995. Rockens text: ord, musik och mening. *Brutus Ostling Bokforlag Symposion*, Stockholm/Stehag.

Lipovetsky, M., Glanc, T., Engström, M., Kukuj, I., Smola, K. (eds.) 2021. *The Oxford Handbook of Soviet Underground Culture*. New York: Oxford University Press (online edition).

Luvaas, B. 2013. 'Exemplary Centers and Musical Elsewheres: On Authenticity and Autonomy in Indonesian Indie Music'. *Asian Music*, 44, 2, pp. 95–114.

MacFadyen, D. 2002. *Estrada: Grand Narratives and the Philosophy of the Russian Popular Song since Perestroika*. Montreal: McGill-Queen's University Press.

Marc, I. 2015. 'Travelling Songs: On Popular Music Transfer and Translation'. *IASPM Journal*, 5, 2, pp. 1–21.

McLuhan, M. 2001 (1962). *Understanding Media: The Extension of Man*. London and New York: Routledge.

McLuhan, M. 2011 (1964). *The Gutenberg Galaxy: The Making of the Typographic Man*. Toronto: University of Toronto Press.

McMichael, P. 2005. '"After All, You're a Rock Star (At Least, That's What They Say)': Roksi and the Creation of the Soviet Rock Musician'. *Slavonic and East European Review*, 83, 4, pp. 664–84.

McMichael, P. 2009. 'Prehistories and Afterlives: The Packaging and Re-Packaging of Soviet Rock'. *Popular Music and Society*, 32, 3, pp. 331–350.

McMichael, P. 2014. '"A Room-Sized Ocean": Apartments in the Practice and Mythology of Leningrad's Rock Music'. In Risch, W.J. (ed.) *Youth and Rock in the Soviet Bloc*. Blue Ridge Summit: Lexington Books, pp. 289–330.

McMichael, P. 2019. '"That's Ours. Don't Touch". Nashe Radio and the Consolations of the Domestic Mainstream'. In Strukov, V., Hudspith, S. (eds.) *Russian Culture in the Age of Globalization*. London: Routledge, pp. 68–98.

Mjør, K.J., Turoma, S. (eds.). 2020. *Russia as Civilization: Ideological Discourses in Politics, Media, and Academia*. Abingdon: Routledge.

Moore, A. 2002. 'Authenticity as Authentication'. *Popular Music*, 21, 2, pp. 209–223.

Moskva 24. 2016. 'Moskovskie tusovka: ot 'Gorbushki' do Gorbushkina dvora'. 28 January. URL: https://www.m24.ru/articles/gorod/28012016/95284 (accessed 11 March 2025).

Moss, L. 2007. 'Encouraging Creative Enterprise in Russia'. In Henry, C. (ed.) *Entrepreneurship in the Creative Industries: An International Perspective*. Cheltenham: Edward Elgar Publishing, pp. 142–158.

Mulligan, M. 2017. 'Global Recorded Market Music. Market Shares 2016. *Midia*, 26 February. URL: https://musicindustryblog.wordpress.com/2017/02/26/global-recorded-market-music-market-shares-2016/ (last accessed 7 May 2020).

Mulligan, M. 2021. 'Recorded music revenues hit $23.1 billion in 2020, with artists direct the winners – again'. *Midia*, 15 March. URL: https://www.midiaresearch.com/blog/recorded-music-revenues-hit-231-billion-in-2020-with-artists-direct-the-winners-again?utm_source=MIDiA+Research+Newsletter&utm_campaign=0cc5a95cbc-EMAIL_

66 *Independent Music in Russia*

CAMPAIGN_2019_01_14_12_03_COPY_01&utm_medium=email&utm_term=0_8602b921cd-0cc5a95cbc-523334714 (accessed 8 October 2021).

Neumann, I.B. 2017. 'Russia's Return as True Europe, 1991–2017'. *Conflict and Society: Advances in Research*, 3, pp. 78–91.

Nooshin, L. 2017. 'Whose Liberation? Iranian Popular Music and the Fetishization of Resistance'. *Popular Communication*, 15, 3, pp. 163–191.

Parkinson, T. 2018. 'Indiestanbul: Counter-Hegemonic Music and Third Republicanism in Turkey'. *Popular Music*, 37, 1, pp. 40–62.

Pennycook, A. 2007. *Global Englishes and Transcultural Flows*. London: Routledge.

Pennycook, A. 2010. *Language as a Local Practice*. Abingdon: Taylor & Francis.

Petrova, Z., Kurakin, V. 2016. *Geroi sovetskogo n'iu-veiva*. 'Khrushchyovka.Org.' URL: https://www.youtube.com/watch?v=alTI7kCUmXE (last accessed 7 May 2020).

Pilkington, H., Omelchenko, E., Flynn, M., Bluidina, U., Starkova, E. 2002. *Looking West? Cultural Globalization and Russian Youth Cultures*. Philadelphia: Pennsylvania State University Press.

Platonov, R. 2012. *Singing the Self: Guitar Poetry, Community, and Identity in the Post-Stalin Period*. Evanston: Northwestern University Press.

Power, E. 2019. 'How landfill indie swallowed guitar music in the mid-Noughties', *The Independent*, 28 July. URL: https://www.independent.co.uk/arts-entertainment/music/features/landfill-indie-kaiser-chiefs-album-razorlight-the-kooks-ricky-wilson-a9022051.html (accessed 5 May 2020).

Prokof'ev, P. 2019. 'Skol'ko prinosiat nezavisimym muzykantam proslushivaniia na 'Yandeks.Muzyke', Apple music i drugikh strimingovykh servisakh'. *VC.ru*, 5 December. URL: https://vc.ru/media/95834-skolko-prinosyat-nezavisimym-muzykantam-proslushi-vaniya-na-yandeksmuzyke-apple-music-i-drugih-strimingovyh-servisah (accessed 6 October 2021).

Putin, V. 2021. 'Poslanie Prezidenta Federal'nomu Sobraniiu'. 21 April. http://kremlin.ru/events/president/news/65418 (accessed 11 August 2023).

PwC.ru. 2020. 'Muzykal'naia industriia'. https://www.pwc.ru/ru/publications/mediaindustriya-v-2020-2024/muzykalnaya-industriya.html?fbclid=IwAR0SELXCCBFoOKIaGUwLuZ-kybvUFK7UJ6ZhBXazt3AXJzPjVGp-W1k-wo8 (accessed 7 October 2021). PwC has ceased operation now in Russia and the website is defunct. Similar information can be found here: https://vk.com/@musuniversecom-pwc-vylozhili-issledovanie-muzykalnogo-rynka-rossii-s-progno.

Qu, S., Hesmondhalgh, D., Xiao, J. 2021. 'Music Streaming Platforms and Self-Releasing Musicians: the Case of China'. *Information, Communication & Society*. DOI: 10.1080/1369118X.2021.1971280.

Rabow-Edling, S. 2012. *Slavophile Thought and the Politics of Cultural Nationalism*. Albany: State University of New York Press.

Radishchev, A. 2020 (1790). *A Journey from St. Petersburg to Moscow*. New York: Columbia University Press.

Rafaeli, J.S. 2016. 'The Definitive History of Landfill Indie in Seven Songs, Narrated by Johnny Borrell'. *Vice*, 5 April. URL: https://www.vice.com/en_uk/article/rmjdvp/landfill-indie-johnny-borrell-razorlight-the-strokes-kooks-definitive-history (accessed 5 May 2020).

Redkin, K. 2022. '2022 – god, kogda kakonchilas' samodel'naia kul'tura 2010-kh'. *Slomannye pliaski*, 3 March. URL: https://t.me/brokendance/697 (accessed 6 March 2022).

Regev, M. 2013. *Pop-Rock Music: Aesthetic Cosmopolitanism in Late Modernity*. Cambridge: Polity Press.

RIA Novosti. 2022. 'Putin zaiavil, chto kollektivnyi Zapad vo glave s SSHA vedet sebia agressivno'. 7 July. URL: https://ria.ru/20220707/putin-1801060019.html (accessed 25 July 2024).

Riabova, I. 2022. 'Sergei Mudrik: 'chem bol'she slushatel' otkryvaet dlia sebia novykh imen, tem luchshe'. *IMI*, 25 April. URL: https://i-m-i.ru/post/mudrik-vk-interview (accessed 27 April 2022).

The History, Structures and Politics of Nezavisimaia Muzyka   67

Robertson, R. 1995. 'Glocalization: Time-Space and Homogeneity-Heterogeneity'. In Featherstone, M., Lash, S., Robertson, R. (eds.) *Global Modernities*. London: Sage, pp. 25–44.

Ryback, T. 1990. *Rock around the Bloc: A History of Rock Music in Eastern Europe and the Soviet Union, 1954–1988*. Oxford: Oxford University Press.

Sadkov, S. 2020. 'Skol'ko platiat za proslushivanie VK (Boom), Apple Music, Spotify, Yandexs.Muzyka i dr. v 2020 godu'. *Sadkov.info*, 28 January. URL: https://sadkov.info/ instrumenty-dlya-muzykantov/skolko-platyat-za-proslushivaniya-vk-boom-apple-music-spotify-yandeks-muzyka-i-dr-v-2020-godu-onlajn-kalkulyator-doxodov-ot-striminga/ (accessed 7 October 2021).

Safronov, E., *et al.* 2019. *Kul'tura i kul'turnye industrii v RF 2017–2019*. Moskva: Intermedia. URL: https://www.intermedia.ru/uploads/culture-of-russia-2019_web.pdf (accessed 15 August 2021).

Saprykin, Y. 2023. 'Balalaika i Ko'. *Kommersant*, 27 October. URL: https://www.kommersant.ru/doc/6283696 (accessed 30 October 2023).

Schiffrin, D., Tannen, D., Hamilton, H.E. (eds.) 2003. *The Handbook of Discourse Analysis*. Oxford: Blackwell.

Schiller, H. 1976. 'Communication and Cultural Domination'. *International Journal of Politics*, 5, 4, pp. 1–127.

Sezneva, O. 2013. 'Re-Thinking Copyright through the Copy in Russia'. *Journal of Cultural Economy*, 6, 4, pp. 472–487.

Sezneva, O., Karaganis, J. 2011. 'Russia'. In Karaganis, J. (ed.) *Media Piracy in Emerging Economies*. Social Science Research Council, pp. 149–218.

Sheveleva, S. 2015. 'Chto my nadelali. Glavnye redaktory The Village raznykh let – o tom, kuda vsyo katitsia'. *The Village*, 24 April. URL: https://www.the-village.ru/village/city/5-let-the-village/213567-razgovor-s-glavredami (accessed 11 March 2019)

Small, C. 1998. *Musicking: The Meanings of Performing and Listening*. Hanover, NH: Wesleyan University Press of New England.

Smith-Maguire, J., Matthews, J. (eds.) 2014. *The Cultural Intermediaries Reader*. London: Sage.

Sprengel, D. 2020. 'Neoliberal Expansion and Aesthetic Innovation: The Egyptian Independent Music Scene Ten Years After'. *International Journal of Middle East Studies*, 5, 3, pp. 545–551.

Steinholt, Y. 2003. 'You Can't Rid a Song of Its Words: Notes on the Hegemony of Lyrics in Russian Rock Songs'. *Popular Music*, 22, 1, pp. 89–108.

Steinholt, Y. 2005. *Rock in the Reservation: Songs from the Leningrad Rock Club 1981–1986*. Bergen – New York: The Mass Media Music Scholar's Press.

Stokes, M. 2013. 'Afterword: a Worldly Musicology?. In Bohlman, P. (ed.) *The Cambridge History of World Music*. Cambridge: Cambridge University Press, pp. 826–842.

Strong, C., Canizzo, F. 2021. 'Pre-Existing Conditions: Precarity, Creative Justice and the Impact of the COVID-19 Pandemic on the Victorian Music Industries'. *Perfect Beat*, pp. 10–24.

Tarassi, S. 2018. 'Multi-Tasking and Making a Living from Music: Investigating Music Careers in the Independent Music Scene of Milan'. *Cultural Sociology*, 12, 2, pp. 208–223.

Taylor, T. 2012. *The Sounds of Capitalism: Advertising, Music, and the Conquest of Culture*. Chicago: University of Chicago Press.

Taylor, T. 2013. 'Globalised New Capitalism and the Commodification of Taste'. In Bohlman, P. (ed.) *The Cambridge History of World Music*. Cambridge: Cambridge University Press, pp. 744–764.

Thornton, S. 1995. *Club Cultures: Music, Media, and Subcultural Capital*. Cambridge: Polity Press.

Thussu, D.K. 2015. 'Reinventing 'Many Voices: MacBride and a Digital New World Information and Communication Order'. *Javnost - The Public*, 22, 3, pp. 252–263.

Tolstad, I. 2021. 'We Have No Music Industry!' Exploring the Context of Post-Soviet Music Making Through the Lens of Contemporary Swedo-Russian Collaborations'. In Galuszka,

68 Independent Music in Russia

P. (ed.) *Eastern European Music Industries and Policies after the Fall of Communism: From State Control to Free Market*. Oxon: Routledge, pp. 62–78.

Tolz, V. 2001. *Russia: Inventing the Nation*. London: Hodder Education.

Tolz, V. 2010. 'The West'. In Leatherbarrow, W.J., Offord, D. (eds.) *A History of Russian Thought*. Cambridge University Press, pp. 197–216.

Toomistu, T. 2018. 'Such a Strange Vibration: Rock Music as the Affective Site of Divergence among the Soviet Estonian Nonconformist Youth'. *Res Musica*, 10, pp. 11–27.

Toynbee, J. 2000. *Making Popular Music: Musicians, Creativity and Institutions*. London: Bloomsbury Academic.

Troitsky, A. 1988. *Back in the USSR: The True Story of Rock in Russia*. London: Faber & Faber.

Turino, T. 2008. *Music as Social Life. The Politics of Participation*. Chicago: The University of Chicago Press.

Vaughan Williams, R. 1987 (1963). *National Music and Other Essays*. Oxford: Oxford University Press.

Vermeulen, T., Van den Akker, R. 2010. 'Notes on Metamodernism'. *Journal of Aesthetics & Culture*, 2, 1, pp. 1–14.

Voronin, I. 2022. 'Gorbushka i fantiki: kak bylo ustroeno muzykal'noe piratstvo v 1990-kh'. *Afisha*, 26 October. URL: https://daily.afisha.ru/music/24288-fantiki-prodigy-i-gorbushka-kak-bylo-ustroeno-muzykalnoe-piratstvo-v-1990-h/ (accessed 14 September 2023).

Ward, C. 2014. 'Rocking Down the Mainline: Rock Music during the Construction of the Baikal-Amur Mainline Railway (BAM), 1974–1984'. In Risch, W.J. (ed.) *Youth and Rock in the Soviet Bloc: Youth Cultures, Music, and the State in Russia and Eastern Europe*. Lanham: Lexington Books, pp. 81–100.

Way, L. 2016. 'Protest Music, Populism, Politics and Authenticity: The Limits and Potential of Popular Music's Articulation of Subversive Politics'. *Journal of Language and Politics*, 15, 4, pp. 422–445.

Webb-Gannon, C., Webb, M. 2019. '"More than a Music, It's a Movement": West Papua Decolonization Songs, Social Media, and the Remixing of Resistance'. *The Contemporary Pacific*, 31, 2, pp. 309–443.

Wikström, P. 2014. *The Music Industry: Music in the Cloud* (2nd Ed.). Cambridge: Polity Press.

Wikström, P., DeFilippi, R. (eds.) 2016. *Business Innovation and Disruption in the Music Industry*. Cheltenham: Edward Elgar.

Wojnowski, Z. 2020. 'The Pop Industry from Stagnation to Perestroika: How Music Professionals Embraced the Economic Reform That Broke East European Cultural Networks'. *The Journal of Modern History*, 92, pp. 311–350.

Yaffa, J. 2020. *Between Two Fires. Truth, Ambition and Compromise in Putin's Russia*. New York: Penguin.

Yoffe, M. 2013. 'The Stiob of Ages: Carnivalesque Traditions in Soviet Rock and Related Counterculture'. *Russian Literature*, 74, 1–2, pp. 207–225.

Yurchak, A. 2006. *Everything Was Forever, Until It Was No More: The Last Soviet Generation*. Princeton, NJ: Princeton University Press.

Yurchak, A. 2011. 'A Parasite from Outer Space: How Sergei Kurekhin Proved That Lenin Was a Mushroom'. *Slavic Review*, 70, 2, pp. 307–333.

Zav'ialov, V. 2020. 'Pochemu v Rossii net edinogo charta?'. *IMI*, 29 September. URL: https://i-m-i.ru/post/chart-in-russia?fbclid=IwAR145q2WosF2BPeWWOJJr2FLBopKrU0k7uhGDQ5kqGkfSwgqnF-xBZ1uMoA (accessed 20 October 2021).

Zhitinskii, A. 2007a (1990). *Puteshestvie rok-diletanta*. Sankt-Peterburg: Amfora.

Zhitinskii, A. 2007b (1990). *Vtoroe puteshestvie rok-diletanta*. Sankt-Peterburg: Amfora.

Zhuk, S. 2010. *Rock and Roll in the Rocket City: The West, Identity and Ideology in Soviet Dnipropetrovsk 1960–1985*. Washington: Woodrow Wilson Center Press.

2 "We also can. We're not worse"

The Anglophone Wave (2008–2012)

Introduction: "Everyone back in 2010 was singing in English"

In late 2012 Tesla Boy, a three-piece band from Moscow, performed their single "Electric Lady" on *Vechernii Urgant*, a very popular late-night show on Russia's most-watched channel, *Pervyi Kanal* (Channel One).[1] The presenter, Ivan Urgant, introduced the performance of the band with these words:

> Dear friends, people often write to us asking why we don't always host bands that are on the peak of music trends. Well, today, we have that very band here as guests. These people know how to correctly shave the sides of their head and leave a nice shrub on the top. These people know how to play fashionable new songs on an old synthesiser. And they know how to wear jeans three sizes smaller. Because they are *fashionable*. Friends, please welcome, Tesla Boy!
>
> (Urgant in *Vechernii Urgant* 2012)

The term "fashionable" (*modnyi*), with which Urgant described the band, was not only an indicator of the popularity, especially amongst the youth, that Tesla Boy enjoyed in 2012, but it also suggested that Tesla Boy were not alone at the "peak" of music in vogue. On 26 April 2012, Pompeya, another local Anglophone band, had performed their single "Slow", also on *Urgant*. This occurred only ten days after the first broadcast of the programme, when the audience share was around 12% (Borodina 2012). But Pompeya and Tesla boy were not the only English-singing bands whose performances were being televised in that period. On 6 June of the same year, another Anglophone group, Everything Is Made in China (EIMIC) played on Russia-1 (*Rossiia-1*) during the talk show *Profilaktika*. The same show hosted the performances of other local Anglophone bands: Coockoo (19 April 2012) and Moremoney (5 May 2012). Another channel, *Dozhd* (TV Rain), broadcast the live shows of On-The-Go (3 March 2011) and Human Tetris (2 October 2011). While *Channel One* and *Russia-1* were state-controlled, *Dozhd'* was part of the liberal oppositional media,[2] which points to the wide appreciation of the Anglophone bands across Russian society beyond political agendas.

The appearance of so many domestic Anglophone groups on national TV was both unprecedented and abnormal, yet TV was the most visible manifestation of a

DOI: 10.4324/9781003248699-3

70   *Independent Music in Russia*

much larger and widespread trend. For example, Anglophone bands participated in all the relevant indie-rock festivals of the time, becoming a consistent presence in their line-up after the turn of the decade. Between 2007 and 2010, Moscow-based *Piknik Afishi*, organised by the trendsetting magazine *Afisha*, held a special stage for local Anglophone bands called "Idle Conversations". *Piknik* also featured on its bill On-The-Go (2011, 2014 and 2017), Pompeya (2012) and Tesla Boy (2013 and 2016). These three bands experienced a popularity which, as evidenced by their participation in later festivals, outlived the Anglophone Wave. For instance, Moscow's *Bosco Fresh Fest* hosted On-The-Go on six occasions (2012, 2013, 2015, 2016, 2017 and 2018), Pompeya on three (2012, 2014 and 2016) and Tesla Boy on two (2013 and 2016). St. Petersburg's *Stereoleto*'s programme also included On-The-Go (2012 and 2016), Pompeya (2010 and 2017) and Tesla Boy (2009 and 2015). Judging by the capacity of the clubs hosting local Anglophone bands, in the early 2010s these bands could fill clubs with a capacity that ranged between 500 and 1500 people. For instance, Moscow's indie haven 16 Tons, which hosted at least one, sometimes two, gigs of Pompeya, Tesla Boy and On-The-Go every year during the 2010s, has a capacity of 550.

This trend was not exclusively concentrated in Moscow. These bands regularly toured across Russia's territory once or twice a year, witnessing approximately a similar attendance. Ekaterinburg, located 1700km from Moscow in the Ural region, represents a good example of this spread. In 2013, On-The-Go filled the local Dom Pechati (Printing House), which has a capacity of 600, whereas Pompeya and Tesla Boy gigged the Teleklub, which has a capacity of 1500.[3]

The appearance and popularity in Russia of home-bred English-singing groups – which I term the "Anglophone Wave" – did not occur by chance nor suddenly. Domestic Anglophone bands had increasingly gained momentum since 2008, when trendsetters started promoting them as part of a youth movement that looked westward. Since all artistic work involves the joint activity of a large number of people (Becker 1982), the exposure Russian Anglophone bands received was only the culmination of a collective effort undertaken over time. Correspondingly, the rise of the Anglophone Wave in Russia's alternative music panorama represented a symptom of a broader change in Russian society: the perceived internationality carried by English as a language reflected the cosmopolitan image that the youth were attempting to construct. Interviewee 25, the singer of an Anglophone post-punk band, observed that when they founded the project at the end of the 2000s, there was no doubt about which language to use; the choice of English was "natural". Interviewee 28, the leader of another Anglophone collective, summed up the spirit of the time: "everyone back in 2010 was singing in English". This perception was not only reiterated by virtually all the participants interviewed but also evident in the production of music media at the time, online and off. The taken-for-grantedness of the use of English was paired with close attention to contemporary sonic trends in Western indie and ultimately aimed at fashioning a transnational product that could be qualitatively equal to those. This, in turn, evidenced the intention to situate Russia on a par with its constitutive Other, the West.

"We Also Can. We're Not Worse" 71

The period of the Anglophone Wave coincides roughly with the presidency of Dmitry Medvedev (2008–2012) and with Russia's last glimmer of democracy before the authoritarian shift of Putin's third presidency. As I argue below, local Anglophone bands constituted one of the products of this period, aided by a perceived Russia-West political relaxation, Russia's tentative openness to the West and Moscow's modernisation. Such favourable conditions encouraged the formation of a Westernising discourse among independent music participants, who assembled, shared the resources available and eventually mobilised the *nezavisimaia muzyka* world westward with conviction and intensity. What follows below also situates the emergence of independent English-singing bands at the crossroads of a horizontal cultural movement and vertical financial investment. The horizontal movement comprised the young "hipster" intelligentsia, that is, the "creative middle class" newly formed as a product of Putin's first two mandates as president. The vertical investment came both from the state and from private companies often led by state-aligned oligarchs, in the shape of funding for culture, infrastructure, and city reconfiguration. The basis of both horizontal and vertical projects, again, was the Western model, the idea that Moscow (and by extension, Russia) could compete with other Western capitals (and by extension, the West) in terms of cultural innovation, technology and urban comfort. As explained in the next chapter, the grassroots, horizontal impulse to situate Moscow in an imagined global community was thwarted considerably between winter 2011 and spring 2012, when the police violently repressed the protests against Putin's return to power, in which many of the same young creatives and professionals took part.

Despite its novelty for Russian culture, intensity, collective dimension and significance for the youth, and despite emerging at the intersection between popular music, society, and politics in Russia at the turn of the 2010s, the Anglophone Wave has hardly attracted scholarly attention.[4] This chapter seeks to fill such a gap. In unearthing the aims and scope of the Anglophone Wave, and in contrast to Russia's current isolation from Europe and opposition to the West, I aim to show that, not long ago, a large portion of Russian independent cultural producers successfully constructed a bridge toward the Other: the escapism that these Anglophone Wave performed was "productive", in the sense that it repeatedly projected the utopian image of a West European, globally integrated and cool Moscow, until this image eventually materialised. Such escapism was also political, because through these spaces, the independent community entered into a public conversation regarding the direction, values and future of Russian culture. The music in which they performed such a task, correspondingly, was a sunny, "chilled" and upbeat indie, sung in English and looking in a different direction from where the storm was coming. Indeed, at that time, practitioners did not pay enough attention to what would become clear after 2012: the fact that Westernisation in architecture, technology and urban comfort was a state project, and that modernisation did not in fact correspond to democratisation.

In what follows, I first provide a brief overview of the debates surrounding the influence of Western (particularly Anglophone) popular music in Soviet and Russian popular music before the Anglophone Wave, linking these debates to

72 *Independent Music in Russia*

broader issues of derivativeness and authenticity (as perceived by practitioners). I then analyse how Western and Anglophone popular music made way into the post-Soviet Russian media and cultural landscapes in the period leading up to 2008. Next, I explore the main traits of the Anglophone Wave, linking the phenomenon to wider cultural and social trends and to a discussion of the political nature of escapism, before offering some conclusions.

Anxieties of influence: from Western rock to *russkii rok* and from *russkii rok* to the Anglophone Wave

"In terms of sound, *russkii rok* is Western rock", claimed Interviewee 13, one of the most influential music critics in Russia: "musically, our musicians didn't invent anything new. What they invented is a literary tradition". What Interviewee 13 suggests here is that *russkii rok* achieved its distinctive character through the absorption and adaptation of its main sonic influence, Western popular music. This encompasses domestic styles beyond *russkii rok* too. In the Soviet and Russian independent music tradition, echoes of Western music are more recurrent than "Russian" folk melodies; electric instruments are more used than traditional acoustic ones; Bob Dylan is more referenced than Vysotsky.[5] The influence of Anglo-American popular music, however, does not make Russian independent musicians derivative, but is instead indicative of their struggle in finding different coordinates within but also outside the broader musical system with which they aesthetically identified.

In his eponymous book on literary theory, Harold Bloom (1997 [1973]) calls such a quest for ownership "anxiety of influence". Bloom explains that the legacy of other previous poets constrains the aesthetics of subsequent poets, who are always confronted with the eventuality that their work may be derivative or weak if compared with that of their predecessors. This anxiety ultimately drives the "new" poets to look for innovation: if "strong" and persistent, the poets will find their own voice, become an influence themselves and integrate their name in the canon.

The first to experience such anxiety in Russian independent music were the Soviet rockers who founded *russkii rok* in the 1970s. Anglophiles and "cosmopolitan par excellence" (McMichael 2019, 77–78), they experienced anxiety not in relation to the Russo-Soviet literary tradition, but to Western musicians such as John Lennon, Bob Dylan, Mick Jagger, Marc Bolan and others, whom they recognised as key figures for their craft (see also McMichael 2005, 2008). Reflecting on the task of shaping music of equal aesthetic value as Western rock performers but without copying them, Soviet unofficial musicians identified their positive difference in literary proficiency. Partly because of the perceived supremacy of Western musicians and partly because of the scarcity of resources available (e.g., studios, producers and equipment), they did not place the emphasis of differentiation on sonic innovation, and they channelled their creativity into something that they perceived as unimportant in Western music: the word.[6] Poetic competence was therefore where they focused their attention. As Iurii Shevchuk, the frontman of the band DDT,[7] declared: "what's most important in rock music is poetry. The music is only secondary, and what you need to do is to make sure, first and foremost, that the quality of your poetry is the best it can be" (Shevchuk in Cushman 1995, 105). Of course, the adaptation from Western to Soviet forms did not end with poetry: literariness came often with the Russian (or local) language as its vehicle and reflections on local realities as its subject matter.

For Russian Anglophone bands like Pompeya, Tesla Boy and On-The-Go, who rose to national popularity between 2008 and 2012, the anxiety of influence was reversed, and experienced towards the Russophone Soviet rockers, not towards Anglo-American music, leading them to funnel their creativity into what the Soviet predecessors had in their view neglected: the sound. In this process, admiration mixed with criticism, but *russkii rok*'s constraining legacy emerges quite clearly in the participants' discourse. For example, Interviewee 15, a member of one of these Anglophone bands, observes:

I grew up listening to Kino[8] and *russkii rok*, and that also had an impact on me, but didn't make me want to sing in Russian anyway. I thought I could never do something as cool as that by singing in Russian.

Interviewee 4, frontperson of another Anglophone collective, comments:

The first band I had was Russophone. I didn't sing on that one, though, but I was contributing with my stuff every now and then and I learned a lot from it. Then, the next band I joined was Anglophone. I immediately felt some sort of song-writing freedom [*songvraiterskaia svoboda*] and started writing my own lyrics. It just seemed a more natural process in order to express my thoughts. It may seem peculiar, but I did try to write in Russian, and it just was a very difficult process.

Interviewee 12, then leader of another Anglophone group, adds:

When you write in Russian you're suddenly confronted with the tradition of *russkii rok*. You need to write incredibly clever lyrics. [...] In English you can take a step back from that literary rock-hero, be less strict and less harsh with yourself.

Interviewee 32, main writer of an internationally renowned Russian Anglophone band, muses:

Initially the idea was to do [the band] in Russian, but we could not write lyrics that we liked. [...] I always thought that the quality of the lyrics in '80s Russian rock and post-punk was very important. They were logocentric bands, if you like. English groups are more... well, you can convey emotions and energy with simple images. This might not work out in the case of a Russian band.

74 *Independent Music in Russia*

Thus, instead of looking inwards, the Anglophones looked outwards, discarding lyrical proficiency as unattainable and therefore inadequate. At the same time, they acted like a "system crash", claiming that the poetic ability of Soviet unofficial musicians was not enough to shape tangible difference from the Western canon. The following excerpt from an interview between Tesla Boy leader Anton Sevidov and Aleksandr Gorbachev evidences this point:

Sevidov: I don't quite understand why I should acknowledge my belonging to Russian culture as a musician. For example Kino are considered a classic of *russkii rok* – nonetheless some of their recordings sound the same as The Smiths. I well remember, and it struck me at that time, how those guys tried to be fashionable [...]

Gorbachev: but Tsoi had very recognisable Russian melodies....very direct.

Sevidov: Oh, come on! Didn't Joy Division have very direct melodies? There's a funny thing about this Russianness [*russkost'*]: imagine if all these people – Tsoi, Maik, BG – sang in English.[9] There wouldn't be anything Russian left. Because there's nothing Russian there as it is. And that's not a bad thing. On the contrary, it's great. I think that's the beauty of art: music washes away boundaries between countries.

(Gorbachev 2013)

The perceived boundlessness of music, for Sevidov, overcame national tradition. Furthermore, the commodification of *russkii rok*, which had seen its most-representative bands perform in stadiums since the late 1980s-early 1990s, contributed to the "difference" that Anglophone bands embodied when they entered the domestic popular music scene in the late 2000s. By that time *russkii rok* had crystallised as a mainstream style, thanks also to media such as like *Nashe Radio* (a radio station established in 1998, which was dedicated to Soviet rock and *russkii rok*) and its "emanation" *Nashestvie* – the largest festival in Russia, which was set up in 1999.[10] In shaping the difference of the Anglophone Wave bands, the choice of another language (English) played an important role. For musicians and fans, as another music critic put it, "English functioned as the most immediate door to another world" after "the cultural trauma" of the 1990s (Interview 5), in which Russia became perceived by the youth as culturally provincial (see also the surveys in Pilkington et al. 2002). English came therefore to represent an antidote to the datedness of *russkii rok*, a means to express distinction from the dominant Russophone context. As Interviewee 13 explains:

At the end of the 90s the term 'Govnorok'[11] was coined, and partially some bands started singing in English because they were tired of that 'Govnorok'. In a way, English became a protest against that degradation, that degeneration of classic *russkii rok*.

However, the linguistic and sonic differences of the Anglophone Wave were not signs of protest proper – many of the bands from the Anglophone Wave had significant admiration for the *rokery* – but they instead constituted a distancing from a *russkii rok* sound that had become dominant, together with the exploration of musical avenues that were perceived to be new. Thus, the Anglophone Wave at the end of the 2000s represented the latest stage in the journey of the Other into Russian rock music territory. The way in which Soviet musicians adapted from English to Russian and post-Soviet Russian musicians adapted from Russian to English presupposed a continuous interrogation of Western popular music and its symbolic power.

The tangible West

"It was the striving towards the West, the love towards the West… like, we also can, we're not worse [*my tozhe mozhem, my ne khuzhe*]". With these words, verging between admiration, need for validation and competition, Interviewee 12 – ex-leader of a popular Anglophone indie group around 2010 – explained the impulse behind the Anglophone Wave. Bands were singing in English as a long-term consequence of the political and cultural opening towards the West. During the 1990s and 2000s, indeed, "the flow of Western commodities and cultural forms […] increasingly shaped the cultural world of the Russian youth" (Pilkington et al. 2002, 101). Russia, however, had been at the receiving end of West-defined global popular music discourses (with a few exceptions, such as t.A.T.u.). For this reason, musicians had the urge to demonstrate that they stood at the same qualitative level as their Western colleagues: that they had "caught up" with the West on the one hand, and that Russia was part of the global musical discourse on the other. As discussed in the previous chapter, these motivations were embedded in a historical framework of Russia's perceptions of inadequacy, uncertainty and admiration in relation to its Other, which at times translated into collective inferiority complexes, at times drove Russian artists to embark on creative journeys towards difference, and often inspired imaginative practices.

The latter state is best captured by Alexei Yurchak's (2006) concept of "Imaginary West". Analysing the society of the late Soviet period, he defined the "Imaginary West" as a local construct that was based on the forms of knowledge and aesthetics associated with the "West", but not necessarily referring to any "real" West" (35–36). This, in his view, constituted one of the primary drives for informal Soviet culture and youth habits after the death of Stalin, and "contributed to "deterritorialising" the world of everyday socialism from within" (Yurchak 2006). Yurchak argues that this Imaginary West comprises objects and actions that created a connection with the West when the actual West was impossible to encounter physically. For instance, wearing Western clothing, connecting to Western radio channels, listening to Western rock, covering songs by The Beatles and decorating one's own pirate vinyl with names and drawings of Western bands all fall under the category of practices related to the Imaginary West. These practices were devoted to making the West appear in the private spaces of Soviet individuals and at the same time take Soviet individuals where they likely could have never gone in the flesh. Accounts of Western influence on late Soviet unofficial music that highlight

76 *Independent Music in Russia*

this collective psychological voyage to foreign domains, including playing, performing and listening to rock music, are well-documented in cultural artefacts and scholarship.[12] Soviet musicians listened to and performed Anglo-American tunes regardless whether they understood the lyrics and, while fashioning their own identity, modelled themselves on Anglo-American performers in attitude and style. These ways of connecting with the Other provided them with considerable pleasure and represented an escape from official ideology.

Yurchak maintains that the "Imaginary West" ended with the fall of the Soviet Union, and "that with it were lost all those intimate worlds of meaning and creativity that were so indivisible from the realities of socialism and so constitutive of its forms of 'normal' life" (206). While this is true of the "Imaginary West" in the context of socialism, it is debatable in relation to the concept of "Imaginary West" overall.

The Imaginary West changed its appearance, rather than vanishing altogether: the West, the Other, remained something "imaginary" for most post-Soviet Russians, insofar as the cultural gap, perceived to separate Russia from the "West", continued to be upheld across music participants (while the political elite failed to address the economic gap). True, the material encounter with the West in the 1990s did not hold to expectations in some cases, and its image crashed in others. This is not only evidenced by the one-way flow of Western cultural products into Russia, but also by the criticism contained in Russian discourses around globalisation as a manifestation of American imperialism (Pilkington et al. 2002, 4–13). This disillusion was also expressed in cultural artefacts, particularly in Aleksei Balabanov's blockbusters *Brat* and *Brat 2* (*Brother* and *Brother 2*), which came out in 1997 and 2000, the latter coincidentally the year of Putin's first election (Putin himself embodies the outcome of this post-Soviet ressentiment). In music, Russian cultural products failed to leave a mark in the "arrogantly Anglophone market" (Christgau 1991) despite considerable corporate investment in some cases.[13] But while the expansion of Western capitalism into Russia was seen as rapacious and ruinous, the construction of the West was still that of an "imaginary world" (Hashamova 2007, 10) which held and exerted significant symbolic power in Russia. As the most powerful representative of this West, America became for the Russian youth a fantasy place onto which to project everything that was questionable *morally* (vulgarity, individualism, consumerism, coldness, etc.), but at the same time, thanks to its relentless apparatus of soft power, America was also identified as the source of everything that was *culturally* exciting and authentic, in particular music, style and fashion, including alternative ones (Pilkington et al. 2002). In music, the West continued to dictate trends (reflected in youth magazines such as *OM* and *Ptiuch*), and its symbolic power remained desirable and psychologically attractive. As a result, the Russians' ressentiment towards the West as a political system grew together with the appeal for the Russian youth of Western music, styles and cultural products, irrespective of the very youth's knowledge that these were symbols of soft power propelled by the American consumerist machine (Pilkington et al. 2002, 98–100).

Hence, in the 1990s new barriers preserved the deterritorialisation of the post-Soviet Russian generation, upholding the Russians' myth-making of the West as a magical land. Frontiers did open, but, as before, only a few "chosen" people

"We Also Can. We're Not Worse" 77

could cross them. Like in Soviet times, the average salary did not allow travel (Gorbachev and Zinin 2014, 17, Barker 1999, 13). Also, as in Soviet times, Western musical products were more available and affordable across the black market than in shops, and they were scarcely to be found outside big cities. Fans would get what they could lay their hands on. As in Soviet times, individuals overcame the paucity of Western music available through a set of ingenuous practices, which engendered fantasy journeys into the West and then inspired these people to pursue careers in music. Interviewee 1, the singer of a Russian Anglophone band, recalls:

In 1993–94 the guys that worked for our local television [in a town in the Far East, around nine thousand kilometres from Moscow] managed to latch onto MTV, obviously illegally. I remember seeing Nirvana's *Unplugged in New York* and other videos, and I thought it was cool, that music is cool. Plus, my dad had a huge collection of vinyl records, and I started listening to The Beatles, The Stones, and all that '60s rock. I went mad. I couldn't play any instrument and I'd already been in three bands. That is, I used to sit on the bench with my schoolmates and go: 'you'll be on guitar, we're going to conquer the whole world, we'll travel there and there'... And that alone was so cool. I would have goose bumps, and I would come back home and say: 'mom, I've founded a rock band!' And my mom would say: 'you finish year three, then we'll see'.

Parental habits played an important role in upholding the symbolic appeal of the West for the new generation of performers. Rather than rupture, continuity of taste and listening habits informed the passage between the last Soviet generation (coming of age in the 1970s and 1980s), and the first post-Soviet one (coming of age between the 1990s and the 2000s). As Interviewee 4, the leader of a major Anglophone Wave group, elucidates:

We grew up with the same records that our father had, first on vinyl, then on cassettes, then on CDs, and that was varied rock music, with different levels of 'heaviness', [from] both the British and American scenes, [including] the main representatives from back then: The Beatles, Pink Floyd, The Doors, Led Zeppelin, and so on. Pop music was also present, Madonna, Michael Jackson... All this reached us, we absorbed it one way or another.

For all these reasons, Anglo-American music, as Russia's musical Other, remained an object which Russian musicians could compare themselves to, and which continued to exert a great degree of fascination through its symbols and imageries. As Western music remained the model for musical production, Russian practitioners committed to catch up with it on the one hand, while on the other they were confronted with the disparity between cultural flows created by unequal power relationships, which reinforced perceptions of Russian popular music's belatedness or, worse, backwardness. The youth, as shown in the surveys conducted by Pilkington et al. (2002), considered Western popular music more evolved and

78 Independent Music in Russia

generally qualitatively "better" than the Russian equivalent (in terms of "sound" and "drive", not in terms of lyrics), whereas Russia was felt to imitate and dwell, internationally, on the cultural margins.

What journalist Aleksandr Gorbachev calls Russia's "European Project" emerged in this context and, to an extent, aimed at culturally redressing the balance between Russia and the West. As shown in the previous chapter, Gorbachev focused mainly on musicians, yet this project was holistic and involved loose assemblages of people in various fields of society. Indeed, the foundations of the "European Project" were laid at the end of the 1990s and during the first half of the 2000s through a few key initiatives led not just by musicians, but mainly by private investors. The method of such enterprises entailed, as its first step, the outsourcing and importing into Russia of Western commercial models of entertainment.

MTV Russia began broadcasting in 1998 and for the first few years proposed a mixture of Western (65%) and Russian (35%) rock, pop and indie songs through a combination of American-derived and Russia's "own brand" shows – 60% and 40%, respectively (*Argumenty i Fakty* 1999). In its "golden age" (1998–2002), MTV Russia inspired a new understanding and taste in music to the generation born during perestroika by introducing local bands with more alternative sounds that were different from the mainstream *russkii rok*. The figure of the VJ (video jockey), devised in the 1980s in the West but until then unknown to the Russian public, embodied a new way of performing music entertainment. With their laid-back attitude, humour, youth, English fluency and an aura of cosmopolitanism (Sorokin 2013), MTV Russia's VJs spoke straightforwardly and as peers to their young viewers, functioning as role models and as "tellers" of the stories of the Other. This, united with MTV's televising of ground-breaking mass events like the Red Hot Chili Peppers concert on Moscow's Red Square in 1999 and Paul McCartney's in 2003 (the latter with Putin and his ministers in the audience), framed the Other as increasingly close.

At around the same time, in 1999, Russian entrepreneur Ilia Oskolkov-Tsentsiper and American businessman Andrew Paulson founded the entertainment guide *Afisha*, which soon became Moscow's (and, to a lesser extent, St. Petersburg's) go-to magazine for music, fashion and urban culture. In St. Petersburg, *Afisha* competed with *Sobaka* and, in Moscow, with the Russian spin-off of *Time Out*, established in 2004. The format of these other two magazines was also Western-inspired. *Time Out Moscow* in particular was very similar to its British counterpart, and for the first issues the headings were in English, including a section called "Gay & Lesbian" (a legacy of Russia's liberal policies regarding individual expression in the 1990s), while the magazine nicknamed itself "the diary of a free person" (Boiarinov 2014). *Time Out Moscow* and *Afisha* often featured Western cinema, fashion or music stars on their covers. For their no. 1 issue cover, for example, *Time Out* had Colin Farrell, while *Afisha* had Gwyneth Paltrow.

For emerging local musicians, being on the radar of *Afisha*'s fortnightly release represented one of the best tools for expanding their fandom and gig opportunities.[14] For a decade, *Afisha* was the main tastemaker in Russia, defining what was "good" and "cool" in Muscovite culture (and, by extension, in the country at large).

"We Also Can. We're Not Worse" 79

Its former editor Iurii Saprykin (*Eshchenepozner* 2019) called it "a factory of desire" (*fabrika zhelanii*), running according to the motto "it will be as we say" (*kak skazhem tak i budet*). A banner with such an inscription hung in Pushkin Square, one of the busiest and most central places in Moscow. According to Saprykin (*Eshchenepozner* 2019), *Afisha* was both visionary and effective, because it saw nascent trends in the West and immediately transferred them to Russian ground a few years before Russians started perceiving them, thus enacting a vital shift from the "Imaginary West" to a tangible "Russian West". *Afisha* also shaped its own Anglicised jargon, including popularising the word *khipster* (hipster) and introducing in the everyday slang of the youth: words like *gërlfrend* (girlfriend) *boifrend* (boyfriend), *dedlain* (deadline), *messedzh* (message), *open speis* (open space), *feiskontrol* (face control), etc. (Sycheva 2010).

In 2006, Tsentsiper sold *Afisha* to Prof-Media (which also owned MTV between 2007 and 2013). Pro-Media would be bought out by Gazprom-Media Holding in 2013. As the name suggests, Gazprom-Media is in turn a subsidiary company of Gazprom, Russia's gas giant, of which more than 50% is owned by the state. Gazprom-Media controlled numerous outlets in Russia, including the (politically oppositional) radio station *Ekho Moskvy* (since 2001, closed in 2022), the TV channel NTV (since 2001), the online video platform *Runet* (since 2008), and the newspaper *Izvestiia* (since 2005). While Gazprom-Media's acquisition did not turn *Afisha* into a propaganda mouthpiece, the corporate buyout of *Afisha* evidenced the interests of state actors in establishing their presence in youth culture and entertainment, at a time when the oligarchs were doing a similar thing with physical spaces (see later).

Afisha promoted itself through the creation of a yearly music festival as well, *Piknik Afishi* (Afisha's Picnic), which took place for the first time in Moscow in 2004. As Interviewees 5 and 19, who worked in the magazine for a long time, put it, *Piknik Afishi* aimed at enhancing the journal's reputation, expanding its outreach, and enacting in practice what the journal was talking about in its pages. Over the years the festival brought a considerable number of Western indie artists to Russia for the first time (Beirut, Mùm, Black Lips, Editors, Metronomy, Franz Ferdinand, Blur, Suede, Sohn, Foals, Everything Everything, Arcade Fire, etc.), while showcasing also Russian ones (On-The-Go, Pompeya, Tesla Boy, Mujuice, Markscheider Kunst, Manicure, SBPCh, Padla Bear Outfit, etc.).

Afisha was not the only one involved in this operation of local and foreign indie discovery. Concert promoters like Igor' Tonkikh (founder of one of the first Russian indie labels, *Feelee*, in 1988), together with *Afisha*'s ex-music editor and *Piknik* developer Greg Goldenzwaig, opened Ikra, a club in the Eastern part of Moscow that regularly featured not only Western indie artists (Róisín Murphy, Amon Tobin, 65daysofstatic, NoMeansNo), but also local ones (Tesla Boy, Alina Orlova, Peter Nalitch). Together with Solyanka, between 2007 and 2011 Ikra remained at the centre of a growing *nezavisimaia muzyka* community whose underlying process was the assimilation of the Western Other into the Russian musical fabric.

Meanwhile, in 2002 Muscovite pop duo t.A.T.u. released the single "All the Things She Said" and succeeded in what many other Soviet and post-Soviet musicians had failed before them: reaching global acclaim. The duo rose to worldwide

80 *Independent Music in Russia*

fame without being contracted with any major label, relying instead on the initiative of manager and producer Ivan Shapovalov, whose role in the group's popularisation was fundamental. A child psychologist turned entrepreneur, Shapovalov actively constructed t.A.T.u.'s transgressive image, including the band's relationship with the political. For example, in 2003 t.A.T.u. performed on American TV with t-shirts carrying the inscription "fuck the war" (*khui voine*), a reference to the then-recent US invasion of Iraq, while their kiss onstage was censored by the camera. This episode, and the duo's failure to win the Eurovision in the same year, prompted Russian commentators to accuse "the West" of homophobia (see Heller 2007). Yet their success was due not just to their provocative homoerotic videos and live performances, but also to the refinement of the sonic product and the carefully packaged Western sound, in which English lyrics were an integral part. t.A.T.u. are still one of Russia's most successful music export products to this day, with more than eight million records sold worldwide (*www.tatu.ru* 2019), four weeks at the top of the UK chart (Cherrytree Records 2012), and several international music awards. Most importantly, t.A.T.u. showed the Russian musicians, including the ones gravitating around the *nezavisimaia muzyka* world, that singing in English could be paired with commercial success and public recognition globally.

Thus, the first half of the 2000s provided the indie scene with new resources that paved the way for the subsequent strengthening and expansion of the Muscovite *nezavisimaia muzyka* community in the second half. This transformation occurring at the level of popular culture reflected another transformation on a larger scale, which was equally influential in recent Russian history: the architectural renovation of Moscow.

"They imagined a comfortable, hipstery Moscow": time, city and soundtrack

The sociocultural significance and audience recognition of Russian Anglophone bands in the post-Soviet space are entwined with the time and space that those bands inhabited. "Many bands in Russia had performed in English before Tesla Boy and Pompeya", says Interviewee 18, a Moscow-based music journalist, manager and promoter, "but they were not influential". "There were lots of Russian groups singing in English, especially in the 1990s, we had many Britpop imitators, but no one made a career out of it", echoes his colleague (Interview 17), who is also a musician. Domestic Anglophone collectives, as music observer (Interview 11) puts it, "had remained in the past, completely forgotten". To be sure, domestic Anglophone musicians had sporadically reached some local notoriety before the Anglophone Wave. Among the most notable examples we can list: the Rostov-based post-punk band Matrosskaia tishina (The Sailor's Silence, in honour of the famous Moscow prison), which began in 1987 and was particularly active in the first half of the 1990s; the rock project Tandem, founded in 1991 in Vladivostok; the alternative rock band Team Ocean, which started in Moscow in the same year; the progressive rock group Extrovert from Irkutsk, Siberia, established in 1993; the St. Petersburg ska collective Spitfire, founded in the same year; the metal band

"We Also Can. We're Not Worse" 81

Catharsis, established in 1996 in Moscow; and the grunge band Moi rakety vverkh (My Rockets Up), formed in Moscow in 2001, which achieved radio rotation and TV appearance in the mid-2000s. These projects, however, did not experience the same public resonance and they did not appear consistently, as a movement.[15]

What created the conditions for the exceptionality of the Anglophone Wave as a full-fledged, networked and structured music world (in addition, of course, to the qualities of Pompeya, On-The-Go and the other Anglophone bands) resided in the socio-political milieu, specifically in Russia's economic growth (2000–2014), Moscow's modernisation (2008–2018), and the perceived political openness of Dmitri Medvedev's presidency (2008–2012). Interviewee 33, a journalist and former head of an important independent label and artist management company, has put the Medvedev years in relation to the local *nezavisimaia muzyka* scene in this way:

> We had four years of Medvedev, who acted like he was a liberal, hung around with an iPhone, a bike, as if we were a cool European country as well. And we actually were. The crisis hadn't started yet, and everything looked somehow very good. And we, on our verandas, gathered up, had fun [*tusovalis'*] and listened to Pompeya.

Similarly, Interviewee 35, a music columnist for a national newspaper, explains:

> From the second half of the 2000s, when 'Putin's wellbeing'– let's call it that way – started, when, in general, people started to earn money, and socially everything was more or less alright, new interesting bands began to appear on the scene. These bands preferred to sing in English, and predicated according to the British indie school. We can list them, it's such an obvious list: Tesla Boy, Motorama,[16] On-The-Go, Pompeya.

The quotations above illustrate how two members of the music community viewed the political, economic and societal context in which local Anglophone bands appeared at the end of the 2000s, and how they saw such bands as celebratory soundtracks of that particular time of "innocence". The socio-political conditions encouraged musicians and the community around them to create space for an enthusiastic vision of renewal.

First of all, Russia's economy improved extensively. In the years 2000–2014 (with the exception of 2009), Russia's GDP experienced a constant growth, averaging annually around 7% during Putin's first two terms (2000–2008) and 4% during the second half of Medvedev's term in office (2010–2012) (World Bank 2016a). Moreover, Russia recovered more speedily than many other countries, including the US, from the economic crisis that hit the world in 2008 (World Bank 2016b). Secondly, in 2008 Dmitry Medvedev became the new president of the Russian Federation, aged 42. Whereas many – not unreasonably – viewed Medvedev as Putin's puppet (Hale 2015; Wilson 2015), it needs to be acknowledged that Medvedev, at first, wore the mask of a young and progressive politician. Many, for instance, would remember his love for Western hard rock (especially Deep Purple) and his ecstatic

82   *Independent Music in Russia*

visit to Apple's headquarters in Cupertino in 2010, where Steve Jobs gifted him with a brand-new iPhone 4. Anti-corruption, social reforms, political liberalisation and orientation of Russia towards the West stood out in his agenda and public rhetoric, giving the impression of a real change in Russian society, which some tentatively called new "thaw" or "perestroika 2.0" (Hahn 2012). Medvedev worked in tandem with Putin, who momentarily took the role of prime minister. The pair enacted a "good cop/bad cop" strategy (with Medvedev as the friendly Westerniser and Putin as the tough Slavophile guy) which created both uncertainty about Russia's future and an opening of the political space (Hale 2015, 281; 2017, 34). However, while Medvedev's gesture at political reform on the whole ended up strengthening the regime and introducing more of the same (Wilson 2015), his administration succeeded in enhancing public perceptions of Russia as belonging both to the Western world and to Europe. For example, in 2008, 52 percent of Russians identified their country as European (Levada Centre 2021), in a moment when talks of a visa-less policy were held between the EU and Russia. Russians' enthusiasm reached its apex in 2010, when 78 percent of respondents thought Russia should strengthen its relationship with the West, compared to 61 percent in 1999 (Levada Centre 2018), while 69 percent held a favourable view of the EU, a record to this day (Pew Centre 2019).

Crucial to Russia's European rapprochement was the modernisation of one of its key elements: Moscow. During Medvedev's term, large amounts of funds were invested in the renovation and development of Russia's capital city. In 2008, one trillion rubles (£11.5 billion) were allocated as the capital's budget, an amount then similar to that of London (Olifirova 2007). The city's budget grew consistently over the years, due partly to the prospect of hosting the FIFA World Cup in 2018, the year in which it doubled to two trillion rubles (£23 billion) (Moscow Official Website [www.mos.ru] 2018). The street kiosks, which were so typical of the Russian capital's landscape, but became viewed by the administration as shabby remnants of the past, were removed. Central streets were paved and closed to the traffic, and pavements were enlarged to host the flow of pedestrians. The rusty rollercoasters in Gorky Park were dismantled and replaced by museums, pavilions, sport areas and cafes. Parks were replanted, decorated and embellished. Historical buildings were restored and polished. New bars, restaurants and clubs mushroomed at an unprecedented rate, resembling those of Shoreditch in London or the East Village in New York. In the central and old district of Kitai Gorod, as Skolkov (2009a) noted on *Look At Me*, "a whole venue route began to take shape".

Since "space produces as space is produced" (Leyshon et al. 1995, 425), two consequences occurred. Firstly, Moscow attracted a large number of young musicians seeking to make a career, supplanting St. Petersburg in the role of epicentre of musical culture. Having moved from the city of Togliatti (1000 km east of Moscow) at the end of the 2000s, Interviewee 4, vocalist of an important Anglophone band, reveals:

There was a period when we were deciding where to go: Moscow or Piter [St. Petersburg]. Having toured a bit, though, we could assess the atmosphere, the scene, how it could develop in practice, and we understood that Moscow was the best choice for us, because there were more venues [...]

"We Also Can. We're Not Worse" 83

Piter was for a long time the cultural capital, and I suppose that the scene there is still influential and the artistic *tusovka* is still very interesting. But we thought we needed something more. [...] What attracted us at the time was to develop as a band but also to make money with music.

In addition to Interviewee 4 and his band, other influential Anglophone indie bands (or members of bands) such as Therr Maitz (Magadan – 10,000 km away), Parks, Squares and Alleys (Khabarovsk – 8,000 km), Moremoney (Kogalym – 3,000 km), The Jack Wood (Tomsk – 3,500 km), Vosmoy (Perm – 1,500 km) and Hospital (Komsomolsk-na-Amure – 9,000 km) moved to Moscow from other parts of Russia's vast territory. Participants in the Anglophone independent world thus converged, resources were shared and musicians began to overcome the threshold for the popularisation of the genre.

Secondly, Moscow's landscape became populated with cultural hubs and art centres that soon became crucial platforms and junctions for the creative youth. This happened in less than three years: Winzavod opened in 2007, Artplay and Garage in 2008 and Flacon and Strelka in 2009, to name only the most influential ones. Creative industries scholar Margarita Kuleva (2019, 6–8) describes such spaces as "new, sexy and international" (in Strelka, for example, the teaching was conducted only in English). Winzavod ("Wine Factory"), a centre for contemporary arts located near Kurskaia station, featured 11 art galleries and six institutes of art, media, design and music, as well as a few shops and bars. It hosted various musical events, including the independent music and experimental art summer festival *Forma*. Artplay, a 65,000-square-metre centre for creative industries located also near Kurskaia, comprised around 60 different small creative businesses, the underground music club Pluton and the RMA Business School (the first in Russia to offer degrees in music management). The last delegates' conference of *Moscow Music Week*, Russia's annual showcase of upcoming musical talent, took place here in 2019. Artplay also hosted disparate musical events, including the independent music festival *Endless Summer*. Located on Red October Island, Strelka (Arrow) consisted of an institute of architecture and design, a publishing press, a venue and a summer concert arena. Flacon, an art territory of 50,000 square metres, included art and design galleries, bars, and a large open-air concert stage. In the summer, the cluster hosted numerous festivals, including *Summersound* and *Panki v gorode* (Punks in the city). Garage, a museum of contemporary art, emerged in the middle of Gorky Park as a symbol of Moscow's renewed coolness and international appeal. The museum featured a bookshop and regularly hosted conferences and talks. Dozens of concerts took place around Garage every summer, often in various sites simultaneously.[17]

These new spaces materialised at the intersection of the interests of rich private investors and the Moscow administration. For example, oligarch and Chelsea FC former owner Roman Abramovich stood behind the development of Garage, billionaire and Rosneft adviser Roman Trotsenko founded Winzavod (Rosneft is Russia's largest oil company and is state-controlled) and media tycoon Aleksandr Mamut financed Strelka. At the same time, the development of privately owned cultural institutions gained political support because this process coincided with the

84 *Independent Music in Russia*

urban policies pursued by the city government itself (Suvorova and Mudryi 2017; Kuleva 2019, 7). The change was initiated already under Yurii Luzhkov (mayor of Moscow between 1992 and 2010) and then pursued with more intensity by Sergey Kapkov (Moscow's Head of Culture between 2011 and 2015, himself a long-time collaborator and friend of Abramovich's) and the new mayor Sergey Sobyanin (2010–present). Sobyanin explicitly revealed his intentions to make Moscow look like a European capital (Bush 2016), whereas Kapkov, who was 36 at the time of his appointment, aimed to turn the "spectators" of this urban change into "participants" in the change (Kapkov in *Moskva 24*, 2014). Moscow city authorities thus contracted private companies which in turn consulted with young creatives for ideas that would radically redefine the face of the city and urban culture. Strelka, for example, oversaw the reconstruction of Gorky Park, Moscow's most iconic central park. The renovation, which started in 2011 and finished in 2015, was one of the major architectural projects of the last 20 years in Russia. Strelka's founder, Il'ya Oskolkov-Tsentsiper (the former owner of *Afisha*) had among his collaborators some of the people who were putting on Anglophone indie nights in Solyanka and ran a stage at *Afisha's Piknik*. Invested with the responsibility and seizing the opportunity, the creative youth tailored this urban redefinition to themselves.[18]

The new clusters hosted a plurality of cultural forms and spaces for entertainment, relaxation and fashion activities: concert halls, art galleries, design schools, clothing shops, fancy cafes and craft-beer bars were all concentrated in one territory. The polyfunctionality of the spaces, which would reflect the versatility of its practitioners (see later), actively encouraged interaction between the professionals involved, leading to the formation of a creative community of young people who viewed the West as increasingly near and locally realisable. Established in 2010, the webzine of urban culture *The Village*, itself a tribute to (and a driving force of) the changing city, proclaimed as its motto:

> We write about the comfortable city, broadly discussing how we understand it: comfort of life in the big city depends simultaneously on global city-building initiatives and on the amount of places where good coffee is served.
>
> (*The Village* 2019)

Coffee, comfort and global initiatives were part of a design to turn Moscow into a European space. Indeed, it was the clear intention of the participants involved in Moscow's creative community (which included independent music) to promote a Westernising approach across the whole entertainment industry, an approach that consciously embraced globalisation and dismissed differences between Russia and the West. Interviewee 8, one of the witnesses of this change, observed:

> Pompeya, Tesla Boy and On-The-Go […] imagined playing music as if Russia wasn't any different from New York, London, Paris, Manchester. […] And together with other bands, parts of *Afisha*, some media, designers, writers, actors and directors, they imagined a comfortable, hipstery Moscow. And at some point this came true, and to a significant extent.

"We Also Can. We're Not Worse" 85

Similarly, Interviewee 33 talks about "a complete renaissance" that affected the lifestyle of the up-and-coming Muscovite *tusovka*. Yet, this *tusovka* promoted changes in the city that were significantly endorsed by politicians and businessmen too. This collective effort created a new, Westernised and "cool" Moscow, out of which domestic Anglophone music emerged as soundtrack.

The renovation of Moscow, therefore, inspired the transformation of independent culture and empowered the community of cultural producers that led it. Together with the urban geography, the cultural perceptions of its inhabitants changed: there was no need to seek the Other elsewhere, as it was finally visible and within reach. Muscovites realised that their city could now compete on all grounds with West European capitals, that they had been liberated from the "elsewhereness" that had been influencing the youth since the late Soviet generation, that the West, the Other at which Russia had constantly gazed – at times with resentment and envy – was now perceived as no longer "imaginary", no longer "better", and no longer "other".

Emerging as epitomes of this change in perceptions, Russian Anglophone bands generated a substantial local following that identified them as the music of the ongoing modernisation. The intensification of Russian Anglophone music in the years 2008–2012, therefore, did not simply concern production, but also reception. People increasingly listened to fashionable local bands who sang in English: the high-quality production and dancing rhythms of Pompeya, On-The-Go and Tesla Boy celebrated a hopeful time and matched the optimistic climate.

"You want to organise a gig, play it and then talk about it": *nezavisimaia muzyka* networks

The success of the Anglophone collectives around 2010 depended also on the growth and strengthening of the network of people involved in various ways in the independent music business. In Chapter 1, I discussed Crossley's concept of "music world" – a cultural space formed by tight and sympathetic networks of music participants who mobilise as they expand in numbers; when this mobilisation rises beyond the "threshold", it has a knock-on effect on the popularisation of the genre, and personal interaction is paramount to its success: "a critical mass [of participants] will achieve nothing, […] in the absence of relationships between its members" (Crossley 2015, 238). To achieve change networks must have four conditions: connection, coordination, large numbers and a large city.

All these factors came together in the Moscow *nezavisimaia muzyka* community at the end of the 2000s. The core of this world, identifying the dense connectivity of 31 Moscow-based musicians, label owners, promoters, festival organisers and journalists, is shown in the graph below (Figure 2.1). As participants recall, the ties were strong: "we all knew each other", says Interviewee 16, then frontwoman of a popular Anglophone group. Sergei Poido, the mastermind behind the "Idle Conversation" events, argued: "we saw people who were ready to change the city, and we knew all of them, they were our friends or friends of friends" (Poido in Sheveleva 2015). These members were usually directly linked; when this did not occur, they had a tie of second degree. For example, Maria Melnikova, the leader of the Anglophone

86 *Independent Music in Russia*

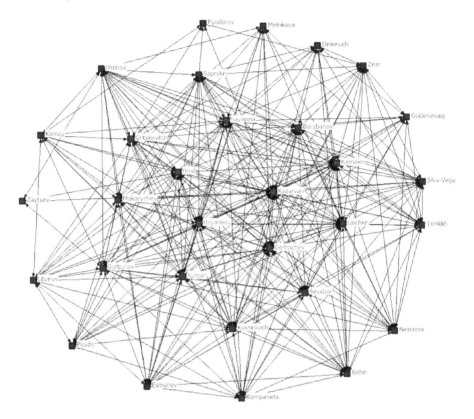

Figure 2.1 UCINET graph showing the interconnections between 31 of the main participants (musicians, journalists, venue promoters, festival organisers, label owners) of the Moscow *nezavisimaia muzyka* world in 2010. Source: Graph created by the author.

band Coockoo, was not directly connected with Oleg Nesterov (owner of the indie label Snegiri), but the two were linked with each other through a considerable number of other members. The nodes with most connections were the journalists Gorbachev and Boiarinov, the musicians Gritskevitch and Ustinov, the festival organisers Kusnirovich and Silva-Vega, the concert promoter Kazarian and the venue promoter Kamakin. This meant that when Melnikova and her band released a new song or performed at a gig, Nesterov was likely to know about it quickly. Indeed, in 2019 Melnikova did sign a deal with Snegiri with her new Russophone project Masha Maria.

An important fact is that many of the 2010 *nezavisimaia muzyka* network "hubs" are represented by the leaders of Anglophone bands: Sevidov (Tesla Boy), Brod (Pompeya), Gritskevitch (Moremoney), Makarychev (On-The-Go) and Xuman (Xuman). These musicians were supported in each stage by other members of the community in recording and distributing albums, organising gigs, participating at festivals and advertising. The ties among promoters, journalists and label owners served to create hype around the musicians' product.

"We Also Can. We're Not Worse"   87

Another characteristic of the *nezavisimaia muzyka* network was the versatility of its participants. Different roles in the community were often taken up by the same person. In the Russian case, this multitasking enthusiasm blurred the lines between musicianship, journalism, cultural mediation and entrepreneurship, and compensated for infrastructure underdevelopment (as discussed in the previous chapter). This versatility greatly aided the expansion of the network. Poido, for example, was the main editor of *The Village* (a branch of the influential fashion and music portal *Look At Me*, which Vasily Esmanov was in charge of) and the organiser of the "Idle Conversation" nights at the club Solyanka, one of the focal venues of *nezavisimaia muzyka*, for which Kompaniets did PR and in which all other key members of the *nezavisimaia muzyka* scene were one way or the other involved ("Idle Conversation" had its own stage at *Afisha's Picnic*, a festival devised by Goldenzwaig, and its own column in the magazine *Look At Me*, founded by Esmanov). Gorbachev was the music editor of *Afisha*, friends with Lisichkin (himself the editor of *Vice Russia* and owner of the label Kometa), organiser of the music showcases "Sredy Gorbacheva" (2009–2010) at Ikra (which was the club managed by Tonkikh and Goldenzwaig), and collaborated with the head of the Snegiri label, Oleg Nesterov, on the release of a compilation of new *nezavisimaia muzyka* called *No Oil. No Stress. No Noise* (2010).

These are only a few examples. Interviewee 17, himself a musician, editor of a musical webzine, editor of a music publishing house, freelance journalist, concert promoter and writer, has summarised the elasticity of the *nezavisimaia muzyka* community thus: "you want to organise a gig, play it and then talk about it". Multitasking created a dynamism that was crucial in developing the independent music industry, through which networked actors were capable of recruiting new participants. Out of this network expansion, the community reached a critical mass and overflowed.

Independent music is in English: an Anglophone-only label

It was *nezavisimaia muzyka*, and not pop or mainstream rock, that consistently adopted English as the language for song lyrics. This can be explained by the fact that English, in a landscape populated by *russkii rok* and pop, was associated with a sense of anti-commercialism and aesthetic nonconformism that in turn equated with traditional indie values. Indeed, the use of the English language in Russian popular music does not correlate with commercial success. This point has been raised in previous studies. Eddy (2007, 186), for example, observes that English in Russian popular music becomes less present as the genre becomes more commercial. In his investigation of Russian blues, Urban and Evdokimov (2004, 9) came to a similar conclusion: blues in Russia is a niche genre, and "blues in Russia is almost invariably sung in English". Therefore, English language and mainstream music are often inversely proportional in Russian music culture: the more alternative or independent the music style, the more the artists sing in English.

The Anglophone *tusovka* assembled along focal sites and figures: Solyanka, Ikra and the new creative clusters functioned as hubs for clubbing, listening and

88 *Independent Music in Russia*

informal socialisation (*obshchenie*); *Afisha* and *Look At Me* as style and taste makers; Pompeya, Tesla Boy and On-The-Go as major exponents; to these we can add an Anglophone-only label as one of the focal points for production. The label, founded by Interviewee 14 in 2009, nurtured the sound of Pompeya, On-The-Go and many more groups of the Anglophone Wave. The studio, located on the North-East of the Moscow area, had as its logotype four hands holding each other in solidarity. In this regard, the studio had bedrooms for the musicians, so that they could live communally. At least in the beginning, the label did not require a contract with its artists (reminiscent of Tony Wilson and Factory Records) – collaboration was undertaken based on reciprocal sympathy and common vision (Skolkov 2009b). Interviewee 14 remembers the first steps of the label:

> In 2009 we started to assemble around us musicians who were similar to us in terms of music vision. At that moment it was something more or less 'Daft-Punky', reminiscent of the 80s, that sort of indie-dance. We soon realised it had to be in English, it just didn't sound good in Russian, even when we tried. So it turned out that we release music in English, despite the fact that if we did it in Russian we would sell twice as much. You see, there was no indie music in Russia before us. However, someone should take care of the development of music, so we took the cross on our shoulders.

"Indie" as a mode of production in Russia had of course existed before Interviewee 14's label. What was different here was the quality of the production. For the label's founder, this quality had to stand a comparison with the West and parallel the community's effort towards the global, epitomised by the English-language lyrics. English functioned as one of the main tools for, and manifestations of, the international flavour that the youth community endeavoured to create: as a movement stretching out towards the Other, it also adopted the sound and the language of the Other. This systemic model of doing things included sound production and techniques of mixing and mastering. In order to achieve a sound similar to Western indie equivalents, Interviewee 14 imported high-quality equipment from the US and hired one of the most promising sound engineers in the *nezavisimaia muzyka* world at the time – Kornei Kretov. The sound of *nezavisimaia muzyka*, in many aspects, became Kretov's sound, "as if brought here [to Russia] from the outskirts of London where dubstep and grime originated".[19] Kretov collaborated on influential indie releases since 2009 as a sound producer, mixing engineer and/ or mastering engineer. Given the success of the first works by Pompeya and On-The-Go, Kretov's sound generated demand, amongst other indie bands, for the studio and more of that sound. Similarly to what engineer/producer Andrei Tropillo had done in the 1980s with Leningrad rock,[20] Kretov fashioned his sound using the studio as an added instrument (Prorokov 2013). And just like Tropillo calibrated his sound to bands in vogue in the West like Joy Division and the Cure, so did Kretov, using as a reference contemporary Western indie-rock bands like

"We Also Can. We're Not Worse" 89

Daft Punk, MGMT, Arctic Monkeys, Foals and so on. Both Tropillo and Kretov looked at the Other as a source.

Interviewee 14 entered the loop of the *nezavisimaia muzyka* tusovka not only with his label, but also with his band, which he then promoted through the channels of the *nezavisimaia muzyka* community. The label's first compilation of *nezavisimaia muzyka* songs in 2009 had its own release party in Solyanka during one of the "Idle Conversation" nights. Before that, *Look At Me* had already dedicated a long interview to the band and the studio (Skolkov 2009b). As Interviewee 14 reminisces: "*Look At Me* wrote about us, and all our label history began". The studio gradually became one of the nodes of the community.

The aim of the label was to promote "good, clever, but not commercial music", and not limited to the domestic market (Skolkov 2009b), in the belief that "sooner or later a Russian artist can become successful abroad" (Interview 14). Packaging a product for export was both a challenge and a mission; once the sound was attuned to Western standards, the next element to adjust was the lyrics. Yet it was not enough for English to be simply a marker of belonging to an imagined community of international artists: English had to be flawless. David MacFadyen, one of the finest connoisseurs of the Russian independent scene and the author of several books on Soviet and Russian popular music,[21] has confessed that listening to Russian bands singing in English could be a struggle: "I often have to look for lyrics of songs performed in English simply because I can't understand the original" (MacFadyen in Gorbachev 2015). Intelligibility for Interviewee 14 was dependent on good English pronunciation, which was considered a skill belonging to "innate" good hearing: "you can tune a note if they [the singers] are out of tune, but you can't teach someone to sing in English" (Interview 14). The presence of an accent was viewed as off-putting for a supposed Western audience as well as for the local public:

> We can't conceive of Russian accent as fascinating. It's impossible, it's fucked up! And of course I pay attention to the accent, it's the most important thing. That is, the lack of an accent, or at least, that it should be as little significant as possible in order not to annoy the hearing.

The singers of the Anglophone bands who passed through the Anglophone studio, at least on record, sounded "native", and their English was very difficult to locate geographically. The concealment of the accent aligned with the image that its founder – and more broadly the entire *nezavisimaia muzyka* community – was striving to create: that of a Westernised – almost "Swedenised" – Russia, in which evident elements of Russianness (not only the Russian language, but also the Russian accent in English) were removed. Despite the scarce knowledge of English among the population,[22] Russia could now become a non-Anglophone country producing Anglophone music that could appeal to both domestic and international markets. And even though such music did not significantly impact Western audiences, for reasons that include a hierarchical global industry dominated by "actual" Anglophone countries (see Chapter 5), it widely spread domestically.

90 *Independent Music in Russia*

Political escapism

When Pompeya released their debut album *Tropical* in 2011, Aleksandr Gorbachev (2011) dubbed it in his *Afisha* review "the chronicle of an internal emigration". The album, a milestone of the Anglophone Wave, was composed of nine songs bursting with airy synthesisers, funky guitars and upbeat rhythms that conveyed a cheerful and carefree atmosphere. Lyrics lacked explicit references to political contexts, were infused with abstractness, and dealt mostly with the desire to create a different reality for the lyrical hero to inhabit – usually with another person, the addressee of the song. The album cover featured a Moscow underground station populated by tropical animals, and a policeman standing and observing the scene (see Figure 2.2).[23] The whole album aimed at creating a microcosm out of the ordinary, sheltered from the world surrounding it. Key in this operation was the act

Figure 2.2 Screenshot of the front cover of Pompeya's debut album *Tropical* (2011).
Source: YouTube.[26]

"We Also Can. We're Not Worse" 91

(or the idea) of "running". Gorbachev (2021) aptly explains how "running" (*begstvo*) has represented a recurrent theme throughout Russian popular music (including where from, where to and who with). This was particularly evident in the works of the main Anglophone Wave groups,[24] of which *Tropical* represents the apex:

> We like songs
> We write songs
> To keep you out
> On the dancefloor [...]
> Gimme gimme gimme
> Chance to answer
> To your daily problems
> On the dancefloor. ('We Like Songs')

> I was run, run, run, running from that dream
> What can I say, this is the day
> When I'm run, run, run, running all the way
> To stand next to you. ('Y.A.H.T.B.M.F')

> I'm paranoid about the world I know
> This miserable show
> We got no way to go
> Paranoid
> We're getting too depressed
> We're dreaming of escape
> Uncertain and unsaved [...]
> We'll ride the path between the stars
> We'll find a new life. ("Cheenese")

Here the movement from something is displayed (the "daily problems", the world's "miserable show") as well as the movement towards something else ("the dancefloor", "a new life") and the like-minded companion (a loved individual, or a dancing community). *Tropical* fits quite consistently with Gorbachev idea of "running".

It was therefore quite surprising that the critic, at that time one of the primary musical intermediaries of the country, did not like the record: "relaxed Balearic pop and Chill-wave are employed in their most opportunistic manifestations: smarmy grooves, flirtatious male falsetto, beach whim" (Gorbachev 2011). The critic's contention regarded two areas: originality and social context. As for the former, in Gorbachev's view, Pompeya's music lacked hybridisation; it had failed to adapt Western cultural flows to the local context, and therefore did not possess any cultural relevance.[25] As for the latter, he concluded that Pompeya, in their music, "pretend that the policeman doesn't exist, even though they perfectly know he's there. This is the most off-putting thing" (Gorbachev 2011). For Gorbachev, the deterritorialisation

92 *Independent Music in Russia*

of *Tropical* from Russian realia, including from the policeman, a trope that has historically represented in Russian culture systemic disorder, power abuse and corruption, meant ignoring a problem that instead needed urgent addressing.

But the band wanted to focus on the unknown surroundings, rather than on the known ones. On the other side of the argument, a Pompeya member claimed that *Tropical* originated by contrast, with imagination playing a fundamental role: "We were sitting in the studio [the Anglophone-only label's] and it was winter outside. That's perhaps why *Tropical* is so sunny and marine" (Interview 15). The figure of the policeman on the cover, who "got in the picture by chance" and was not photoshopped in it like the exotic animals, could therefore be imagined anew, lose his threatening association with the authoritarian state and assume parodic traits. Re-imagined and re-imaged, the policeman can simply do nothing about the merry disruption taking place despite, regardless, or even because of his presence. Being cast in an odd habitat, the exotic creatures are not only decontextualised, but in turn also actively decontextualise the policeman, who ultimately becomes silly, bizarre, ridiculous. His dethroning (or, better, decrowning) denotes carnivalesque mockery.

In Bakhtin's (1984, 107–122) conceptualisation, the "carnival" implies a pause of the current order, in which the "laws, prohibitions, and restrictions that determine the structure and order of ordinary, that is noncarnival, life, are suspended". An atmosphere of "joyful relativity" weakens any one-sided rhetoric, seriousness, rationality and dogmatism, and the subject of the serious (and at the same time the comical) is presented in an everyday situation, without revering distance and in the "living present". The carnival enacts a dissolution of social hierarchies and presupposes "active participation", that is, no distinction between performers and spectators. The carnival, in other words, "is the place for working out, in a concretely sensuous, half-real and half-play-acted form, a new mode of interrelationship between individuals, counterposed to the all-powerful socio-hierarchical relationships of noncarnival life".

In carnivalesque fashion, the exotic birds in Pompeya's album cover, like Pompeya's songs, unsettled the routine and invited the listener to break away into another place, a utopia in the sense of *eu-topos*, a "good place", in which everyday structures are put on hold and relationships redefined, even if temporarily. This utopia was located inside the psyche of the author as well as in the realm of the Other. The "psychological attractiveness of the 'other'" (Myers-Scotton 2006, 63), however conceived of by the subject, encourages the individual to make that journey, to imagine a new identity, to break conventions and to create new symbolic realities, turning a feeling of displacement in the everyday context into the gratification of another imagined world (Kramsch 2009). As Yurchak (2006) describes, it was in a similar guise that Soviet citizens connected to the "Imaginary West" through private practices (including singing in English) and enacted the momentary separation from omnipresent Soviet ideology. Physical constraints enabled a creative escapism in which English functioned as the "ticket" to a journey into another, "extra-ordinary" realm. Similarly, Anglophone Wave authors and audiences accentuated this escapism by employing and celebrating a language different from their mother tongue. Singing in Russian anchored the *tusovka* to everyday

"We Also Can. We're Not Worse"   93

contexts that were perceived as uneventful and out of touch with the international community to which the community strived to belong. Conversely, singing in English helped the community to dissociate, travel to unexpected domains, forge an alternative social identity and turn displacement into affirmation.

Contrary to Gorbachev, who saw *Tropical*'s runaway aesthetics as mere imitation, the band did not consider escapism as negative, but actually as productive and, crucially, as intrinsic to the artist's condition: "Any sort of artist can be named an internal emigrant. Any musician, a priori, is already emigrating towards his own self" (Interview 15). The retreat within the self, apart from bringing solace from unpleasant realities, is active and has social vitality. The retreat produces something that is then projected externally (be this a lifestyle, a taste, a way of dressing and so on) which can then be shared. In the musician's case, internal migration creates the preconditions necessary for aesthetic creation. But since escapism is as integral to music-making as it is to music-listening (Schäfer 2013), the music initially produced "to run away" may actually become a meaningful and unifying factor when heard by an audience, as listeners emotionally connect with what the music conveys to them. Thus, escapism is an activity from which individuals gain pleasure, enacting task absorption and temporary dissociation while reducing self-evaluation (Stenseng et al. 2012, 20), but has a simultaneous social potence.

The trope of internal emigration, used by both the artist and the critic to characterise the record albeit with contrasting meaning, rendered very well the intrinsic transformative charge and political (though not oppositional) dimension contained in escapism. As explained above, Bakhtin's carnival forms an alternative space which is both inside and outside the order into which it irrupts, a social world animated by a desire to pause reality as it is known and produce another one. Such a space of possibility, to use Fredric Jameson's (2004, 43) words, "emerges at the moment of the suspension of the political" but also carries "extimacy" (exteriority in intimacy) in relation to the political.[27] For Jameson, the utopian possibility is born when the subject steps into a position of externality, which allows the subject to take "unimaginable mental liberties with structures whose actual modification or abolition scarcely seem on the cards" (45). Crucially, this external viewpoint remains partly within the context (in Jameson's words – "the stillness at the centre of the hurricane") and simultaneously generates the utopian impulse that aims beyond it, that which "leaps outside" (Ricoeur 1993). This state corresponds to the dialectical process between what is and what is yet to be, revealing utopia as Ernst Bloch (1996) famously envisaged it: an open space and an open-ended process, as well as a "concrete" engagement with the world rather than mere abstraction or contemplation. Therefore, the utopian movement from something that exists towards something that could be enacts real behaviours, cultural products and social values that are at the same time non-involved and political. Its manifestations coalesce in the world as a suspension of, and therefore an alternative to, what is commonly known.

Going back to the Pompeya case analysed, two positions seemed delineated, both concerning the purpose of music: socially engaged (Gorbachev's) and apparently

94 *Independent Music in Russia*

disengaged (Pompeya's). Such issues are not just typical of Russian popular music, of course, but have represented one of the cruxes of music discourse historically. Music scholar Simon Frith (1996, 20), for example, asked:

> How should we distinguish between the ways in which people use culture to 'escape', to engage in pleasures that allow them a temporary respite from the oppressive relations of daily life […] and those uses of culture which are 'empowering', which bring people together to change things?

Frith, however, knew that this question constitutes a false dichotomy. As he worded it: "what's at stake is not a simple matter of either/or: 'resistance' shifts its meaning with circumstance" (Frith 1996). This is because, as we have seen, escapism can be (and indeed is) political: the "temporary respite" – the "escape" – does not preclude empowerment and change, precisely because it contains in itself a utopian drive that stretches towards the social. As Walser (1993) also noted in his study on heavy metal, escapism is guided by the vision of an alternative community. In other words, escapism – as a primary component of the artistic process – does not ignore problems but rather copes with them. In the process of "coping", the subject finds a way out of quotidian cul-de-sacs by imagining and engineering a world that is different from the one they came from. The enactment of the "vision of the world", which drives the musician's personal creativity, may overlap with networks of like-minded people, who eventually coordinate and mobilise a larger community towards change. This community, by refashioning values, may impact the musical and cultural history of a country (and beyond).

As we have seen in this chapter, the appearance of new venues and platforms that endorsed local Anglophone bands was made possible by the concerted efforts of various people involved in different businesses but united by a common vision of placing Russia on an equal footing with the West. From magazine editors to fashion artists, and from concert promoters to the bands themselves, the people performing escapism redefined youth culture. Moreover, the rise of a community of consumers of local Anglophone music was directly linked not only with the improvement of domestic musical infrastructures, but also with the investment of significant state funds in the Westernisation of Moscow's cityscape and lifestyle – investment, in other words, in a collective utopian drive towards the West that was performed until the West actually materialised. Hence, escapism can also be political and transformative, even if its starting point is rooted in playful personal creativity and is devoid of straight political messages.[28]

The political element in escapism did not mean oppositional: the discourse of the independent music community did not counter the ambitions of political and economic elites. On the contrary, these elites were well on board with the project of renovation and took active part in it. Moreover, the utopian drive promising the possibility of material community realisation (Gardiner 1992, 39–40) instigated the Anglophone Wave to annul the hierarchy between the West and Russia in terms of musical development. Practitioners did this, however, by espousing West-defined styles and promoting West-defined tastes, as well as by leaping towards a

West-centric, imagined and globalised world community.[29] This brought to the fore the tensions between forging new conventions of local practice borrowed from the global centre and remaining excluded from actually entering such global centre in terms of market participation and critical recognition (several of these Russian Anglophone musicians did not meet any international popularity). Moreover, the political turmoil of 2012 and the beginning of the conflict in Ukraine in 2014, which signalled Putin's authoritarian shift and ushered Russia into international isolation, seemingly turned the independent participants' hopes of global participation into illusion. Faced with new challenges, the *nezavisimaia muzyka* community had to reinvent itself along different parameters and vis-à-vis a different milieu.

But alongside rupture there was also continuity: some of the Anglophone bands continued their careers and exerted influence over the new generation of musicians (including Russophone ones); other Anglophone acts which emerged slightly later achieved national popularity (particularly Therr Maitz and Little Big); and notwithstanding the end of community foci such as Solyanka – to which *Afisha* recently dedicated a nostalgic documentary (Bebutov and Konchalovskaia 2023) – many of the spaces used by the Anglophone Wave continued to function as creative clusters and to nurture networks of cultural producers. However, these actors, who would then shape the New Russian Wave, already oriented music, style and language in the direction of Russia as a culturally intimate and deeply enigmatic object. And while the Anglophone Wave subscribed to a grand narrative of global integration, the music movement that came after 2012 already articulated a metamodern condition that, to use Khrushchëva's (2020, 18) formulation, was conscious of "the meaninglessness of grand narratives but want[ed] to believe in one of them anyway".

Conclusions

This chapter has illustrated the social context in which Russian Anglophone musicians emerged as a significant cultural phenomenon in Russian culture at the end of the 2000s. The modernisation of Moscow, the changes in the economic landscape, the perceived dialogue with the West, and the connectivity and solidarity of the network paved the way for the rise of the Anglophone Wave and its fan base.

Domestic Anglophone musicians were only the tip of the iceberg of a whole system of people with the same commitment to social change and innovation, and they were representatives of such transformation because they embodied modernisation in terms of sound – indie – and in terms of language – English. Both elements were part of the toolkit employed by the *nezavisimaia muzyka* community participants to express a new cosmopolitan identity and shape a new cultural milieu. These practitioners endorsed the idea that music knew no boundaries and nationalities. As Pompeya's vocalist Daniil Brod maintained: "music is like science: it's international" (Brod in Gorbachev 2015).

In this process, the young Muscovites were aided by political, public and private actors. These contributed to create new resources and urban spaces, designed on Western blueprints, that the community utilised as hubs for cultural production and

96 *Independent Music in Russia*

the creation of its networks. Thus, the construction of a new, modern and Westernised taste at a micro level was entwined with the construction of a modern and Westernised city at a macro level. Thanks to the development of new facilities for participants' meetings, crossovers, as well as for playing and recording music, the *nezavisimaia muzyka* network strengthened and expanded, while the Other – the West – finally materialised. The "Imaginary West" was now not only tangible, but also culturally reproducible in local settings through a constant, collective escapism.

The union with the Other gave the community an empowered image of itself. In the eyes of tastemakers and fans, local Anglophone performers had overcome the perceived sonic inferiority towards the Other from which Russia had until that moment suffered. Now it was possible to create a Moscow that was equal to London or New York, and a Russia that was no different from the West.

As we will see in the next chapter, however, this enthusiasm was short-lived. As it happened numerous times before in Russian history, in domestic politics modernisation eventually did not come with democratisation, in foreign politics the tentative idyll with the West turned sour and in society hopes for integration in a global imagined community left the stage for nationalistic reassessments.

Notes

1 Between its inception in April 2012 and its suspension in February 2022, the programme aired at 11.30 pm, five times a week. *Vechernii Urgant* was one of the most appreciated and longest programmes of *Pervyi Kanal*, maintaining an audience share of around 15 percent over the years (Borodina 2012; Danilov 2017), and representing a prestigious platform for musicians to expand their audiences.

2 *Dozhd'* was declared a "foreign agent" by the Kremlin in August 2021 and banned in Russia in March 2022.

3 If such numbers (500–1500) may appear small, it needs to be considered that successful independent acts in Russia at that time, whether Anglophone or Russophone, rarely experienced more attendance than that for a solo gig. The numbers of *nezavisimaia muzyka*, if compared to those of Western equivalents, were and are much smaller. This applies to other types of platforms as well (e.g., view counts on YouTube). For example, On-The-Go's video for "In the Wind" gathered, at the time of writing, 220,000 views, Pompeya's single "90" collected 2.5 million views, and Tesla Boy's "Spirit of the Night" gained 1 million views; these were important numbers, especially if we take into account that YouTube was still a limited phenomenon around 2010 and, in Russia, it was also flanked by other domestic platforms of video sharing, such as Rutube.

4 Issues related to the use of English in popular music genres in non-Anglophone countries have been covered in South America (Pacini-Hernandez et al. 2004), Africa (Perullo and Fenn 2003), Indonesia (Wallach 2003), Malaysia (Pennycook 2007), Germany (Larkey 2003), France (Cutler 2003; Guibert 2003; Spanu 2014; 2015), Italy (Mitchell 2003) and Nepal (Greene and Henderson 2003), to mention a few. As for Russia, we find brief remarks in Cushman (1995, 285–297), Urban and Evdokimov (2004, x, 9–13) and Eddy (2007, 176–185), none of which deal with the period studied. One contribution from Aleshinskaya and Gritsenko (2017) on multilingualism in the TV show *Golos* (equivalent of *The Voice*) is the extent of current publication on the subject of language choice in Russian popular music. *Golos*, however, is a mainstream programme, while this chapter hopes to fill a gap in scholarship by focusing on independent music culture.

"We Also Can. We're Not Worse" 97

5 Vladimir Vysotsky (1938–1980) was a Soviet singer, songwriter, poet and actor, and one of the main representatives of the genre of "guitar poetry" (also known as *avtorskaia pesnia* – "author's song"). At the crossroads between popular music and poetry, guitar poetry consists of a singer-songwriter performing intimate songs under the unobtrusive accompaniment of an acoustic guitar. Both guitar poetry and Soviet rock shared a dimension of marginality in the Soviet Union, an ambivalent treatment by the authorities between condemnation and accommodation, and the primacy of word over sound. On guitar poetry see Platonov (2012) and Smith (1984).

6 It is worth stressing that this is a perception – Western popular music has paid great attention to the word too, as testified, for example, by the award of the Nobel Prize for literature to Bob Dylan in 2016.

7 Founded in Ufa in 1980, DDT is one of the most celebrated Soviet and post-Soviet rock bands in Russia.

8 A legendary post-punk Soviet band from the 1980s, fronted by iconic singer Viktor Tsoi (1962–1990).

9 Viktor Tsoi (1962–1990); Boris Grebenshchikov (1953–); Maik Naumenko (1955–1991), leader of the band Zoopark.

10 For the connections between Nashe Radio and nationalism, see McMichael (2019).

11 *Govnorok*, a union of *govno* (shit) and *rok* (rock), became popular to describe a certain type of *russkii rok* that was perceived as formulaic, repetitive and unoriginal.

12 See for example: *Roksi 1-3* (Aa. Vv. 1977–78), Troitsky (1988), Apted (1989), Cushman (1995), Steinholt (2005), McMichael (2005; 2008), Rybin (2010) Fürst and McLelland (2014).

13 The substantial failure of the exportation of Soviet and Russian bands in the Anglo-American sphere, which started during perestroika and continued in the early 1990s, renewed perceptions of derivativeness among participants. After the initial hopes for a "Red Wave" in music, with numerous Soviet and Russian artists presenting their music to the Western public and press, only the band Gorky Park managed to acquire some degree of fame. This, however, entailed a certain compliance with Western audiences' stereotypical perceptions of Russian bands, and was enacted through self-exoticisation: in the video for "Bang", for example, the balalaika, sickle and hammer and slogans in Cyrillic letters are indiscriminately jammed together. Those musicians who refused to trade off their image for the stereotype-defined rules of the market failed to raise commercial interest in their music, for example rock guru Boris Grebenshchikov. His long-awaited, Anglophone album *Radio Silence* (1989), produced by a major label (Columbia), flopped spectacularly and was sentenced as "romantic claptrap" and "more déjà vu than anybody with access to media should be asked to stomach" (Christgau 1989).

14 At its prime, *Afisha* distributed 184,300 copies across Russia, 84,300 of which in Moscow alone (*Afisha* 2012). While the paper issue was discontinued in 2015, the journal's website remained popular, counting 11 million monthly visitors in 2019 (*Afisha* 2019).

15 One of the reasons for this lay in the deficiency of music networks and infrastructures. The independent music scene lacked foci capable of systematically sponsoring performers to audiences. The general view, as journalists Gorbachev and Zinin (2014) write, is that 1990s indie bands were a "lost generation" (*poteriannoe pokolenie*), playing "songs into the void" (*pesni v pustotu*) in a period in which "history won over culture" (Gorbachev and Zinin 2014, 5).

16 Motorama are a band from Rostov-On-Don, Southern Russia. The band has achieved considerable international popularity in Europe and especially in Central and South America (see Chapter 5).

17 All these sites are still open at the time of writing (2024).

18 The reconstruction of Gorky Park was a success which extended way beyond Moscow, and Tsentsiper was contracted to realise similar urban projects in 40 other Russian cities. In 2021, Tsentsiper's company had more than 80 clients (including state institutions), 200 projects, and a turnover of 520 million rubles (£4.3M) a year (Kiniakina 2021).

98 *Independent Music in Russia*

19 Description of Kretov as advertisement for one of his seminars: https://theoryandprac-tice.ru/presenters/1867-korney-kretov/seminars.
20 As mentioned in the previous chapter, Andrei Tropillo was a sound producer credited as being the master behind Soviet rock. In the early 1980s, Tropillo recorded many of the unofficial Soviet rock bands that would gather wide popularity during perestroika.
21 See: MacFadyen (2001, 2002a, 2002b).
22 A survey conducted in June 2008 by the independent institute for statistics Levada Cen-tre (2008) on 1600 Russians in 128 cities revealed that only 15% of the population could speak a foreign language. In 2014 the Centre conducted another poll on the knowledge of foreign languages among Russians (Levada Centre 2014) and found that only 11% of the population self-identified as fluent in English. This number doubled among young-sters (aged 18–24) to 22% and nearly doubled in Moscow, where 20% claimed to speak English. The data showed that the spread of English among Russian speakers was quite limited. Rather than involving actual fluency, English was functional to the construc-tion of a "cool", "trendy", cosmopolitan image of the individual and the community (Kramsch 2009), and as a means to gain the "real or imaginary rewards" (Fishman et al. 1977) that it symbolized. This does not impinge on the profound aesthetic and social meaning that Anglophone performers and audiences attribute to English as a badge of belonging to an imagined, global community.
23 Security personnel (*okhrana*) are very common on Moscow's underground platforms.
24 Take, for example, Tesla Boy's "Speed of Life" (2010), or On-The-Go's "Into the Wild" (2012).
25 I have explained elsewhere (Biasioli 2022) that this process of hybridisation happens re-gardless of whether it is reflected overtly in music's sound, lyrics or lyrics' language, as cultural flows must go through a mediation that is private, personal, covert and therefore not always visible.
26 https://www.youtube.com/watch?v=vaCJXfoEgKE (author of cover: Misha Gannushkin).
27 Jameson borrows the term "extimacy" from Lacan (1986), who dispenses with the stand-ard difference between exteriority and interiority in psychology, stressing instead how the private and the collective are in a state of constant interaction. Extimacy connotes no distinction between the outside and the inside, the outer world and the psyche, "culture and the core of personality, the social and the mental […] and states explicitly the inter-penetration and mutual transformation of both spheres" (Pavón-Cuéllar 2014, 661).
28 See also Huizinga's (1949) concept of "play", defined as: "A free activity standing quite consciously outside 'ordinary' life as being 'not serious,' but at the same time absorbing the player intensely and utterly (13). 'Play' is simultaneously 'fun' and 'serious', but while seriousness seeks to exclude play, "play can very well include seriousness" (p. 45). Cushman (1995, 143) applies this framework of play to *russkii rok*: "Play, especially in restrictive or confining social situations, becomes a means of transcending the world, a means of subjectively removing oneself from the world while still remaining in it".
29 This by no means implies that the Anglophone Wave was purely imitative in its result. As I explained elsewhere (Biasioli 2022), Russian Anglophone music was the product of a mediation between the global and the intimate.

References

Aa. Vv. 1977–1978. *Roksi 1, 2, 3*, St Petersburg, samizdat (self-publication).
Afisha. 2012. 'Mediakit.' URL: https://www.afisha.ru/Afisha7files/File/mediakit/Afisha-mag_mediakit_2011-02_RU_.pdf (last accessed 12 March 2019).
Afisha. 2019. 'About.' URL: https://www.afisha.ru/article/about/ (last accessed 12 March 2019).
Aleshinskaya, E., Gritsenko, E. 2017. 'Language Practices and Language Ideologies in the Popular Music TV Show The Voice Russia'. *Language & Communication*, 52, pp. 45–59.

"We Also Can. We're Not Worse" 99

Apted, M. 1989. *The Long Way Home*. Granada. URL: https://www.youtube.com/watch?v=dd7eztULWOE (last accessed 7 May 2020).

Argumenty i Fakty. 1999. 'Pochemu MTV pobedilo MuzTV.' 23 June. URL: http://www.aif.ru/archive/1635245 (accessed 7 May 2020).

Bakhtin, M. 1984. *Problems of Dostoevsky's Poetics* (ed. by Emerson, C.). London and Minneapolis: University of Minnesota Press.

Barker, A.M. 1999. 'The Culture Factory: Theorizing the Popular in the Old and New Russia'. In Barker, A.M. (ed.) *Consuming Russia: Popular Culture, Sex and Society Since Gorbachev*. Durham: Duke University Press, pp. 12–45.

Bebutov, T., Konchalovskaia, L. 2023. *Puteshestvie na krai nochi: effekt Solyanki. Afisha*, 13 March. URL: https://www.youtube.com/watch?v=9MXdXNcypqA&t=7s (accessed 20 March 2023).

Becker, H. 1982. *Art Worlds*. Berkeley, CA: University of California Press.

Biasioli, M. 2022. 'Between the Global and the Intimate: Russian Popular Music and Language Choice'. *Modern Language Review*, 117, 2, pp. 164–90.

Bloch, E. 1996 (1959). *The Principle of Hope (Volume One)*. Cambridge, MA: The MIT Press.

Bloom, H. 1997 (1973). *The Anxiety of Influence. A Theory of Poetry*. New York: Oxford University Press.

Boiarinov, D. 2014. 'Taim-Aut navsegda'. *Colta*, 23 December. URL: https://www.colta.ru/articles/media/5787-taym-aut-navsegda (accessed 28 June 2022).

Borodina, A. 2012. 'Urgant i Gyul'chatai'. *Kommersant*, 25 April. URL: https://www.kommersant.ru/doc/1916727 (accessed 20 August 2018).

Bush, J. 2016. 'Small Businesses Cower after Moscow's Night of Bulldozers'. *Reuters*, 17 February. URL: https://www.reuters.com/article/us-russia-economy-bulldozers/small-businesses-cower-after-moscows-night-of-bulldozers-idUSKCN0VQ1W5?fbclid=IwAR34_7E1BrBXakpBO8UC1SWY90kQktY3uvjDf-AHZhF-TKFsWUTq-geAU9M (accessed 18 February 2019).

Cherrytree Records. 2012. 'Cherrytree to Reissue "200km/h in the Wrong Lane" with Unreleased Song "A Simple Motion" and Special Remixes'. 2 October. URL: http://www.cherrytreerecords.com/profiles/blogs/cherrytree-to-reissue-200km-h-in-the-wrong-lane-with-unreleased-s (accessed 1 May 2017).

Christgau, R. 1989. 'Consumer Guide'. *Village Voice*, 25 July. URL: https://www.robertchristgau.com/xg/cg/cgv789-89.php (accessed 14 October 2021).

Christgau, R. 1991. 'Perestroika, Glasnost, Art-Rock'. *Village Voice*, 15 January. URL: https://www.robertchristgau.com/xg/rock/russia-91.php (accessed 12 November 2018).

Crossley, N. 2015. *Networks of Sound, Style and Subversion. The Punk and Post-Punk Worlds of Manchester, London, Liverpool and Sheffield, 1975–80*. Manchester: Manchester University Press.

Cushman, T. 1995. *Notes from the Underground: Rock Music Counterculture in Russia*. Albany, NY: State University of New York Press.

Cutler, C. 2003. 'Chanter En Yaourt: Pop Music and Language Choice in France'. In Berger, H.M., Carroll, M.T. (eds.) *Global Pop, Local Language*. Jackson: Mississippi University Press, pp. 329–48.

Danilov, I. 2017. 'Itogi televizionnoi nedeli: Urgant operezhaet Solov'eva, Malahov, Galkin i Men'shova idut na dno'. *Kultura VRN*, 26 November. URL: https://culturavrn.ru/cinematv/22403 (accessed 29 June 2022).

Eddy, A. 2007. 'English in the Russian Context: A Macrosociolinguistic Study'. M.Phil. Thesis, Wayne State University.

Eshchenepozner. 2019. 'Iurii Saprykin: Limonov i Parkhomenko, filosofy i khipstery'. 7 March 2019. URL: https://www.youtube.com/watch?v=GvqVow4e01E&feature=youtu.be&fbclid=IwAR17ni26p2DCrkMaH7lYFh-YvDYf4UEWCgwq_5T6C_S1IZx_w8QazI5v1Xo (accessed 8 May 2020).

Fishman, J., Cooper, R., Conrad, A. 1977. *The Spread of English. The Sociology of English as an Additional Language*. Rowley: Newbury House Publishers.

100 *Independent Music in Russia*

Frith, S. 1996. *Performing Rites. Evaluating Popular Music*. Oxford: Oxford University Press.

Fürst, J., McLelland, J. (eds.). 2014. *Dropping Out of Socialism: The Creation of Alternative Spheres in the Soviet Bloc*. London: Lexington Books.

Gardiner, M. 1992. 'Bakhtin's Carnival: Utopia as Critique'. *Utopian Studies*, 3, 2, pp. 21–49.

Gorbachev, A. 2011. 'Albom Tropical i khronika vnutrennei emigratsii'. *Afisha*. URL: https://daily.afisha.ru/archive/volna/archive/9562/ (accessed 3 February 2017).

Gorbachev, A. 2013. 'A pochemu my dolzhny rasti iz russkoi muzyki? Prem'era novogo al'boma Tesla Boy'. *Afisha*. 21 May. URL: https://daily.afisha.ru/archive/volna/archive/tesla_boy_tumod/ (accessed 7 May 2020).

Gorbachev, A. 2015. 'How to make it in America, Russian indie band-style'. *Newsweek*, 6 June. URL: https://www.newsweek.com/russian-indie-bands-take-america-340003 (accessed 12 March 2019).

Gorbachev, A. (ed.). 2021. *Ne nado stesniat'sia: istoriia postsovetskoi pop-muzyki v 169 pesniakh, 1991–2021*. Moskva: IMI.

Gorbachev, A., Zinin, I. 2014. *Pesni v Pustotu*. Moskva: Corpus.

Greene, P.D., Henderson, D.R. 2003. 'At the Crossroads of Languages, Musics, and Emotions in Kathmandu'. In Berger, H.M., Carroll, M.T. (eds.) *Global Pop, Local Language. Jackson*: Mississippi University Press, pp. 87–108.

Guibert, G. 2003. 'Chantez-Vous En Français Ou En Anglais?' le choiz de la langue dans le rock en France'. *Volume!*, 2, pp. 83–96.

Hahn, G.M. 2012. 'Perestroyka 2.0: Toward Non-Revolutionary Regime Transformation in Russia? *Post-Soviet Affairs*, 28, 4, pp. 472–515.

Hale, H.E. 2015. *Patronal Politics*. Cambridge: Cambridge University Press.

Hale, H.E. 2017. 'Russian Patronal Politics Beyond Putin'. *Dædalus*, 146, 2, pp. 30–40.

Hashamova, Y. 2007. *Pride and Panic: Russian Imagination of the West in Post-Soviet Film*. Bristol: Intellect Books.

Heller, D. 2007. 't.A.T.u. You! Russia, the Global Politics of Eurovision, and Lesbian Pop'. *Popular Music*, 26, 2, pp. 195–210.

Huizinga, J. 1949. *Homo Ludens. A Study of the Play Element in Culture*. Boston: Routledge & Kegan Paul.

Jameson, F. 2004. 'The Politics of Utopia'. *New Left Review*, 25, pp. 35–54.

Khrushcheva, N. 2020. *Metamodern v muzyke i vokrug nego*. Moskva: RIPOL Klassik.

Kiniakina, E. 2021. 'Istoriia kompanii 'Tsentsiper''. *Kiosk (Inc.)*. URL: https://cb.kiozk.ru/article/istoria-kompanii-cenciper (accessed 8 November 2024).

Kramsch, C. 2009. *The Multilingual Subject*. Oxford: Oxford University Press.

Kuleva, M. 2019. 'Turning the Pushkin Museum into a 'Russian Tate': Informal Creative Labour in a Transitional Cultural Economy (the Case of Privately Funded Moscow Art Centres)'. *International Journal of Cultural Studies*, 22, 2, pp. 281–297.

Lacan, J. 1986 (1960). *Le séminaire. Livre VII. L'éthique de la psychanalyse*. Paris: Seuil.

Larkey, E. 2003. 'Just for Fun? Language Choice in German Popular Music'. In Berger, H.M., Carroll, M.T. (eds.) *Global Pop, Local Language*. Jackson: Mississippi University Press, pp. 131–51.

Levada Centre. 2008. 'Znanie inostrannykh iazykov v Rossii'. 16 September. URL: http://www.levada.ru/old/16-09-2008/znanie-inostrannykh-yazykov-v-rossii (accessed 30 October 2016).

Levada Centre. 2014. 'Vladenie inostrannymi iazykami'. 28 May. URL: https://www.levada.ru/2014/05/28/vladenie-inostrannymi-yazykami/ (accessed 30 October 2016).

Levada Centre. 2018. 'Rossia-Zapad'. 14 May. URL: https://www.levada.ru/2018/05/14/rossiya-zapad-2/ (accessed 14 September 2023).

Levada Centre. 2021. 'Rossia i Evropa'. 18 March. URL: https://www.levada.ru/2021/03/18/rossiya-i-evropa-2/ (accessed 14 September 2023).

Leyshon, A., Matless, D., Revill, G. 1995. 'The Place of Music'. *Transactions of the Institute of British Geographers*, 20, 4, pp. 423–33.

"We Also Can. We're Not Worse" 101

MacFadyen, D. 2001. *Red Stars. Personality and the Soviet Popular Song 1955–1991*. London: McGill-Queen's University Press.

MacFadyen, D. 2002a. *Estrada?! Grand Narratives and the Philosophy of the Russian Popular Song Since Perestroika*. London: McGill-Queen's University Press.

MacFadyen, D. 2002b. *Songs for Fat People. Affect, Emotion, and Celebrity in the Russian Popular Song, 1900–1955*. London: McGill-Queen's University Press.

McMichael, P. 2005. "After All, You're a Rock Star (At Least, That's What They Say)': *Roksi* and the Creation of the Soviet Rock Musician'. *Slavonic and East European Review*, 83, 4, pp. 664–84.

McMichael, P. 2008. 'Translation, Authorship and Authenticity in Soviet Rock Songwriting'. *The Translator*, 14, 2, pp. 201–28.

McMichael, P. 2019. "That's Ours. Don't Touch'. Nashe Radio and the Consolations of the Domestic Mainstream'. In Strukov, V., Hudspith, S. (eds.) *Russian Culture in the Age of Globalization*. London: Routledge, pp. 68–98.

Mitchell, T. 2003. 'Doin' Damage in My Native Language: The Use of 'Resistance Vernaculars' in Hip Hop in France, Italy, and Aotearoa/New Zealand'. In Berger, H.M., Carroll, M.T. (eds.) *Global Pop, Local Language*. Jackson: Mississippi University Press, pp. 3–17.

Moscow Official Website. 2018. http://budget.mos.ru/ (accessed 25 October 2018).

Moskva 24. 2014. 'Interv'iu, Sergei Kapkov: Kultura, vzgliad v budushee.' 14 October. URL: https://www.youtube.com/watch?v=_8P8LiEaBK0 (accessed 22 May 2020).

Myers-Scotton, C. 2006. *Multiple Voices: An Introduction to Bilingualism*. Oxford: Blackwell Publishing.

Olifirova, S. 2007. 'Biudzhet Moskvy – 2008: Bolshe trillion rublei na raskhody'. *Komsomolskaia Pravda*, 20 August. URL: https://www.kp.ru/daily/23958/72267/ (accessed 5 May 2020).

Pacini Hernandez, D., Fernandez L'Hoeste, H., Zolov, E. (eds.). 2004. *Rockin Las Americas: The Global Politics of Rock in Latin/o America*. Pittsburgh, PA: University of Pittsburgh Press.

Pavón-Cuéllar, D. 2014. 'Extimacy'. In Teo, T. (ed.) *Encyclopedia of Critical Psychology*. New York: Springer, pp. 661–64.

Pennycook, A. 2007. *Global Englishes and Transcultural Flows*. London: Routledge.

Perullo, A., Fenn, J. 2003. 'Languages Ideologies, Choices, and Practices in Eastern African Hip Hop'. In Berger, H.M., Carroll, M.T. (eds.) *Global Pop, Local Language*. Jackson: Mississippi University Press, pp. 19–51.

Pew Centre. 2019. 'Views of the European Union over Time'. 9 October. URL: https://www.pewresearch.org/global/2019/10/14/the-european-union/pg_10-15-19-europe-values-04-015/ (accessed 14 September 2023).

Pilkington, H., Omelchenko, E., Flynn, M., Bluidina, U., Starkova, E. 2002. *Looking West? Cultural Globalization and Russian Youth Cultures*. Philadelphia: Pennsylvania State University Press.

Platonov, R. 2012. *Singing the Self: Guitar Poetry, Community, and Identity in the Post-Stalin Period*. Evanston: Northwestern University Press.

Prorokov, G. 2013. 'Zvukorezhissyor Korney Kretov o tom, kak delat' pesni luchshe'. *Afisha*, 8 November 2013. URL: https://daily.afisha.ru/archive/volna/heroes/zvukorezhisser-korney-kretov-o-tom-kak-delat-pesni-luchshe/ (accessed 11 March 2019).

Ricoeur, P. 1993. 'Imagination in Discourse and in Action'. In Robinson, G., Rundell, J. (eds.) *Rethinking Imagination*. London: Routledge, pp. 118–35.

Rybin, A. 2010. *Maik. Vremia Rok-n-Rolla*. Sankt Peterburg: Amfora.

Schäfer, T. 2013. 'The Psychological Functions of Music Listening'. *Frontiers in Psychology*. URL: https://www.frontiersin.org/articles/10.3389/fpsyg.2013.00511/full (accessed 30 May 2020).

Sheveleva, S. 2015. 'Chto my nadelali. Glavnye redaktory The Village raznykh let – o tom, kuda vsyo katitsya'. *The Village*, 24 April. URL: https://www.the-village.ru/village/city/5-let-the-village/213567-razgovor-s-glavredami (accessed 11 March 2019).

102 Independent Music in Russia

Skolkov, S. 2009a. 'Kolonka Idle Conversation vypusk 2'. *Look At Me*, 16 September. URL http://www.lookatme.ru/flow/muzyika/idle_conversation/72771-kolonka-idle-conversation-2009-09-16 (accessed 11 March 2019).

Skolkov, S. 2009b. 'Xuman Records'. *Look At Me*, 29 October. URL: http://www.lookatme.ru/flow/posts/music-radar/76167-xuman-records-2009-10-29 (accessed 11 March 2019).

Smith, G.S. 1984. *Songs to Seven Strings (Russian Guitar Poetry and the Mass Song)*. Bloomington: Indiana University Press.

Sorokin, I. 2013. 'V kontse proshloi nedeli stalo izvestno, chto v iiune 2013 goda telekanal MTV Rossiia zakroetsia navsegda'. *Afisha*. URL: https://daily.afisha.ru/archive/volna/archive/mtv_rip/ (accessed 5 May 2020)

Spanu, M. 2014. 'Sing it Yourself! Uses and Representations of the English Language in French Popular and Underground Music'. *KISMIF 2014 Conference Proceedings*, pp. 513–23.

Spanu, M. 2015. 'Global Noise, Local Language: A Socio-Anthropological Approach of Language Authenticity in French Metal'. *Modern Heavy Metal: Markets, Practices and Cultures Conference Proceedings*, pp. 122–30.

Steinholt, Y. 2005. *Rock in the Reservation: Songs from the Leningrad Rock Club 1981–1986*. Bergen – New York: The Mass Media Music Scholar's Press.

Stenseng, F., Rise, J., Kraft, P. 2012. 'Activity Engagement as Escape from Self: The Role of Self-Suppression and Self-Expansion'. *Leisure Sciences*, 34, 1, pp. 19–38.

Suvorova, N., Mudryi, S. 2017. 'Issledovanie: kak ustroen biznes Strelki'. *Inc.*, 11 February. URL: https://incrussia.ru/fly/issledovanie-kak-ustroen-biznes-strelki/ (accessed 29 June 2022).

Sycheva, A. 2010. 'Sovremennye yazykovye protsessy v SMI (na premere zhurnala *Afisha*)'. MA thesis, Togliatti University.

The Village. 2019. 'About'. URL: https://www.the-village.ru/pages/about (accessed 12 May 2020).

Troitsky, A. 1988. *Back in the USSR: The True Story of Rock in Russia*. London: Faber & Faber.

Urban, M., Evdokimov, A. 2004. *Russia Gets the Blues: Music, Culture and Community in Unsettled Times*. Ithaca, NY: Cornell University Press.

Vechernii Urgant. 2012. 'Tesla Boy's performance'. 28 November. https://www.youtube.com/watch?v=9taIFbS_7Cs (accessed 20 August 2018).

Wallach, J. 2003. 'Goodbye My Blind Majesty: Music, Language, and Politics in the Indonesian Underground'. In Berger, H.M., Carroll, M.T. (eds.) *Global Pop, Local Language*. Jackson: Mississippi University Press, pp. 53–86.

Walser, R. 1993. *Running With the Devil: Power, Gender, and Madness in Heavy Metal Music*. Hanover, NH: Wesleyan University Press.

Wilson, K. 2015. 'Modernization or More of the Same in Russia: Was There a "Thaw" Under Medvedev?' *Problems of Post-Communism*, 62, 3, pp. 145–58.

World Bank. 2016a. 'GDP Growth, Russian Federation'. URL: https://data.worldbank.org/indicator/NY.GDP.MKTP.KD.ZG?end=2016&locations=RU&start=1990 (accessed 27 October 2017).

World Bank. 2016b. 'GDP Growth'. URL: https://data.worldbank.org/indicator/NY.GDP.MKTP.KD.ZG?end=2014&locations=RU-IT-US-DE&start=2000&view=chart (accessed 27 October 2017).

www.tatu.ru. 2019. 'About'.

Yurchak, A. 2006. *Everything Was Forever, Until It Was No More: The Last Soviet Generation*. Princeton, NJ: Princeton University Press.

3 "I live in Russia and I'm not scared"

Russia's conservative turn, the new Russian Wave and metamodernism (2012–2018)

Introduction

Vladimir Putin's third term as Russia's President from 2012 to 2018 ushered Russia into a significant recalibration of its post-Soviet identity. This process involved defensive responses to Western influences, which ran in tandem with endeavours to cultivate a renewed sense of "pride" in the country's cultural heritage, endorse notions of exceptionalism, limit or suppress political opposition and present a unified image of Russia as the "moral champion" of the world against the "corrupt West" (Sharafutdinova 2014). The annexation of Crimea in 2014 propped up, both within the political establishment and among the general populace, perceptions of Russia's autonomy from the West, its burgeoning global significance and its distinctiveness as a standalone civilisation. The idea of a multipolar world, according to which Russia should act as the leader of one of the world's spheres of influence, gained traction during this period, before becoming one of the official rhetoric tools for justifying Russia's full-scale invasion of Ukraine in 2022.[1]

This chapter asks how *nezavisimaia muzyka* practitioners artistically processed this change in the political sphere. It argues that this top-down reconceptualisation of Russian identity, primarily rooted in nationalistic narratives, indirectly provoked a reassessment in independent music as well: here, English made way for Russian; the cosmopolitan hopes animating the Anglophone Wave made way for the patriotism of low-life of the New Russian Wave; and metamodernism emerged as a type of artistic sensibility in which the author became progressively invested in Russia as subject matter but at the same time removed from expressing any clear moral judgements about it.

Some of the discourse produced in *nezavisimaia muzyka* during Putin's third term oscillated between nationalism and patriotism. Although in common usage the two terms have often become synonyms, it is useful to distinguish them for the purpose of this chapter. Patriotism is understood here as pride for one's country, informed by reason and dedicated to the country's improvement (Viroli 1995). Patriotism values freedom above everything else, aims to defend the country from abuses of individual power from within and prevents descent into illiberalism (so, for the patriot, "it matters if"). Conversely, nationalism underlines unconditional loyalty to the nation and irrational, permanent devotion to it (so, for the nationalist,

DOI: 10.4324/9781003248699-4

104   *Independent Music in Russia*

it is "no matter what"). Patriotism is open to cultural contamination and diversity, whereas nationalism emphasises the nation's uniqueness and oneness, denying difference internally and (re)producing it externally (Beck 2006, 56). Indeed, one of nationalism's crucial aspects is binarism when it comes to "the other(s)".

The relationship between popular music and authoritarian regimes has of course been studied in contexts outside Russia.[2] However, studies have traditionally oriented themselves on the character of resistance of popular music, or on the official uses and appropriations of music at the expense of whole genres and artists. The framework that is usually endorsed in scholarship and media pits the resisting, liberal (often West-looking) artist against the authoritarian, oppressive state.[3] In Russia, where music-state relations have historically been complex and multi-faceted,[4] this framework is too rigid and limiting. Without discarding binaries and oppositions (they do exist), we should not ignore another widespread manifestation of state-music relations, namely that grassroots music practitioners can write into nationhood not in entirely subversive or resisting ways, but rather through reassessments that may simultaneously compete with, overlap, ironise and/or complement the state's vision.

Several products of *nezavisimaia muzyka* produced in Putin's third term showed signs of both nationalism and patriotism – in fact, they swung between the two. On the one hand, Russia became a totalising feeling, a permanent repository of devotion and artistic investigation "no matter what" which was fuelled by the Russia-West dichotomy. On the other hand, cultural producers also articulated, though ambiguously, the country's problems and denied, rationally, any alliance with the state ("it matters if").

Because of Russia's historically multifaceted and fluid criteria of national identification, Russian culture is a prime example of how the country/nation as affect can drive artistic creation and produce enduring myths. In some strands of the 2010's mainstream, as Laruelle and Engström (2018) have shown, this attitude gave rise to what they called "new second-world aesthetics", an art steeped in the recycling of the Soviet, positioning itself as an up-and-coming alternative to first-world, tedious, politically correct culture. Referring to the works of fashion stylist Gosha Rubchinsky and the rock band Leningrad, they saw these products as characterised by "transgressive consolidation": "a post-glamour parody of Hollywood, show business, corporate culture, the fashion industry and their Russian counterparts" (Laruelle and Engström 2018, 14), which may at first appear as transgression or protest against the status quo, but which was ultimately in tune with the conservative discourse of the "first world crisis" endorsed by the Kremlin as well. Perceived backwardness could then be turned on its head as a sign of national authenticity. Second-world art evoked the idea of "subaltern empire" formulated by Morozov (2015), whereby Russia – a world superpower and a colonialist force – spoke internationally from a perspective of colonial subalternity and victimhood.

Another mainstream example was Russia's biggest festival, *Nashestvie* (established in 1999 and on a hiatus since 2019), which during the 2010s attracted around 150,000–200,000 people each summer (*Nashestvie* 2016). *Nashestvie* was an extension of the work of *Nashe radio* (Our Radio), the main organiser of the festival. *Nashe radio*, founded in 1998, promoted and crystallised the genre of *russkii rok*, airing almost exclusively Russophone music and placing great emphasis on the idea of *nashe* (ours) as a symbol of pride in Russia's cultural heritage. *Nashestvie*, a play on the words *nashe*, *shestvie* (march, parade), and *nashestvie* (invasion), showcased mostly artists that fitted into the same limited format of *Nashe radio*: Russophone and/or *russkii rok*. Because of these rigid criteria, *Nashestvie* hardly changed its line-up over the years, preferring instead genre consolidation through its "regular" artists. Even though the festival introduced a second stage for upcoming bands in the late 2010s, groups playing more experimental music were excluded from participation for stylistic and linguistic reasons. Similarly, the internal otherness of domestic Anglophone bands placed them on the opposite pole of *Nashe radio* and *Nashestvie*'s ethos, making these musicians not qualifiable, on linguistic grounds, to play at a festival with more than one nationalistic overtone. *Nashestvie*'s commitment to depicting a homogeneous image of post-Soviet music stood at the intersection between state rhetoric and cultural nationalism. In 2015, for example, an exhibition of tanks and war weaponry endorsed by the Ministry of Defence was introduced on the site of the festival, not far from the artists onstage.[5] Thus, Nashestvie disseminated not only music, but also the unnerving social atmosphere pervading Russian society, espousing state-endorsed nationalism and relying on its active support.

Approval of, and support from, state nationalism was not the case of independent music, even though similar binarisms and exclusionary processes surfaced here too. In the *nezavisimaia muzyka* of the same period, the construction of the national entailed the highlighting of the difference between Russian music and the music of the Other, together with an isolation and devaluation of those domestic musicians perceived as not fitting in the new parameters. Such reconfiguration, which was initiated by the practitioners responsible for filtering cultural content before it trickled down to the public, did not move along the lines of ethnicity (many famous Russian performers in today's industry are ethnically mixed or non-Russian), but of language and, to some degree, style.

In the *nezavisimaia muzyka* of the mid-2010s, the misfits became the local Anglophone bands. If these bands rose to popularity in the late 2000s and early 2010s, towards the end of the decade they were regarded amongst cultural intermediaries (journalists, critics, trendsetters, and so on) with scepticism. For some pundits, these artists were not representative of Russia's evolving milieu, not attuned with the times, deficient in poetic content, originality or significance for the youth. One of the main reasons why local Anglophone bands received such criticisms was that, as internal others presenting domestic traits (Russian nationality of the composers) mixed with foreign ones (use of English for the lyrics), they represented an oddity in a music scene that strived towards maximising expressions of Russianness (Biasioli 2021, 674). The debate they originated and the consequent treatment they received from cultural intermediaries highlighted the struggle for the "national" in the Russian independent scene of the mid-2010s, as well as the interplay between political rhetoric and "alternative" music, two worlds apparently apart, but, as this chapter argues, involuntarily intersecting on a few ideological planes.[6] Indeed, *nezavisimaia muzyka*, as one of the arenas for the production of cultural discourses, was not immune to the new zeitgeist saturated with official

106 *Independent Music in Russia*

rhetoric: once the Kremlin produced its nationalistic discourse, this discourse travelled around, bounced in multiple directions, morphed and caught on horizontally and loosely. Because this discourse – like any discourse – was composed of several different parts, it could be resisted by grassroots cultural producers as it could be subjected to selective readings, filtering, ironisation and/or appropriation. To an extent, therefore, the evolution of what was perceived as worthwhile in the Russian independent music industry in the 2010s responded to the transformation of what was perceived as culturally appropriate by the government.

Because the ways in which these interactions occurred were multiple and were subject to the exercise of the practitioners' agency, they had varied outcomes: some artists chose to overall comply with (or even enthusiastically espouse) the new status quo; others decided to vocally oppose it, following the example of Pussy Riot (though hardly with the same level of exposition); some others – likely, in a new, original mode – delivered more subtle responses based on ambiguity in order to deal with the authoritarian turn of their country while maintaining high levels of artistic autonomy and, on top of this, accessing large audiences. On the one hand, in this latter group in particular, Russia's "second-world" status was articulated no longer as a source of embarrassment, but with pride; on the other hand, the official discourse of nationalism was in many instances transformed, bent, ridiculed. Some of the outcomes of such cultural production are presented in the second part of this chapter and grouped as manifestations of a sensibility which seemed increasingly on the rise in 2010s Russia, featuring equivocality, indirectedness and post-irony as its main ingredients; following Engström (2018) and Khrushchëva (2020), this trend can be called "metamodern".

Metamodernism was theorised by Dutch philosophers Vermeulen and Van den Akker in 2010 to describe a new, global and widespread approach to culture-making, characterised by an oscillation between "a modern enthusiasm and a postmodern irony" (2010, 1). Rather than rejecting postmodernism, the metamodern "structure of feeling" (Vermeulen and Van den Akker 2010, 2) incorporates its ironic detachment and disillusion about grand narratives, but simultaneously goes beyond it by subscribing to the reconstruction of the very grand narratives of modernism. In other words, metamodern artists know they cannot accomplish this reconstruction, but they try all the same: as Khrushcheva (2020, 16) maintains, metamodernism is a "nostalgia for devalued big meanings". As a result, metamodernist art fluctuates with, between and through (post)modern poles. Put vis-à-vis the authoritarian state and its nationalistic narratives on one side, and the desire to reflect and comment on this reality on the other, metamodernism became in Russian popular music a sensibility that overcame binaries of critical art vs. the status quo, investment vs. detachment, action vs. inaction, criticism vs. compliance. Through this response (consciously or not), musicians "interrogated back", interacted with, filtered, altered and downplayed the pervasive interpellation of ideology while performing their own version of patriotism, Russianness and even dissensus without risking the retaliation from the authorities that characterised the Pussy Riot affair. Indeed, the exaggerated punishment for the punk activist group functioned as a cautionary tale for independent artists to be aware of when stepping into the territory of state

"*I Live in Russia and I'm Not Scared*" 107

politics. Pussy Riot purported to represent large portions of the population who took to the streets between December 2011 and May 2012 against state abuse of power, corruption and Putin's third term. As the liberal movement was squashed and the new political climate veered towards conservative values, reactionary policies and authoritarianism, some artists shifted to metamodernism as a realisation that frontal political clash was both futile and dangerous.[7]

This chapter therefore delineates the various stages in the development of metamodernism as a widespread artistic "condition" and civil tactic: firstly, it offers an account of how some aspects of state nationalism (e.g., defensiveness against foreign influence, revival of tradition and the idea of a Russian identity) were accepted and integrated in independent music, and how this led to the demise of the Anglophone Wave as a dominant movement in *nezavisimaia muzyka*. At the same time, it also recognises the impact on this demise of the Crimean annexation and the deterioration of political relationships between Russia and the West. Secondly, it provides a few examples of how new independent music was produced in this new climate, and how it was influenced by official discourse but at the same time attempted to defamiliarise it. In particular, I examine: *Festival' Bol'* (Pain Festival), the most relevant catalyst of the New Russian Wave; the bands Buerak and Pasosh, among the main representatives of this movement; and the singer Monetochka, the queen of post-irony.

"Why don't Russian bands sing in Russian?"

In April 2011, Aleksandr Gorbachev, then the editor of the music section of *Afisha*, organised a roundtable about the use of English in *nezavisimaia muzyka*, to which he invited Anglophone and Russophone musicians. The aim of the roundtable was to understand why domestic groups were singing in English at such an unprecedented rate: "The question is not new, but as before topical: new interesting and talented Russian bands appear every day, but a large part of them do not sing in their native language, preferring English to Russian" (Gorbachev 2011).

The excerpts were published soon after on *Afisha*'s website under the title: "English First: *pochemu russkie gruppy ne poiut po-russki*" (English First: Why Russian Bands Don't Sing in Russian). Summarising the content of the debate, the reasons leading bands chose English were:

a Phonetic and syntactic (regardless of fluency). Kirill Ivanov, leader of the band Samoe bol'shoe prostoe chislo (The Largest Prime Number),[8] and Gleb Lisichkin, founder of the indie label Kometa Records, editor of Vogue Russia and artist manager, were of the opinion that in English it is "easier" to sing. Nadezhda Gritskevich, then singer of the Anglophone band Moremoney, commented that "English sounds softer", while musician Vasilii Zorky maintained that "for a music that's based on melody, English suits better".[9] Ivan Smirnov, leader of the band Krasnoznamënnaia diviziia imeni moei babushki (The Red Banner Division by the Name of My Grandma),[10] observed: "I don't know English, but I write lyrics in English".

108   *Independent Music in Russia*

b Psychological. Ivanov and Gorbachev saw English as an "escapism", while Evgenii Gorbunov, guitarist of the bands Glintshake and NRKTK and, later, leader of the band Inturist, claimed that English continues "a tradition of copying".[11]
c Inherent to globalisation. As Gorbunov observed: "English is a universal language", which, echoed Gritskevich, was "deeply integrated" in society.
d Tradition. Some musicians formed their taste by listening to Anglo-American music. As Zorky stated: "I didn't belong to the Russian music context".

As an external contribution to the roundtable, Gorbachev invited eminent rock critic Artemy Troitsky, who accredited the main motives for the choice of English to:

e Degradation of traditional *russkii rok*, from which younger musicians wanted to dissociate.
f Development of the internet with subsequent disruption of national boundaries.
g Russia's socio-political situations.

However, the question regarding the likelihood of this Westernised fashion in *nezavisimaia muzyka* to continue was not asked: could the Anglophone Wave last? As explained in this chapter, the verdict that history passed was *no*.

Gorbachev himself was not entirely on board with the ethics and aesthetics of the Anglophone Wave. As discussed in Biasioli (2021), Gorbachev offered an unfavourable review of the works of the main local Anglophone groups, mocking their attitude, clothing and effort at international recognition. About *Modern Thrills*, Tesla Boy's first LP, Gorbachev commented: "in the end, no one is going to put it on BBC One, are they?" (Gorbachev 2010). About Pompeya, he stated: "recording in Los Angeles seems like a pose" (Gorbachev 2012a). Particularly interesting was his comment on On-The-Go's second album *November*: "On-The-Go's sound does not have any national identity" (Gorbachev 2012b). This observation aimed to reassess Russian independent music along parameters of Russianness which, for Gorbachev, seemed at odds with the activity of many domestic Anglophone artists. This judgement was based not only on the foreign language they used, but also on the lyrical content that these bands proposed, which, in the critic's opinion, did not tally with the milieu in which the lyrics were written. Arguably Russia's most prominent tastemaker in the *nezavisimaia muzyka* scene of the early 2010s, Gorbachev worked at *Afisha* between 2005 and 2014, becoming the editor of the journal's music section in 2011 and its main editor in 2013. What the critic strived for was a music that could comment on, and engage with, Russia's present and pressing issues – not necessarily antagonistically, but at least reflectively – with sounds and lyrics that could evidence the tensions within Russian society. In his numerous interviews with the Anglophone bands, published in *Afisha* between 2010 and 2014, Gorbachev confronted the musicians in regard to the absence of a territorial marker in their music. Here is an extract from a 2012 interview with Pompeya:

Gorbachev:	Your ties [to Russia] are on the level of the visual. In your music there's nothing Russian or Muscovite.

Agafonov [Pompeya's bass player]:	I don't understand how you can tie music to Moscow. Music is international. You can highlight your identity only through visual elements.
Simonian [Pompeya's drummer]:	[...] I don't understand, do you want us to play the *gusli*? [a Russian traditional string instrument]
Gorbachev:	I would like to feel your connection with the time and place in which you exist. When there's no such thing, for me it's a minus.
Simonian:	And for me it's a plus.

(Gorbachev 2012a)

The object of the debate – and the reason for Gorbachev's contending – was the search for a principle that could locate the band to its "time and place". Pompeya felt they belonged to an international tradition, while Gorbachev opined that this international tradition needed to be reimagined and transformed within a paramount national one, rooted in the zeitgeist. Gorbachev's arguments gained momentum as the zeitgeist changed and more trendsetters began to label local Anglophone bands as dated or out of place in the new political climate. Decisive in this reassessment were Russia's authoritarian turn and imperial actions between 2012 and 2014, which made musical internationalism seem professionally unrealistic: if Russia is not part of the Western world politically, how can it be part of the Western world culturally? Some new form of musical identity, therefore, had to be sought.

Cracking the magical Anglophone world: protest and Pussy Riot

By the time of Gorbachev's interview with Pompeya in 2012, the political context had begun to shift, and shadows were looming upon the Anglophone *nezavisimaia muzyka* world. In late 2011 Putin announced his candidacy in the 2012 presidential elections. Prior to that, in 2008, Putin's party Edinaia Rossiia had secured a modification in the constitution, whereby the duration of the presidential term was prolonged from four to six years. The likely possibility of Putin's return and the unchanged leadership of the party rang the alarm bells of several Russians, for whom this represented a step back in Russia's uncertain democratic process. The most intense protest movement of the decade ensued: across the country, and especially from December 2011 to May 2012, hundreds of thousands of Russians openly contested the government and demanded change. But the brutal response of the police led to clashes, which culminated in the arrest of 30 demonstrators during the "March of the Millions" in May, and the imprisonment of almost all of them (*Lenta.ru* 2012; *Meduza* 2017). The repression of the protests ushered Russia into a period of human rights restrictions and cast more than a doubt about the

110 *Independent Music in Russia*

future of the country, including of domestic liberal media. As former *Afisha*'s editor (2003–2008) and journalist Iurii Saprykin observes:

> We just didn't want Putin to come back. We wanted to prolong that light, soft, comfortable life of the Medvedev period, which, for my circle – *Afisha, Telekanal Dozhd', Ekho Moskvy* – was actually quite alright.
>
> (Saprykin in *Eshchenepozner* 2019)

With Putin's return, the liberal intelligentsia suffered a loss of innocence that put into question the effectiveness and implementability of their ideas. Unsurprisingly, it was in this context of anxiety that a direct blow to the Anglophone Wave and its cosmopolitan image came, in the form of an actionist art performance which included music as one of its components.

In February 2012, the activist group Pussy Riot performed "Mother of God, Drive Putin Away" (*Bogoroditsa, Putina progoni*), later known as "A Punk Prayer", in the Cathedral of Christ the Saviour in Moscow. A few days later, the police opened a case of hooliganism against the group, on the grounds of the strong language used in a religious place, containing expressions such as "the shit of the Lord" (*sran' gospodnia*) and "the motherfucking patriarch believes in Putin more than in God", referred to the Patriarch of the Orthodox Church Kirill. The trial commenced in July 2012 and ended the following month with the sentencing of two Pussy Riot members – Maria Alekhina and Nadezhda Tolokonnikova – to two years in a penal colony. One of the activists' aims was to criticise the increasing closeness between the Kremlin and the Orthodox Church (Putin was seeking support in the Orthodox Church in view of the upcoming presidential elections in spring 2012), but ended up sealing their alliance, as the Kremlin was able to cynically exploit the activists' actions to push its neo-traditionalist agenda (Rutland 2014). In doing so, the Russian authorities framed Pussy Riot as degenerates at the mercy of Western corrupt values (e.g., feminism, LGBT+ rights, atheism), from which Russia had now the imperative of defending itself. Thus, as Sharafutdinova (2014) argues, the affair stood at the intersection of some major changes in Russian politics and society: domestically, it served the purpose of legitimising the government; internationally, it projected Russia as the last bastion of traditional moral standards vis-à-vis an increasingly decaying, encroaching and inimical West.

While several studies have analysed the group's significance in Russia's recent history (Rutland 2014; Sharafutdinova 2014; Yusupova 2014), as well as its musical inspirations and endeavours (McMichael 2013; Wiedlack 2016), little has been said about the impact the Pussy Riot affair had on the local independent music scene. Steinholt (2013) commented that it is difficult to frame Pussy Riot as an instance of "punk music vs power", because the group was not part of that world and punk musicians did not see them as members of their community. Borenstein (2021) claimed quite the opposite by centring the debate on the perspective of "punk" as ethics rather aesthetics. During my fieldwork, which covered some of the Muscovite punk scene, respondents were inclined to situate Pussy Riot outside punk (and music in general), and in negating the group's authenticity. Interviewee

33, a former magazine editor, label owner and music manager, argued that Pussy Riot were "something in-between Putin and Matrioshkas"; Interviewee 17, a punk journalist and musician, laconically asserted that "Pussy Riot songs are useless"; Interviewee 58, a Pussy Riot former collaborator and musician, calls them "the Spice Girls of protest", who were "put together by their 'manager' [Pëtr Verzilov] like a pop act", and who "sought publicity at all costs". This view of Pussy Riot as a fabricated and commercial project (which converges with how they were often framed in domestic state-controlled media) may explain the scarce support for the activist group among local musicians (*Afisha* 2012a), despite the solidarity of international pop and rock stars like Madonna, Franz Ferdinand and Red Hot Chili Peppers (*Radio Free Europe* 2012a, 2012b). Such a detached stance was in line with the abstraction from, and non-involvement in, political matters by Russian musicians in the early 2010s, for music was seldom used as a platform for the practitioners' political beliefs even when the practitioners were politically active. As Interviewee 5 maintained: "the fact that musicians go to the demonstrations doesn't mean that they have to sing about the demonstrations". In another *Afisha*'s (2012b) roundtable, called "*Muzyka dolzhna oskorbliat' chuvstva: pochemu russkie gruppy ne poiut o politike*" (Music must offend feelings: why Russian bands don't sing about politics), organised by Gorbachev in the aftermath of Pussy Riot's sentence, *nezavisimaia muzyka* participants remarked precisely on this scarcity of political reflections in Russian popular music, pinning it down to historical and aesthetic reasons. The rapper Ivan Alekseev (known as Noize MC) observed that, because bards and *russkii rok* musicians were used to communicate protest subtly as a survival strategy, post-Soviet Russian culture now developed "a stereotype that speaking in allegories and metaphors is normal, but speaking directly is stupid and vulgar" (*Afisha* 2012b). Pompeya singer Daniil Brod considered political enunciations as "inappropriate" to the recreational function of music (*Afisha* 2012b), whereas Glintshake guitarist, Evgenii Gorbunov, noted: "In addition to politics, there are much more important things which music is about. You don't have to be highly socially engaged to be a good musician" (*Afisha* 2012b). Thus, aesthetics still triumphed over ethics in music-making across the independent community.

The scepticism surrounding Pussy Riot, however, does not negate their major impact on the *nezavisimaia muzyka* world. To start with, Pussy Riot contributed to the gradual demise of the Anglophone Wave and its utopian project of international Russia and participation in global popular music. The splinters originating from the deflagration of the scandal cracked the magical world that the cosmopolitan hipsters had built, demonstrating that the blanket of modernisation, progress and globalism thrown over Russia was too short. By diverting the course of aesthetic investigation towards socio-political issues, Pussy Riot showed that there was another side to Russia's reality, one in which political problems had never left. Secondly, the activist group prompted musicians to redefine how protest could be expressed through music without running the risk of retaliation from the authorities – in other words, to mix ethics with aesthetics and get away with it. Partly as an artistic style of political allusion, and partly as a survival tactic, musicians adopted metamodernism as a stance to refrain from the revolutionary attempts of actionism

112 *Independent Music in Russia*

without being politically apathetic (Engström 2018). But before this stance became channelled into the organised activities of the New Russian Wave, another major historical event would contribute to a redefinition of musical values in independent music: the start of the conflict in Ukraine.

The new Russian isolation and the New Russian Wave

If the Pussy Riot affair destabilised the ideal world of the Anglophone Wave, the outbreak of the conflict with Ukraine in 2014 and its repercussions eventually destroyed it. Between November 2013 and February 2014, Ukrainians protested president Viktor Yanukovich's decision to sign trade agreements with Russia instead of the EU. The protest movement, which acquired the name of "Euromaidan", advocated for closer bonds with the EU and more autonomy from Russia. Protests were initially peaceful but became violent in February 2014 when the clashes between the police and the demonstrators resulted in 113 casualties and the overthrowing of Yanukovich, who fled to Russia. In the Southern and Eastern regions of Ukraine, in which ethnic, linguistic and cultural ties with Russia were stronger, pro-Russian forces started separatist anti-Euromaidan movements, taking control of several strategic positions in Donetsk and Lugansk in the East, and Crimea in the South, aided by Russian military support. After a controversial referendum, the Kremlin annexed Crimea in March. The referendum and subsequent annexation were not recognised by the US, the EU and other countries of the Global North, which enacted economic sanctions on Russia. These were prolonged in 2019, 2020 and 2021 (*TASS* 2021) and eventually replaced with new and more substantial packages of sanctions following Russia's invasion of Ukraine in February 2022. The 2014 sanctions reduced access to foreign finance to Russian companies and introduced an embargo on import of arms (at that time Russia's largest export after oil and gas). Russia responded with an embargo on the import of food from the EU, the US and the other countries involved. Although studies have disagreed on the significance of their impact, the mutual sanctions generated a crisis in the Russian economy with a GDP reduction between –0.2% and –1.5% per year between 2015 and 2017 (Korhonen 2019). Even though Russia's Prime Minister Dmitry Medvedev framed the countersanctions as part of a strategy to incentivise Russia's own production of goods (especially in the agricultural sector) and to seek new commercial agreements with other non-Western countries, in 2014 the ruble fell by 40% against the dollar, fuelling inflation and the evaporation of tens of billions of dollars for Russia (Golubkova and Baczynska 2014). At the same time, the crisis initiated a process of de-Westernisation of Russia's economy, as exemplified by the establishment in 2015 of the Eurasian Union with Armenia, Kyrgyzstan, Kazakhstan and Belarus, as well as the intensification of ties with the BRICS countries.

While economically in recession, Russia experienced an upsurge in nationalistic sentiment. Crimea was officially fashioned as the proof of Russia's renewed geopolitical importance. As Kolstø (2016, 6) noted, "the annexation of Crimea allowed Putin to ride two horses": imperial nationalism and ethnonationalism. Both nationalisms, Kolstø maintained, were on the rise as grassroots movements and at times conflicted with each other, with the Kremlin often having to keep the balance in check. Crimea, however, appeased both parties, since its population was primarily ethnically Russian and its acquisition projected the image of a strong state (Kolstø 2016). As Russia's isolationism from the EU and the Global North grew after the annexation, the idea of Russia as part of Europe was replaced with a new national identity, redefined through opposition to European values – or, better, to the perceived degeneration of those values, which had now moved to the East, making Russia their prime inheritor and custodian (Laruelle 2016; Sakwa 2017, 216). The fall of the Russian ruble and the financial crisis of 2014–2016 did not weaken popular consensus for Putin, which reached 85–87% in the immediate post-Crimea period (Kolstø 2016, 6). The numerous polls conducted by the Russian Public Survey Centre (VTsIOM) and the independent Levada Centre[12] reported widespread anti-Western sentiment and overall support for Russia's foreign policies. According to a Levada Centre (2017a) survey, 72% of Russians perceived Russia as a world superpower, compared to 47% in 2012 (Levada Centre 2020). Likewise, 67% of the Russians surveyed felt proud to live in Russia (Levada Centre 2017a). Fifty-seven percent of Russians viewed the sanctions against their country as "not significant", 76% would not want Russia to remove them (VTsIOM 2017) and 69% agreed with the country's support for the rebels in the Donbas (VTsIOM 2015a). Fifty-one percent saw China as the friendliest country for Russia, while 73% perceived the US as the unfriendliest (VTsIOM 2015b). In addition, for the first time in the post-Soviet period, the majority of Russians polled had a negative attitude towards the European Union, which peaked at around 70% in late 2014/early 2015 (Levada Centre 2018a, 2018b). As these surveys suggest, nationalist sentiments were caused by an emotional reaction fuelled by Russians' perceptions of the West. It is not a coincidence that the relevant shifts in public opinion coincided with geopolitical crises and international tensions, as this reaction engendered a defensive mechanism in which isolation became an empowering condition for waking up latent ressentiment, turning inferiority into superiority and fashioning a "third path" (Malinova 2014; Neumann 2016; Surkov 2018).

Patriotism and its binary entrenchment, nationalism, have always found fertile ground in Russia. Neumann (2016, 1382) observes that to proselytise Russians about patriotic pride, regardless of any political orientation they might have, is often like preaching to the converted: "It is a given in the debate [on Russian foreign policy] that Russia should be great". Similarly, "reactive nationalism" vis-à-vis the West and Eurocentrism (Tolz 2010, 211) has been articulated in Russia long before other non-Western nations and in comparable post-colonial terms. In contemporary times, such nationalism, as Laruelle (2019, 7) maintains, has become "polyphonic", meaning that it is voiced simultaneously by different actors with different political beliefs and social backgrounds, who may well be in opposition to each other. In fact, when we talk about patriotism and nationalism in Russia, we are dealing with discursive formations that, to use Deleuze and Guattari's (1987) image, are no longer arborescent – they do not originate in a tree-like hierarchical order, for example from the intellectual or political elite down onto the masses. Rather, they are rhizomatic, they emerge horizontally and loosely: official propaganda may

114   *Independent Music in Russia*

enhance such sentiments, but the sentiments themselves are already there, and operating as active sediments of history.

These dynamics affected 2010's independent musicians. Irrespective of their
political views, they existed in a nationalistic zeitgeist which influenced decisions
concerning their careers. Here is an excerpt from my conversation with Interviewee
2, the singer of an indie collective, in 2016:

MB: Which language [between Russian and English] do you think will
                   be more used in the near future in Russian independent music?
Interviewee 2:   It is a difficult question. *This is almost a geopolitical issue.* […]
                   Russian language, the revival of Russian culture, and all the rest
                   of it, I think, is the main focus of the political course now. So I
                   think Russian will gain popularity. Politics often causes a lot of
                   changes in our lives, whether we are interested in politics or not,
                   and regardless of what point of view we hold in politics, it still
                   has a great impact on our lives. And people are now less likely to
                   travel to other countries, quite a large part of the Russian popula-
                   tion is much more hostile to Western culture, and this greatly af-
                   fects the kind of music they will listen to. I am also affected by all
                   this [emphasis added].

Interviewee 2's observation about language choice constituting a geopolitical
issue evidences the level of musicians' awareness of the interplay between international politics and local cultural phenomena, no matter how small these cultural
phenomena may be (and how independent or apolitical their participants self-
profess). Interviewee 2 places themselves within this situation and within their
imagined community, not outside of it. Indeed, musicians are integral members of
the societies in which they reside and are, therefore, subject to the political decisions of their respective governments, much like other citizens. In the context of
non-Western musicians working in authoritarian regimes, it would be reductive
to assume that they wholly reject the official values of their government or fully
embrace those promoted in the West.

What happened during Putin's third term was something else: while *nezavisimaia
muzyka* distanced itself from and ironised some aspects of top-down politics, political developments reinforced the idea, across its practitioners, that Russia needed
to find a new musical identity no longer centred on identification with the Other
but rather on the rejection of it. This new sonic identity took the name of the New
Russian Wave (*novaia russkaia volna*).[13] The coinage of the term was attributed to
the organiser of the *Pain Festival* and the major promoter of the movement, Stepan
Kazarian, in 2015 (Romakhov 2016). Interviewee 61, member of one of the main
NRW bands, explains how the movement came about and gained traction, and how
shifts at the geopolitical level gave an impulse on grassroots musical communities:

In Moscow around 2014 there were some groups making a different type of
music. But they were on their own, not a community. Then several events
started bringing them together, like Tantsy nizkogo kachestva ['Poor Quality

Dances'], Atmosfernoe davlenie [Atmospheric Pressure], Ionosfera[14]. The organisers did not pay the bands, or paid them very little, but you could write to them and they would put you on the bill straightaway. It was at these mini-festivals that we started to gather some audience, mainly people that came to see the other bands. I remember a gig in which it was us, Ic3peak,[15] Shortparis, and many other artists who are now big. They were all playing at these mini-festivals. Also, media [pages] on VKontakte developed really quickly around this time, Rodnoi Zvuk [Native Sound], for example. Basically, around that period we were playing two, three times a week because there were many clubs and all you needed to have were a few songs uploaded on VKontakte. Any quality would do. Gigs were free, or maximum 200 rubles, the organisers' model was to do small events, but a lot of them, so that they would earn a small income but often. There was a lot of audience exchange, after some time everybody got to know everybody in the *tusovka*, musicians from different bands started to collaborate and form other bands. That's how we grew, and it was something new. Everybody was singing in Russian, which was something unusual for the scene, because before we had bands like Pompeya and Tesla Boy and we thought that we were one with the rest of the world. […] I think the main episode was Crimea. We kind of realised that the relationship between Russia and the West was deteriorating and there was no more need for international music projects.

The lines above sum up how artistic conventions (practices accepted as norm in the art world) started to change in relation to the general climate around the art world. Once the Medvedev's honeymoon period with the West was evidently over, a sense of resignation mixed with ressentiment and desires of cultural autonomy kicked in, translating in musical practice into a shift in language, style and attitude. The NRW made its first steps when practitioners turned their focus away from hopes about the internationalisation of Russian music, and spaces as well as resources were shared in a re-energised fashion devoted to the establishment of new conventions. Immediacy and unassuming (low) quality took over the sonic refinement and attention to detail typical of the Anglophone Wave as the normative way of doing things. Interviewee 79, member of another NRW group, adds:

It started around 2014. A bunch of bands started doing something fresh and kind of got together, not just by themselves, but thanks to the festivals they played at, for example Bol' [Pain]. Some of them were friends, but it was a collective experience. The audience played a big role. Some bands were different in terms of sound, others more similar, but these places accumulated the same kind of energy and attracted the same type of audience. The New Russian Wave wasn't about the bands, but about the people that it attracted. It was who we were playing to, rather than who was playing.

Interviewee 79's ideas about the importance of audiences in shaping a genre's symbolic relevance reflect well DiMaggio's (1987) concept of "ritual classification" in art. This means that audiences "may explicitly label new musical forms but also,

116   *Independent Music in Russia*

less explicitly, classify artists and works through the structure of their preference" (Crossley 2015, 7). In other words, musicians are grouped together as a "movement" because, alongside other classifications that may derive from record labels, journalists or the artists themselves, they share the same audiences (Crossley 2015).

Overall, the quotations above capture the intersection between musicians (performing), gatekeepers (enabling musicians to perform) and audiences (listening to the performers) in the creation of a music movement. Hailing from a marginal point, the New Russian Wave acquired symbolic and commercial capital not only as a relevant commentary of a change in society, but also as a music world in which a whole assemblage of people, in different roles, did things together and in the same direction, while growing in scope and size in the process. This, eventually, led to a diversification of subgenres within the movement. As explained by Interviewee 37, a key concert promoter and artist manager who helped shape the movement, the New Russian Wave became a fluid concept thanks to its expansion:

> Initially, I thought that it was only one thing, but now I'm not so sure anymore. Initially, the New Russian Wave seemed to me like post-punk and new wave. Then the kids that come to my events made me realise that they perceive this wave differently. They say that Ic3peak is New Russian Wave, for example. Eventually I understood that the New Russian Wave is made of a few genres, a specific aesthetics and a specific atmosphere, all together. Besides, I'm sure that there will be many alternative Russian Waves.

The specific aesthetics and atmosphere in question, however broad, can be spelled out. Despite the heterogeneity of the artists involved, many artists belonging to the New Russian Wave shared in their colour palette elements such as the use of Russian, a good degree of stereotyped suffering (in lyrics as well as attitudes), rougher sounds and darker visual aesthetics (in videos as well as performances), a tinge of curiosity for the "pre-Putin era", a revivalism of Soviet post-punk in various forms, metamodern sensibility, and a mixture of patriotism and protest. Stepan Kazarian, the creator and curator of the festival *Bol'*, concisely judged the New Russian Wave as "the honest, dirty, gloomy, Russian sound" united with a certain "love for the drum machine" (Biasioli 2021, 680).

NRW musicians, born after the dissolution of the USSR, found inspiration in late Soviet and early post-Soviet aesthetics. Around them, the strong legacies of two of its main representatives, Kino's singer Viktor Tsoi and Granzhdanskaia Oborona's leader Egor Letov (1964–2008), were heightened through events, concerts, tributes and films.[16] Additionally, new independent bands like Buerak (Gully), Ploho (Bad) and Gde Fantom? (Where Is the Phantom?) continued to carry Kino's influence, evident in their deep vocals, detached delivery, reverb-heavy guitars, straightforward drum machine patterns and melodically prominent basslines. In contrast, Egor Letov, who passed away in 2008 at the age of 43, experienced a posthumous rediscovery after a decade of relative obscurity, and was celebrated by the New Russian Wave musicians as the embodiment of an anti-commercial, rebellious and DIY ethos.

"I Live in Russia and I'm Not Scared"   117

In concert with cultural recycling and nostalgia (see Engström 2021), the obsession of today's Russian culture with Tsoi and Letov has made them both "undead". Apart from opposite factions trying to appropriate their legacies and contending whether they would have taken the Russian or the Western side in the war in Ukraine (Puchkarev 2022; *Vecher s Kiber Frontom* 2023), their spectral presence in Russian popular culture is further emphasised, for example, in the return of Kino's arena concerts since 2021, in which the band's original members played under the accompaniment of Tsoi's recorded voice. Or in the song "Vse kak u liudei" (Just Like Everyone Else), where the rapper and multi-instrumentalist Noize MC sampled Letov's voice for the chorus while adding new lyrics describing today's Russia as a repressive state. Letov's criticism of the Soviet regime earned him the reputation of an uncompromising and anti-establishment poet, a legacy that resonates in today's indie scene as a form of protest against power, notwithstanding Letov's adherence to Limonov's and Dugin's National Bolshevik Party in 1994.[17]

But it was not only Tsoi and Letov: 1980s groups like Alyans, Tsentr, Nii Kosmetiki and Igri, once Joy Division disciples, reunited in the second half of the 2010s after long hiatuses and started touring again, acquiring new status as "precursors" of the New Russian Wave. This included their participation as headliners of music festivals targeted to the youth, such as the main New Russian Wave incarnation, *Festival' Bol'*.

Emerging performers conceived of such revival of 1980s Soviet post-punk music in the second half of the 2010s as a return to the roots of a domestic tradition and consequently, closer to what "Russian" music should sound like according to its trendsetters and intermediaries. This idea of authenticity was constructed as distinct from the Anglophone Wave and its myths. As Interviewee 77, leader of an internationally renowned NRW band, said: "first Kino, then Joy Division". Or, as Interviewee 79, member of one of the early NRW groups, remarked: "We did things less professionally than the previous generation [of musicians] thought necessary. It was lo-fi, it was DIY, it was in Russian, it was provocative, it was eccentric".

The New Russian Wave reflected well what Herzfeld (2004) calls "cultural intimacy". As Herzfeld (2004, 19) states, cultural intimacy is: "the recognition of those aspects of a cultural identity that are considered a source of external embarrassment but that nevertheless provide insiders with their assurance of common sociality". Pushing the argument a little, cultural intimacy can be articulated thus: "it is a country full of problems, but it is *my* country". Cultural intimacy explains, according to Herzfeld, why people can be "fiercely patriotic and fiercely rebellious at the same time" (91). It is the intrinsic coalescence of the "despite" and the "thanks to" that animates people's actions and thoughts, and that has the nation/country as its origin, projection and endpoint. Within this framework, patriotism and protest may well coexist (what I call *patrioprotest* – see next chapter).

In Russia, cultural intimacy has often offered the basis for a shared system of feeling in which even the supposedly negative stereotypes, such as backwardness or secondariness, could be overturned and acquire a special and cherished social significance. This has regularly provided cultural figures with endless material for their works and for building the difference from the West that they so longingly

118 *Independent Music in Russia*

sought. Russia's cyclical, multiple and unfinished identity quests have sharpened cultural intimacy as a constant civic condition and as an aesthetic, productive drive. Interview 82, the concert promoter of an important Moscow venue, explained this reversal of roles between English and Russian and the embracing of one's own "shame" as "pride":

> In general, in terms of poetics and meaning, the way of conveying emotions in English is more simplified than in Russian. Russian sounds vulgar, it just sounds disgusting. A very simple phrase in English inspires and awakens feelings exactly the same as a very talented poetical phrase in Russian. [but] People are tired of going out of their way to create some kind of impression, just tired. They don't want to waste most of their lives running after something fake, and not one or two people are tired of it, but the whole society. They want to do what they want. Musicians are singing about real things, the new generation is realist. If they sing about new buildings in Chertanovo [a residential district of Moscow filled with concrete buildings] instead of pretty girls dressed in Gucci is because the new buildings in Chertanovo are real and the pretty girls in Gucci are not. [...] You can go to some cafe here – and there is Europe, and you go outside – and it's a bazaar. [...] People who grew up in this fake [thing], they now understand that it is fake, and they understand that they had been looking at this fake [thing] all the time, and they want something real. [...] This realism, with the younger generation, is displayed in some kind of post-punk mess.

Interviewee 82 interpreted this shift to the NRW as the end of the pretending and the discovery of the "real", regardless but also thanks to the fact that alongside pride this "realism" may expose societal problems and evoke feelings of embarrassment (indeed, such metamodern realism did not resolve this tension between problems, embarrassment and pride, but embraced all of them). The NRW wake-up call did not only refer to language but to a holistic project (attitudes, aesthetics, ethics, etc.), which waved goodbye to Medvedev's dream and became manifest in a humble, perhaps even trashy, but nonetheless more appropriate, post-punk. The binaries between "the West" (Gucci, European cafes) and "the East" (the bazaar) were also interesting, as they hinted at another historical trope in Russia's fluctuations of nationhood (meaning, Russia's relationship with Asia as alternative to Europe) (see Bassin 2012). The former pair was infused with sophistication and refinement, but ultimately also with extraneity and foreignness in relation to the Russian context. The bazaar, instead, was characterised as disorderly, but ultimately also as close and familiar.

The contrast between the two Waves – the Anglophone and the New Russian – became evident as a means to fashion a new authenticity grounded in cultural intimacy. As seen in Chapter One, Gorbachev (2019) connected the rise of the New Russian Wave with the end of the "European Project". In his article, published in *Meduza* (one of the most renowned oppositional media outlets in the Russian language),[18] Gorbachev pointed out that the musicians of the previous generation

(2000s and early 2010s) were often renamed in the Russian press on Western parameters: "our Interpol", "Russian Arcade Fire", "local Elliott Smith" and so forth. They were so renamed, Gorbachev maintained, partly because of their mirroring of Western trends, and partly because cultural intermediaries strived to position these artists in the global community with which they identified *nezavisimaia muzyka*. However, Gorbachev argues – not without postcolonial overtones – that in this way Russian popular music perpetuated its own secondariness. Conversely, with the rise of NRW, "everything was turned upside down". As he claimed, "when it became clear that no one needs us in the 'global world', it emerged that being on our own can also be quite interesting". By dismissing a Westernised image of themselves, he argued, NRW artists were reestablishing a connection with their surroundings: they were employing a "more direct, domestic and physical" language, singing "a lot about sex and little about dreams" and taking high literature and internet memes as equally valuable sources of inspiration. This, for Gorbachev, was "perhaps shameful, but more honest". As for the European project, he continued, it disintegrated under the weight of the socio-political events of Putin's third term, becoming "an illusion" in which some Anglophone bands kept living. For Gorbachev, "striving to resemble Radiohead and The XX looks provincial in today's context". Hence, in addition to language, which was one of the most evident contentious arenas, Gorbachev's critique took place also on symbolic and epistemic grounds. The whole "European" (read: Westernised) attitude that inspired the bands, their lyrics and their sound was put under fire. The dichotomy was rearticulated: on one side, the West as an imagery of dependence; on the other, liberating and quintessential Russian tropes.

The issue at stake was therefore not only a musical or cultural one, but part of a larger societal, intellectual and political debate – indeed, the most heated and recurrent in Russia since the nineteenth century – consisting of finding a place, a way of development, and an identity for Russia. The answer that Gorbachev offered in the article delineated a path for Russia's own musical autonomy. This judgement, on the one hand, echoed long-standing Slavophile discourses around Russia's own cultural path, and, on the other, displayed rhizomatic resonances with the political environment of late 2010's Russia, in which "autonomy" (political, cultural, economic) from the West became a tenet. Around the same time, Putin's former advisor Surkov (2018), for example, commented that Russia, as a "half-blood" and a "mixed-race" entity, was expected to face at least 100 years of geopolitical solitude (this was before the full-scale war in Ukraine), because the journey to the West had at last ended. In a mixture of postcolonial and imperial language, Surkov assessed the idea of a solitary third path as unique and positive in finding Russia's identity, despite all the difficulties ahead: "there will be stars", he said (Surkov 2018).

In an uncoordinated, loose manner, both political and musical transformations occurred at the same time and with similar dynamics, even though these two factions (music practitioners and the political elite) disagreed with each other on multiple points of the political agenda. It cannot be stressed enough that the spread of patriotic and nationalistic discourses from politics into the independent music scene during Putin's third term was unsystematic and occurred without

120 *Independent Music in Russia*

orchestration from above. The intermediaries interviewed in this chapter worked in non–state-funded media. Most of them were often quite critical of the actions of the Russian government, usually employing social media to voice their civic position. Several among them participated in oppositional demonstrations. The majority of them left Russia in protest after the invasion of Ukraine in 2022. These intermediaries were not mouthpieces of the government – quite the contrary. This suggests that in mid-2010s Russia, love for the country that is conditional and non-dichotomous (patriotism) and love that is unconditional and binary (nationalism) – were not just coercively imposed from above. Rather, thanks to their intra-relational and emotional nature, they travelled across society multi-directionally and across different domains, providing the tonic notes onto which a variety of polyphonies were built. Of course, as presented later in this chapter and in the next, top-down messages were also disassembled, re-assembled and estranged by grassroots music practitioners into strident counterpoints, but the coexistence of cultural patriotism and political protest indicated forms of resistance that, while contesting the state, were also attuned to some of its values.

Banal and irrelevant: the devaluation of Anglophone bands as internal others

The change in the conventions of thinking and doing independent music in Russia did not occur without conflict within the community. Key in this was the role of the intermediaries, who, situated after production and before consumption (Smith-Maguire and Matthews 2014), mediated between artists and listeners. As always happens in culture, fashions come and go. Here, however, the trendsetters and gatekeepers that championed the New Russian Wave linked the movement with a national identity which, in their opinion, the previous movement lacked. In the distinction that was made between "authentic" and "inauthentic" music, bands that sung in English ended up occupying the inauthentic side of the scene. For instance, Interviewee 18, a musician, journalist and concert promoter, viewed the Anglophone groups as clones with nothing to say:

> Musicians are people who run away from reality very often, they like to live in an illusion. It seems to them that in Russia everything is bad, and if they sing in English everyone will need them. And secondly, they simply have nothing to say. And this is the key moment when people don't have their own thoughts, they hide behind another tongue and say 'look, we are cool…'

A similar judgement was offered by Universal talent scout and music journalist Oleg Karmunin, who marked Anglophone bands as banal:

> All of those people who send me demos in English disappoint me. I say: 'sorry, not my cup of tea'. […] It's always some sort of dreamy soft rock. The dullest music in the world. […] That's why I insist: do not sing in English.
>
> (Karmunin 2019)

"I Live in Russia and I'm Not Scared"   121

Likewise, Interviewee 35, an important music journalist, labelled the Anglophone bands as commercially unwise and qualitatively deficient:

I sincerely wonder why a young man who has such a huge country in front of him, why does he sing in English? The only answer suits me is 'I want to have a career abroad'. [...] But when you sing in English in Russia... Well, you need an argument in the form of a very good song so that I say: 'Yes, OK, well, since you can't do it in a different way...' But most of these bands don't have good songs.

Such discourses had a significant impact on local audiences and on the performers themselves. As I evidenced elsewhere (Biasioli 2021), interviews personally conducted at festivals and gigs in 2017 already signalled a shift in the perception of Anglophone and Russophone music among music aficionados. Many respondents highlighted a development (*razvitie*) in the quality of Russophone music as well as a growth in the amount of new Russophone musicians who appeared on the scene in the mid- and late 2010s. Lyubov, 30, observed: "There has been a clear development because when we grew up there were music channels like MTV... and back then they didn't show Russian performers.[19] Now the situation has changed". Ekaterina, 28, claimed: "Now it's evident how bands relate to music more responsibly and try to craft something original". Maria, 20, said: "In Russia now there has been a development of rock, punk and rap culture that school students really like". Margarita, 19, reflected: "There's been an improvement because although our scene started to develop much later than the Western one, it's only a matter of time now before we catch up". Vitaly, 26, argued that the development lied in the fact that "many local performers who sang in English have now converted to Russian". When asked what the main difference between Russophone and Anglophone music consisted of, the most common answer was also that music in Russian was closer (*blizhe*) and soulful (*dushevnaia*), whereas music in English was finer and more energetic. Alevtina, 21, for instance, argued that Western music was qualitatively better (*bolee kachestvennaia*) but music in Russian resonated more with her, even though it was poorer in quality. Nikolai, 18, claimed that "Russian people have nothing left but soul, and that is what they put in their songs". Sasha, 18, maintained that "Anglophone music is for everyone, and is easier to listen to. Russian music is the content, you need to dig deeper, not everything is on the surface, it's not ephemeral". Dmitry, 38, contended that Russophone music presents "themes that are well-known and very near to the listener. There's no need to translate them, they are thoughts that I live with every day". Such commentaries evidenced a contrast between the West (the form, the body) and Russia (the content, the soul), not dissimilar from what reported in Pilkington et al.'s (2002) surveys (conducted in the late 1990s and early 2000s), in which the youth associated the West as qualitatively "better" but "superficial", and Russia as qualitatively "worse" but "sincere". However, unlike those surveys, Russian youngsters now did not recognise their country as a marginal receiver of Western trends, even if the term of comparison was the same.

122 *Independent Music in Russia*

In terms of shifts in the musicians' practice, several artists who reached popularity in the independent world towards the end of the 2010s (e.g., Glintshake, Shortparis, Ic3peak) abandoned English for Russian between 2014 and 2016. For some of them, the choice may have been dependent on many factors, including the willingness to creatively experiment in their own language, but also on self-interest, to advance their career (e.g., obtain more gigs and media attention). In any case, language-switching paralleled the changes in perceptions amongst the audience, and both tendencies evidenced the efficacy of the discourse promoted by the *nazavisimaia muzyka* intermediaries. Nikolai Komiagin, singer of the dark pop group Shortparis, who once sang in French and English, for example, claimed:

> We want to sing about Russia. [...] There's an entire generation, between 16 and 35 that feels more autonomous, and I say this with a certain pride. [...] Especially in culture, we are independent, self-sufficient. The awareness of our own national identity, our traditions, is being expressed in music. We look less at the West, we take less from the West.
>
> (Komiagin in *3voor12 extra* 2020)

As evidenced here, Russia in the second half of the 2010s became increasingly seen in affective terms and as the subject matter of urgent artistic investigation. According to Komiagin, the music community's self-sufficiency in terms of tropes, traditions and language sidelined Western influence to the role of secondary source.

Nonetheless, the spotlight on bands from the New Russian Wave did not imply the disappearance of domestic Anglophone groups. Rather, as the dominant narrative in *nezavisimaia muzyka* became Russophone, local Anglophone artists who chose not to adapt to the new cultural climate were relegated to a more ancillary position, and their presence in the music media and at music festivals decreased. As I discussed in Biasioli (2021), such decrease corresponded to the intermediaries' filtering. For instance, surveys personally conducted during summer 2017 evidenced discrepancies between the linguistic preferences of 300 Muscovite indie bands (Russophone 42%; mixed 27%; Anglophone 31%) and the overwhelming majority of Russophone bands showcased on the main indie music festival stages in European Russia at the same time. Since festivals are sites where cultural and social capital are developed, networks are consolidated and tastes are amplified (Wilks 2009), the limitation of Anglophone acts underlined the intent of gatekeepers to construct and disseminate the new Russophone trend.

Mixed results were yielded through linguistic inquiries into the main public pages on VKontakte (*pabliki*) dedicated to Russian indie music and crucial to its promotion (incidentally, all of them boasting names with patriotic echoes): *Storona* (Side), *Motherland* and *Rodnoi Zvuk* (Native Sound). Through this analysis, conducted between 19 March and 9 April 2018, it emerged that *Storona* (then followed by over 30,000 people), published Russophone and Anglophone Russian musicians on a percentage of ten to one; *Motherland* (at the time followed by 100,000 subscribers), published one Anglophone Russian artist for every four Russophone ones. *Rodnoi Zvuk* (then totalling 120,000 subscribers) published one Russian

Anglophone artist for every two Russophone ones. These numbers, however, varied through time, as further proof of the performativity of the Russifying discourse. A second analysis conducted on *Rodnoi Zvuk* between 9 and 19 October 2021, for example, showed that the *pablik* had published during that period 70 Russophone artists, 12 instrumental, 4 mixed and only 3 Anglophone ones.

Moreover, if we consider the language of the demos received by some *nezavisimaia muzyka* venues, numbers similar to those of the above-mentioned survey appear. Interviewee 83, former art director of a well-established Muscovite club, reported to have received in 2018 between 20 and 30 demos a day, with 40% in English, 50% in Russian and 10% instrumental or in other languages. Interviewee 84, an ex-concert promoter at another famous music bar in Moscow, said that even though the trend was becoming increasingly Russophone in 2018, in 2015 the majority of the demos received were still Anglophone. Interviewee 18, who in November 2017 was working as a concert promoter for another important venue in central Moscow, revealed that in terms of guitar music, the linguistic proportion of the demos received was two Anglophone bands to one Russophone band. These numbers, however, did not match those extracted from chief indie *pabliki* and, above all, festivals. This divergence reinforces the idea that, in the mid- to late 2010s, a substantial portion of gatekeepers and tastemakers was actively forcing a "nativisation" of *nezavisimaia muzyka*.

At times, Anglophone events were outright ignored. For instance, in July 2016, a specific festival for Anglophone bands called the "Russian Anglophone Festival" took place in Moscow for the first (and so far only) time. Over two days, 15 local Anglophone bands shared the stage. The festival was set in Sokolniki, one of the largest and most iconic Moscow central parks and one of Muscovites' favourite weekend destinations. Entry was free and the festival was, according to the practitioners involved, well-attended. Despite this, all the major music zines, such as *Afisha*, *Colta*, *The Village*, *Snob* and *The Flow*, did not review the event. The Russian Anglophone festival was, according to one of its curators, "an attempt to build a dialogue and overcome internal and external barriers" (Biasioli 2021, 685). Yet it was practically ignored by the independent music media. The showcase of Russian Anglophone bands, according to Interviewee 30, one of the other co-organisers, aimed to portray a "fresh" and positive image of Russia as an open country. English was seen as an instrument through which Russia could establish a culturally enriching dialogue with the rest of the world. However, as Interviewee 30 recognised, this aim was not exactly accomplished:

When we did the festival we went against the trend. Our government said they would raise the amount of songs in Russian on radios to 70%, and there seems to be a certain paradigm 'patriotism equals Russian language'. But I think that patriotism is to meet half-way [*idti navstrechu*], to build a dialogue. […] I love my country, but the fact that I'm promoting English doesn't mean I'm despising Russian or Russia in general. I'm actually doing my country good publicity in the eyes of other countries. If we don't build a dialogue, if we don't open, we run the risk of building curtains again, of closing. . . why should we do that?"

124   *Independent Music in Russia*

The version of patriotism given by Interviewee 30 corresponded quite well to the one given in the beginning of the chapter: love for one's country open to external influences and conditioned to that rational openness beyond binaries. However, history was already at the time showing that the Russian Anglophone festival was running against local musical trends and global geopolitical ones, as a fragment spun out of the bygone era of the Anglophone Wave.

These transformations in the hierarchies within *nezavisimaia muzyka* were contested or accepted with bitterness by Anglophone practitioners. For instance, Interviewee 26, a now-former guitarist of an Anglophone indie collective, admitted in 2017: "We are not fashionable, we are an Anglophone band". As many Anglophone musicians observed in discussions on social media at the time, the "alternative of the alternative" in Russian music became embodied by bands singing in English. Pompeya singer Daniil Brod identified the beginning of the shift in music taste with the inception of the Ukrainian conflict in 2014. In a Facebook public conversation with Aleksandr Gorbachev, he said: "Without 2014, the European project would have continued" (Brod on Gorbachev's Facebook page, 2 January 2019). Brod himself admitted in 2018 that the "hipster generation was dead" (Brod in *Kvartirnik NTV* 2018), thus sealing the relegation of local Anglophone music to the role of secondary narrative – the niche of the niche – in *nezavisimaia muzyka*. Interviewee 14, the founder of the label-studio in Moscow discussed in the previous chapter, elaborated:

> It's all politicised crap. That is, we see a direct correlation between official messages and people's intolerance to everything Anglophone. As soon as we have relaxation, we immediately see an instant correlation, a warming up, and more people come to concerts, for example, of On-The-Go or Tesla Boy. That is, there is a direct correlation there. Of course, all people have their own head on their shoulders, and it seems like everyone thinks with it. But, for large masses, for large volumes of people, this propaganda still works.

According to Interviewee 14, there was a correlation between state policies and how Russian bands singing in English were perceived in the country. This link between language choice in songs and political developments was observed also by Interviewees 25 and 24, vocalist and bassist of a renowned post-punk Anglophone band, who argued:

Interviewee 25:   You know, in 2010, everyone said that it was awesome to sing in English, there can't be a Russophone band. Now the same dudes say: 'why do you sing in English, do you not live in Russia?'

Interviewee 24:   In the 'rich' years, in 2008, everyone travelled everywhere, to the West, there was a feeling of openness. Yes, this is one of the aspects, maybe it is a macro-level, but nevertheless. . . and then all the events that you already know began, and with them, the return of our spiritual foundations, and that also played a big role.

"I Live in Russia and I'm Not Scared" 125

Interviewee 25:	There are people who used to organise festivals for English-speaking groups, and now they have switched to only Russian-speaking groups, because it's just like… it brings more money and it's kind of fashionable now.

Similarly, Interviewees 26 and 27, guitarist and vocalist of another Anglophone indie band, discussed this change in attitudes:

Interviewee 26:	We played songs in English, and it was all good. Then 2014 happened.
Interviewee 27:	Crimea…
Interviewee 26:	Yes. And then there were people sometimes at our concerts who were like 'Why are you singing in English, why not in Russian?' […]
Interviewee 27:	Practically all groups are now switching to Russian, and I think it's like… to concede, that is, to give up. That is, *to give up in a global sense* [*sdat'sia v global'nom smysle* – emphasis added].

For Interviewee 27, to concede or to give up in a global sense meant to concede to the official narrative, to submit to its interpellation and to give up the holistic idea of Russia as an internationally integrated unit. According to Interviewee 3, binary thinking also meant giving up to the politicisation of art, which was detrimental to artistic freedom:

This is again some kind of trend set by stupid critics who want to put you right away either in a box of Russian-speaking bands or in a box of English-speaking bands. What for? Well, it will probably be easier for them to dig into these boxes later. But, unfortunately, it seems to me that this also has an impact on the bands themselves, and it can affect their style, regardless of their desire, that is, they can follow some trends regardless of whether they want to. It just seems to them that some direction in the media has changed, and that this is wrong, because artists themselves may not feel at ease with it. Creativity should be 100% expression of what you want.

For Interviewee 3, as well as for Interviewee 27, the impositions of the media turned into impositions in music-making (what to sing about, in which language, with what tone), and in musicking (music as a social activity involving a collective effort). These changes in turn became new conventions, new accepted ways of doing things that replaced the old ones.

All the enunciations in this section underscore how national and international political situations strongly influence local practices, including the language in which a song is sung. In Chapter One, I examined Turino's (2008) discussion of *habits* and their permutations: habits shape and are shaped by social life, and the discourses they create are both fashioned from the bottom up and influenced from the top down. This may seem trivial and obvious in theory, but its effects in practice

126 *Independent Music in Russia*

are often overlooked, especially in the context of authoritarian Russia during the 2010s, where the scholarly tendency has been to pit creators and politicians in binary, oppositional terms. On the contrary, in 2010s Russian independent music, participants (and their audiences), despite their various positions in relation to state politics (indifference, scepticism, non-involvement, support, dissent and so on), were not immune to the official narratives permeating the zeitgeist (be this Westernisation, as we saw in the previous chapter, cultural sovereignty, patriotism or, in some instances, nationalism), precisely because they interacted with this zeitgeist. The re-orientations around Russianness of habits, conventions and meaning-making within post-2014 *nezavisimaia muzyka* were stimulated by the changes in habits, conventions and meaning-making within the Russian political milieu, in the same way that the Anglophone Wave was animated by and with the cosmopolitan façade that politicians like Kapkov, Sobyanin and Medvedev wanted to build at the beginning of the decade. Therefore, while music intermediaries in the Anglophone Wave promoted the internal otherness embodied by the English-singing artists within a holistic project of Westernisation, after Crimea this internal otherness was often ignored, criticised or devalued.

Russianness and post-irony: the Pain Generation

The NRW relied on paradigms of Russianness in order to construct its immediacy and be authenticated by audiences. In broad terms, Russianness is what makes a particular cultural or social practice (perceived as) typically "Russian". In more concrete terms, Russianness is a construct, invented by the Russian intelligentsia in the nineteenth century, which consists of (but is not limited to) certain moral values that are supposed to belong "acutely" to the Russian people and their culture, such as the endurance of suffering, compassionate altruism, love for the nation and the belief in the special role of Russia. Russianness semantically overlaps with the equally elusive idea of the "Russian soul" (Pesmen 2000; Olson 2004) which several Russian writers, including Dostoevsky, and composers, such as Glinka, have tried to express in their works (Frolova-Walker 1997; Hudspith 2004). Russianness, as Huttunen (2012) argues, is an auto-generated, "timeless" concept with which Russians have invented and endorsed their and their country's uniqueness and mission. As Ryazanova-Clarke (2012) points out, Russianness has needed the West in order to exist and function in the Russian imaginary and culture: through the continuous reference to what Russia is *not*, Russians have constructed a significant part of their national identity.

Russianness, in addition to the values above, became manifest in mid- to late 2010s popular music through concrete objects from Russia's recent past (for instance, Soviet architecture), and established negative stereotypes, like ideas of Russia's backwardness and provinciality, since all of them were equally appropriated and refashioned by the new generation of Russian musicians as a cultural, intimate legacy. Such an aesthetic operation was informed by the rediscovery of perceived national roots and the creation of an autonomous cultural space (goals that were not so dissimilar, as we have seen, to those pursued in parallel at state level).

"I Live in Russia and I'm Not Scared" 127

Crucially, however, practitioners played with the nationalism propagated by the state and turned on its head through the deployment of post-irony as well as the emphasis on the unassuming "lousiness" of the Russian condition. In this process straight statements were turned over twice, so that the first statement and its opposite coexisted in an indiscernible continuum of irony and seriousness (Khrushchëva 2020, 30), while the author abstained from any final moral judgement.

The most important catalyst of this new aesthetic trend was undoubtedly the *Bol'* (Pain) Festival, established in Moscow by music manager and promoter Stepan Kazarian in 2015. From a one-day showcase of Russian underground music, *Bol'* became in a few years the primary event in the independent scene. In contrast to a bunch of bands that performed in front of a few hundred people in 2015 (Levchenko 2019), *Bol'* hosted more than 90 performers over the course of three days in 2019 (including international acts), attracting almost 17,000 spectators in total.[20] The year 2019 was also the festival's final year before the coronavirus pandemic and its subsequent closure in 2022 (most of the organisers have relocated abroad since the start of the full-scale war).

Kazarian, like other cultural intermediaries in the NRW, tapped into the pool of Russia's history and self-perceptions to increase shared symbolic capital. When he founded *Bol'*, for example, Kazarian talked about a return in independent music of the "honest, dirty, gloomy, Russian sound", which he equated with authenticity. Yet, what was this Russian sound? On the one hand, it descended from the nineteenth-century idea, constructed by the Russophile intelligentsia, that the folk song reflected the "invincible tragic Russian soul [...] a sadness at the core of every Russian" (Frolova-Walker 2004, 121–124), which composers strove to replicate in their works. On the other hand, this sadness, a foundational element of *Bol'*'s poetics of low life, was accompanied and disrupted by the irony cast over it. Indeed, Kazarian claimed that the name *Bol'* was conceived of as a joke, a four-letter word (in Russian the soft sign is considered a letter) that echoed the names of some indie bands at that time, such as Trud (Labour), Srub (Log-House) and Utro (Morning). Nonetheless, *Bol'* soon became the trademark for the landscape of the NRW: "impudent, noisy, sometimes dirty and uncomfortable" (Barabanov 2019). These attributes, however, were evaluated positively as markers of genuineness: Aleksandr Gorbachev, for example, praised *Bol'* as "a zone of discomfort"[21] (*zona diskomforta*) in contrast to the Westernised urban comfort of *Afisha's Picnic* – the other, well-established and somehow rival Muscovite festival. As observed during fieldwork in 2017, *Bol'*'s discomfort was also reflected in the excruciatingly long queues for the very few food and drinks kiosks, and for the even fewer toilets.

On a societal level, the festival's uneasiness reflected the uneasiness of an entire generation, which almost entirely coincided, in the case of *Bol'*'s attendees,[22] with "Gen Z" (people born after 1994). This "Pain Generation", on the one hand, witnessed only one ruling establishment in their adult life (Putin's); on the other, it became fascinated with the immediate pre-Putin past (the 1990s and the Soviet 1980s) as a missed opportunity and as a foreign land worth exploring. One of the musical representatives of the Pain Generation, the singer Elizaveta Gyrdymova –

128   *Independent Music in Russia*

known by the stage name of Monetochka (Little Coin) – epitomised both tendencies. In 2018 Gyrdymova released "90", a song whose video followed the footsteps of the popular (nationalistic) film *Brother* (*Brat*, 1997) and whose lyrics addressed the 1990s as a time of chaos but also freedom. Two years later, in an interview with journalist Iurii Dud', she said: "I was born in 1998, I lived two years without Putin. I don't remember a time without Putin. [Living without him] would be at least interesting" (*VDud'* 2020). This unattainable desire was reflected within the Russian Gen Z as a cause of pain. As Kazarian put it, the Pain Generation was:

> Resolutely hedonistic and fully part of a twenty-first-century lifestyle, indistinguishable from that of their Western peers, but somehow unable to shrug off a kind of weltschmertz [a feeling of melancholy and world-weariness] that also reflects a sentimental – if knowing – view of Russia's recent history.
>
> (Kazarian in Foster 2019)

Kazarian here argues that, while lifestyle and hedonism may be analogous everywhere, the Russian system of feeling presented differences from that of the West. Socio-political occurrences, be these the fall of the USSR, the shock of the 1990s, Putin's hold of power and increasing autocracy, seeped through to the Russian youth, set them aside from their Western contemporaries and mutated into pain. In these terms, *Bol'* and the Pain Generation could be regarded as an instance of Russia's "cult of suffering" (Rancour-Laferriere 1995), a certain inclination that Russians have, or we think they have, towards sadness, misery and tragedy. This idea, solidified by the works of nineteenth-century writers like Tolstoy, Dostoevsky and Chekhov, has long been fixed in the Western imaginary. Rainer Maria Rilke, for example, argued that Slavic people are equipped with "the capacity not only to suffer but to find meaning in suffering" (Rilke in Pesmen 2000, 328), whereas Virginia Woolf (2017 [1925]) was convinced that Russian suffering was common, shared and produced a "sense of brotherhood". It is also thanks to these views that "the tragic soul myth [has] retained much of its hold over the Russian literary imagination and continued to appeal to many Westerners as the essence of Russianness" (Frolova-Walker 2004, 125).

Pain was also appropriated by the Putin's administration and made one of the foundational pillars of official discourse, deployed to "harness group emotions for the political aims of the regime" (Sharafutdinova 2020, 110). The political elite did not have to look far, but only to feel the pulse of the population in relation to Russia's recent history. As Oushakine (2009, 262) demonstrated, the suffering that emerged from the various traumas of Russia's 1990s, evident particularly in the neglected provinces, served as a shared language for people to bond together and form "communities of loss", united in solidarity of grief and ultimately in a "patriotism of despair". Putin's government, from the very onset, was able to capitalise on this embodied trauma and turn suffering into a potent ideological and emotional weapon. The official go-to myths became not only the pain caused by the chaos of the 1990s but also the heroic suffering that Russians endured during World War II (Malinova 2017), omnipresent in state-sponsored TV, films and other media. In both cases, mediated pain served to propagandise a particular image: the great resilience of the Russians and their glorious victory over Nazism in one case, and the arrival of Putin to save the country in the other. It is in the memory of the terrible transition from state-controlled to market economy that Putin still has one of his main sources of popular support, and this is why the pain that the 1990s evoke in the Russians needs to be kept alive as a scarecrow, including through media and culture (Sharafutdinova 2020, 110–129).

At the same time as it became an object of authoritative discourse, the trope of suffering was reinvented by the Pain Generation along different lines. Thanks to the peculiar mode of post-irony (discussed in Chapter One), pain (and resilience to it) was treated ambivalently, at the same time mocked as rubbish rhetoric and sincerely endorsed as quintessentially national, while the author's intention became irreducible to one or the other (or indeed, to any) interpretation. Because of this excess of suffering across the Pain generation and the New Russian Wave, it was ultimately impossible to understand where the agony began and the posturing ended. As Interviewee 37 maintained, showing a great deal of awareness of contemporary cultural debates: "All *Bol'* festival is founded upon post-irony".

Post-irony was a response – more subtle than the oppositional actionism of Pussy Riot – to address the contradictions and fragilities of Russian society, caught in the revival of national greatness but also in authoritarianism and isolation from Europe, a society in which the modernisation of the urban landscape and the technological innovation championed by Moscow did not correspond to the development of the country's democratic structures at large. On the contrary, Moscow's modernisation, initiated by Mayor Yurii Luzhkov in the 2000s and furthered by his successor Sergei Sobyanin in the 2010s, relied heavily on distraction as a tool for power consolidation. This distraction was aimed at the "creative" middle class, the most likely to engage in contestation with the government (Etkind 2017) and therefore the one that needed to be co-opted with less evident means. The more Moscow was rebranded as "European" at an infrastructural level, the more human rights and freedom of speech in Russia became endangered. The innovations of the Russian capital's architecture, lifestyle and public amenities under Medvedev continued during Putin's third and fourth terms in tandem with Russia's autocratic turn and the erosion of civil rights (see also Gel'man 2017). Renovated parks with free beach volley courts and ping-pong tables, new pedestrian areas, new Metro lines, new art museums and fully Europeanised cultural centres – all praised by, and catered to, the politically critical intelligentsia – helped divert public attention from, if not sugar-coat, the parallel introduction of restrictive civic measures such as the anti-LGBT laws, the laws against public gatherings, the expansion of police and judicial powers and the 2020 changes to the constitution designed to prolong Putin's time in power until 2036. Taking their inspiration from the West, where the concept originated, Moscow authorities understood how the "smart city" could ultimately serve the interests of power, with the state working in unison with corporations and tech companies within the neoliberal framework (see Kitchin 2022). Music, in the

130 *Independent Music in Russia*

process, became one of the instruments for power consolidation, through which the state deflected the focus from political participation to hedonism (Biasioli 2023).

Caught up between improved living standards and political stagnation, Muscovite youth had indeed more than one reason for aching, as indicated by the mass protests of 2012 and 2019, in which the "creative class" that was tentatively forming up had a leading role (*Colta.ru* 2012; Beumers et al. 2017). But together with this pain came the resignation to the impossibility of change and the irony on one's own condition. Etkind (2017, 10) observed that laughter represents the best hope for civil society when there is no other hope. In the case of post-irony, laughter made way to a "faint smile" (Khrushchëva 2020, 32).

Post-irony emanated in multiple directions: at oneself, at pain itself and at those who ironised on pain. The latter category therefore incorporated *Bol'* and its bands as objects of derision. The argument was along the lines of: "If Russia is an uninterrupted landmass of pain, why pay [to go to the festival] to see a fake version of this pain?" (*Smertach Daily* 2019). In 2017, for example, the name *Bol'* was appropriated by another festival (once called *Strukturnost'* – "Structuredness"). The organiser of this "second" Pain Festival, Leonid Kotelnikov, made public a private conversation he had with Kazarian on Facebook (now deleted); when Kazarian demanded an explanation for the copying of his festival's name, Kotelnikov replied: "yes, we do a festival of the same name, but with real pain inside" [*s real'noi bol'iu vnutri*]. The reply, which became instantly a meme within *nezavisimaia muzyka*, showed the "competition" for authenticity over the cult of suffering – the "realer" the pain, the more authentic the festival – and simultaneously pointed to irony as a destabiliser of this very same pain. *Bol'*'s values, aims and hype were also deconstructed through visuals (see Figure 3.1). The picture is taken from the Telegram Channel *Smertach Daily* (*smert'* in Russian means "death"), which dealt with ironic commentaries on the Russian way of (low) life, with particular focus on the provinces. The picture showed an advert for various housing maintenance services. Some of the names on the advert are "Lock Change", "Insect Disinfestation", "Plastic Windows", "Plumber", "Sewage Cleaning" and so on.

The irony rested, on one hand, upon the recontextualisation of a house maintenance advert into a festival poster, based on the names of the bands who played the Pain stage in the previous years, and, on the other hand, upon the actual similarity between the services listed on the advert and these bands' names: Ssshhhiiittt, Ploho (Bad), Vlazhnost' (Humidity), Sewage Sour, Oleg Musor (Oleg Garbage), Brom (Bromine) and so on (Figure 3.2).

Another example was the post-punk band Buerak (Gully), who made the irony of Russian post-punk and the Pain Generation one of their aesthetic signatures (and, for this reason, became a prime representative of the New Russian Wave). In 2020 the band released a re-recorded version of "Konokrad" (Horse Thief), a song they initially published in 2014 when they were just starting out. Buerak singer, Artem Cherepanov, explains that:

It's a note of sarcasm on Russian post-punk. We promised to release some dark post-punk but actually rerecorded a song from 2014, showing that in

"*I Live in Russia and I'm Not Scared*"   131

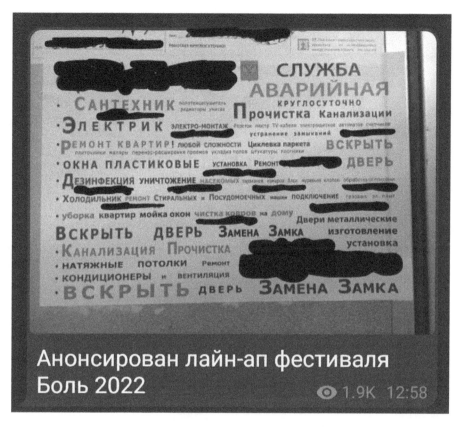

Figure 3.1 House maintenance advert mockingly turned into the line-up for *Bol'* 2020. The headline says: "The line-up of Festival *Bol'* 2020 has been announced". Source: Telegram Channel *Smertach Daily*, 13 September 2019.

2020 it is very stupid to write this sort of material with a serious approach. Here for you is an ideal post-punk track, sounding better than everything else that is released in that style now, and even fresher.

(Cherepanov in *Colta.ru* 2020)

Cherepanov mocked the triteness of many bands from the New Russian Wave that appeared after them. However, Buerak themselves hardly ever changed their sound and approach (see below), which turned the singer's mockery to the direction of his band too. Operating within a post-ironic framework, in the same interview Cherepanov declared that the "essence" of the Russian song resides in its lyrics (*tekst*) and sad atmospheres (*minor*), thus upholding the historical view on most Russian popular musicians. In the end, both pain and irony on pain, as discourses, were not conflicting, but testified to the engagement that Russians have had with the idea of suffering as an essentialised pillar of their identity, however truthfully experienced.

132 Independent Music in Russia

Figure 3.2 Line-up of *Bol'* 2019. Source: *Concertinfo.ru.*[23]

"I Live in Russia and I'm Not Scared" 133

An endless cigarette: boredom and low life as provincial plenitude

Strictly connected to "pain" were imaginings of "boredom", "low life" and, of course, their container: "the province". In Buerak's case, this is Siberia (the band hails from Novosibirsk), the land of suffering par excellence.[24] Buerak's songs featured simple and lo-fi arrangement, short compositions (usually less than three minutes in length and rarely featuring a bridge), unobtrusive drum machines, a minimal amount of chords, a low, monotone, almost detached vocal delivery and lyrics on the border between the serious and the ridiculous, which nonetheless described the Russian way of (low) life and the new ethics of the Russian youth. Let us consider, for instance, the song "Strast' k kureniiu" (Passion for Smoking), released in 2016:

> Got up early in the morning, smoked a cigarette
> Before eating, I took out a cigarette
> I had a very big lunch yesterday
> And lit a cigarette without leaving my chair
> I really like smoking every Wednesday
> One cigarette and a second cigarette
> I'm blowing smoke in rings on Saturday before lunch
> When I smoke a cigarette, I smoke a cigarette
> I really like my passion for smoking
> I smoke a cigarette and then another one
> I love watching the ash fall from it
> I smoke a cigarette and then another one.

"Strast' k kureniiu" is structured more like a series of monotonal utterances than a pop song,[25] as evidenced by the absence of a chorus, the composition's short length (just over two minutes) and the lack of any noticeable musical development (e.g., new instruments joining in or changing parts). The repetitive character of the music matched the recurrent image of the cigarette upon which the lyrics obsessively centred as the simple (and only) pleasure available, the pinnacle of the unvaried routine of ordinary (Russian) life (*byt*).

The meaning is, however, double-voiced. On the one hand, smoking could be seen as engaging in self-harm as the only way to temporarily escape the unbearable boredom of a Russian provincial town. On the other hand, the song could be interpreted literally as an ode to smoking, as a poeticisation of a commonplace act and as a feverish and emotional activity that brings gratification to the protagonist. Over one and the other interpretation lingers the post-irony contained in the lyrics. The provincial hero, by disengaging from the uninspiring external context and by pursuing easy and unassuming goals, may retreat in the private space of the *byt* as both a comfort zone and an articulation of Russianness, in a circular, closed and invariable rhythm. But the listener does not – and should not – know whether this routine is praised or frowned upon.

Both interpretations contain more nuances within themselves, which oscillate further like metamodernist matrioshkas within the bigger piece. If we are to interpret the

134 *Independent Music in Russia*

song as an ironic take on provincial life, then, of course, smoking functions as a noxious, dangerous tranquiliser, and the cigarette burns like the days of the hero, trapped in an uneventful existence. But the reappropriation of boredom serves also as the door to contemplation, to the *vita contemplativa*, of which cigarettes have become in visual culture an essentialised trait. One can think, for example, of the recent global phenomenon of "Russian Doomer" and the transnational romanticisation of (Russian) sadness (discussed in Chapter Five). In the compilations of the genre on YouTube, the meme of the "doomer" is embedded, smoking, against the background of Soviet residential blocks.[26] Boredom thus becomes much an end in and of itself as it is overcome. No longer driven by a desire without an object (in the Schopenhauerian sense), the subject defeats boredom through the acceptance that there is nowhere to run to: with the aid of an endless series of cigarettes, he keeps himself occupied and satisfied, eventually reaching the absence of desire (what more can be desired if one is content with simple pleasures?). The ironic reading stores within itself the serious one.

If we are to interpret "Passion for Smoking" positively, then we can look at it as a hymn to laziness and as an act of defiance towards pervasive discourses of (toxic) productivity. As Boris Groys (2009, 4) maintains, even if today we are stuck in a reproduction of the present that does not lead to any future but to unproductive, wasted time, we can also assess this wasted time positively "as excessive time, as time that attests to our life as pure being-in-time, beyond its use within the framework of modern economic and political projects". The repetitiveness of ordinary, banal and unproductive actions is elevated in the case of Buerak to a metanarrative in itself and to a defining criterion of Russianness as it is experienced in the provinces. In doing this, it both defies and reasserts the political: boredom and wasted time are epitomised as a quiet resistance to economic overstimulation or authoritative interpellation, but simultaneously essentialised as a proud embracing of the common low life in Russia. It is not an overstretch to see in this apology of political idleness and low life the looming of the figure of the Soviet *bezdel'nik*, the good-for-nothing loafer that lived in the interstices of Soviet society not least because he was enabled to do so by a paternalistic state in which basic needs were guaranteed (indeed, *vnye*). In addition to the band's sonic rootedness in the Soviet New Wave, the visual aesthetics of "Strast' k kureniiu" (and of Buerak in general) are indebted to Soviet heritage too, as evinced by the concrete residential buildings, built on the Soviet model, that constitute the background of the video for the song (many of them appear to be in construction, thus reproducing the past into the present). Like in the song, hardly anything happens in the video: against an average urban background, in black and white, the two band members sing, play or smoke. The serious reading becomes therefore a playful take on the Russian condition (Figure 3.3).

Keti Chukhrov (2020) argues that most of Soviet cinema in the 1960s and 1970s was not cinematic (in other words, it was boring, from an external perspective) because its goal was not to display innovative aesthetic methodologies but to inscribe the goodness of the ideology in the moving image. That is why these films were flat and conflict-less: in a realised, de-alienated society "virtue confronts virtue, rather than evil" (113), and what looked like a reality full of squalor and boredom was supposed to be perceived by its participants as plentifulness liberated from the vices

"*I Live in Russia and I'm Not Scared*" 135

Figure 3.3 Still frame from Buerak's video for "Strast' k kureniu". Source: YouTube.[27]

of capitalism. Chukhrov maintains that "in any other—non-communist—context, the same things would be seen otherwise: as poor, inefficient, badly designed, unattractive, raw, cheap, and tasteless" (107). But because these things guaranteed "cultural intimacy", the reassurance of common sociality and a shared cultural code, they would in effect acquire a "halo", extra meaning, exceeding value, and would become "both basic and perfect at the same time". In this way, participants treated "the reality of basic need" as spiritual and ontological plenitude (107). In other words, boredom functioned as an indentitarian, affirmative tool vis-à-vis the Western system of morally loose entertainment.

Indeed, many of Buerak's songs (and those of the post-punk strand of the NRW at large) were uneventful and purposefully constructed as such. Buerak's lo-fi, short, basic, "boring" tunes, most of which end in the same way as they begin, turned the inferiority complex that many Russian musicians experienced towards Western music into a statement of Russianness: there was no need to look for fully fledged structures composed of an alternation of verses, choruses, bridges; no need to vary the vocal delivery; no need for sonic refinement, complex chord progressions, melodies, harmonies, arrangements; no need to introduce new instruments, lines, or effects; national identity was already expressed through the mantra of the *byt* and the plainness of the song, and any change in this balance would be counter to the overall affective mode, to the construction of aesthetic authenticity and to the metamodern irreducibility of the text to a straight understanding.

I live in Russia and I am not scared… Or am I?

The investigation and poeticisation of the ordinary traversed much of the work of another representative band of the NRW and the Pain Generation: Pasosh.[28] In

136   *Independent Music in Russia*

their songs, cosmopolitanism and provinciality, life and death, youth and old age, hope and disillusion coalesced in fluctuations informed, in turn, by the youth's need to transform future-related anxieties and nationalistic top-down messages into a bottom-up, valuable inquiry into what made the Russian youth "Russian". The epitome of this attitude was the song-manifesto "Rossiia" ("Russia", 2015):

> I live in Russia, and I'm not scared of what the currency exchange will be tomorrow
> I live in Russia, and I'm not scared not to feel my pulse in the morning
> We died here a long time ago, and we don't feel the cold
> We were born old, and we are waiting for our youth
> And we are not cold in winter, and we are not hot in summer
> After all, you and I will die somewhere in a suburban park
> I live in Russia, and I'm not afraid of what the weather will be tomorrow
> I live in Russia, and I'm not scared, I'm not scared, I'm not afraid
> We died here a long time ago, and we don't feel the hunger
> We were born old, and we are waiting for our youth
> I live in Russia and I'm not scared [×4]

A metamodern oscillation animates the song throughout. On the one hand, the song is a statement of defiance, strength and bravery, which is connected to the country – Russia – and relies on established tropes, like the volatility of the ruble, the harsh Russian climate, or the poor living conditions of the people. These negative tropes – well-known to foreigners as well as locals – are nonetheless embraced in the song as social poetics and used to create a positive movement from old age to youth and to underline the resilience of the Russian character in spite of the unfavourable circumstances (another historical trope). On the other hand, however, references to death populate the song (how can you be afraid if you are already dead?),[29] and the life of the hero appears powerless in relation to the system enclosing it, liminal, unsafe and confined to vagrancy around the periphery. The emotional contrast is emphasised through the music too. The boldness of the statement "I live in Russia and I'm not afraid" is immediately downplayed by (or, rather, integrated into) the raucous, desperate and frightened scream of the voice singing the line. Ambiguity, thus, arises: is the lyrical hero not scared because he lives in Russia, or in spite of the fact that he lives in Russia? Is the country a benevolent or malign entity? As usually happens in the case of the NRW, the answer is: both. The entire song is built on this ambivalence, and its firm aim is not to resolve it. The ultimate defiance is indeed about the political. Interviewee 77 explains:

> 'Rossiia' was a big hit and probably the first anthem of the scene [NRW]. Conservatives would say it's like a pro-Russia song, like 'we are not afraid and blah blah blah'; leftists would say this is a leftist song because it is ironic about how everything is good when everything is bad. In reality, it's just not a political song at all. It's a bizarre view on what living in Russia feels like.

"I Live in Russia and I'm Not Scared" 137

A lot of it came from going abroad and meeting people who, when knowing you are from Russia, would say: 'wow, do they really kill people on the
street there?'

Good or bad, it does not matter: Russia here is presented in the form of prolonged
emotion, as an affect "no matter what". It is telling that in the album track list the
song "Rossiia" is embedded between the song's "suffering" [*stradanie*] and "forever"
[*navsegda*], forming the triptych: suffering-Russia-forever. Equally indicative of the
shared experience of these feelings is the fact that many songs in the album adopt the
perspective of the "we", a collective group which can likely be identified with the
Russian youth. The title of the album, *We Will Never Be Bored (Nam nikogda ne budet skuchno)* represented the affirmative statement of the coming-of-age of the "Pain
Generation" in the face of contingencies: whatever political elites will decide to do,
we, in our own world, will find ways to make life interesting for ourselves because
we have the resources – internal and external – to do so. This was a new, enthusiasti-
cacceptance of one's condition of insider-outsider, of *vnye*, in reaction to the ideological comeback. As evidenced in the videos for some of the songs on the album, ordinary actions such as shopping in night supermarkets, smoking cigarettes, drinking
alcohol, going around in the city, skating and dancing are all invested with meanings
of both defiance and pride. In the video of "Navsegda", for example, unassertive
Moscow houses, alleyways, underpasses and tube carriages coexist with monumen-
tal streets, skyscrapers and historical buildings (interestingly, the Kremlin is never
shown), in a declaration of love for the city in all its breadth. Here, however, ambiguity kicks in once again to inform the listener that this declaration of love is not unconditional. It is expressed, quite literally, in the conditional: "I would stay here forever,
I would never leave" (*ia by ostalsia zdes' navsegda, ia by ne stal uhodit' nikogda*),
which implies an "if" that does not solely depend on the subject's will, but also on
external factors, and which demonstrates the metamodern dynamics of oscillation
between the determination to commit to a grand project (Moscow, Russia) and the
impossibility of fully committing to it for a number of reasons, including because the
project is morally dubious. The subject would like to espouse it culturally but at
the same time also disaffiliate from the violence it exudes politically.

The formalist literary theorist Viktor Shklovsky (2016) famously proposed in
1917 the concept of "defamiliarisation" (*ostranenie*) to describe the effect produced by art that makes strange what seems habitual (e.g., by looking at it from
an unexpected perspective, or with an unusual language). This device, according
to Shklovsky, has the effect of prolonging the aesthetic perception and is key in
distinguishing the poetic (formed speech) from the prosaic (the everyday, direct,
economical speech).

This distinction between poetic and prosaic language is absent in most NRW
songs (including in Pasosh's "Rossiia"); the two have coalesced into an all-purposes
language that can be used at the bar like in a song, but the effect of defamiliarisation is achieved in another way: precisely, through the crafted impossibility of a
resolution, the ambivalence of the aim of the text. The ambiguous mode with which
the familiar is projected estranges the work. If the pride goes, then we are left with

138 *Independent Music in Russia*

the univocal, straightforward political critique that Russian artists so much discard as dull; if the critique goes, then we are left with a nationalistic anthem, equally banal and uninteresting. Like Shklovsky's "stone", which art must make "stony", the interlocking of these elements (pride/nationalism and critique/contestation) creates the defamiliarisation that makes "Russia" feel "Russian".

Such aim is achieved, of course, also through the indeterminacy of the author's subjectivity in the text, what Bakhtin called "removal" (*ustranenie*) of the author from the field of their hero. According to Bakhtin, a precondition for valuable art is that the author must stand in a position of outsideness (*vnyenakhodimost'*) in relation to their hero, and at the same time in dialogue with the hero. Bakhtin saw this removal as a "loving act" (Bakhtin in Emerson 2005, 641), so that the hero could flourish in a liberated way from the author, while the author could imagine the hero as a full-fledged self. *Ustranenie* is performed not only as an ethical technique (e.g., to prevent direct political statements, to reveal an ethical stance), but also as an aesthetic device which, like *ostranenie*, prolongs the time of perception of the work of art, makes such perception difficult, elevates it and indefinitely delays any conclusive, unidirectional interpretations (it "unfinalises" them).[30] In Pasosh's "Rossiia", a crucial distinction here is that removal means "distance" only in the moral sense, whereas it means the opposite – "overidentification" – in the emotional sense: the author is so invested in their hero that it creates an "excess of vision" from within, not from without. That is why the listener is not able to understand what the author thinks: the removal is moral, not affective.

In sum, *ostranenie* (defamiliarisation) of the common and *ustranenie* (removal) of the author from the political coexisted across most of the NRW and were made audible in Pasosh's work. As the distinction between objects as they are perceived and objects as they are known collapsed, what remained was a prolonged aesthetic and emotional effect, which re-created and looped back into the permanent mood from which it started: that of Russia as an affective discourse. Together with this, what was also prolonged was the multi-voiced as well as multi-directional contradictions, nuances and ambiguities of this affective condition.

The Russian Ark

Elizaveta Gyrdymova (aka Monetochka), born in 1998 in Ekaterinburg, was the musician from the Pain Generation who, perhaps more evidently than anyone else, epitomised the metamodern fluctuations in contemporary Russian culture (Engström 2018) as well as the systematic utilisation of post-irony. From her name to her voice, from her sound to her lyrics, Gyrdymova reached mass popularity in late 2010's Russia through a musical image that was simultaneously profound and superficial, authentic and fake, mature and childish. In her most notorious work to this date, *Colouring Books for Adults* (*Raskraski dlia vzroslykh*), released in 2018 when the singer was only 20, such ambivalence extended to the realm of the sociopolitical.[31] For instance, in the opening track of the album, called "Russian Ark" ("Russkii kovcheg") and inspired by Aleksandr Sokurov's 2002 film of the same

"I Live in Russia and I'm Not Scared" 139

name, Monetochka reflected on the Russian condition. The track is all about the past, present and future of Russia:

[Verse 1]
Smelling of alcohol, gentlemen are smoking,
Their ladies are hiding their fluffy eyebrows into shawls that smell so sweet.
Our journey has been so long we no longer remember where we come from,
where we are going,
Which dock we started from, and what prize awaits us in the end.
The chains, the chains are dragging us down to the bottom,
Right into the nets with octopi, right into the poachers' nets,
But there's a lot of us, and not many of them.
Where is their Apple Feast of the Saviour?[32] Where is their oil, where is their gas?
They've got unisex, we've got *kvas*,[33]
Iconostasis, Mikhailov Stas...[34]

[Chorus]
The broken ark is going up from the bottom,
And we're going to live forever, and our journey is endless.
We will search for happiness there, where even
The icons of the scary five-storey buildings are crying.

[Verse 2]
They say there's no final destination, we're doomed, and, somewhere
On the shore, someone evil can't stop staring at us angrily,
GMOs and UFOs are sent to us by Satan with cheers,
Garbage and dirt have been lying around here for a long time, soon we'll go
right to the bottom,
But I'm shouting!
Down with the troubled atheistic thoughts,
With the Protestants' dirty feet!
The devil won't take down the unsinkable homeland!
All the people on the streets of Petersburg have seen how
In cursive Cyrillic a great word is neatly formed out of shapeless garbage
and dirt:
Russia! Russia!
Ukraine! Ukraine!

[Bridge]
The heart doesn't long for changes,
Tired Tsoi is napping in the cabin,
The hum of sirens resounds like the singing of a nanny,
And the bullet holes are just like her face.
Sadly, Pussy Riot have taken
The colourful masks off their faces,
They look so good without them, they're so beautiful.

140   *Independent Music in Russia*

Not only did Gyrdymova reinterpret here the same questions of Russia's "special path" that had animated the Russian salons of the nineteenth century, but she also presented them as incomplete and ambiguous. The journey ("where from" and "where to?"), which does not presuppose an end or a start ("we no longer remember"), exemplified the unresolved issues that Russia has faced in its self-identification throughout its history. The West is obviously called into the mix, but it is in this juxtaposition that irony invades both objects of discussion. First of all, the two are immediately and automatically posited in confrontation. Secondly, they are reduced to symbols: the West to unisex toilets, while Russia to natural resources, *kvas*, Orthodoxy and a pro-Putin chanson singer. Thirdly, the image of the West as diabolical Other ruining the fabric of Russian society is reinforced throughout the text: poachers, capitalist Protestants, atheists and even GMOs (partially banned in Russia in 2020 through a "food security" legislation) all conflate into an imagined Western strawman. The point of view coincides with mainstream pro-Putin propaganda, but it is exaggerated to the point of ridicule. On the other hand, Russia, with which the hero overidentifies, stands undefeatable and spiritually pure, yet this equally nationalistic stereotype is undermined by the fact that Russia is an unhappy land, made of junk and doomed. Therefore, to the parody of mainstream messages about the morally decaying West, Monetochka attaches the parody of equally neo-traditionalist enthusiasm about backward, desolated Russia.

Yet, seen through the lens of post-irony, the entire song could be also read in the opposite way – as devotion to the country. The device of defamiliarisation, the impression that something usual is not presented as we know it, together with the emotional overidentification and moral removal of the author, makes laughter give way to doubt, and separating the text's sarcasm from sincerity becomes impossible.

This textual ambivalence is also upheld by the tropes scattered around the lyrics. Oil and gas may well be symbols of power, certifying (as the war in Ukraine then exacerbated) Western dependence on Russia. The crying icon, a good omen in Orthodox religion, symbolises not sadness but an imminent miracle. The crying icon was also featured on *Raskraski*'s cover, echoing the artwork "Freedom to Pussy Riot" painted by Novosibirsk artists Artem Loskutov and Maria Kiseleva, which was displayed in Novosibirsk during the Pussy Riot trial in 2012. Monetochka likely hinted at the commodification Pussy Riot underwent in global popular culture (e.g., by featuring on the American TV show *House of Cards*). The substance of the protest (the balaclava) is replaced by the superficiality of the glamour (their looks), and the painful experiences of Tolokonnikova and Alëkhina are turned upside down. Famously, Tolokonnikova said from prison that "the only person who can legitimately represent the group is a girl in a balaclava" (Marcus 2012). Now that the balaclava is no longer worn, Monetochka seems to ask, what is left of the group and its dissident spirit? As Maria Engström (2018) noted, Pussy Riot are evaluated in "Russkii kovcheg" "as an outdated type of ideological and aesthetic expression". This outdated type, Engström continues, was the open and direct confrontation of art-actionism with the state, rejected by musicians in the late 2010s in favour of more subtle and suspended political enunciations. Rather than pushing the boundaries of whatever was permitted in late 2010s' Russia at their own peril,

"I Live in Russia and I'm Not Scared" 141

musicians preferred the insertion of dissent into a broader and readily available patriotic framework.

Another identifiable trope of the song are the cheap housing buildings (*piatietazhki*) that mushroomed in the late Soviet period. Like the crying icon, these buildings acquire a positive value: they are no longer remnants of a harrowing past, but rather constitute cultural heritage, manifestations of the long and ongoing construction of national character through the endurance of pain. Journalist Yury Saprykin (2018), in an article about Monetochka, commented that such buildings:

> Have their own beauty, but this beauty is born through hardship, tragedy, trauma, inherent discomfort and wrongness [*nepravil'nost'*] of that place. And right there in the strength of hardship and wrongness, this place deserves – let's say it clearly – love.

A recurrent mechanism of inversion is at play here: ugliness becomes beauty, tragedy becomes a test for resilience and, generally, a positive emotional outcome (love) is made out of a negative concrete process (hardship). Both icons and Soviet buildings seem to refer, historically, to the Russians' supposed ability to see sense in pain.

The most important and overarching theme of "Russkii kovcheg" was, however, the future of Russia as a country. The perspective adopted by Monetochka, like in Pasosh's "Rossiia", is one of a collective "we" and from within the action. The image of the Russian ark represents chaos; the disparate people in it are not driving towards a fair system, yet they are united by a strong sense of communal belonging. This is opposed to the nets of the poachers – the West and its values – which are dragging the ark down. And even if broken and facing an uncertain journey, the ark is coming up. It is, as Engström (2018) observed, an upward movement, revolutionary and conservative at the same time. It is not a coincidence that Gyrdymova was coveted by both the liberal intelligentsia and government authorities. On the most famous oppositional media *Meduza*, as well as state-controlled cultural outlet *Russia Beyond*, for example, *Raskraski* was crowned album of the year and the singer elevated to the voice of a generation (Gorbachev 2018; O'Callaghan 2018); at the same time, the Kremlin saw Monetochka in exactly the same terms and tried to co-opt her (*Meduza* 2018), particularly because she joined social critique with patriotism. Conscious of these pulls and ambivalences, the singer did perform on state-controlled Channel One (Vechernii Urgant) but then refused to take the stage in 2018 at *Nashestvie*, Russia's largest music event, due to the display of war weaponry on the festival territory (Kozachenko 2018).

Monetochka exploited the ambiguities around her work playfully and provokingly. For example, during the early live performances of "Russkii kovcheg", Gyrdymova used to raise her fist in the air and shout "Russia! Russia!" ("*Rossiia! Rossiia!*") during the bridge of the song. The crowd, quite expectedly, would join in loudly (Monetochka 2018).[35] In a concert held at Moscow's GlavKlub in January 2019, Monetochka introduced the track by inviting the fans to shout "*Rossiia, Rossiia*". To what seemed like a feeble reaction, the singer teased the fans: "it

142   *Independent Music in Russia*

is very unfriendly and very unpatriotic, as if you came here from another country. Let's try once more!" The fans then shouted "*Rossiia*" increasingly louder, Monetochka incited them but then abruptly cut short: "right, you're ready for it now", after which the music started (Monetochka 2019).

However, such patriotism was also destabilised. If one listens to the album recording of the song in mono, the chant "Russia, Russia!" is counterpointed by the chant "Ukraine, Ukraine!", which is otherwise swallowed in the stereo mix. Monetochka used a recording from a 2014 demonstration in Crimea, in which people of both factions simultaneously shouted the name of the nation to which they wanted to belong (*TV Rain* 2016). Apart from the valence of this metaphor (Russia attempting to overpower and absorb Ukraine), this ingenious audio trick added another layer of unresolved "either/or" and confused the listener further as to what narrative – imperialistic or decolonial, nationalistic or critical – should transpire from the song. The double-voicedness articulated through post-irony, encompassing both studio techniques and live performances, invalidated any unidirectional interpretation. On the one hand, Russia was depicted as a reactionary and regressive organism. On the other hand, this organism was infused with affection in spite of, regardless and because of its flaws, as the recipient of love "no matter what", broken but undefeatable, disorderly but rising. These tensions (or better, metamodern oscillations) were purposefully crafted in "Russkii kovcheg" as irresolvable, in a way that hardly exhausted the song's layers of meaning. The mass popularity of Monetochka as the *enfant prodige* of Russian popular music demonstrates that this was also a highly viable commercial strategy: by nodding simultaneously in multiple liberal and conservative directions, Monetochka was able to attract listeners of different political backgrounds and increase the outreach of her work.

Conclusions

This chapter has illustrated the main changes in *nezavisimaia muzyka* in the mid-2010s in conjunction with the tectonic shifts in Russia's domestic and foreign politics. It has detailed the emergence of the New Russian Wave as the new dominant movement in independent Russian music, which can be broadly defined as DIY, influenced by Soviet post-punk, built on sombre atmospheres, informed by Russia's political isolation, preoccupied with the exploration of nationhood and animated by ambiguous post-irony. In the quest for Russianness, the NRW engaged with culturally intimate tropes of suffering, endurance, *byt*, backwardness and pride which were embedded in the Russians' long-standing investigations around the myth of their country's special path and in the history of Russia-West relations. In *nezavisimaia muzyka*'s exploration of the national character, therefore, similar questions of cultural autonomy affecting politics surfaced in a rhizomatic manner.

At the level of linguistics, the NRW hailed a return to the use of Russian after a period of Anglophone prominence in *nezavisimaia muzyka*. Influenced by the socio-political changes around them, independent practitioners fashioned an aesthetic aura around music in the vernacular to the detriment of domestic Anglophone groups. However binary or essentialised this opposition may seem, it was strongly

"*I Live in Russia and I'm Not Scared*" 143

felt (and constructed) by the participants themselves. For the community, English and Russian were not simply languages. When applied to music they embodied two distinct sets of values: the former epitomised global membership, and the latter signified aesthetic difference and cultural specificity. Both sets of values, however, originated from the same idea of membership in an imagined community (Anderson 1983). As discussed in Chapter One, the fact that individuals join a specific group on the perception of having something in common with its members (but without knowing them) can be used to fashion both nationalism and cosmopolitanism. It is the difference in the participants' affiliation that creates dynamic tensions, out of which dominant and subordinate narratives take shape within cultural communities.

However small-sized, commercially niche, or self-professed as independent, a music movement is therefore not immune to internal struggles for leadership over meaning-making that are influenced by geopolitical events and external official discourse, regardless of the political orientation of its participants. The linguistic conflict in *nezavisimaia muzyka*, for example, signalled not only the end of Medvedev's cosmopolitan Russia, but also unveiled the blur between anti-globalist pushbacks and the return of "the national" both in politics and in independent culture.

Nonetheless, these various points of convergence between *nezavisimaia muzyka* and party politics did not signify their complicit alliance. Grassroots practitioners hacked, mocked, reworked, plasticised and eventually ambiguated top-down nationalism. The musical products that emerged in mid-2010s Russia and achieved widespread popularity among the youth, while informed by cultural intimacy, created a version of Russianness that fluctuated between pain and posturing of pain, backwardness and pride in backwardness, condemnation and commendation, reprobation and enthusiasm. Key in this operation was the use of post-irony as a twice-turned-over statement that simultaneously maintained its literal connotation, advanced its ironic contradiction and created a defamiliarising blend of the two. Practitioners interacted dialogically with this blend, by refraining willingly from giving any ultimate moral judgement while dissolving themselves into their subject matter, Russia, through overidentification with it.

This was not a postmodernist closed circle, but an open-ended spiral, its movement not repetitive or mirrored, but dialectical and progressive: in one word, recursive (Hutchings 2022, 169). In this spiral, the nationhood projected by grassroots music practitioners was at the same time full of anxieties and irony but also interactive with official discourse. Similarly, this interaction showed not just signs of postmodern resignation to an invincible doom, but also modern vitality in adding one's own personal voice to discussions about the country, whatever the circumstances. In a metamodern fashion, independent music practitioners were conscious of the inevitable disruption or even insignificance of their grand narrative of Russia but sought to project it all the same. In order not to exhaust the song's aesthetic, ethical and commercial potential, what was imagined to be "Russian" was indeed post-ironised and made elusive to any final explanation, in a survival strategy that addressed the nations' problems and evaded the authorities' scrutiny. The next chapter will detail how this subtle response concerned also the performance of political protest, as well as how the state, in chaotic and contradictory ways, reacted to it.

144 *Independent Music in Russia*

Notes

1 Up until Putin's third term, the idea of multipolarity had been popping up in different fields of Russian society and among actors with different political beliefs, in a rather non-linear, rhizomatic fashion. It was for example championed by Yeltsin's prime minister Yevgeny Primakov in the late 1990s (and re-presented by Putin in his 2007 Munich Speech), articulated by Neo-Eurasianist, "far-right" philosopher Aleksandr Dugin (one of the main ideologues of Russia's civilisational turn but in the 1990s dwelling on the fringes of discourse), and by a series of intellectuals of various camps concerned about Russia's post-Soviet Americanisation (see Pilkington et al. 2002).
2 See for example Randall (2005); Illiano and Sala (2010); Machin-Autenrieth et al. (2023) whose edited volumes deal with disparate authoritarian contexts in South and Central America, Europe, Asia and Middle East.
3 With exceptions, such as Party (2010) and Ibrahim (2016).
4 See, for example: Cushman (1995); McMichael (2005); Steinholt and Wickström (2009); Wickström (2014); Rogatchevski and Steinholt (2016); Engström (2021).
5 As observed during fieldwork in 2017, the arsenal attracted considerable interest among the festival goers. Children and youngsters – some even dressed as hippies – climbed onto the tanks, took photographs and interacted with the military officers.
6 As I argued previously (Biasioli 2021), the tendency to sideline English-speaking groups could also be seen a bottom-up inflection of cultural sovereignty. As Krasner (2007) has it, cultural sovereignty is the existence of an authoritative decision-making structure (the state) within the culture of a political entity. This structure decides what type of culture is adequate (or inadequate) in relation to the idea of the nation that the state is trying to achieve. In the case of Russia, this cultural filter was embedded, top-down, in a project of "national security" (*natsional'naia bezopasnost'*) devoted to the preservation of national values, and, consequently, to the defence from threats to these national values. Clause 79 of the "Decree of the President of the Russian Federation" (31 December 2015), *On the National Security Strategy of the Russian Federation*, said:

> Threats to national security in the field of culture are the blurring of traditionally Russian spiritual and moral values and the weakening of the unity of the multinational people of the Russian Federation by *foreign cultural and information expansion* (including the distribution of substandard products of *mass culture*) […] and the *reduction in the importance of the role played by the Russian language* in the world.
> (Putin 2015) [emphasis added]

This defensive attitude served to counter the spread of foreign cultural artefacts (in the policy's view, this culture is in all likelihood West-defined) perceived as detrimental to presupposed traditional values and interests. Regardless of the political view of the *nezavisimaia muzyka* practitioners, this dichotomy between inside and outside, between "ours" and "not ours" was often replicated on a smaller scale in their daily practice of fashioning meaning around music. Thus, over the 2010s, the official values animating the zeitgeist influenced grassroots cultural producers, irrespective of whether these values were resisted, endorsed or both.

7 As explained in the next chapter, the coalescence between artistic and civic position in *nezavisimaia muzyka* gave rise also to direct forms of protest towards the end of the 2010s and the beginning of the 2020s. Metamodernism is therefore one of the responses to the increasingly authoritarian political climate in Russia.
8 Samoe bol'shoe prostoe chislo is an indie band, established in St. Petersburg in 2006. The band emigrated after February 2022.
9 Vasily Zorky is a Russian musician, journalist and writer. In 2022–2023, he travelled around Europe playing small gigs, raising funds and trying to contribute to build a sense of unity and purpose for the Russian anti-war émigré community (Kanunnikova 2023).

10 Krasnoznamĕnnaia diviziia imeni moei babushka is an alternative rock collective founded in Moscow in 2008.

11 Glintshake is a Russian avant-garde/indie rock band, known for their eclectic sound, experimentation and absurdist lyrics, formed in Moscow in 2012. NRKTK (short for Narkotiki [Drugs]) was an indie duo, active in Moscow between 2007 and 2012. Inturist is an art rock project, established in the late 2010s.

12 Levada Centre was labelled a foreign agent by the Russian government in 2021.

13 Note the difference between "New Russian Wave" and "Russian New Wave" – the latter may overlap too much with the Soviet New Wave of the 1980s. Changing the order of the words allowed this "wave" to be refashioned as something new, while linking with the Soviet predecessor. Also interesting is that the title alone aimed to attach the sound to the nation, as in the case of Brit-Pop, K-Pop, J-Pop, It-Pop and so on, in the attempt to mould a form of music that could epitomise the country's "essence". However, here this essence is not *rossiiskaia*, but *russkaia*: while this may be a result of the willingness to stress the linguistic aspect of the movement (the Russian language was a fundamental component of the genre), the formulation had ethnic overtones and revealed a certain unawareness of Russia's status of empire.

14 The St. Petersburg festival stemming from the activity of the club Ionoteka, managed by music entrepreneur Aleksandr Ionov.

15 An electronic, dark witch-house band (see next chapter).

16 Some examples are: "Simfonicheskoe Kino" (Symphonic Kino), an orchestral and instrumental remake of Tsoi's songs, which premiered at indie festival *Stereoleto* in 2017; "My vse vyshli iz Kino" (We all came out of Kino), a compilation of Kino's cover songs performed by contemporary musicians as a tribute to Tsoi's 55th birthday, which came out also in 2017 thanks to the initiative of *Meduza* and various *indi* labels; Kirill Serebrennikov's film *Leto* (Summer), released in 2018, which describes the early days of the Leningrad independent scene and has Tsoi as one of its protagonists; and Aleksei Uchitel's 2021 release of *Tsoi*, a film centred on the car accident in which the singer lost his life. But Viktor Tsoi's legacy as a post-Soviet pop icon has made him appealing to power as well, which has sought to appropriate his image and influence over the youth (Hillen 2020).

17 The National Bolshevik Party (NBP) was a mixture of far-left and far-right discourse united under the banner of nationalism, and it represented a fringe party in the Russian system (it never made it to the parliament). Nonetheless, in the 1990s it attracted a considerable number of musicians, including Sergei Kurĕkhin. Aleksandr Dugin, currently one of the most renowned ideologues of Russian nationalism and the multipolar world, was its co-founder.

18 *Meduza* is a news company registered in Riga, Latvia. It was declared a foreign agent by the Russian government in 2021.

19 This is factually inaccurate, as MTV Russia showed Russian performers as well as foreign ones. However, it may be indicative of a certain perception of foreign musical initiatives as stifling the development of Russia's own culture.

20 Similarly to *Nashestvie* in the mainstream, *Bol'* relied on a consistent line-up of "regular" bands. Out of the five iterations of the festival, 35 bands played twice, and eight performed three times.

21 Aleksandr Gorbachev, public Facebook post, July 8, 2019.

22 As observed during fieldwork in 2017.

23 https://concertinfo.ru/gig/9977/

24 Siberia has occupied a particular place in the Russians' mind. Because of its remoteness from the centres of the Empire and its harsh weather conditions, Siberia became a dumping ground for exiles in Imperial Russia, and gulag camps proliferated there in the Soviet Union. The discourse of Siberia was constructed in European Imperial Russia on terms borrowed from the West European colonial experience, such as Russia's "own Peru" or "Russian Brazil", even if the majority of the local population consisted already

146　*Independent Music in Russia*

of ethnic Russians since the mid-eighteenth century (Bassin 1991, 770; 2012; Tolz 2001, 163). Siberia thus became in the Russian imagination an unappealing land where the opposites of European Russia were consigned (Figes 2002, 379). At the same time, Siberia is also what makes Russia such a vast expanse, and geographical vastness constitutes one of the reasons for pride in Russian political and intellectual discourse. With the discovery of natural resources, the region became the source of most of Russia's wealth as well. Because of its isolation and lack of infrastructure until very recently, Siberian music, particularly punk, developed distinctive forms and ideas that originated from the constraints of every-day low life. As Gololobov et al. (2014, 26–27, 37–41) observe, one of them was "shittiness" (in sound, equipment, fashion and technique) as a distinctive, positive marker. As the authors write, local punks "did not try to avoid [this] "shittiness", but promoted and celebrated it as the true enactment of punk. Thus, in the Russian regions, lived and performed low life became an ambiguous but powerful gesture of exhibiting the social status of local subculture. This gestured was performed vis-à-vis the centres of Moscow and St. Petersburg as an embodiment of authenticity, in the same way in which NRW musicians working in the capitals would construct their low life vis-à-vis Western music and trends (see also Drew 2023).

25　Cherepanov's singing style is very similar to that of Vasily Shumov, leader of the Soviet band Tsentr (Centre), who also deployed Russian stereotypes in his art and, not coincidentally, can also be seen as a (proto)metamodernist (see Saprykin 2018).

26　https://www.youtube.com/watch?v=wcaZcbain2s&t=26s.

27　https://www.youtube.com/watch?v=jxLYYf5bz0M.

28　*Pasosh* means "passport" in Serbian. The band's singer, Petar Martic, was born in Serbia and moved to Russia during his childhood.

29　This theme of the "dead undead" would be reprised by the band Ic3peak a few years later, for their famous single "Smerti bol'she net" (Death Is No More).

30　On the combined use of Shklovsky's *ostranenie* and Bakhtin's *ustranenie* see Emerson (2005).

31　In her later works (2020–2022), Monetochka took an increasingly clear stance of political opposition. After Russia's invasion of Ukraine, she and the rapper Ivan Alekseev (Noize MC) went on a charity tour around Europe fundraising for victims of the war. During the concerts Monetochka would read one of her latest poems, "Khui voine" ("Fuck the War"). An excerpt goes: "My voice will be brave/even if they tie my hands/ and press my cheeks against the wall/I will whisper 'fuck the war'". Upon her return, Gyrdymova left Russia and relocated in Riga, Latvia. To explain the move, the singer said she was tired of speaking in metaphors and wanted to feel free about her words (RBK 2022).

32　Apple Feast of the Savior (Iablochnii Spas) is a Slavic folk celebration day (19 August) in honour of the Transfiguration of Jesus.

33　Traditional Russian beverage made out of fermented rye bread.

34　Stas Mikhailov is a famous Russian pop and chanson singer, a People's Artist of Russia and an ardent supporter of Putin's politics, including the war in Ukraine. Whilst very successful in the Russian mainstream, he has been criticised for his "utter mediocrity" (Troitsky in *Ekspress Gazeta* 2011) and "bad music, disgustingly arranged and with horrible vocals" (Grishkovets 2012 in *Argumenty i Fakty* 2012).

35　During her 2022 charity tour around Europe, Monetochka replaced the lines "Russia, Russia" with "*net voine*" (no to war).

References

3voor12 extra. 2020. 'Shortparis: dismantling ideas about Russian identity'. 7 March. URL: https://www.youtube.com/watch?v=Jr-u8bLJXG4&fbclid=IwAR096HAnDINaOj1T2u HQYI2kzEYtUomU1G4fBjqLSHBvtnFf9ySze769yUU (accessed 7 May 2020).

Afisha. 2011. 'Afisha sostavila spisok samykh iarkikh i zapomnivshikhsia russkikh pop-khitov za poślednie 20 let'. Undated. URL: https://daily.afisha.ru/archive/volna/archive/pop/ (accessed 26 September 2023).

Afisha. 2012a. 'Russkie muzykanty o Pussy Riot'. *Afisha*, 6 August. URL: https://daily.afisha.ru/archive/gorod/archive/russkie-muzikanti-o-pussy-riot/ (last accessed 7 May 2020).

Afisha. 2012b. 'Muzyka dolzhna oskorbit' chuvstva. Noize MC, Vasia Oblomov, Evgenii Gorbunov, i drugie obsuzhdaiut, pochemu molodye russkie gruppy ne poiut o politike'. 11 September.

Anderson, B. 1983. *Imagined Communities: Reflections on the Origin and Spread of Nationalism*. London: Verso.

Argumenty i fakty. 2012. 'Evgenii Grishkovets: 'ia ne hochu zhit' nigde, krome Rossii''. 15 February. URL: https://kuzbass.aif.ru/culture/theatre/96244 (accessed 7 May 2020).

Barabanov, B. 2019. 'V poryadke khaosa'. *Kommersant*, 7 July. URL: https://www.kommersant.ru/doc/4025227 (accessed 6 July 2020).

Bassin, M. 1991. 'Inventing Siberia: Visions of the Russian East in the Early Nineteenth Century'. *The American Historical Review*, 96, 3, pp. 763–94.

Bassin, M. 2012. 'Asia'. In Rzhevsky, N. (ed.) *The Cambridge Companion to Modern Russian Culture*. Cambridge: Cambridge University Press, pp. 65–93.

Beck, U. 2006. *The Cosmopolitan Vision*. Cambridge: Polity.

Beumers, B., Etkind, A., Gurova, O., Turoma, S. (eds.). 2017. *Cultural Forms of Protest in Russia*. London: Routledge.

Biasioli, M. 2021. 'Russophone or Anglophone? The Politics of Identity in Contemporary Russian Indie Music'. *Europe-Asia Studies*, 73, 4, pp. 673–90.

Biasioli, M. 2023. 'Songwashing: Russian Popular Music, Distraction, and Putin's Fourth Term'. *The Russian Review*, 82, 4, pp. 682–704.

Borenstein, E. 2021. *Pussy Riot: Speaking Punk to Power*. New York: Bloomsbury Academic.

Chukhrov, K. 2020. *Practicing the Good: Desire and Boredom in Soviet Socialism*. Minneapolis: University of Minnesota Press.

Colta.ru. 2012. 'Kreativnyi klass v Rossii: kto eti liudi?' 28 August. URL: https://archives.colta.ru/docs/4829 (accessed 5 November 2021).

Colta.ru. 2020. 'Buerak: "tekst i minor, vot v chem dusha russkoi pesni"'. 1 April. URL: https://www.colta.ru/articles/music_modern/23960-geroi-novogo-russkogo-roka-duet-buerak-rasskazyvayut-v-chem-ih-identichnost?fbclid=IwAR1E84I0BoRcHWkx5GOXRrFff4THXHwQ6wve63rsZhxgsWMkQpP6M-Uo-sU (accessed 7 May 2020).

Crossley, N. 2015. *Networks of Sound, Style and Subversion: The Punk and Post-Punk Worlds of Manchester, London, Liverpool and Sheffield, 1975–80*. Manchester: Manchester University Press.

Cushman, T. 1995. *Notes from the Underground: Rock Music Counterculture in Russia*. New York: State University of New York Press.

Deleuze, G., Guattari, F. 1987. *A Thousand Plateaus*. Minneapolis: University of Minnesota Press.

DiMaggio, P. 1987. 'Classification in Art'. *American Sociological Review*, 52, 4, pp. 440–55.

Drew, T. 2023. *Situating Svoi: Nonconformism and Intrainstitutional Autonomy in Late-Soviet Novosibirsk*. Unpublished PhD thesis, University of Manchester.

Ekspress Gazeta. 2011. 'Prigozhin i Troitsky razgadali secret uspekha Vaengi'. 17 February. URL: https://www.eg.ru/showbusiness/24192/ (accessed 7 May 2020).

Emerson, C. 2005. 'Shklovsky's *Ostranenie*, Bakhtin's *Vnenakhodimost'* (How Distance Serves an Aesthetics of Arousal Differently from an Aesthetics Based on Pain)'. *Poetics Today*, 26, 4, pp. 637–64.

Engström, M. 2018. 'Monetochka: The Manifesto of Metamodernism'. *Riddle*, 26 June. https://www.ridl.io/en/monetochka-the-manifesto-of-metamodernism/ (accessed 7 May 2020).

Engström, M. 2021. 'Recycling of the Post-Soviet Counterculture, and the New Aesthetics of the 'Second World'. *Novoe Literaturnoe Obozrenie*, 169, pp. 70–88.

148 *Independent Music in Russia*

Eshchenepozner. 2019. 'Iurii Saprykin: Limonov i Parkhomenko, filosofy i khipstery'. 7 March. URL: https://www.youtube.com/watch?v=GvqVow4e01E&feature=youtu. be&fbclid=IwAR17ni26p2DCrkMaH7lYFh-YvDYf4UEWCgwq_5T6C_S1IZx_ w8QazI5v1Xo (accessed 8 May 2020).

Etkind, A. 2017. 'Introduction: Genres and Genders of Protest in Russia's Petrostate'. In Beumers, B., Etkind, A., Gurova, O., Turoma, S. (eds.) *Cultural Forms of Protest in Russia*. London: Routledge (e-book version).

Figes, O. 2002. *Natasha's Dance. A Cultural History of Russia*. London: Penguin.

Foster, R. 2019. 'New Weird Russia – Part One: Sampler'. *The Quietus*, 10 January. URL: https://thequietus.com/articles/25864-new-weird-russia-shortparis-glintshake-review (accessed 7 May 2020).

Frolova-Walker, M. 1997. 'On "Ruslan" and Russianness'. *Cambridge Opera Journal*, 9, 1, pp. 21–45.

Frolova-Walker, M. 2004. 'Music of the Soul'? In Franklin, S., Widdis, E. (eds.) *National Identity in Russian Culture*. New York: Cambridge University Press, pp. 116–31.

Gel'man, V. (ed.). 2017. *Authoritarian Modernization in Russia: Ideas, Institutions and Policies*. London: Routledge.

Gololobov, I., Pilkington, H., Steinholt, Y. 2014. *Punk in Russia: Cultural Mutation from the 'Useless' to the 'Moronic'*. Oxon: Routledge.

Golubkova, K., Baczynksa, G. 2014. 'Rouble fall, sanctions hurt Russia's economy: Medvedev'. *Reuters*, 10 December. URL: https://www.reuters.com/article/us-russia-medvedev-sanctions-idUSKBN0JO0SR20141210 (accessed 16 October 2021).

Gorbachev, A. 2010. 'Tesla Boy, 'Modern Thrills': Moskovskii sint-pop na eksport'. *Afisha*, 24 May.

Gorbachev, A. 2011. 'English First: pochemu russkie gruppi ne poiut po-russki'. *Afisha*, 13 April. URL: https://www.afisha.ru/article/englishfirst/ (accessed 20 May 2020).

Gorbachev, A. 2012a. 'A ty chego hotel by? Chtoby my igrali na gusliakh'. *Afisha*, 2 November.

Gorbachev, A. 2012b. 'Premera al'boma On-The-Go 'November''. *Afisha*, December. URL: https://daily.afisha.ru/archive/volna/archive/on-the-go_november/ (accessed 7 May 2020).

Gorbachev, A. 2018. 'Avtor pesni "Mama, ia ne ziguiu" Monetochka zapisala luchshii russkii pop-al.'bom goda. Ser'ëzno? (Da)'. *Meduza*, 25 May. URL: https://meduza.io/ slides/avtor-pesni-mama-ya-ne-ziguyu-monetochka-zapisala-luchshiy-russkiy-pop-album-goda-seriezno-da (accessed 3 November 2023).

Gorbachev, A. 2019. 'Epokha Zemfiry i mumiy troll zakonchilas. Teper' vsyo inache'. *Meduza*, 2 January. URL: https://meduza.io/feature/2019/01/02/epoha-zemfiry-i-mumiy-trollya-zakonchilas-teper-vse-inache (accessed 30 May 2020).

Groys, B. 2009. 'Comrades of Time'. *E-Flux*, 11, pp. 1–11.

Herzfeld, M. 2004. *Cultural Intimacy: Social Poetics in the Nation-State*. New York and London: Routledge.

Hillen, S.P. 2020. *Nationalism and Its Discontents: Transformations of Identity in Contemporary Russian Music on and off the Web*. Doctoral dissertation, Arizona State University.

Hudspith, S. 2004. *Dostoevsky and the Idea of Russianness*. London and New York: Routledge.

Hutchings, S. 2022. *Projecting Russia in a Mediatized World Recursive Nationhood*. London: Routledge.

Huttunen, T. 2012. 'Autogenesis in Russian Culture: An Approach to the Avant-Garde'. In Alapuro, R., Mustajoki, A., Pesonen, P. (eds.) *Understanding Russianness*. Oxon: Routledge, pp. 165–82.

Ibrahim, Z. 2016. 'Disciplining Rock and Identity Contestations: Hybridization, Islam and New Musical Genres in Contemporary Malaysian Popular Music'. *Situations*, 9, 1, pp. 21–47.

Illiano, R., Sala, M. (eds.) 2010. *Music and Dictatorship in Europe and Latin America*. Turnhout: Brepols Publishers.

Kanunnikova, O. 2023. 'Seichas ia vizhu ogromnuiu set' vzaimopomoshchi: rossiiskii muzykant i zhurnalist Vasilii Zorkii'. *Novaia gazeta*, 14 February. URL: https://novayagazeta. ee/articles/2023/02/15/seichas-ia-vizhu-ogromnuiu-set-vzaimopomoshchi-rossiiskii-muzykant-i-zhurnalist-vasilii-zorkii (accessed 2 April 2024).

Karmunin, O. 2019. Post on his Telegram Channel. *Russkii Shaffl*, 25 September. URL: https://t.me/rushuffle/878.

Khrushcheva, N. 2020. *Metamodern v muzyke i vokrug neë*. Moskva: Ripol Klassik.

Kitchin, R. 2022. 'Afterword: Decentering the smart city'. In *Equality in the City: Imaginaries of the Smart Future*, ed. Susan Flynn (forthcoming), pp. 1–8 (online working paper), https://mural.maynoothuniversity.ie/14646/1/RK-Decentring-2021.pdf.

Kølsto, P. 2016. 'Introduction: Russian Nationalism Is Back – but Precisely What Does That Mean?' In Kolstø, P., Blakkisrud, H. (eds.) *The New Russian Nationalism: Imperialism, Ethnicity and Authoritarianism 2000–15*. Edinburgh: Edinburgh University Press, pp. 1–17.

Korhonen, I. 2019. 'Economic Sanctions on Russia and Their Effects'. *CESifo Forum*, 4, 20, pp. 19–22. URL: https://www.ifo.de/DocDL/CESifo-Forum-2019-4-korhonen-economic-sanctions-december.pdf (accessed 16 October 2021).

Kozachenko, D. 2018. Poshlaya Molli, Monetochka i eshe neskolko artistov otkazalis' ot uchastia v festivale Nashestvie. *Afisha*, 24 July. Available from: https://daily.afisha.ru/ news/18625-tri-gruppy-otkazalis-ot-uchastiya-v-nashestvii-festival-sotrudnichaet-s-ministerstvom-oborony/ (accessed 6 July 2020).

Krasner, S.D. 2007. 'Sovereignty'. In Ritzer, G. (ed.) *The Blackwell Encyclopedia of Sociology*. Hoboken, NJ: Wiley Blackwell. URL: https://doi.org/10.1002/9781405165518. wbeoss213 (accessed 19 March 2020).

'Kvartirnik NTV u Margulisa: Gruppa Pompeya.' 24 November 2018. URL: https://www. youtube.com/watch?v=a15cEECAP6Q (last accessed 17 May 2020).

Laruelle, M. 2016. 'Russia as an Anti-Liberal European Civilisation'. In Kolstø, P., Blakkisrud, H. (eds.) *The New Russian Nationalism: Imperialism, Ethnicity and Authoritarianism 2000–15*. Edinburgh: Edinburgh University Press, pp. 275–97.

Laruelle, M., Engström, M. 2018. 'Vizualnaia Kultura i Ideologiia'. *Kontrapunkt*, 12, pp. 1–17.

Laruelle, M. 2019. *Russian Nationalism. Imaginaries, Doctrines, and Political Battlefields*. London: Basees/Routledge.

Lenta.ru. 2012. 'Sledstvennyi komitet izuchit video s izbieniem uchastnitsy 'Marsha millionov". 10 May. URL: https://lenta.ru/news/2012/05/10/skrf/ (accessed 30 May 2020).

Levada Centre. 2017a. 'Gordost' za stranu i narod'. 21 December. URL: https://www.levada.ru/2017/12/21/17311/ (accessed 15 February 2019).

Levada Centre. 2017b. 'Velikoderzhavnye nastroeniya v Rossii dostigli istoricheskogo maksimuma'. 21 December. URL: https://www.levada.ru/2017/12/21/velikoderzhavnye-nastroeniya-v-rossii-dostigli-istoricheskogo-maksimuma/ (accessed 15 February 2019).

Levada Centre. 2018a. 'Otnoshenie k stranam'. 12 February. URL: https://www.levada. ru/2018/02/12/otnoshenie-k-stranam/ (accessed 26 May 2020).

Levada Centre. 2018b. 'Rossiya i Zapad'. 2 August. URL: https://www.levada.ru/2018/08/02/ rossiya-i-zapad-3/ (accessed 26 May 2020).

Levada Centre. 2020. 'Velikaia derzhava'. 28 January. URL: https://www.levada. ru/2020/01/28/velikaya-derzhava/ (accessed 30 July 2024).

Levchenko, L. 2019. 'Bol konkuriruet s festivaliami so vsego mira'. *The Village*, 2 June. URL: https://www.the-village.ru/village/weekend/industry/355295-bol (accessed 30 May 2020).

Machin-Autenrieth, M., Castelo-Branco, S.E.-S., Llano, S. (eds.). 2023. *Music and the Making of Portugal and Spain: Nationalism and Identity Politics in the Iberian Peninsula*. University of Illinois Press.

Malinova, O. 2014. 'Obsession With Status and *Ressentiment*: Historical Backgrounds of the Russian Discursive Identity Construction'. *Communist and Post-Communist Studies*, 47, pp. 291–303.

150 *Independent Music in Russia*

Malinova, O. 2017. 'Political Uses of the Great Patriotic War in Post-Soviet Russia from Yeltsin to Putin'. In Fedor, J., Kangaspuro, M., Lassila, J., Zhurzhenko, T. (eds.) *War and Memory in Russia, Ukraine and Belarus*. London: Palgrave.

Marcus, S. 2012. 'Reading the Pussy Riot Act'. *Book Forum*, 19 October. URL: https://www.bookforum.com/culture/reading-the-pussy-riot-act-10340 (accessed 3 November 2023).

McMichael, P. 2005. "After All, You're a Rock Star (At Least, That's What They Say)': Roksi and the Creation of the Soviet Rock Musician'. *Slavonic and East European Review*, 83, 4, pp. 664–84.

McMichael, P. 2013. 'Defining Pussy Riot Musically: Performance and Authenticity in New Media'. *Digital Icons: Studies in Russian, Eurasian and Central European New Media*, 9, pp. 99–113.

Meduza. 2017. 'Piat' let 'Bolotnomu delu'. Desiat' istorii ego uchastnikov'. 6 May. URL: https://meduza.io/feature/2017/05/06/pyat-let-bolotnomu-delu-desyat-istoriy-ego-uchastnikov (accessed 30 May 2020).

Meduza. 2018. The Kremlin is Supposedly Looking for Russia's Next Patriotic pop Star, and it Reportedly wants Monetochka. 3 August. Available from: https://meduza.io/en/feature/2018/08/03/the-kremlin-is-supposedly-looking-for-russia-s-next-patriotic-pop-star-and-it-reportedly-wants-monetochka (accessed 6 July 2020).

Monetochka. 2018. 'Russkii kovcheg'. URL: https://www.youtube.com/watch?time_continue=1&v=WPXY38Zq8Os (accessed 7 May 2020).

Monetochka. 2019. 'Russkii kovcheg'. https://vk.com/video52244129_456239050 (accessed 7 May 2020).

Morozov, V. 2015. *Russia's Post-Colonial Identity: A Subaltern Empire in a Eurocentric World*. Basingstoke: Palgrave Macmillan.

Nashestvie. 2016 'www.nashestvie.ru' (accessed 5 December 2016).

Neumann, I.B. 2016. 'Russia's Europe 1991–2016: Inferiority to Superiority'. *International Affairs*, 92, 6, pp. 1381–99.

O'Callaghan, T. 2018. 'Meet Monetochka, the Popstar Fast Becoming the Face of Young Russia'. *Russia Beyond*, 9 July. URL: https://www.rbth.com/arts/328716-meet-monetochka-popstar-adult-coloring-books (accessed 20 June 2024).

Olson, L.J. 2004. *Performing Russia: Folk Revival and Russian Identity*. London and New York: Routledge.

Oushakine, S. 2009. *The Patriotism of Despair: Nation, War and Loss in Russia*. Ithaca, NY: Cornell University Press.

Party, D. 2010. 'Beyond 'Protest Song': Popular Music in Pinochet's Chile (1973–1990)'. In Illiano, R., Sala, M. (eds.) *Music and Dictatorship in Europe and Latin America*. Turnhout: Brepols Publishers, pp. 671–84.

Pesmen, D. 2000. *Russia and Soul*. Ithaca, NY: Cornell University Press.

Pilkington, H., Omelchenko, E., Flynn, M., Bluidina, U., Starkova, E. 2002. *Looking West? Cultural Globalization and Russian Youth Cultures*. Philadelphia: Pennsylvania State University Press.

Puchkarev, A. 2022. 'Otets Tsoia zaiavil, chto ego syn był patriotom i podderzhal by spetsoperatsiiu na Ukraine'. *Daily Storm*, 16 May. URL: https://dailystorm.ru/kultura/otec-coya-zayavil-chto-ego-syn-byl-patriotom-i-podderzhal-by-specoperaciyu-na-ukraine (accessed 19 September 2023).

Putin, V.V. 2015. 'Ukaz Prezidenta Rossiiskoi Federatsii ot 31 dekabria 2015 N 683, 'O strategii natsional'noi bezopasnosti Rossiiskoi Federatsii''. *Rossiiskaia Gazeta*, 31 December. URL: https://rg.ru/2015/12/31/nac-bezopasnost-site-dok.html (accessed 9 March 2020).

Radio Free Europe. 2012a. 'More Western Rock 'N' Roll Solidarity for Pussy Riot'. 23 July. URL: https://www.rferl.org/a/transmission-pussy-riot-red-hot-chili-peppers-franz-ferdinand-support/24653735.html (accessed 5 May 2020).

Radio Free Europe. 2012b. 'Madonna Protests Pussy Riot Detention at Moscow Concert'. 2 August. URL: https://www.rferl.org/a/madonna-protests-pussy-riot-detention-at-moscow-concert/24670081.html (accessed 30 May 2020).

"I Live in Russia and I'm Not Scared" 151

Rancour-Laferriere, D. 1995. *The Slave Soul of Russia: Moral Masochism and the Cult of Suffering*. New York: New York University Press.

Randall, A. (ed.) 2005. *Music, Power and Politics*. New York and London: Routledge.

RBK. 2022. 'Pevitsa Monetochka ob'iasnila ot'ezd iz Rossii'. 8 May. URL: https://www.rbc.ru/society/08/05/2022/6277dba49a79472b193e5931 (accessed 31 July 2022).

Rogatchevski, A., Steinholt, Y. 2016. 'Pussy Riot's Musical Precursors? The National Bolshevik Party Bands, 1994–2007'. *Popular Music and Society*, 39, 4, pp. 448–64.

Romakhov, D. 2016. 'Muzykal'nyi festival' "Bol": zdes' Bolshe vsego griazi, zhira i eksperimentov'. *Afisha*, 1 July. URL: https://daily.afisha.ru/music/2123-muzykalnyy-festival-bol-zdes-bolshe-vsego-gryazi-zhira-i-eksperimentov/ (accessed 5 May 2020)

Rutland, P. 2014. 'The Pussy Riot Affair: Gender and National Identity in Putin's Russia'. *Nationalities Papers*, 42, 4, pp. 575–82.

Ryazanova-Clarke, L. 2012. 'The 'West' in the Linguistic Construction of Russianness in Contemporary Public Discourse'. In Alapuro, R., Mustajoki, A., Pesonen, P. (eds.) *Understanding Russianness*. Oxon: Routledge, pp. 3–18.

Sakwa, R. 2017. 'The Age of Eurasia'? In Bassin, M., Pozo, G. (eds.) *The Politics of Eurasianism: Identity, Popular Culture and Russia's Foreign Policy*. London and New York: Rowman & Littlefield International, pp. 201–20.

Saprykin, Y. 2018. 'Neprivichnaia Rossiia. Molodost' v mnogoetazhkakh'. *Seans*, 23 August. https://seance.ru/articles/neprivychnaya-rossiya-2/ (accessed 2 March 2020).

Sharafutdinova, G. 2014. 'The Pussy Riot Affair and Putin's Démarche from Sovereign Democracy to Sovereign Morality'. *Nationalities Papers*, 42, 4, pp. 615–21.

Sharafutdinova, G. 2020. *The Red Mirror: Putin's Leadership and Russia's Insecure Identity*. Oxford: Oxford University Press.

Shklovsky, V. 2016 (1917). 'Art as Device'. In Berlina, A. (ed.) *Viktor Shklovsky: A Reader*. London: Bloomsbury, pp. 73–96.

Smertach Daily. 2019. Post on Telegram Channel. 5 July 2019. URL: https://t.me/russ-death/4050 (accessed 30 October 2023).

Smith-Maguire, J., Matthews, J. (eds.). 2014. *The Cultural Intermediaries Reader*. London: Sage.

Steinholt, Y. 2013. 'Kitten Heresy: Lost Contexts of Pussy Riot's Punk Prayer'. *Popular Music and Society*, 36, 1, pp. 120–24.

Steinholt, Y., Wickström, D.E. 2009. 'Visions of the (Holy) Motherland in Contemporary Russian Popular Music: Nostalgia, Patriotism and Ruskii Rok'. *Popular Music and Society*, 32, 3, pp. 313–30.

Surkov, V. 2018. 'Odinochestvo polukrovki'. *Rossiia v globalnom politike*, 9 April. URL: https://globalaffairs.ru/global-processes/Odinochestvo-polukrovki-14-19477 (accessed 5 May 2020).

TASS. 2021. 'Russian Diplomat Zakharova Slams EU's New Set of Sanctions Against Russia as Hypocrisy'. 14 October. URL: https://tass.com/world/1349691 (accessed 16 October 2021).

Tolz, V. 2010. 'The West'. In Leatherbarrow, W.J., Offord, D. (eds.) *A History of Russian Thought*. Cambridge University Press, pp. 197–216.

Turino, T. 2008. *Music as Social Life. The Politics of Participation*. Chicago: The University of Chicago Press.

TV Rain. 2016. 'Miting v Krimu v marte 2014: polovina tolpy skandiruet 'Rossiia!', drugaia – 'Ukraina!'". YouTube, 18 March. URL: https://www.youtube.com/watch?v=CDaPtGQ6Jog&t=7s (accessed 2 November 2023).

Vdud'. 2020. 'Monetochka – novyi zhizn', novyi dom, novyi al'bom'. YouTube, 20 October. URL: https://www.youtube.com/watch?v=SgV0-0puqWM&t=4148s (accessed 10 November 2024).

Vecher s Kiber Frontom. 2023. 'Esli by Egor Letov dozhil do nashikh vremën, kakuiu by storonu on prinial v konflikte s Ukrainoi'? *Rutube*, February. URL: https://rutube.ru/video/0e5c1c9a15cc29132e13d8466fe5ef3a/ (accessed 19 September 2023).

152   *Independent Music in Russia*

Vermeulen, T., Van den Akker, R. 2010. 'Notes on Metamodernism'. *Journal of Aesthetics & Culture*, 2, 1, pp. 1–14.

Viroli, M. 1995. *For Love of Country: An Essay on Patriotism and Nationalism*. Oxford: Oxford University Press.

VTsIOM. 2015a. 'Sanktsii protiv Rossii: derzhim oboronu?'

VTsIOM. 2015b. 'Kak vy otnosites' k SSHA'.

VTsIOM. 2015c. 'Kholodnaya voina'. URL: https://wciom.ru/index.php?id=236&uid=115071 (accessed 15 February 2019).

VTsIOM. 2017. 'Rossiya—velikaya derzhava'. 15 March. URL: https://wciom.ru/index.php?id=236&uid=116111 (accessed 15 February 2019).

Wickström, D.E. 2014. *Rocking St. Petersburg - Transcultural Flows and Identity Politics in Post-Soviet Popular Music*. Stuttgart: Ibidem Verlag.

Wiedlack, K. 2016. 'Pussy Riot and the Western Gaze: Punk Music, Solidarity and the Production of Similarity and Difference'. *Popular Music and Society*, 39, 4, pp. 410–22.

Wilks, L.J. 2009. *Initiations, Interactions, Cognoscenti: Social and Cultural Capital in the Music Festival Experience*. PhD thesis, The Open University. URL: http://oro.open.ac.uk/25570/1/wilks_final_post-viva_thesis_11-06-09.pdf (accessed 15 June 2020).

Woolf, V. 2017 (1925). *The Common Reader (the 1925 edition)*. Musaicum Books: online version.

Yusupova, M. 2014. 'Pussy Riot: A Feminist Band Lost in History and Translation'. *Nationalities Papers*, 42, 4, pp. 604–610.

4 Patrioprotest

The ambiguous resistance of *nezavisimaia muzyka* (2018–2022)

Introduction

How was political protest articulated in *nezavisimaia muzyka* at the turn of the 2020s? And in what ways did the state respond to it? Can a common denominator between music and power be found during occurrences of protest? These questions wish to test whether Russia at the turn of the 2020s fit the widely assumed framework that sees non-Western autocratic regimes and independent musicians who contest them in a relationship of antagonism. The analysis below reveals a very fragmented and diverse picture: contrary to general assumptions, often reinforced in Western media, Russian practitioners positioned themselves in relation to the authoritarian zeitgeist through a wide array of strategies and counterstrategies, informed not only by a desire to "challenge" the status quo but also by an intention to blur the lines between challenge, support and indifference towards it. This suggests continuity with the Russian/Soviet tradition of placing the work vaguely and ambivalently in relation to the political. Jonson and Erofeev's (2017) edited volume captured some of the multiplicity of the positioning choices in question, including those artists hailing from conservative and reactionary milieus. Yet the framework that informed most of the scholarly analysis of artistic production (Rancière's dissensus) still pitted cultural producers against the authoritarian regime by default. In a similar guise, Morozov, Reshetnikov and Gaufman (2024) employed metamodernism – that is, a framework that excludes any straight, ultimate and definite statement about politics – to analyse the cultural actors within it in seemingly predetermined positions of, again, dissensus.

In Rancière's (2010) conceptualisation, dissensus is that which polemises with, destabilises or disrupts the consensus, that is, the established, univocal, undivided distribution of what can be seen, said and done. For Rancière, consensus implies the general acceptance of shared values and norms, but what is considered legitimate, just or acceptable is often the result of the dominant or ruling groups projecting or imposing their values and norms as the common ground for everyone else. Dissensus, on the other hand, stands for the challenge to this order, emphasising the existence of different perspectives, voices and positions that are often marginalised or excluded by the dominant consensus.

DOI: 10.4324/9781003248699-5

154 *Independent Music in Russia*

I do not wish to contend that dissensus does not occur (it does), yet this is only one of the possible manifestations of creative protest. In other cultural products, for example, dissensus is inextricably bound up with – and indistinguishable from – consensus. For example, if the art work stems from a metamodern condition – with, across and beyond (post)modernism (Vermeulen and Van den Akker 2010) – then the political element contained in it will involve metaprotest – with, across and beyond protest. This means that its political aesthetics will question, polemise and invent new trajectories between what can be seen, said and done (Rancière 2010, 149) and simultaneously endorse what can be seen, said and done already. There will be no opposition or contrast, but rather oscillation and merging, between what Rancière (2010, 138) calls *aesthetic distance* (the suspension of relation between the art work and a specific, intended social function),[1] traditional critical art[2] and, crucially, a third, added category of preservation of the status quo. In this form of political aesthetics, which I term *patrioprotest*, the vagueness and strangeness of dissensus meet the vagueness and strangeness of consensus, leaving, as before, the viewer to subjectivise as they please, often in a wide range of interpretation between and including opposite poles.

The mutual imbrication of consensus and dissensus was one of the multiple responses, or coping mechanisms, that Russian creatives adopted to face the authoritarian zeitgeist in late 2010s/early 2020s, yet it was a significant one that has not received sufficient scholarly attention. Engström (2018, 2021) and Semenenko (2021) have been among the few to productively nuance the relationship between popular music and power,[3] and to acknowledge that separating positions of agreement from critique may be impossible with those practitioners who construct ambiguity in their art work purposefully, switch camps continuously or whose art work is interpreted, mediatised and re-mediatised in opposing ways by different actors – including state actors – trying to inscribe their own reading on it (see also: Strukov 2016; Hutchings 2022). Dissensus alone is not enough to explain "the dual position in which one can support the ruling regime and at the same time pose as its critic", which "is not only extremely comfortable but also profitable" (Semenenko 2021, 82).

The objective of this chapter is thus to capture the complexity of forms of creative protest animating Russian independent music culture at the turn of the 2020s – as well as the state's reaction to them – including those forms of *patrioprotest* involving political aesthetics that do not squarely fit in categories of either contestation or validation of the accepted order. This chapter is tripartite: the first section puts the relationship between musicians and politics in Russia in an historical perspective, highlighting musicians' typical attempts at self-removing from political matters; the second part analyses protest in independent music produced during Putin's fourth term; the third part defines and examines instances of *patrioprotest* – a peculiar, ambiguous and inextricable blend of elements of protest and patriotism, which can be interpreted radically differently depending on the viewer's standpoint. *Patrioprotest*, I hope, may prove useful as a framework for scholars studying culture–politics relations not only in Russia, but also beyond, particularly in other authoritarian regimes.

Protest, patriotism and the state

The start of Putin's fourth term in 2018 displayed an important similarity to the start of his third term in 2012, as the waves of contestation surged to comparable high levels in 2018–2019, with 1,443 public protests across the country in the first three quarters of the year, a record number considering the yearly average between 1,200 and 1,500 (Starikova 2019).[4] Police brutality reached heights unseen since 2012,[5] while one of the summer rallies in 2019 became the largest since 2012, attracting over 50,000 participants (Piatin 2019).

At the same time, an independent survey conducted in the same period (Levada Centre/Ebert Fund 2020) showed that Russia's youth (14–29 years olds) were far from being against Putin. While 87% were very satisfied with their lives and 81% looked positively into their personal future, only 20% were interested in politics and only 11% claimed to have a clear grasp of it. Even if trust in state institutions was overall low, high level of trust were shown for the president and the armed forces as protectors of national security and stability, two values the youth regarded as key (moreover, distrust equally concerned international organisations like the EU, NATO and countries such as the US). Two third of respondents supported the annexation of Crimea and would not give the region back even if sanctions were lifted. Lastly, 76% of the youth did not identify with what is commonly perceived as "Western" culture, 58% did not view Russia as a European country and 67% saw Europe and Russia as caught in severe confrontation. These results did not differ much from the general surveys conducted during Putin's third term that were presented in the previous chapter. The Ebert Fund's survey showed a Russian youth that was as nationalistic as it was disinterested in politics. But how to explain, then, the amalgam of high levels of contestation, but also of support and indifference?

In 2020, journalist Iurii Dud' asked his colleague Mikhail Kozyrev which line from a song in Russian music since 2000 was more representative for him. Kozyrev, tellingly the former director of the nationalist outlet Nashe Radio but also one of the faces of the oppositional channel TV Rain (*Dozhd'*), replied: "the line from the Ufa-based band Lumen, 'I love my country so much but I hate the state" (Kozyrev 2020). Released in 2006 and titled "State" (*Gosudarstvo*), the song presented the following chorus: "It's a kind of democracy here, but actually it's Tsardom/I love my country so much, but I hate the state". Kozyrev vividly captured the relationship between "country/nation" (*strana*) and "state" (*gosudarstvo*) that informs *patrioprotest* to a significant level. The *strana* here was a beloved, historical and cultural entity, while the *gosudarstvo* was the repressive system that unjustly ruled it. Yet, throughout Russian cultural history, lines could become blurred, and the imaginings of the country/nation could fluctuate or drift from democracy into an illiberal territory that may overlap with the anti-democratic state: for instance, an émigré writer such as Limonov and an oppositional subcultural figure like Egor Letov converged in the foundation of the National Bolshevik Party in 1993. Nobel laureate Aleksandr Solzhenitsyn was a dissident in the Soviet Union and an Orthodox nationalist in 1990s Russia. Before them, the history of Russian literature is full of examples: the national poet Aleksandr Pushkin was twice internally exiled

156 *Independent Music in Russia*

for his anti-government verses and yet fully defended the country's imperial greatness; Gogol lucidly exposed the social problems of nineteenth-century Russian society, and yet towards the end of his life defended serfdom; Dostoevsky was nearly killed by the Tsar for his socialist sympathies, was confined to Siberia for ten years and also became a pro-Tsarist conservative who advocated for Russia's messianism in Europe and colonial expansion in Asia. In short, intellectuals and artists in Russia have usually presented both traits: on the one hand, they were repressed and punished by the authoritarian state; on the other hand, they cultivated a genuine love for their country and praised its special role, greatness and difference from the other countries of "the West", which sometimes merged with the nationalism promoted by the state. While projections of the "nation" could be placed in a relationship of rivalry with those of the "state", the two could also be used to justify each other in Russian cultural history.

Kozyrev himself embodied this hybrid condition, actively contesting the government but simultaneously being blamed for promoting a type of music – *russkii rok* – that ended up mutating in some cases in reactionary, chauvinistic or progovernmental rhetoric, with several Nashe radio performers actively supporting the invasion of Ukraine (Kozyrev 2022, see also McMichael 2019). In the interview, Kozyrev, who regretted some of his past artistic choices, was consoled by Dud', who had also dealt with a number of musicians in his career as Russia's most famous YouTube interviewer: "Misha, I wonder, why is this so serious for you? You can't be responsible for everyone you gave a chance to! [. . .] These are artists! Their psyche is mobile. They get carried away and everything else. Why do you have such a high demand from them?" (Dud' in Kozyrev 2020).

Scholarship has indeed addressed this "psychic mobility" of Russian musicians in relation to the political. Rogatchevski and Steinholt (2016), for example, have investigated how the extremist National Bolshevik Party (NBP) attracted several independent musicians in the 1990s, including Sergei Kurekhin and Egor Letov. Steinholt and Wickström (2009) have analysed the extent to which the identity transformations of some *russkii rok* musicians were informed by nationalism, Orthodoxy and nostalgia. Friedman and Weiner (1999) have studied how Russianness in Russian rock constitutes such an all-encompassing idea that sometimes it turns into Russophilism and nationalism.

A few more cases may provide an update of this common trend of fluctuation between support and protest in Russian music culture. *Russkii rok* musicians, with some exceptions such as Iurii Shevchuk, never tread a straight line.[6] Andrei Makarevich, leader of Mashina vremeni (Time Machine), one of the most influential Russian rock bands of all time, advocated for music's political neutrality for most of his 50-year career and has written anti-establishment songs since 2014. In 2003, Makarevich sat at a chair of honour next to Putin at Paul McCartney's concert on Red Square, while in 2010 he amicably drank with Dmitri Medvedev in an informal rendezvous between the president and some *russkii rok* musicians (*REN TV* 2011). Then, in 2014, he signed a letter in support of Ukraine and started participating in rallies against Putin's politics. The same letter was signed by another attendee of the 2010 presidential get-together, Boris Grebenshchikov, leader of the band Akvarium and cult rock figure in Russia.[7] Viacheslav Butusov, another staunchly self-professed apolitical performer (Tass 2017), took part in 2014 in a public apology against the annexation of Crimea, save continuing going there for his gigs (Shenkman 2022). In September 2022, Butusov sang his song "Poslednee pis'mo" (The Last Letter), written in 1985, together with the director of VTB Bank from the stage of the Eastern Economic Forum in Vladivostok (*Kommersant* 2022). The famous lines of the song, already popularised by the nationalistic film *Brat 2*, went: "Good-bye America/Where I've never been. [...] They've become too small for me/Your worn jeans/ We've been taught for so long/To love your forbidden fruits". The reference to Russia's proud detachment from the Western economic market was obvious.

Even performers who showed unshakable loyalty to power could oscillate: pop artist Oleg Gazmanov, author of the anthem for Edinaya Rossiya (former Putin's party) and the post-Soviet hymn to Soviet nostalgia "Sdelan v SSSR" (made in the USSR), had his single "Novaia tsaria" (New Dawn) removed from TV and radio broadcasting due to its political criticism (*REN TV* 2011). Oleg Likhachëv, a chanson performer and a (now former) Duma member, after singing "Vladimir Putin – molodets" (Vladimir Putin Is Right) in 2014, released "Ia otrekaius' ot Putina" (I Renounce Putin) in 2018 (Zagrutdinov 2020). Lastly, rappers were also unpredictable. In 2017, Viacheslav Mashnov, better known by the pseudonym of Slava KPSS, released "Vladimir Putin", a song in which he compared himself (as the king of rap) to Putin, and his challengers (as losers) to Navalny (though it was not evident whether the song was a form of endorsement or mockery of the Russian president). In 2018, his manager confirmed Mashnov had taken two million rubles (£20,000) from the Kremlin to compose a song which "dissed" Nikolai Sobolev (Gerasimenko 2018), a popular video blogger who could hardly be considered an oppositional figure at that time (Levchenko 2018). In 2021, Mashnov was arrested at one of the "Free Navalny" rallies and jailed for seven days (*Izvestia* 2021; Shanina 2021).[8]

The musicians' socio-political protest did not address all the points of the government's agenda, but, rather, involved only a selection of those at any given time: through the exercise of their agency, musicians chose what to endorse and what to contest. In other words, musicians did not subscribe to opposition (or compliance or indifference) tout court, but their performance of resistance went along personal and varied paths that they carved in response to the zeitgeist in which they were enclosed. Interviewee 12, singer in an independent band, for example, argues:

> Because now state propaganda imposes a specific image of being Russian and patriotic that you have to experience towards your country if you are Russian, it [the choice of Russian over English in lyrics] is like an internal protest. It's not an open protest. Well, in a way it is open, because obviously musicians don't support the party agenda. It [singing in Russian] is like a means to understand what makes you Russian, what your personal patriotism is, and what your personal Russian language is and what your personal culture is, instead of what they tell you. And people, young people, are trying to find their real roots.

158   *Independent Music in Russia*

As discussed in the previous chapter, despite the social critique, Russia as a problematic yet beloved entity was one of mid- to late-2010s *nezavisimaia muzyka*'s most frequent topics, and Russianness the lens through which this message was projected. But however different in the means, the protest Interviewee 12 talks about had similar goals to the Kremlin-sponsored narrative: the construction of Russia's cultural significance as distinct from the West.

Therefore, the compatibility of objectives between state propaganda and protest music (e.g., constructing pride in the nation's present, finding Russia's roots, re-evaluating Russia's past and projecting it into an exciting future) could thus be exploited by the state through defusing, co-opting or commodifying the contrasting elements within the songs. By reframing antagonism into a continuum, the state could hijack competing visions about nation-building and selectively exploit them for its own legitimation. For instance, pro-Kremlin music producer Igor Matvienko (founder and composer of Liube,[9] Putin's favourite band) maintained:

> For the first time in my life, I realized—and this was a true revelation for me—that Russian youth began to listen to Russian music […] If you go to the Patriarch's Ponds [a famous recreational site in the centre of Moscow], you will hear Russian tracks, booming loudly from passing cars. […] Perhaps they won't be very good ideologically, […] but they will be in Russian.
> (Matvienko in Nechepurenko 2019)

Matvienko, who sat at the table with Putin during the concert crackdown meeting in December 2018 (more on that below), seemed to suggest that there was something higher than ideology: it was the outcome – if that works, why worry? Having different ideological standpoints did not necessarily represent an insurmountable obstacle if those differences were directed at similar goals concerning nationhood. The linguistic switching to Russian equated, in Matvienko's view, to productive (read: usable) nation-building. Firstly, the youth's consumption and appreciation of Russian-language products was an instance of cultural autonomy, which is what the Kremlin, after all, advocated as well. Secondly, in some cases, the state could attempt to boil down the image of the nation articulated in musical products to the common denominator of patriotism, exploiting this shared ground to overcome the remonstration which may have been encoded in the music. Lastly, protest music could also be a potential victory for state-legitimation, if listeners could be persuaded of the benignity of a system which even allowed (some forms of) criticism to exist within it.

Politics is dirty: indifference and non-involvement

Ambiguity was obviously not the only positioning strategy for musicians in late 2010's Russia: open protest, dissensus and indifference were also available. A quick account of how musicians have historically positioned themselves in relation to authoritative discourse can be useful to better understand their attitudes in the contemporary period studied. Traditionally, Soviet musicians located themselves outside political antagonism, activism or open protest, preferring to subtly articulate dissensus, use *stëb* or be unconcerned with criticising the system altogether. While early studies on Soviet rock highlighted the oppositional character of *russkii rok* towards the apparatus (Rauth 1982; Troitsky 1988; Ryback 1990), other studies, especially after 2000, have increasingly called this opposition into question, evidencing the musicians' non-involvement, cynicism or indifference to Soviet rhetoric (Steinholt 2005; McMichael 2005, 2008; Yurchak 2006), as well as the efforts made by the Soviet state to direct youth culture towards an ideologically acceptable version of rock (Pekacz 1994; Steinholt 2005; Kveberg 2013). There were exceptions, of course,[10] but even the most famous protest song of Soviet rock, "Khochu peremen" (I Want Changes) by Kino, explored the inner changes of the heart, not the changes to the system of power that audiences attributed to it (*Komsomolskaia Pravda* 2012; *Dozhd'* 2014; Sokolov 2021). As explained in Chapter 1, a state of being *vnye*, simultaneously inside and outside the system, seems to describe Soviet musicians better than the figure of the rebel.

The personal creativity that musicians pursued by shutting the door on Soviet rhetoric engendered a position of aestheticism and a disassociation from public engagement. Music came to constitute the sacred and politics the profane (Cushman 1995). Andrei Makarevich, leader of Mashina vremeni, interviewed by Cushman (1995, 94), exclaimed: "why do you always ask about politics? I'm sick of politics. I thought you wanted to talk about music. [...] Music is outside of politics". Similarly, Viktor Sologub, singer-bassist of Igry (band he formed after Strannye igry split up in 1985), argues that:

> Energy [...] is what's more important in music. And I don't mean energy in order to dance. I mean energy in the sense of something meditative. [...] In the end there will be a differentiation of cultural forms, and rock will simply be considered art. It will be completely depoliticised, outside of politics. [...] We, rock musicians, have to propagandise spirituality and the soul.
>
> (Sologub in Cushman 1995, 98–9)

This inner spirituality, with its sacredness, which separated the central aesthetic pursuit from the goal to openly antagonise the state, constituted one of the pillars of many Soviet rock and *russkii rok* musicians. The *tusovka* performed an intentional distancing from the trivial dimension which it saw embodied by state politics.

This detachment was passed on by Soviet practitioners to their post-Soviet colleagues. When the USSR collapsed and the new system incorporated *russkii rok* into mainstream entertainment, the new generation of musicians orbiting around the St. Petersburg club Tam-Tam dissociated themselves from *russkii rok* at the level of sound but at the same time they kept their predecessors' depoliticised aesthetics, which continued to be seen as coinciding with autonomy from the political system and alternativeness to the commercial mainstream. The 2000s, marked by economic growth, further drifted independent music away from protest. As Interviewee 13 (the famous critic) summed up: "All everyone wanted was to make money and have a good time".

160   *Independent Music in Russia*

Some members in 2010's *nezavisimaia muzyka* upheld the tradition of non-involvement and continued to profess a music voluntarily detached from politics. Being apolitical was synonymous with being both "clean" and "about art", as politics was seen as a contaminating agent as well as a distant and ineffable territory. Interviewee 6, leader of an internationally renowned indie band, argued:

> I don't like to meddle in that, because I understand that I am a person who is distant from all that, and people who think they understand politics are deeply wrong. They have no idea of what's going on. I, at least, am not afraid to admit it, and so I don't make conclusions or judgements, I don't say 'this is good', or 'this is bad', I just prefer not to think about it. Because politics is a lie, it is a game, it is always a chessboard.

The inexplicability of Russian politics, which made the effort of understanding politics a vain endeavour, contributed to making apoliticism a chiefly aesthetic factor. According to Interviewee 69, drummer of an experimental rock collective, politics hinders the process of "shamanism" (*shamanstvo*), the entrance into a state of spiritual trance and elevation which is key to the musical experience. Even if political convictions are held, these are best kept away for music's sake. Interviewee 15, member of an internationally famed group, mused that he could swear against Putin in a song, but this would be "uninteresting". Interviewees 26 and 27, guitarist and vocalist for an indie band, maintained:

> *Interviewee 27:*   We are ordinary guys, we have something to say about ourselves, but we don't want to write a manifesto for some other group of people.
> *Interviewee 26:*   We would want everything to be different. But we don't sing about that. We sing about *something else*. [emphasis mine]

Interviewee 10, leader of a well-known indie pop group, also talked about the apolitical, artistic idea:

> I don't quite like when musicians use art as a demonstration of their – sometimes not even theirs – civic position. I think music should be about *something else*.
>
> > [emphasis mine]

This "something else" was indeed a perceived aesthetic purity and spiritual energy, no different from what 1980s *russkii rok* musicians looked for in their songs. As the decade progressed, the political climate of the 2010s acquired elements of similarity with that of the 1980s in terms of Russia's partial isolationism, renewed East–West tensions, media control, censorship and implementation of freedom-restricting laws. For some, this was enough to tip them over the engaged camp (especially in conjunction with the wave of protests of 2018–2019); for others, it was not.[11] Up until 2022, and as in the late-Soviet era, several musicians regarded

Patrioprotest 161

disengagement from political activism as a means to purify their art from the incomprehensible and uninspiring language of politics, as well as a defence from its interference.

Concert crackdown, decentralisation and participatory consolidation

Open protest was another option at the musicians' disposal, just as interference was another option at the disposal of the state. Between October and November 2018, around 30 pop, rap and indie concerts were either cancelled or disrupted by regional authorities (*Meduza* 2018a), while the rapper Khaski (Husky) was arrested and jailed for 12 days for hooliganism (see later). Most of these cancellations were carried out in the name of the law "On the Protection of Children from Information Harmful to Their Health and Development", implemented in 2012. This law banned material that could lead minors to violence, self-harm, suicide, drug and alcohol use and, from 2013, "non-traditional" sexual relationships (the so-called anti-LGBTQ+ laws).[12] It was not the first time that concerts were cancelled by the authorities after the introduction of such restrictive measures, of course, but cancellations never occurred with such intensity.[13] Civil right activist and lawyer Pavel Chikov reported that the FSB held a "black list" (*chërnyi spisok*) of musicians, like in Soviet times (*Meduza* 2018b),[14] and debates over freedom of speech, state interference and cultural repression in Russia increased (MacFarquhar 2018).

However, the authorities' parameters were blurred and the decisions on censorship varied from case to case. The most targeted performers, for example, were not politically engaged indie bands or scandalous rappers, but the independent teenage pop group Frendzona (Friendzone). The group, founded just a year before, saw their music go under the magnifying glass of the authorities at least on seven occasions, which disrupted the band's tour and caused it major economic damage.[15] The casus belli were the lyrics from the song "Askorbinka" (Ascorbic Acid) ("I will teach your young sister how to smoke"), and from the song "Butylochka" (Spin the Bottle), which tells the story of a female teenager kissing her girlfriend during a pajama party and falling in love (see also Figure 4.1):

> The smell of lips, why is there something pounding under the T-shirt
> I've kissed a hundred times, but boys don't know how to do it like that
> Everyone laughed and immediately forgot about it
> But not me, wait, I think I've fallen in love, stop. [...]
> It says here – love does not depend on gender
> Fate is screaming at you – baby, do experiment

In nearly all cases, the cancellations were demanded by the (quasi)non-governmental activist group Antidiler (Anti-Dealer). The Antidiler movement, founded in Krasnoyarsk in 2013 by the former Liberal-Democratic MP Dmitrii Nosov, consists of volunteering vigilantes who have as their primary aim the ending of drug consumption in Russia. Even if they may at times function as a double-edged sword due to excessive zeal or create conflict along class dynamics

Figure 4.1 Screenshot from Frendzona's video for "Butylochka" (2018). Source: YouTube.[16]

(Gabdulhakov 2018; Trottier et al. 2020, 11), vigilante groups have been supported by the state as a grassroots extension of its powers and ideology. According to *Komsomolskaya Pravda*, in 2018 Antidiler carried out more than 100 anti-drug raids with the collaboration or assent of the police, and concerts became one of the main targets of their campaign (Karpitskaia 2019). In reference to Frendzona, on 13 November 2018, the Krasnoyarsk Antidiler committee announced: "singing to children about drugs, same-sex love and libertine lifestyle is a crime against the nation" (*Rossiia 24*, 2018). Nosov told *Rossiia 24* he had received numerous warnings from parents about Frendzona's upcoming gig and had then turned to the Siberian State University for evaluation of the bands' lyrics. The scholars confirmed that Frendzona incited drug use and homosexuality. When Antidiler put pressure on the local authorities, these summoned the venue's owner, the band's tour manager and the concert promoter, strongly advising them not to carry out the concert. As Zaitseva (2018) reports:

> The procurator's office concluded that most of the band's songs contain profanity, propaganda of same-sex relationships, suicide, and information that can make children want to drink alcohol or other prohibited substances. They stressed that if minors hear these songs during the concert, this will violate their right to 'normal physical, intellectual, mental, spiritual and moral development', and the organisers will be fined for violating the law.

The claims of incitement to homosexuality against Frendzona showed once again the authorities' enigmatic and malleable standards. In 2014, t.A.T.u., Russia's

Patrioprotest 163

most notorious (albeit semi-fake) non-heteronormative act, whose acronym means *ta liubit tu* (This girl loves that girl), performed at the opening ceremony of the Sochi Winter Olympics in front of millions of international TV viewers.[17] In 2016, live on state-controlled Channel One, the duo performed their hymn to lesbian freedom "Nas ne dogonyat" (They're Not Gonna Get Us) at the jubilee of the children's studio academy Neposedy (The Fidgets), sharing the stage with its pupils.[18]

It may be inferred that, in the instance of Frendzona, the interference of local authorities into the ordinary activities of teenage pop acts served as a reminder about the length of the radar of power. Lobbied by crowds of worried parents and vocal activists, the authorities applied bureaucratic vehemence towards apolitical performers, in an implementation of ideology that was not only corrective, but also formative, aimed at asserting the presence of the state even in unexpected environments. The witch-hunt warned musicians that no one was exempt from the censorial machine, should the authorities decide to investigate.

At the same time, this interpretation, which attributes a high level of centralising capacities to the state, does not exclude another one: specifically, that this witch-hunt was primarily generated at grassroots level and as a spin-off of recent Russian social policies, which local authorities had to survey and the central apparatus had to manage. In other words, the crackdown could be seen also as a manifestation of the decentralisation and disconnection ingrained in Russia's vast bureaucratic machinery and federal system. As Goode (2018, 265) has shown, when "patriotism became the only game in town" in post-Crimea Russia, Putin significantly boosted Russia's State Programme for Patriotic Education (SPPE),[19] funding disparate non-commercial organisations with the intent to foster "civic accountability for the fate of the country" (Goode 2018, 268). Russia, as a relatively new entity, was still "improvising" its governing institutions (Studin 2018), and one of these experiments involved creating, funding or backing para-governmental and non-governmental groups for the promotion of state-approved values, from the institution of the family to parking cars in a considerate way.[20] Non-governmental and non-profit organisations, such as Antidiler or parents' associations, are examples of a "participatory consolidation", that is, of an activism that upholds state narratives from the bottom up. Being decentralised, horizontal and difficult to control, such activism at times exceeds the state in ideological zeal. When this happens and the matter spins out of the regional authorities' control, the state (at the central level) is faced with the dilemma of firmly intervening, appeasing or ignoring. In the context of late 2010s Russia, the political elite managed to kill two birds with one stone, whatever the real origin of the crackdown: on the one hand, it could claim distance from repressive measures by blaming them on the initiative of local actors; on the other, it could extend its powers over popular music (one of the few industries it could not regulate) by scaring and scarring practitioners.

"Common vampires": the Ic3peak case

On ten different occasions in the space of two weeks, the authorities' meddling into musicians' affairs extended to the New Russian Wave band Ic3peak (pronounced:

164   *Independent Music in Russia*

"I speak" or "Ice Peak"). Ic3peak, who play a mixture of dark wave and electro, had switched to Russian around 2017 after starting their career in English, and together with the linguistic change came an engagement with social and political topics. In October 2018 the band released the video for the song "Smerti bolshe net" (Death Doesn't Exist Anymore). Unlike Frendzona, this was a case of direct and open dissent. In the song, Nastia Kreslina, the duo's vocalist, sings:

> [Intro]
> I fill my eyes with kerosene
> Let it all burn, let it all burn
> All of Russia is watching me
> Let it all burn, let it all burn
>
> [Verse]
> Now I'm ready for anything
> I've done my time in the internet jail
> I'm going out in the street to play with my cat
> But the cops' car runs it over
> I'm going through the city in my black hoodie
> It's cold as usual and people are wicked
> Nothing awaits me ahead
> But I'm waiting for you, one day you'll find me
>
> [Chorus]
> I drown in the swamp in golden chains
> My blood is purer than pure drugs
> They will beat you in the square, together with other people
> While I roll a spliff in my brand new home.
> Death doesn't exist anymore.

The lyrics alluded to the normalisation of police brutality during protest demonstrations ("they will beat you up in the square"), and the selfish hedonism of the current generation in response to it ("while I roll a spliff in my brand new home"), hinting at the coexistence of the authoritarian state with economic comfort and political apathy, which renders in vain any possibility of change. Kreslina later stated that she wrote the lyrics for the song after the 2018 general election, which saw Putin win for the fourth time: "It ['Smerti bolshe net'] talks about your internal state. When you feel you're in a situation from which it's impossible to get away, death doesn't scare you anymore, because the way you live isn't life at all" (Kreslina in *Nezhnyi redaktor* 2018). Kreslina was adamant to speak not only for herself, but on behalf of many people belonging to her generation, who could not, or were afraid to, vocalise their feelings of anxiety (*Nezhnyi redaktor* 2018).

In the video, scripted by the band themselves and set in Moscow, Kreslina and the other duo member, Nikolai Kostylev, feature as vampires occupied in disparate sinister affairs. They cover themselves in kerosene in front of the Russian White House, sit on top of two anti-riot guards (OMON) in front of the ex-KGB

Patrioprotest 165

headquarters (connecting the oppression of the Soviet past to the contemporary era), smoke a joint in the VDNKh (a park built for hosting the display of economic achievements in the USSR) and feast on raw meat and bloody drinks by the Kremlin (a reference, perhaps, to contemporary power feeding on the remnants of Soviet ideology and the blood of the people) (see Figures 4.2 and 4.3).

"Smerti bolshe net", as Kreslina envisaged, became a new generational anthem, as the attempt to ban Ic3peak's concerts backfired and enhanced the band's

Figure 4.2 and 4.3 Two screenshots from Ic3peak's video for "Smerti bol'she net" (2018). In Figure 4.2, the two band members play on top of two antiriot policemen in front of the former NKVD and KGB (and today's FSB) headquarters at Liubianka, Moscow. In 4.3, Kreslina and Kostylev eat raw meat on Red Square, in front of the Lenin Mausoleum. Source: YouTube.[21]

166   *Independent Music in Russia*

popularity: "we will always be thankful to the FSB [Russia's security service] for the advertising campaign" (Kreslina in *Nezhnyi redaktor* 2018). The Ic3peak affair, like the other concert bans, had a vast echo on national media, including national television coverage. The YouTube views of "Smerti bolshe net" soared in the days of the controversy, climbing up to 30 million by the end of the year. Numerous commentators on the video admitted to having discovered the band – until then barely known outside of *nezavisimaia muzyka*'s circles – through the news. For their part, the band politically radicalised, voicing their dissatisfaction with the current political system in national and international media (see *Fontanka* 2018; Roth 2018), as well as in subsequent musical outputs.

Interestingly, however, while local authorities disrupted the duo's gigs, the official reaction among the high echelons of power was ambivalent, as evidenced by the fact that the video for "Smerti bolshe net" was not banned – contrary to what happened to other controversial artists' videos, e.g., Khaski's "Iiuda" (Judas). As *RTVI* (2018) reported, the Kremlin did not find "anything bad" [*nichego strashnogo*] with the song's message, despite its explicit reference to drugs, internet policing and state repression: "[it is a] common vampire-gothic emo-clip, a hype that allowed [the band] to enter YouTube's top-charts". Thus, an enigmatic situation presented itself: on the one hand, local authorities attempted to disrupt Ic3peak concerts, on the other hand the Kremlin did not find any particular anti-government propaganda in the band's songs. Arguably, the lack of connection between central state organs and local authorities in the periphery played a role in this. Kreslina noticed that:

> Perhaps the whole thing [the order to crack down] was initially centralised, but then it acquired a chaotic character, as everything in Russia does: everything got out of control and began to happen in its own way, locally. I think we are still in the galaxy of artists with whom people in power would not even bother to talk.
>
> (Kreslina in *Wonderzine* 2019)

In the same rapid way in which it became chaotic, however, the crackdown on concerts stopped. The order came from the top of the central apparatus: on 15 December, none other than Putin discussed the subject of concert bans during an official meeting with his team. While worried about the references to drugs, the president commented that "to grab and not let go is the worst, most ineffective way one can possibly think of, and the consequences will be the opposite of what expected" (*Lenta.ru* 2018). He then added that "if one cannot stop youth culture, it is necessary to offer a guide to direct it" (*Lenta.ru* 2018). Putin's words signalled a truce in the authorities' harassment of musicians across Russia.

Ic3peak's completion of their tour and growing nationwide fame did not seal the victory of cultural independence over the authoritarian state but rather proved the flexibility typical of spin dictatorships (illusion of pluralism and democracy, avoidance of hard-line repressive measures, randomness of punishment, co-optation of media actors, etc.). Like in the case of Frendzona, two interpretations can be proposed, and they by no means exclude each other. The first views the Ic3peak case as evidence that the boundarylessness of state intrusion in cultural niches could be justified as a lack of communication between central and regional organs. The other sees the state's démarche and the return to a managed laissez-faire approach, as the Kremlin realised that the musicians' protest against the system was not harmful to the system, but advantageous, because it provided the political elite with the opportunity to elevate itself to the level of magnanimous arbiter. Instead of fighting music subcultures (like in the case of a fear dictatorship) or commodifying and incorporating them (like in the case of a capitalist democracy), the state allowed them to continue operating as a monitored safe space where participants could express their dissent, punishing only selectively and randomly.

"I was silent, a cop was born": the New Russian Wave and the new Russian protests

Despite the efforts of the Kremlin to accommodate and manage discontent in independent music, the 2019 protests sharpened the political participation of several musicians and increased their open contestation. Some of the acts associated with the New Russian Wave performed at oppositional rallies,[22] while, between August and November, rap, rock and NRW musicians released an unprecedented number of protest songs, many of which starred the figure of the cop (*ment*) in a leading role (Table 4.1).

The subjects of police violence and state despotism are also addressed on some of the most influential NRW releases of 2020, as a further demonstration that the residue of the 2019 protests carried over into the new decade. In Khadn dadn's "Zvezdy na plechakh" (Stars on Shoulders),[23] the main character, in a marijuana-altered state, is beaten by policemen, while Ic3peak's video for "Marsh" (March) is an explicit critique of the militarisation of Russian society.

Table 4.1 List of bands and songs' videos released in conjunction with the protests in Moscow in 2019.

Artist	Song	Release (2019)
Andrei Makarevich	"Pesnia pro rossiiskie OMON" (A song about the Russian Anti-Riot policemen)	July
Marketing*	"Ledenets" (Candy)	August
Jars*	"Ment" (Cop)	August
Monetochka*	"Gori gori gori" (Burn Burn Burn)	August
Ploho*	"Zakladka" (The Stash)	September
Tarakany	"Delo molodykh" (A youth affair)	September
Pussy Riot	"1937"	September
Noize MC, Egor Letov	"Vsyo kak u lyudei" (Just like Ordinary People)	September
GSPD*	"Zariazhennyi" (Loaded)	October
Khaski*	"Sedmoe Oktiabria" (October the 7th)	October
The Villars, Groza*	"Politsiia" (Police)	November
Shortparis*	"Tak zakalialas' stal'" (Thus the Steel Was Tempered)	November

Note: Those with a * indicate musicians loosely belonging to the NRW.

168 *Independent Music in Russia*

Figure 4.4 Screenshot from Jars' video for "Ment" (2019). Source: YouTube.[25]

All these songs had two common objects of aesthetic investigation: first, the normalisation and interiorisation of authoritarianism and violence in the very thoughts and behaviours of the Russian population; second, as journalist Lev Levchenko (2019) argued, the unviability of the traditional artist's stance of indifference to this process. As the lyrics of the chorus of Jars' song "Ment" (Cop) summarised:[24] "I was silent/a cop was born" (*ia molchal/rodilsia ment*). The song's video depicted a day in the life of an ordinary young man: he wakes up, has breakfast, exercises, attends the band's concert, drinks, dances, goes back home (Figure 4.4). The next day, he puts on a police uniform and goes to work. Jars' singer, Anton Obrazina, stated:

> A cop is someone who wants to preserve the status quo, someone who believes that what the state does is right. It is right to repress demonstrations, it is right to put Golunov in jail, it is right to torture. It's become disturbing that many friends and acquaintances are beginning to share this view, even those who were once in the punk movement. They've begun to believe what they read in pro-government media and Telegram channels. I've decided to call all these people (and my own inner indifferent part) 'cops'.
>
> (Obrazina in Levchenko 2019).

While indifference turned to connivance, the figure of the "cop", "one of the main characters of contemporary Russian music" (Rondarev 2020), became a symbol, half material, half imaginary. The material one exerted violence on people and legitimised autocracy, the imaginary one prevented the individual from rebelling to the real one. It was the "inner cop", a pervasive and contagious figure, whom the indie-rap band Marketing addressed in their song "Ledenets" (Candy):

> I go out on the street and one person out of two is a cop
> I don't know if I even exist or not
> Am I here or not
> Am I or cop [*ya est' ili ment*],
> My inner cop
> Says I'm not here.

Figure 4.5 Screenshot from Monetochka's video for "Gori gori gori". Source: YouTube.[26]

In all *nezavisimaia muzyka*'s production of the time, the various images of the cops represented the state, in particular, the invasion of the state in the habits of the citizens, which not only blurred the lines between life and death (like in the case of "Smerti bol'she net") but also clouded the distinction between the public and the private. In the first video of "Gori gori gori" (Burn Burn Burn) in 2019, for example, Monetochka sits still in her apartment with an idiotic smile and a fixed expression (again, half alive, half dead), while everything else around her is devoured by the flames (see Figure 4.5). One of the few objects to feature in her flat is a TV. As the camera zooms out, we see that the entire building, and then the entire city, is burning. She sings: "It doesn't matter where you spit, it doesn't matter where you look, the state is everywhere [*sploshnoe gosudarstvo*]". The message is that, by being indifferent (or sedated by official propaganda through TV), people have let the state appropriate even their intimate sphere, allowing it to burn both the private space (the apartment) and the public space (the city) (Monetochka's fire appears to be the continuation of Kreslina's implied self-immolation in "Smerti bol'she net"). "Burn Burn Burn" can thus be read as a metaphor for the contemporary condition of apathy and powerlessness associated with the Russian population.

As observed in the previous chapter, the Pain Generation, coming of age in the mid-2010s, had tried to create its own new version Russia, however painful and traumatising the present may be. This was an instance of patriotism which remained ambiguous in terms of moral verdicts. However, as the level of authoritarian repression intensified at the cusp of the 2020s, some musicians abandoned metamodernism and post-irony in favour of a seriousness that cleared any doubt as to where the artist stood in relation to the political system (see also Semenenko 2021, 93).

"Speaking up" then aimed both at the limitation of the state's invasion into the individual self and at its replacement with something else. To this extent, the

170 *Independent Music in Russia*

protest of the NRW did not seem to look to the West for inspiration, but rather internally. Contesting the current order did not entail a return to cosmopolitanism or self-identification as Westernisers, but connected with the quest for a new and specifically Russian identity "without Putinism",[27] and patriotism "on one's terms" (*po-svoemu*) (see also Gorbachev 2018). If the NRW embraced Russianness and the ordinary as its primary aesthetic inspirations, it also rejected, and sheltered from, police violence, anti-democratic restrictions and other problematic manifestations of state authoritarianism. But as these problems sharpened at end of the 2010s, for some musicians it was no longer morally good to be silent about the state. Indeed, the spectrum of possibilities for positioning oneself as artist in relation to the status quo comprised also open protest alongside dissensus, indifference, or ambivalence.

Patrioprotest

If, during putin's third term, one could note an oscillation in independent music between nationalism and patriotism, during Putin's fourth term one could see an oscillation between patriotism and protest. *Patrioprotest* describes the process whereby, in order to get messages of resistance across to wider audiences, musicians used patriotism as a device to divert the authorities' attention from the protest encoded in the musical or audio-visual product. In the context of an increasingly interfering state apparatus, the fusion between meanings that were unacceptable and acceptable to the status quo represented a viable negotiation that was also conventional to Russian cultural history. Contemporary writer Dmitry Bykov often cites Soviet writer Leonid Leonov, who, in the context of Soviet cultural repression, used to give the following advice to colleagues: "be sure to give your most cherished thoughts to negative characters" (Bykov 2012). Bykov argues that this was a method for artists to express what they really thought about the system while mitigating the possibilities of being censored or liquidated by power. Framing a positive as a negative, dressing up an attack as a defence or masking a critique in the form of praise gave room to artists to pre-empt reactions from power and to some degree shelter behind an appearance of compliance. But we can go back even further, to Imperial Russia: as Loseff (1984, ix) points out, the history of Russian literature is the history of Russian censorship. In a country that has lived under authoritarian rule for nearly the entirety of its history, artists have long been accustomed to practices of (pre-) negotiation between what could be said and what should not be said, in a triangular relationship that necessarily involved communication with the reader and deception of the censor. From Pechorin to Bazarov through Oblomov, the social critique that corresponded with the author's point of view was endowed to a negatively framed hero.[28] Or, in the case of Pushkin's *The Bronze Horseman* – one of the most celebrated poems of Russian literature and an emblem of Russian's destiny (Figes 2002, 7) – awe for the great achievements of Peter the Great (the Tsar) mixed with rage at the autocratic system (again, the Tsar) that vilified and squashed its own people (with the poet's view impossible to place fully on either side).

Such negotiations with top-down censorship seeped into individual mechanisms of pre-emption of such censorship (meaning, self-censorship) and eventually became ingrained in artistic creation as a convention. As Becker (1982, 190) notes, in art worlds where the state exercises strict control over production, even enormous constraints become internalised by participants to the point that they (the participants) may no longer experience constraints as such, but as the customary way of doing things in the art world. The persistence of the authoritarian regime pairs with the persistence of art production that tries to circumnavigate the regime's interferences. Art produced within this framework becomes legacy for the new generation of artists, who then replicate its modus operandi, and so on from generation to generation, as long as the political milieu remains authoritarian. Throughout this lineage, conventions of "circumlocution" (Loseff 1984, 6) are transmitted, endorsed and solidified. Enduring constraints prompt the birth of new types of art and new aesthetic techniques (e.g., *stëb* or Aesopian language) that constitute fundamental components of the art work. *Patrioprotest* is situated within this creative milieu and refers to a constructed ambiguity in which criticism of some aspects of official discourse is inextricably interwoven with the endorsement of others. Removing the patriotism would turn the art work into an explicit and risky counterculture; taking away the protest would reduce it to state propaganda.

A substantial difference between *patrioprotest* and the metamodern ambivalences examined in the previous chapter can be located in affect and intentionality. While metamodernism can be framed as an affective response, perhaps conscious, perhaps not, *patrioprotest* represents more of a strategy, taken on intellectually, to navigate the higher level of authoritarianism of the zeitgeist. Like Aesopian language, *patrioprotest* is a calculated tactic turned aesthetic convention. The affective dimension is secondary to the rational planning and creation of the art product.

Indeed, what distinguishes metamodernism and *patrioprotest* is also the context, namely the increase in the level of state repression of Putin's fourth term (2018–present) that enclosed the production of cultural products. Such repression did not concern independent music as much as other aspects of public life (e.g., political opposition, LGBTQ+ communities, history and memory) or forms of culture more reliant on government funding and (e.g., theatre, cinema, TV, visual art). Nevertheless, it set the tense environment in which independent music developed, one that discouraged direct engagement with themes of contestation. Crucially, "state" here does not only connote the centre (the Kremlin), but also regional and municipal powers as well as media and religious organisations that are loyal to the centre but can nonetheless take their own initiatives, rewrite, overwrite and co-produce official narrative, or even misinterpret and disrupt it. Artists became more afraid of peripheral authorities and neo-traditionalist zealots than the articulations of Putin's inner circle. Notwithstanding its autocratic character, the "Russian state" up until the invasion of Ukraine (which may have ushered Russia in the direction of totalitarianism) was still a complex entity populated with tensions and fragmentations among the discourses of the various actors who comprised it. As described in the examples at the beginning of this chapter, some degree of non-coordination among them was noticeable. This created confusion, or even contradiction, between the official rhetoric and its implementation throughout Russia's territory. As one editorial in *Nezavisimaya Gazeta* (2019) remarked: "The system in Russia is

172 *Independent Music in Russia*

complicated. On the one hand, it is vertical. On the other hand, this does not mean that who is at the bottom makes no decisions".

The turn of the past decade saw the Kremlin at the crossroads between overt and covert methods of coercion and control, fluctuating between what Guriev and Treisman (2022) identified as "fear" and "spin" operational modes. The fear mode characterised twentieth-century autocracies based on terror, violence, isolationism and media monopoly; the spin mode informed twenty-first century regimes and relied on media manipulation, limitation of public violence, faking of democracy and flexibility. Twenty-first-century dictators rely more on peaceful means of control and less on harsh measures: "if Stalin was 80 per cent violence and 20 per cent propaganda [...], Putin is 80 per cent propaganda and 20 per cent violence" (Yakovenko, quoted in Pomerantsev 2015, 40). Neo-authoritarian states perpetuate themselves by learning from other authoritarian regimes (Hall 2023) and skilfully managing the levels of legitimation, co-optation and repression at their disposal (Gerschewski 2013). Using fear sparingly and punishment selectively, undemocratic political elites give the impression of democracy through illusory media and political pluralism, as well as through the overwhelming projection of their own spin on events and issues in the media sphere, in which they co-opt key actors (Tolz and Teper 2018; Chatterje-Doody and Tolz 2019). The aim is to defuse or discredit oppositional potential as much as possible, rather than block or suppress it tout court: "one can publish newspapers or books that call the man in the Kremlin a dictator. The catch is that most people do not want to read them" (Guriev and Treisman 2022, 6). For a spin dictatorship, apathy towards the regime is almost as good as enthusiastic support for it, as both reproduce, passively and actively, the main objective of the regime: its own legitimation.

Nonetheless, from 2018 and in the run-up to the full-scale invasion of Ukraine, the power apparatus started to resort more and more to traditional methods of intimidation, violence and punishment. For instance, in 2018 the authorities clamped down on live gigs, as mentioned previously; in 2019 they violently repressed cycles of intense public protest; in 2020 they poisoned Putin's chief political opponent Navalny; in 2021 they arrested Navalny, increased the number of foreign agents, further limited independent media and actively conducted internet censorship campaigns against specific cultural figures and musicians. These were still selective episodes, but their intensification was nonetheless sign of a negative change for the independent music world. In 2016, Interviewee 13, the music critic, summarised that, even though Russia was indeed going through "a 1980s light version", *nezavisimaia muzyka* was still situated "below the radar of the state" and, "like before, it was still possible to do a lot of things". In Putin's fourth term, the same could not be said: the two worlds did not live parallel lives anymore, but one (power) was keen to take incursions into the other (independent music). As Interviewee 77, the singer of a post-punk group, maintained: "the independent scene grew over the 2010s and the state didn't pay attention to it because it hardly knew it was there. When the scene grew to the point of being noticed, it was noticed indeed". "Noticed", in the connotation given to the word by Interviewee 77, meant harassed.

To overcome the hostile environment in which independent music production found itself in Putin's fourth term, musicians had, as previously, an array of choices,

Patrioprotest 173

ranging between support, contestation and apoliticism. But these choices were not mutually exclusive and could be combined in order to fashion a product that could be also consumed by as wide an audience as possible: as presented below in this chapter, the rapper Husky blended acute socio-political critique with patriotism; the group Shortparis "smuggled" queer visibility and counter-narratives about the ethnic "other" by embedding them in a framework of nationalism; Manizha articulated LGBTQ+ and feminist messages together with Orthodox imagery. Those who expressed open protest ran the risk of seeing their gigs cancelled or disrupted, often incurring commercial losses (e.g., the rapper Noize MC, the *russkii rok* singer Andrei Makarevich, the punk-rock band Pornofilmy, the dark-electro duo Ic3peak). For those musicians who chose *patrioprotest*, blurring their positionality in relation to state values provided the shelter they needed in order to articulate their resistance more safely while continuing to perform and earn money.

Whether the supportive elements in *patrioprotest* were genuine is another matter. Crucial to the functioning of this strategy is the lack of clear, definite and definitive statements, as in the product itself so in the interviews that artists may give. Like in Aesopian language (Loseff 1984, 227), the poetics of these texts rest on the enciphering of a subversive motif, "such that namely the act of deciphering becomes the work's inner content". If the subversion is given directly, then the subversive "ceases to be in itself the subject". The same goes for the supportive: if stated plainly, audiences may likely see it as a degradation of artistry. The ambiguity, therefore, must not be broken not only for safety or commercial reasons, but also for aesthetic ones.

It is difficult to assess the impact of *patrioprotest*, as a viable form of resistance, on the social life of audiences. Perhaps, this is not even the right question to ask, given the limitations and repressions of public forms of dissent. Interview 80, member of an indie rock collective, encapsulated the situation thus: "those who think that we [musicians] have some kind of influence on the political life in Russia, [...] that we can protest, [...] don't know Russia. They simply don't have any idea of what's going on". Similarly, Interviewee 77 (the author of several socially engaged songs) reasoned that: "There is a monster, we know it's there, we talk about it, but there is no need to wake him up". If you wake him up (by criticising it openly), "it's like asking a shark not to eat you". Nonetheless, if the official cultural policies implemented after 2012 played a major role in "disarming" music's explicit protest by limiting dissemination of oppositional content, the fact that the level of state censorship increased in the period 2018–2022 may well be the authorities' reaction to a perceived danger, and thus testifies to some degree of the impact on public life of such forms of resistance. Moreover, Shortparis's "Strashno" (Scary) was played during anti-government rallies in Moscow (Ovchinnikov 2019); Khaski's arrest in 2018 triggered the organisation of one of the largest "free speech" cultural events in the country's recent history; Monetochka's *Rasskraski* was labelled "Album of the year" in 2018 on the oppositional outlet *Meduza* (Gorbachev 2018); Manizha's participation in Eurovision 2021 caused a huge and nationwide controversy in Russia's public debates. All of this shows that these works were, to a good extent, influential and impactful in society. However, their promotion on state-loyal media

174 *Independent Music in Russia*

(Shortparis, Manizha and Monetochka performed on Channel One) and, in some cases, appreciation within political elites (Khaski) complicated the picture and raised questions about their efficacy in "resisting" the regime.

The elusive measurement of *patrioprotest's* transformative character, as well as participants' attitudes of ambivalence towards it, are not specific to Russian popular music, but intrinsic to resistance itself as a hybrid and situational space. In scholarship, resistance is broadly defined as opposition to dominant structures. This opposition, however, is not monolithic. Hollander and Einwohner (2004), for example, identify seven types of resistance based on internal, authorial factors (such as "intent"), or external, interpretative ones (like "recognition" and "observation"), concluding that resistance is not a pure concept, but often has a dual and contradictory character, in which a single activity may be intended, or interpreted, as resistance to some aspects of power and accommodation to some others. Under capitalism, resistant narratives are also often subject to commodification and trivialisation.[29] Moreover, while "rock", "punk" and "indie" – genres once considered vessels of resistance – have undergone political disengagement in connection with neoliberalism and globalisation in the West, Western studies have tried – perhaps romantically or yearningly – to herald non-Western independent musicians as politically engaged (Steward 2013). As Sprengel (2020) and Nooshin (2017) observe in relation to the Middle East, such reductive discourse reinforces stereotypes about the East and perpetuates Eurocentric logic and condescending attitudes.

Of course, musicians can also inventively exploit the multifaceted nature of resistance in music, but contesting the status quo in illiberal places does not automatically mean espousing Western values. Writing about Ukraine in the Euromaidan context, Sonevytsky (2016, 292) noted that local musicians had then shifted from a stance of "political ambivalence" to one of "political ambivalence as political conviction". She argued that such ambivalence represented a way to go beyond the East–West binary and explore the possibilities of a "third space" for Ukraine. This was done by engaging with charged political aspects of Ukrainian identity while criticising "the received notion of the political as defined either with or against Russia and the West" (Sonevytsky 2016, 294–95).

Similarly, in Russia, the ambivalence (or, more appropriately, polyvalence) of *patrioprotest* resisted instrumentalisation both at home and from outside. In an interview with the Dutch outlet *3voor12 extra* in 2020, Shortparis's singer Nikolai Komiagin mused:

> Western audiences are still accustomed to see Russian culture as it was in the sixties and seventies, when dissidents shaped their identification with an unofficial art that rebelled against state propaganda and was oppressed by it. [...] Now we don't need a social antithesis to power in order to exist [as artists]. Even though this is a topical issue in Russia. Or artificially topical.

A selective and ambiguous resistance can therefore become a tool that may be used to criticise the status quo domestically and simultaneously dissatisfy external expectations, confuse stereotypification and defy West-centric assimilation.

Patrioprotest   175

The force of this type of resistance resides in its multi-functionality, multi-direction-ality and multi-interpretative nature. Depending on the standpoint from which it is observed and decoded, the musical product assumes varying – including opposing – meanings for different audiences.

"A gig ain't a problem": the Khaski case

The coexistence of dissent and patriotism in today's Russia is well-elucidated in the story of Dmitrii Kuznetsov, known by the stage name of Khaski (Husky). Though Kuznetsov was a rapper, during his career he experimented with different genres, crossing into punk, metal and the New Russian Wave (he collaborated, for instance, with Ic3peak), and was never affiliated to any label, remaining an "artist direct". Kuznetsov was known for his eccentric behaviour – in 2018, he deleted his latest album before release (*The Flow* 2018b); a few days later, he streamed his own (fake) funeral (*Intermedia* 2018) – as well as for his engagement with social issues and direct criticism of power. In the song "Panelka" (Panel House, 2017), the rapper compared Russia to a council estate of dubious reputation which offered no escape and no possibility of positive change. In "Sedmoe oktyabrya" (7 Octo-ber, 2013), a reference to Putin's birthday, Khaski equated the Russian president to a despotic tsar. In "Na chto ia drochu" (What I Jerk Off To, 2020) Kuznetsov imagined being raped, with the rest of Russia, by Putin himself.[30] The rapper was heralded as one of the main voices of protest music in oppositional and liberal me-dia (Boiarinov 2021), including in Khodorkovsky's *Open Media* (2019, 2020), but at the same time garnered the support and friendship of conservative figures such as the writer Zakhar Prilepin and the pro-Kremlin rapper Rich, both vocal supporters of the war in Ukraine. "Paradoxicality", as Aleksandr Gorbachev (2017) identified in an article on *Meduza*, informed the rapper's behaviour, not only politically, but tout court, including aesthetically.[31]

On 22 November 2018, Kuznetsov was arrested and jailed for 12 days (then commuted to four) in Krasnodar (1400 km south of Moscow). Against him were accusations of hooliganism and organisation of an unsanctioned meeting (then dropped), together with the refusal to conduct medical tests for the detection of drugs once in custody (confirmed). Earlier that night, the rapper, incited by the fans and frustrated by the cancellation of his concert by the local authorities, jumped on the roof of a car outside the venue and started performing from there before being taken into custody by the police. The venue manager had cancelled the event a few hours before due to pressure from local authorities. In turn, the authorities claimed to have received Khaski's track list too late to be able to undergo the required censorship checks, and, as a consequence, demanded the concert be postponed. The rapper and his team, on a tour across Russia with a tight schedule, refused to comply. At the hearing, Kuznetsov recognised his guilt for jumping on the car and declared himself ready to repay its owner, but he maintained he was led to act in that way by the circumstances. Ultimately, he claimed that the targeting against him was intentional: "the concert was disrupted by people who do not like my work" (Gnatenko 2018).

176 *Independent Music in Russia*

Kuznetsov's arrest in the midst of the concert crackdown of October and November of 2018 had a national media resonance comparable to that of Pussy Riot in 2012. Contrary to what happened with Pussy Riot, though, this time Russia's music communities mobilised, and the reaction was prompt and decisive. On 26 November, only four days after Kuznetsov's arrest, Oxxxymiron, Basta and Noize MC – three of Russia's most influential rappers – organised a solidarity concert in Moscow's 3,500-capacity Glavklub. The concert was called "Ya budu pet' svoyu muzyku" (I Will Sing My Music), in honour of a line from the song "Ai" that Khaski was singing when he was taken into custody. The income from the concert was donated to Kuznetsov as support against the cancellations that his tour had faced. Publicising the concert, Oxxxymiron (2018) announced that the event was centred upon defending freedom of speech and expression: "it isn't just about Khaski, but about all of us and the future of Russian music".

However, when the concert took place, Khaski had already been released. As it emerged, the rapper had left the Krasnodar detention facilities a few hours earlier. Margarita Simonian, chief editor of *RT* (Russia's state-controlled international broadcaster), commented on her Telegram page that the reason behind Khaski's early release was the presidential team:

> Khaski was released and will continue to be left, touch wood, alone, exclusively because two or three people in the presidential team, who have never heard of Khaski, one night heard about Khaski, heard what happened to him, and were, mmm, how should I put it – outraged by what happened. And when two or three people in the presidential team are outraged by what happened, it usually ends well.
>
> (Simonyan 2018)

Kremlin officials then confirmed to the opposition media channel *Dozhd'* that they pressured the local Krasnodar court to discharge the rapper (Churakova 2018). Later, rumors that the government supported the organisation of the solidarity concert also circulated (Barabanov 2018).

The ambiguous reaction of the state, however, had only started. On 29 November, Sergei Naryshkin, head of the Russian Foreign Intelligence Service, suggested: "The topic of rap attracted the attention of the organising committee, and I thought: maybe the Ministry of Culture should think about granting support for this modern form of poetry and music"? (*NTV* 2018a). Promptly on the same day, the press representative of the Ministry of Culture, Iurii Bondarenko, declared: "Prohibition is not a method. It is not a method for spreading culture in a modern society. Rap music is a significant part of our subculture, and subculture is also a part of our general culture" (*NTV* 2018b).

Roundtables between rappers and Duma members took place on 6 December under the banner "Freedom of Speech in Rap" (Bel'kova 2018). Even if it had been organised as an opportunity for dialogue, the roundtable did not lead to an agreement, and one of the rappers involved, Zhigan (Roman Chumakov), abandoned

Patrioprotest 177

the meeting. On his way out, he told his fellow musician Ptakha (David Nuriev): "it's useless, brother" (Bel'kova 2018). Nonetheless, after Putin's call for guidance rather than suppression of youth culture, in late December 2018 the Duma announced a new grant scheme to support rappers in the first stages of their career called "rap without frontiers" (*bezgranichnii rep*) (Golubev 2018). The contest had as theme "tourism across Russia", which required rappers to sing about their own city in a positive way. The competition was won in Spring 2019 by the Muscovite female rapper Ekaterina Iurchenko with the song "Ia khochu byt' merkoi stolitsy" (I Want to Be the Female Mayor of the Capital). The lyrics of the song were arranged to rhyme by artificial intelligence (*RIA Novosti* 2019; *TASS* 2019). Lastly, pro-Kremlin musical entrepreneurs created *Rap Koktebel'*, a rap festival set in Crimea, which opened in summer 2019 and also took place in 2020 despite the coronavirus pandemic and a ban on musical events in most of the country. The festival made no reference to politics and advertised itself as "cloudless sky, warm sea, refreshing breeze and hot girls in bikinis, dancing to the rocking tracks of rap artists".[32] The occurrence of *Rap Koktebel'* in the contested territory of Crimea embodied the government's new vision of cultural "guidance", whereby rap, with its appeal to the youth, was channelled into affirming Russia's presence in a disputed borderland.

The Khaski case epitomised a change in the Kremlin's attitude: from indifference or delegation of sporadic punishment to local authorities,[33] to active participation in co-opting rap as a nation-building tool. In the aftermath of Khaski's release, chief propagandist Dmitri Kiselëv rapped a fragment of a poem by Vladimir Mayakovsky during his prime-time programme on Rossiia-1, adding it was wrong to persecute rappers (Semenenko 2021, 91). At the same time, international audiences were also reassured, as one of *RT*'s presenters commented (in English): "even the busy man [Putin], who's got more than 99 problems, said that a gig ain't one" (*RT* 2018). And indeed, it was not. Even if Putin's words about guiding youth culture were circumstantial (authorities' investigations into rap continued, in the form of sporadic and random sampling, aimed specifically at finding references to drug use in rappers' videos),[34] they were not unfounded. They relied on the fact that rap in Russia is politically diverse, and that a considerable portion of rap tread the line of "adequacy" in relation to the regime,[35] or openly advocated for the status quo (Denisova and Herasimenka 2019). Although rebellion and resistance customarily animated the rap of the disenfranchised black American youth (Lusane 1993), several Russian rappers borrowed the style more than the politics from it. Rap in 2010s Russia displayed a conspicuous presence of ethnically mixed and non-Russian musicians (such as Timati, Guf, Mot, L'One and so on); "Kalyan rap", a peculiar subgenre which emerged in the late 2010s (a mixture of rap, lyrics about love, folk motives and four-on-four drum kick), was also prevalently made by *rossiiskie*, non-white performers (Bahh Tee, Jony, HammAli & Navai, Rauf & Faik). But many of these rappers did not seem to be attracted by protest politics. In fact, some went the other way. Timati, for instance, was included in the Putin's "list of trusted people" (*spisok doverennykh lits*) in 2018, after years of acquaintance with the president

178   *Independent Music in Russia*

(*The Flow* 2018a). The inclusion in the list gave Timati the "right" to officially endorse Putin during the election period. In 2015 Timati, together with his colleague Sasha Fest, had already released the song "Luchshii drug" (Best Friend), whose chorus went: "My best friend is President Putin". In 2018, together with Guf, he released "Moskva" (Moscow), a song in honour of the capital's mayor Sergei Sobianin.[36] In 2022, Timati publicly supported Russia's invasion of Ukraine (*The Flow* 2022). In short, the bottom line of Putin's reasoning was that rap, and youth culture more generally, could be guided because they were already partly compliant with some of the values of the establishment and already routed along the tracks of consensus.

A similar ambivalence characterised Khaski's situation. When the rapper returned on stage on 12 December 2018, in front of 6,000 people at Moscow's Adrenaline Stadium (Barabanov 2018), interrogatives around the causes of his arrest and release remained open. Indeed, the conflicting messages between the local authorities and the Kremlin were another manifestation of the disconnectedness between various segments of Russia's power apparatus, just like in the case of Ic3peak. Yet, united with this deficiency in coordination was an additional and decisive factor at play: Khaski's patriotism. On the one hand, Kuznetsov had been quite vocal on Russia's social problems and rather critical of its political environment (which he continued to sing about after his release as well). On the other hand, his political stance fluctuated between apparently contradictory poles. In 2014, the rapper befriended nationalist writer Zakhar Prilepin, went to the contested territory of the Donbas to visit him, and collaborated with him and the pro-Kremlin rapper Rich on the song "Pora valit'" (Time to Bring Down, 2014). The song was a nationalistic manifesto whose chorus, sung by Khaski, opens thus: "time to bring down those who say it's time to leave" [*pora valit' tekh kto govorit pora valit'*]. *Valit'* in Russian has a variety of meanings, including "to bring down", "to leave", "to beat it" (in the sense of leaving quickly) but also "to beat violently". The line could therefore be read as "it's time to beat those who say it's time to beat it" (with reference to "leaving the country"), although Prilepin did not confirm such an interpretation (*Most.tv* 2015). In any case, the song offered a negative criticism of the internal opponents of the (then just-started) Ukrainian conflict and the participants of the March for Peace in Moscow (Baliuk 2018). To the puzzled liberal intelligentsia, which held him in high esteem because of his criticism of power, Kuznetsov responded: "in Ukraine, I saw a possible transformation of the Bolotnaya Square protests. If there was another Maidan in Moscow, I wouldn't go" (Tukumbetov 2016). Instead, in 2017 the rapper went again to the Donbas to perform at Lava Fest, a patriotic festival organised by Prilepin.[37] In April 2022, Kuzetsov returned to the war zone to shoot a documentary about the experiences of the Lugansk Philharmonic musicians, mobilised at the pro-Russian front since the start of the full-scale conflict.[38]

Hence, without excluding the disjuncture among the various governmental bodies in the Khaski's controversy, it is plausible to infer that the Kremlin endeavoured to use protest music as another tool for nation-building and state legitimation: on the one hand, power reacted by taking the common denominator of patriotism as primary over specific divisions; on the other, it created an illusion of democracy and freedom of speech by allowing selective criticism of the status quo. Exploiting Khaski's and several other rappers' positions, from obliqueness to ambivalence, from adequacy to nationalism, the Kremlin seized the opportunity for extending its role as a key player in youth culture and in the musical art world.

A Russian doll of ambivalences: Shortparis's "Scary"

Crowned by the critic Artemy Troitsky as Russia' most powerful rock group of all time (*Sobaka* 2019a), Shortparis rose to one of the country's most influential bands in the second half of the 2010s. Having experimented with French and English after their inception in 2012, the group switched to Russian alongside many other New Russian Wave bands in the middle of the decade. Shortparis positioned themselves between music and performance art: their stage theatricality as well as the creation of multi-layered and ambiguous audio-visual content contributed to their crafted image of provocation and intellectualism (Sobolev 2019). The singer, Nikolai Komiagin, worked in the Museum of 20th–21st Century Art of St. Petersburg and regularly quoted French philosophers in the band's work and interviews. The collage of hardly combinable elements, engagement with topical themes and sonic experimentation earned Shortparis the interest and endorsement of the progressive intelligentsia (Shenkman 2021), as well as positive coverage on state-loyal media (Nechaev 2021).[39]

The eclectic aesthetics of the band increasingly reflected, and were fuelled by, the social tensions and political evolution of Putin's fourth term. Shortparis portrayed the militarisation of their country, the state of police, violence, aggression and chaos, often adopting – and therefore exposing – the hidden language of power and taking it to the extreme (see, e.g., the video for "Thus the Steel Was Tempered", released in 2019). This idea evoked the Slovenian band Laibach, whose motto is: "All art is subject to political manipulation, except for that which speaks the language of this same manipulation" (quoted in Nevanlinna 2003). With a similar method of overidentification, in its visual and live work the group also tapped into queer iconographies. Shortparis deconstructed fixed images of Russian masculine identity through gender vagueness and homoerotic stage choreography, in line with its intent to defy classifications altogether (Borealis 2019; *MTV Russia* 2019; *3voor12 extra* 2020).

"Queer" might be understood here as disturbance of identity (Edelman 2004, 17), or critique of identity (Jagose 1996). Following Giffney's (2009, 3) theorisations of queerness, Doak (2020, 215) deployed "queer" in the post-Soviet space as "an anti-identitarian term that first and foremost signifies resistance to categorisation in terms of gender and sexuality, but it also points to a broader project of subverting both political systems and aesthetic norms". In "Strashno", as we will see in a moment, queerness was applied in both directions: to the band members themselves and to the Muslim Other. In carnivalesque fashion, difference between the two groups was thus suspended in favour of an anti-identitarian

180 *Independent Music in Russia*

togetherness. As the 2010s progressed, queering traditional gender representations became in and of itself a form of subversion, given the tough anti-LGBTQ+ measures which characterised Putin's third and fourth terms (Engström 2021).[40] To articulate resistance to this repression, and to make it as public as possible, music practitioners had to "smuggle" counter-discourses in inventive ways, often adopting camp and kitsch aesthetics (Brock and Miazhevich 2022), which, despite the official anti-gay discourse, still populated Russia's musical mainstream (Amico 2014), itself an art world based on excess, circus elements and theatricality (MacFadyen 2002).

But to "brutal queerness", aimed at subverting power dynamics in contemporary Russia, Shortparis paired equally potent mechanisms of contradiction, subjective detachment and moral undecidability that also rendered the work readable in the opposite way: as a strengthening of power. Shenkman (2021) noted that Shortparis's production could not and should not be rationally understood by the audience because incomprehensibility was exactly its aim. But incomprehensibility served also another purpose: discomfort, misery, populism and terror – themes that intermingled in Shortparis's work – could be examined as equally foundational and productive elements, and as such explored with both disgust and fascination.

The song "Strashno" (Scary), particularly the video scripted and shot by the band themselves and released in December 2018, illustrated these paradoxes to a paroxysmic extent, mixing Russian identity, otherness, queer visuals, nationalism and violence, and refraining from proposing any synthesis among and beyond them.[41] The video alludes to the 2004 school siege in Beslan, North Ossetia, in which 334 people, including 186 children, lost their lives, most of them during the clashes between the group of Islamic terrorists (who held 1100 people, including 770 children captive inside the school) and the Russian forces. The tragic event left a scar on the Russian imagination while causing controversy about the way senior officials handled the hostage crisis.[42] In the video for the song, the five shaven-headed members of Shortparis, wearing T-shirts with pictures of rifles on them, take over a school, in the gym of which a group of people, inferred as of Muslim religious identity and of Central Asian descent, are staying (see Figure 4.6). The takeover proceeds through camp clothing, glittering guitars, exaggerated jewellery and erotic male dances, which appear to represent queerness and sexual fluidity. The workers, wearing builders' shimmering vests over robes resembling their traditional clothes, take part in the choreography and are themselves also queered (see Figure 4.7). The last, enigmatic scene of the video shows the band and these "internal Others" carrying what can be viewed as a grave (but also a pedestal) in a funeral procession (or a parade) outside the school, while a white boy stands motionless on it, holding a Russian flag (see Figure 4.8). Over this, Komiagin sings in a dramatic voice: "eternal, eternal, honest, honest, nation" (*vechnaia, vechnaia, chestnaia, chestnaia natsiia*).

In the video we see different "fears" that the state rhetoric in the 2010s tried to marginalise in favour of its project of homogeneous and harmonious nation-building: the fear of the Muslim Other and of the Central Asian migrant, of Nazi fascism and of non-heteronormative sexuality. As the band members themselves

Patrioprotest 181

Figure 4.6, 4.7 and 4.8 Still frames from Shortparis' video for "Strashno". Source: YouTube.[43]

182 *Independent Music in Russia*

stated, these internal fears were sidelined in state discourse, but nonetheless sat within the texture of Russian society:

> The video tries to show the condition in which some people of our generation find themselves. It is of course provocative and alludes to a series of social tragedies that have so far been, for some reason, not reflected upon in our visual culture. During the video we see triggers, painful associations, societal taboos and fears popping up: the Arabic script, no matter if used to write 'love' or 'friendship', is linked immediately with terrorism; shaven heads – with neo-Nazism. After this play on meanings, what essentially remains is a feeling that you can't put into words, yet one that creates an anxiety that is shared by everyone.
>
> (Shortparis in *Meduza* 2018c)

In the "Russian doll" structure of ambivalences that purposefully defies any clear interpretative line, anxiety acts as the song's sole unifying factor, an anxiety commonly experienced beyond racial, cultural, religious and sexual divisions. The sense of impending menace is created by seemingly unrelated snippets of actions, over which towers the figure of "the mayor", who appears in the lyrics as being "on the move" (*maior idёt*). This is a reference to Egor Letov's 1986 song "My – lёd" (We Are Ice), but, in Letov's version, the people were the ice that made the mayor slip; in Shortparis's version, the ice "won't save" the people (*lёd ne spasёt*). The lines: "You don't like it, and they don't like it [...] You can't manage, and they can't manage" (*tebe ne nravitsia, i im ne nravitsia [...] tebe ne spravit'sia, i im ne spravit'sia*), also refer to the all-encompassing dysfunctionality and unchangeability of that society. Eventually, the song does not unfold what should be scary and to whom, because everything – the totality of Russia – is scary to everybody – all its citizens (see also Petrova 2022). Ultimately, "Strashno" does not see the separation between Russia the country/nation (the cherished entity), and Russia the state (the frightening government that rules over it): the two are inextricably entwined.

Not only state and nation, but also the other themes of "Strashno" are merged with their opposite, destabilised and counter-destabilised, in accordance with the nested construction of ambivalences on which the video is based. For example, the Central Asian migrants who constitute the backbone of Russia's workforce (the so-called *gastarbaitery*, or guest workers) are Othered, but at the same time portrayed as part of one's own through the carnivalesque suspension of hierarchies taking place in the middle part of the video. Depending on the viewpoint, the message changes radically. From the perspective of the Central Asian Muslims looking at themselves, the robes they wear may represent their traditional clothing. From the perspective of (some) Russians looking at the other, in a reductive and stereotypical representation, the high-visibility jackets may constitute the clothes often associated with the Central Asian worker. Over both interpretations lingers the equally Orientalist conflation of all Central Asian cultures as one indistinguishable whole that overlooks their national differences. However, this projection is complicated further by the portrayal of the coalescence of Slavic and non-Slavic dances, suggesting the possibility of a dialogue, if not a marriage, of cultures (Petrova 2022; see also an interview with the band in Minaev and Yakovlev 2019). The closing scene, with the migrants carrying the pedestal with the white boy, posits them as pillars on which Russian society stands, but also ties them to that role and orders them under the *russkii* future embodied by the boy.[44] And so on, in a never-ending reversal mechanism that constantly disrupts linearity, and in which the pedestal may be a burden imposed on the people and an honour, the white boy himself a victim and an oppressor, the Russian flag a reason of pain and of pride. In short, "Strashno" teases out the double nature of each sign, refusing to provide a resolution other than dread itself.

Whereas "Strashno" was often seen as an instance of protest against the regime (as mentioned before, the song was used during oppositional rallies in 2019), the band categorically denied any political affiliation and issued conflicting statements aimed at muddying the waters further. On the one hand, the group was pleased that "Strashno" became the "soundtrack of life in Russia in 2019" (Ovchinnikov 2019); on the other, they also stated that "'Strashno' doesn't mean that it is scary to live in Russia [..] it is *Meduza*'s job to write headlines like 'It is scary to live in Russia', not ours" (*BBC Russia* 2019). In order to enact their intent to avoid any form of manipulation from the media, liberal or otherwise (Minaev and Yakovlev 2019), Shortparis struck first by manipulating the media themselves. In several of their conversations, the interviewer was disparaged, his progressive political convictions exposed as narrow-minded biases, and oppositional statements carefully dodged. In reference to "Strashno", and responding to the song's use in anti-Putin rallies, the drummer Danila Kholodkov maintained: "It is not a speech against Putin, it is a social videoclip. And the fact that the audience does what they want with it is cool. But I don't understand what the idea of opposition has to do with it" (Ovchinnikov 2019). The "radicalism" that characterised their generation, continued Komiagin, was "of aesthetic nature", while political discourse "alien" to it (Ovchinnikov 2019), and reducing the relation between independent music and politics to one of opposition "would be too simplistic" (*BBC Russia* 2019).

Over direct political criticism, Shortparis articulated patriotic pride dedicated to the fashioning of a culturally autonomous version of Russia. For them:

> It is very important, as a collective, to be a Russian band [*russkaya gruppa*]. Even when we performed in Brighton [at the Great Escape Festival], we shouted words about Russia [*slova o Rossii*] during the whole gig. We regularly make clear that we are a band from Russia, and we emphasise it.
>
> (*BBC Russia* 2019)[45]

From the stage of the Great Escape, Shortparis indeed shouted "*moia bol'naia Rossiia*" (my sick Russia) (Ovchinnikov 2019): the beloved motherland affected by illness functioned as the band's main source of inspiration, despite, because of and thanks to the anxiety and fear it emanated and simultaneously suffered from.

Proceeding by the textbook of *patrioprotest*, Shortparis thus complicated concepts of resistance and subversion with patriotism, both as aesthetic and civil

184 *Independent Music in Russia*

strategy: while the band indeed challenged stable representation of Russian identity, it also held firm the idea of "the Russian soul" (Komiagin in *3voor12 extra* 2020) which could converge with official projections of nationhood. In other words, Shortparis creatively reinvented Russia by subverting some of the norms set by the government, but at the same time subjected these norms to their own version of a patriotic narrative around the nation which seemed to purposefully unresolve oppositional binaries, in the name of Russia as a paramount idea over any divisionary identitarian quests.

Manizha, songwashing and virtue signalling

What happened to protest music in the context of official projections of nationhood? The question does indeed sound like an oxymoron: how could an authoritarian state like Russia be at ease with endorsing on the international stage values that it actively repressed at home? In what follows below, I demonstrate that this indeed was the case through the story of Tajik-born female singer Manizha's participation in the 2021 Eurovision Song Contest (ESC) with the feminist and pro- LGBTQ+ song "Russian Woman". Manizha's entry signaled the state's endorsement of Western progressive ideas – which did not in fact correspond to Russia's internal situation or domestic political aims – for an advertising campaign on the global stage.[46] The state appropriation of Manizha's creativity represented an effort at *virtue signalling* – that is, "the act [of] displaying one's awareness of and attentiveness to political issues, matters of social and racial justice, etc. […] instead of taking effective action".[47] The ultimate aim of this signalling was to mimic the language of the liberal West in order to clean up Russia's reputation. Manizha was not an isolated case, but part of a broader responsive strategy of *songwashing* (Biasioli 2023), that is, the state utilisation of the allure of music to cover up domestic political problems such as its own legitimacy, civic discontent and questions of minority rights, while promoting a different, positive image abroad.

While I coin the term "songwashing" as a musical version of whitewashing (the act of intentionally omitting unfavorable details about something to make it acceptable, usually by diverting the focus to favorable ones), I borrow the idea primarily from sport, where the process is known as *sportswashing* (Skey 2022). This is because music has specific parallels with sport: like sport, music is a free, enjoyable activity with which people engage in their spare time. Like sport, music is organised into international competitions and mega-media events, such as the Eurovision contest, where it represents a nation and where it can be manipulated as a tool for soft power. For this reason, like sport, music was considered by the Kremlin to be of primary importance during the Sochi Winter Olympics in 2014 and the FIFA World Cup in 2018 (on sport mega-events and soft power, see Makarychev and Yatsyk 2014; Wolfe 2020; Arnold 2021). Like athletes, musicians may be more or less political and may share or challenge the values advocated by their government. But by participating in these events or competitions they may – willingly or not – become agents of soft power, ambassadors to some degree of the agenda of the state that sent them there. The fact that this complicity is so entangled with professional accomplishment makes it difficult to resist for athletes and musicians, and equally problematic to judge from a scholar's perspective (Fruh et al. 2022).

The dynamics with which the process of "washing" occurs are fairly straightforward: on the one hand, there is a knowable moral violation; on the other, there is an urge for that violation to attract less attention (Fruh et al. 2022, 3). Pulling off such "washing" requires not simply concealing negative perceptions of an issue but also establishing a positive image for internal and external audiences. This is where the element of distraction comes in, as it is needed to change lenses, swap discourses, and produce acceptable instead of unpleasant representations.

However, unlike sportswashing, songwashing does not seem to involve long-term plans and machinations on the part of the state; instead, it is a product of the state's capacity to improvise, and to adapt quickly as situations change. Put in this way, songwashing is an example of "adaptive authoritarianism", the flexible system of governance that some autocracies use as they learn from the mistakes and failures of other autocratic regimes and incorporate new ruling tools that prioritise pragmatism, opportunism, and fluidity of ideology, all in an effort to maintain power, build legitimacy, and co-opt supporters (Frear 2018; Hall 2023).[48]

When aimed abroad, songwashing extends the "musical branch" of soft power. Several scholars have evaluated the effectiveness of Russia's soft power with skepticism, pointing out that ruble instability, endemic corruption, and the use of hard power (Georgia since 2008, Ukraine since 2014, Syria since 2015) have helped to invalidate the regime's external projections and instead created (or reinforced) a distrustful, negative image of Russia in the global arena (Sergunin and Karabeshkin 2015; Rutland and Kazantsev 2016). The full-scale invasion of Ukraine has confirmed the enduring fears of several former Soviet republics that regarded Russia as a revanchist, imperial threat (Sergunin and Karabeshkin 2015, 356–60). Rutland and Kazantsev (2016, 397) point out, however, that to some extent this negative image has emerged in a context of global soft power that is largely molded and led by the United States and its Western allies, with which Russia has been in increasing confrontation for the past decade. It is partly for this reason that state-affiliated organs have cultivated for Russia an "alternative", "second-world" mediatic stance, which has given Russia the opportunity to vent notions of an alleged "first world crisis" characterised by moral decay, hypocrisy, out-of-control political correctness, Russophobia and so on, and thereby to challenge the Western global order while gaining sympathy among some non–Western countries' political elites, Western anti-capitalist leftists and far-right supporters (Kaczmarska and Keating 2019; Hutchings 2020; Laruelle 2021).

But how did Manziha, a proudly independent and liberal-minded artist, position herself in all this? How did she exercise her agency? In the discussion that follows below, I try to argue that, in order to negotiate between resisting the authoritarian agenda and being sponsored by it, Manizha responded with her own tactics of *patrioprotest*, inscribing her subversion of aspects of officialdom within an overall appeasement of state-sponsored values.

Manizha Sangin was born in 1991 in Dushanbe, Tajikistan, in a Tajik Muslim family. In 1994, during the Tajik civil conflict, her family fled to Moscow. It was

186 *Independent Music in Russia*

there in the Russian capital where she started her musical career at the age of 15, gaining regular airtime on radio and television before quitting the corporate pop business in an effort to preserve creative independence. To this day, Manizha co-authors all her songs and videos and has no affiliation with any label.[49]

On March 8, 2021, International Women's Day, Manizha was selected by popular vote to represent Russia in the Eurovision Song Contest, due in May, with the song "Russian Woman" (initially dubbed "Russkaia zhenshchina" in Russian).[50] The national final was aired live on Russia's state-controlled main TV channel, Channel One, and the finalists shortlisted by the channel's Organising Committee. According to Manizha, it was the TV channel's staff who had approached her, first inviting her to submit an unreleased song to the competition, and then confirming her participation two days before the final (*Skazhi Gordeevoi* 2021). Despite being a relatively unknown outsider, Manizha received 39.7 percent of the televotes, beating the well-known groups Therr Maitz (24.6 percent) and 2Mashi (35.7 percent).

Though she had appeared on state TV before and had developed a decent portfolio, Manizha's name was far less established than her rivals. Curiously, before announcing the winner of the national selection contest, the presenter invited an expert onstage to assure the audience that the voting had gone according to the rules and no infractions had been noticed (to my knowledge, the first time something like this happened). The last time Russia chose its ESC contestant through televoting was in 2012 (normally, the selection is done internally), but even then the votes from home were paired with a jury of experts on a 50/50 basis, and no "observer" took the stage. For this reason, the televoting process was questioned. Reporting information provided by a glossy magazine's website, *Wonderzine* editor Iuliia Taratuta (2021) suggested that Manizha did not win the popular vote, but was selected because her uncle, the millionaire Akmal Usmanov, had strong ties to a few people in the Kremlin with whom he had done business in Central Asia. In any case, the fact that Manizha's upgrade into the mainstream occurred within a state-sponsored environment helped incubate the tensions and contradictions, which would become manifest later, between the articulation of a progressive message about the country and service to an illiberal state.[51]

One of the decisive factors behind Manizha's success was her engagement with social issues. Manizha was a feminist who supported LGBTQ+ rights, endorsed body positivity, campaigned against the domestic abuse of women, was an ambassador of the "Gift of Life" children's foundation and, in December 2020, became Russia's first UN Goodwill Ambassador on behalf of war refugees.[52] "Artists from the new generation don't just do music", she told *Esquire* while summarising the social message of her art; instead, they use music as a means to an end – to improve the conditions of the people (*Esquire* 2019).

If at first Manizha's artistic endeavors seemed at odds with Russia's official discourse, a closer look shows that, compared to Russia's recent ESC entries, Manizha represented both a continuation and a synthesis that were amenable to state appropriation. First, by openly supporting LGBTQ+ rights, Manizha fit into the stream of LGBTQ+-friendly and camp performers whom Russia continued to send to Eurovision despite its increasingly anti-LGBTQ+ measures at home:

Patrioprotest 187

Dima Bilan in 2006 and 2008, Sergey Lazarev in 2016 and 2019 and Little Big in 2020 (even if this Eurovision was cancelled). LGBTQ+ people constitute the majority of Eurovision's audience, and, to appeal to them, Russian entries often fashioned their stage performances as camp and peppered their lyrics with sexual ambiguity (Miazhevich 2010; Cassiday 2014, 5–10). The choice of singing in English, endorsed by both Bilan and Lazarev, enhanced this ambiguity: English, unlike Russian, does not express gender in adjectives, leaving the subject of the lyrics suspended.[53] In general, rather than the demise of a short-term gay trajectory, as Cassiday predicted in 2014, it would be more appropriate to talk about an "occasional" gay strategy, which Russia used intermittently with other approaches, such as provocation of/confrontation with the West (Samoilova in 2017 and 2018), or ethnic inclusivity/denial of empire. The latter, as Emily Johnson (2014) noted, was reminiscent of the Soviet idea of "Friendship of the Peoples" (*Druzhba narodov*), introduced by Stalin to encapsulate the supposedly harmonious and cooperative coexistence of the various Soviet nationalities.

The queer strategy, nonetheless, proved the most fruitful, as Russia secured a second and first place with Bilan, and two third places with Lazarev, which put Manizha in a suitable position to do well too. Second, being a Tajik refugee who relocated in Russia, Manizha accorded well with the well-trodden path of ethnic inclusivity (see, e.g., Natalya Podolskaya in 2005, Anastasia Prikhodko in 2009 and Buranovskie Babushki in 2012). Third, Manizha presented herself as a serious, committed artist with an empowering feminist message that could be easily espoused by the liberal West. Manizha, therefore, combined LGBTQ+ support, ethnic minorities' visibility, cosmopolitanism and feminism, giving Russia the opportunity to advertise itself as earnestly progressive and intersectionally inclusive.

Manizha's victory at the national selection sparked a nationwide controversy. Soon after the announcement, Channel One's social media pages were swamped by people calling the choice shameful and unlawful, and referring to Manizha herself in demeaning ways, including as a foreign agent on the West's payroll.[54] The situation escalated to the point where, in the following days, the singer's own social media pages attracted aggressive abuse, and even death threats (*BBC* 2021). It is important to note that many of Manizha's detractors discussed neither the quality of the song nor the singer's performance, but rather her ethnicity and views on feminism, sexuality, and gender. The essence of these comments could be summarised as something along the lines of "Why is a Western-inspired Tajik LGBTQ+ activist representing Russia, and with a song called 'Russian Woman'"?

Manizha had attempted, on the day of the selection, to preempt the polemic by comparing Russian women to Russia as a country: "This is a song about the most beautiful and incredible women of Russia […] it's about our inner power. […] But the most important thing is that we have our own path, just like Russia itself" (*Pervyi kanal* 2021). Applying the long-standing and official idea of Russia's third path and special fate in history to Russian women did little to quell criticism, but it did nonetheless signal Manizha's desire to shift the narrative from "alien" and "Western" feminism onto the more familiar track of patriotic, state-endorsed values.

188   *Independent Music in Russia*

Despite the turmoil on social media, Manizha garnered solid support not only from across the spectrum of independent journalism but also from state-controlled media outlets, including *RT*, Channel One, and *Rossiiskaia gazeta*.[55] On the state-endorsed news outlet *Moskva 24* (2021), Manizha responded to her denigrators by explaining the following:

> for me, participating in the Eurovision Song Contest is a great opportunity to tell the world what is really important to me. I am Tajik, but Russia accepted and raised me. I would like the world to see our country as I know it: generous, open, bright, and unlike anything else.

This reinforced the singer's tactic of framing Russia as an ethnically inclusive country while promoting the country's positive image and unique character in the global arena. Such affirmative statements against racial stereotypes and ethnic divisions could be packaged by the state as a story of successful integration, a positive portrait of Russia as a welcoming land of opportunities, despite the growing presence of ethnonationalism at the grassroots level and the state's tendency to recalibrate citizenship according to ethnonational terms (Blakkisrud 2016; Kolstø 2016). Manizha, therefore, offered the state the chance to songwash these internal tensions and present Russia as a harmonious blend of cultures, traditions, and languages.[56] These entities, however, were glued together with the paramount concept of *russkii*: Channel One, for example, dubbed the song in Russian as *russkaia zhenshchina*, not *rossiiskaia zhenshchina*, and in several interviews with Manizha (including with independent or "liberal" journalists), the discussion centred on "What is a Russian (*russkaia*) woman"?[57] Manizha herself launched a project on Instagram called "thisisrussianwoman", in which she collected female perspectives on what it meant to be a Russian woman.[58] The descriptions were both in English and in Russian, but, in the latter, the adjective *russkaia* was always used, even when it referred to ethnic non-Russian women. One way to see this would be that Manizha was here subverting the concept of *russkii* from the bottom-up, colouring it with multiethnic valence, asserting ownership of it, and disrupting the homogenising narrative from within. Another way of seeing would be that she was doing the opposite: emanating internalised coloniality, she was overlooking differences at the service of empire and the *russkii* dominant discourse. Thus, an ambiguous premise at home set the stage for a similarly equivocal show in Europe.

Manizha's *cause célèbre* soon acquired international resonance, and before and after the Eurovision final in Rotterdam (May 18–22), some Western newspapers framed it as "the brave artist versus the Kremlin". The Italian edition of *Huffington Post* proclaimed that "she has not won Eurovision, but she has won everything else" (Iaccarino 2021). *The Telegraph* (UK) echoed this thought, asserting that "Manizha has upset the establishment and delighted the country's increasingly progressive youth as she rapped her way to victory" (Vasilyeva 2021). Such interpretations were partly justified by an official inquiry conducted into Manizha's lyrics by the Investigative Committee, a state agency responsible for inspecting federal bodies and local authorities. The inquiry was requested by the Russian Union of Orthodox Women on the grounds that "Russian Woman" humiliated the dignity of women and belittled their role as mothers.[59] The allegations were found to be uncorroborated by evidence, and were therefore dismissed (*RIA Novosti* 2021). A separate investigation into alleged fraud in the voting process of the selection show, initiated by Valentina Matvienko, chair of the Federation Council, yielded no result either, and was dropped (Blinov 2021). Whether these conflicts were themselves part of the show is difficult to assess. If they were the result of genuine concerns, though, they denoted the organisational chaos of the various branches of Russian state power, whose narratives at times conflicted with one another (as discussed earlier in the chapter).

The official line of the Kremlin, as reported by its press secretary Dmitrii Peskov, came later than the investigation and was the following:

> "There [at Eurovision] is where bearded women,[60] singers in chicken outfits and the like perform. We do not consider it our concern and worth our attention. [...] We do not consider it appropriate to interfere and comment".
>
> (*Sputnik Tajikistan* 2021)

This minimising indifference was, however, mere posture: under Putin (and until Russia was banned from participation in 2022) the Russian government made a concerted effort to use the Eurovision competition as a tool for nation-branding (Miazhevich 2010). Unlike many other countries, Russia often sent its most popular performers to the competition, evidence of a strong desire to win in order to regain cultural prestige internationally (Heller 2007; Pajala and Vuletic 2022). When Dima Bilan won in 2008, he received a congratulatory phone call from President Dmitri Medvedev, as well as a telegram from Prime Minister Putin himself, who claimed victory for all of Russia (Cassiday 2014, 2). The Kremlin's strategy, then, was to maintain its characteristic enigmatic stance and await further developments, after which it could either claim ownership or disapprove of Manizha. Moreover, Peskov's derogatory statement about gender in the ESC contradicted Russia's own history of ESC entries, several of whom, as we have seen, displayed elements of queer, camp and non-normative sexuality in their performances and lyrics, before and after the anti-LGBTQ+ laws in 2012–13.

Other Western media outlets took a more cautious approach. For example, *The Guardian*, *The Times*, *Deutsche Welle* and *France 24* all analysed Manizha's selection and performance within the context of the backlash her selection provoked among various factions in Russian society. But they did so without mentioning the Kremlin, thus keeping Russian public opinion and the state as two separate entities, and recognising the relative fragmentation of opinions among state actors (Bennetts 2021; Boutsko 2021; *France 24* 2021; Roth 2021).

This approach was all the more valid considering that in Russia some state-endorsed media continued to back Manizha. The domestic version of *RT*, for example,

190   *Independent Music in Russia*

praised the singer for clearly affirming womanhood and gender in Europe, a place in which, according to the commentator, they had disappeared:

> What happens there is this: the mixing of gender poles, the frantic desire to legitimize the right of women to consider themselves men and the right of men to look and think like women produce a clear image, behavior, way of thinking. In the first semi-final, there were practically no men on the TV screen in the traditional sense of the word. There were jackets that turned into dresses, hairstyles and make-up from women's magazines (if there are still women in Europe) and, of course, mannerisms.
>
> (Kandelaki 2021)

This selective (mis)reading of Manizha's Eurovision performance, offered by a state-controlled media, served the purpose of songwashing thorny issues of gender.[61] First of all, it was selective in the sense that Manizha's intention was to show the diversity of self-perceptions of womanhood, including non-normative femininity, an intent exemplified by the video collage of women singing the song, as we will see below. *RT* hijacked this message, stripped it of its non-aligned connotations, and repurposed gender as a propagandistic weapon. It is important to note that this article was targeted at Russia's domestic audience, which proves once again the discrepancies and even conflicts between the Russia articulated for international audiences and the Russia mediatised for domestic ones (Hutchings 2022, 173). Second, Manizha's message of female empowerment occurred not long after the government's partial decriminalisation of domestic abuse. Russia, which is one of the countries with the worst statistics of violence against women, decriminalised non-aggravated battery in 2017, lowering it to an administrative offense punishable by a fine, detention up to 14 days or 120 hours of community service (*Human Rights Watch* 2017). In response to what she saw as a shocking law, Manizha released a video for the song "Mama" in 2019, accompanied with a link to download an app that allowed women to call for immediate help and provided a list of support organisations (*Meduza* 2019b; Roth 2021). By bastardising Manizha's message and activism, and showing her off to the world as "Russian, woman and proud", state media endorsed the feminist cause on the international stage while trying to keep it acceptable within its borders.

Manizha's exercise of agency took into account the above discourses and potential limitations, and her performance at the ESC stage managed to merge patriotism and Russianness with criticism of state-endorsed patriarchy, as well as gesturing towards Western liberalism. It is notable that most of the politicisation of the stage choreography was packaged especially for the ESC final, whereas during the national selection Manizha had kept visual effects to a bare minimum. First of all, the affirmation of female agency was made visible through a number of lyrical and material devices, including Manizha's costume. Quite unlike her performance at the national selection, at the ESC Manizha sang the introduction to her song while enveloped in a huge dress that constrained her up to the neck, a metaphor for the social restraints faced by women in Russia. At the end of the intro, she broke away from the unwieldy costume, revealing an unassuming (but also Soviet-echoing, working-class) red coverall bearing the inscription "рашн wуман". This Cyrillic transcription of the English pronunciation of "Russian woman" (with the addition of the Latin letter "w") perhaps signalled the singer's intention to avoid backlash by going beyond the *russkii/rossiiskii* identitarian affiliations. The gesture was accompanied by the empowering lines "Why wait? Get up and go!" (*A chë zhdat'? Vstala i poshla!*) in reference to crossing a battlefield – a concept reinforced in the chorus of the song, and which stands for the gender divisions within Russian society. To strengthen the feminist message, the first couple of lines of the next verse ("Every Russian woman needs to know/You're strong enough, you're gonna break the wall") recur several times and are sung in English (the rest of the song is in Russian). They encapsulate the composition's meaning, which is made as understandable as possible via the use of the lingua franca, in a nod to the transnationality of feminism.

However, the chorus complicates this linear interpretation. Manizha sings:

They fight, they fight
All around they all fight, but they do not pray
The son's without a father, the daughter's without a father
But a broken family will not break me.

The reference to religion comes at the most dramatic moment of the song, when what had been a lively and dance-like performance suddenly turns solemn and switches to a minor chord progression. The four backing singers lift their arms in a gesture of invocation while Manizha kneels. During the first chorus, a screen shows the visage of a sad woman wearing a *kokoshnik* (a traditional Russian head-dress) watching a battle between horsemen, which epitomises masculine violence (see Figure 4.9). The gravity of the woman's face, and the *kokoshnik*'s resemblance to a halo, are reminiscent of the iconography of the Virgin Mary. The second chorus is accompanied by a projection of a collage of videos of women singing along, aimed at representing the different ways in which women perceive their womanhood, showing inclusivity as a key feature (see Figure 4.10). The reference to religion, however, seems to offer a solution to the problem of gender inequality: if men could remember to live according to good moral precepts, if men would pray instead of fighting, then injustice could be eradicated. It also needs to be noted that Manizha did not employ these screen projections at the national competition; there, she used a simple, abstract design. Also new to her ESC performance were the inscriptions, all in English, "rise up", "be unstoppable", "be yourself" and "be creative", which complemented the empowering message of the performance according to the neoliberal textbook: to make her critique of stereotypical gender roles in Russia explicit and to appeal to a wider international audience, Manizha banked on motivational mottos which had long been cannibalised by Western corporations (see Figure 4.11). At the same time, while the religious subtext queered the neoliberal inscriptions a little, it also gestured toward Orthodoxy, that is, toward an ultraconservative institution – the clergy – that views women primarily as mothers

192 *Independent Music in Russia*

Figures 4.9, 4.10 and 4.11. Still frames from the video of Manizha's performance at the 2021 Eurovision Final. Source: YouTube.[62]

Patrioprotest 193

and is one of Putinism's strongholds. These apparently conflicting elements lent themselves to songwashing. The ability of Manizha to wink in both directions – East and West, Russia and Europe – made her a valuable intercultural mediator, one who could "translate the language of globalism into that of Russian distinctiveness and back" (Hutchings 2022, 142), voicing cosmopolitanism and Western values while expressing patriotism and Russianness.

Manizha's efforts paid off, and Russia did well in the Eurovision competition: she finished ninth (out of 26 participants), receiving 104 points from the various juries and 100 from the audience. Among the juries that voted most favorably for Russia were Azerbaijan (12 points); Portugal, France and Moldova (10 points); The Netherlands and Slovenia (8 points); and Israel and Belgium (7 points), which testified to her appeal across a broad geographic spectrum. Equally important was the media attention that "Russian Woman" garnered, which surpassed that directed toward any other participant in the 2021 ESC and secured for Russia the "global visibility that it much desires" (Strukov 2016, 43). Even though doubts remain about the effectiveness and long-term success of songwashing (as is the case for any type of washing), it is clear that Manizha's ESC adventure was at least not a failure from the state's point of view.[63] Her disparagement of institutionalised patriarchy boosted Russia's attractiveness among Western audiences, indicating, as Vlad Strukov argued in relation to another famous case (Zviagintsev's film *Leviathan*) "the possibility of counter-hegemonic narratives" within the mainstream (Strukov 2016, 37).

Nonetheless, a small segment of Russia's opposition media took issue with Manizha's performance and questioned the subversive potential of such state-endorsed initiatives. In an editorial in the Russian feminist webzine *Wonderzine* titled, "Why We Shouldn't Be Happy about Manizha's Performance at Eurovision", Iulia Taratuta criticised Manizha's "feminism for dummies", arguing that the arena where her contestation occurred was itself disturbing (Taratuta 2021). The editor unfolded an idea that few had previously considered: those in power who had "placed" Manizha there did so "to defeat an opponent (and in the current situation – practically an enemy) with his own weapons on his own field" (Taratuta 2021). Using the West's rhetoric of inclusivity, Russia could either subvert negative stereotypes about its image abroad (for those who believed the authenticity of the performance), or (for those who did not) ridicule Europe's hypocrisy by demonstrating how easy it was to fake such rhetoric. It would not be the first time that Russia deployed this strategy at ESC: t.A.T.u.'s near-miss in 2003 prompted commentators to blame Western homophobia (Heller 2007), while Iuliia Samoilova's exclusion in 2017 was framed along ableist lines (Samoilova is a wheelchair user) (Kazakov and Hutchings 2019).

The day after her *Wonderzine* editorial, Taratuta clarified that:

> We, like other journalists, made attempts to contact Manizha when she became Russia's delegate at Eurovision. I personally tried to interview her, made an application—we were all sent to Channel One, because they dealt with her contacts as soon as she became a delegate. Someone says that these

194   *Independent Music in Russia*

are her contract obligations [...] but in our country it is so arranged that when a singer goes somewhere from Russia, they become a government official.

(The Village 2021)

Taratuta had to clarify because Manizha in the meantime had decided to sue *Wonderzine* for libel (*Meduza* 2021). The singer was angered by the journalist's "lies", but Taratuta did not back off, saying that the singer's reaction further proved her point. After this, silence set in.[64]

Taratuta's clarification had nonetheless disclosed an important point: the lines between the nation and the state had been blurred, and Manizha had been enveloped in an "assemblage" of "manipulative smart power" (Strukov 2016; see also Hutchings 2022). This horizontal and loose network, formed by different – at times even oppositional – actors, projected a compound discourse of nationhood containing threads of contestation and patriotism, cosmopolitanism and Russianness. As Strukov (2016) put it, "manipulative smart power" describes the process through which Russia creates multi-directional and ambiguous messages that can speak to different actors nationally and internationally. Strukov argues that "manipulative smart power" "traverses the binary dynamic of power—positive/negative, external/internal and vertical/horizontal", and top-down/bottom-up, preferring contradiction over consistency to shape its influence (Strukov 2016, 35). The songwashing surrounding Manizha's "Russian Woman" happened along similar lines: in the background of the huge controversy that it ignited, the performance projected a bottom-up, Western-friendly critique of institutionalised patriarchy that was complemented with an equally bottom-up, unconditioned love for Russia, reinforced in interviews and public statements, which in turn echoed state-endorsed, top-down discourses of Russia's special destiny and *russkii*-led ethnic inclusivity. The context and the dynamics within which this occurred, however, left little doubt about the fact that state-affiliated media enjoyed primacy of place in managing these messages.

All in all (and regardless of Manizha's merits and noble intentions), the support that the singer received from several Russian institutions did not signify any sort of democratisation of Russia's political environment; rather, it equated to a spectacle put on for the West. Due to her ethnicity and activism, Manizha synthesised and reaffirmed those values, minorities, and voices that state politics had marginalised, and offered a resolution to those issues that the government had minimised or mismanaged. The values she advocated for – multiculturalism, feminism, non-heteronormative sexual orientations, freedom of speech and ethnic diversity – could now be endorsed all at once internationally, without promoting or implementing them nationally. The state employed songwashing principles to turn Manizha's committed activism into a tool for virtue signalling on the global stage. Crucial attributes of virtue signalling are emptiness and hypocrisy: while the state talked the talk without walking the walk at Eurovision, at home the reins of control over political opposition were tightened and freedom of speech further eroded. In 2021, Alexei Navalny was arrested and sentenced to two years and eight months in a penal colony, 109 media outlets, political organisations and cultural institutions (including *Meduza* and *Dozhd'*) were labeled "foreign agents"; the human rights group Memorial was liquidated; and the stage was generally set for the totalitarian turn of February 2022.

Manizha presented the state with an opportunity to exploit grassroots cultural products – that is, products that form independently and within civil society – to alter perceptions about the country internationally. The example of Manizha complicated Joseph Nye's (2013) observation that authoritarian regimes like Russia did not understand soft power because they did not give civil society enough freedom and support to develop its talents. If soft power is based on affecting the opinions of others through attraction in order to achieve particular goals, the Russian state endeavoured to wield it by paying lip service to Western narratives of inclusion and by mediatising a false virtuous image of itself. The political aspect of music – traditionally assumed to challenge the status quo and bring about social change – was refashioned by the state through a neoliberal, Western lens. Mimicking the West meant that the commodification of resistance in music was preferred over confrontation with it.[65] Moreover, the image of the nation presented at the 2021 ESC contrasted starkly with the one projected domestically. This proved yet again that the decisions Russia's state institutions made were often opportunistic, disorganised, and shaped by local conditions, concerns, and considerations; at the same time, they were also aimed at spreading "confusion, uncertainty, and deniability" under the (sometimes close, sometimes distant) gaze of the Kremlin (Galeotti 2017, 2). This improvised strategy entailed difference and interplay between the image of Russia projected internally and the one projected abroad, one in which Russia the state relied on a blend of attraction and contradiction about Russia the nation to distract domestic audiences and captivate international ones.

Conclusions

As Michael Herzfeld (2004, 155–56) argued:

> [T]he perceptions of actors engaged in such systems are attuned to the negotiation of social values and they often call the bluff of official rhetoric. In so doing they raise the possibility of an alternative, critical perspective. [. . .] Clearly, people do not think, act, or speak exactly as the schematized ideologies of statism would prefer. Nevertheless, they do continue to serve their national entities with great loyalty [. . .] [S]ensitive actors can negotiate the tensions of social identity and daily life within the turbulent context of the modern nation-state, and [. . .] they can be fiercely patriotic and just as fiercely rebellious at one and the same time. This perspective represents an epistemological militant middle ground.

It is that militant middle ground that this chapter has explored, by focusing on the relationship between protest, in its multiple musical articulations, and the Russian state. Indeed, Herzfeld's argument is all the more valid if we take into account the diglossia (or, as he calls it, "disemia") between bottom-up and top-down

196   *Independent Music in Russia*

actors, and the heteroglossia within grassroots actors and state actors: different discourses, involving protest on one end and authoritarian rhetoric on the other, and comprising different political strategies within each group of actors, at times resonated into shared patriotism.

Putin's fourth term provided excellent ground to assess that, in some cases, authoritarian governments and critical cultural figures operated more as dialogical entities than irreconcilable opposites. Firstly, when contestation was articulated, musicians at times flanked it with signs that could be also associated with power, therefore enabling the "smuggling" of critique through to audiences outside the independent music world. These developments and tactics went beyond fixed and widely established dichotomies of political versus apolitical, or of oppositional versus compliant. They countered widespread claims that all art is political and inevitably chooses a side, like Argentinian philosopher Chantal Mouffe's (2001, 100) assertion that "one cannot make a distinction between political art and non-political art, because every form of artistic practice either contributes to the reproduction of the given common sense – and in that sense is political – or contributes to the deconstruction or critique of it". The first part of the assertion holds true – even declaring one's artistic production apolitical, as Slovenian thinker Slavoj Žižek (1991, 191) contends, could be the utmost political act. Yet the second one did not apply to a significant portion of Russia's cultural products of Putin's fourth term, where it was possible to witness an art that was multi-vectorial, simultaneously against and for the state, resistant and acquiescent, expressing both disapproval and devotion – in one word: *patrioprotest*.

Secondly, power reacted to political songs differently to the direct crackdown on Pussy Riot in 2012. Due to the considerable degree of decentralisation and under-coordination between state structures, official discourse showed a variety of contradictory methods of management of protest music, from (sometimes random) punishment to songwashing, from indifference to guidance, from targeting to incorporation of protest. The variety of strategies indicated the coexistence of methods of spin and fear dictatorships and pointed to the unpredictability, arbitrariness and porosity of the boundary between what was permitted and what was not in Russian popular music. The boundary, as Lotman (1990, 134–142) observed, is the domain of cultural bilingualism, a place of constant dialogue and dialectical processes, in and through which actors shape hybridised sign systems. In late 2010s Russia, one of these hybrid systems was *patrioprotest*, born out of power interference on one side and musicians' agency and social engagement on the other.

This chapter has also shown that, regardless of globalising phenomena, states still influence the production, distribution and reception of domestic popular music (Cloonan 1999; Negus 2019). This happens because the state "sets the scene" where musicians and their communities live and create. In the case of democratic societies, this usually involves the promotion of discourses around national values, but also an overall laissez faire attitude and a renunciation of coercive intervention in cultural matters (save perhaps, the introduction of laws defining quotas on domestic/foreign music in radio airplay). In authoritarian regimes, censorship, co-optation and other interventionist strategies are high on the state musical agenda. In spin dictatorships

Patrioprotest 197

like Russia was at the end of the 2010s, all these methods coexisted. The various actors across the state apparatus could be indifferent as they could make their presence felt, could endorse as they could selectively punish. In any case, the Russian state, in its various manifestations, claimed a decisive role in the music world. As Interviewee 77 argued, when a grassroots cultural movement grows to a noticeable extent in Russia, like independent music did, the state always says: "what about me"?

The enduring presence of the authoritarian state gave Russian independent music a significant part of its own specificity, as musicians busied themselves devising and performing "safe" ways to circumvent and criticise it, thus inventing (or solidifying) conventions and localised styles in the process. However, this did not automatically mean that musicians – as members of the intelligentsia reflecting on the situation of their country – resisted or opposed their government tout court, as it was often reductively and condescendingly expected of them in Western media discourse. It meant, rather, that musicians – like the people at large – enacted a process of selection and negotiation by applying their agency where they saw fit. As Yurchak (2006, 28–29) argued in relation to late-Soviet society, the context acted on people decisively but also diversely in their indifference to, dismissal, embracing or reimagination of official norms and values. This was also the case of the Russian independent music world, in which practitioners have been responding to political stimuli in multiple ways and outside rigid schemes of contestation (see also Wickström 2014). Musicians maintained this diversity of tactics vis-à-vis the national and international developments of the late 2010s, together with a continuation of the investigations around its national identity. This "semiotic dynamism" (Lotman 1990, 134) between the "centre" and the "periphery", rather than antagonistic and incompatible, was dialectic and ambiguous.

Notes

1 This "aesthetic rupture", according to Rancière, is supposed to create dissensus, precisely because the art work neither gives lessons nor has a destination (Rancière, 2010, 140). It is through processes of subjectivation of the political in art that a redistribution of the common (ways of seeing, saying, doing) can occur.
2 This consists of representational mediation (production of a new perception of the world) and ethical immediacy (commitment to transformation of the world, mobilisation of individuals).
3 See, for example: McMichael (2005, 2008); Steinholt (2005); Steinholt and Wickström (2009); Wickström (2014); Rogatchevski and Steinholt (2016).
4 This rise was due to the conjunction of several motives of remonstration, from ecological crises (*Kommersant* 2019) to freedom from political activists (*Snob* 2020), but the two that had the most mediatic resonance were the Golunov case (in which police fabricated evidence of drug dealing against *Meduza*'s journalist Ivan Golunov) and the fraud before the Moscow Duma elections (in which candidates from oppositional parties were denied the right to participate despite having gathered the required number of signatures to do so).
5 During these demonstrations, as reported by human rights organisations and independent media outlets, around 3000 people were taken into custody in Moscow alone (*OVD-Info* 2019a, 2019b; *Meduza* 2019a; *Vedomosti* 2019), 28 arrested, and 10 sentenced from one to five years in prison (*BBC Russia* 2020)

198 *Independent Music in Russia*

6 See also Biasioli (2023, 688–92).

7 In 2022, Grebenshchikov was included in the list of "foreign agents" by the Russian Ministry of Justice and moved abroad permanently.

8 In 2022, Mashnov moved abroad.

9 The band was founded in 1989 near Moscow.

10 See, for example, the open protest of songs by the band Televizor (TV) or Egor Letov's Grazhdanskaia Oborona (Civil Defense); or the dissensus contained in some of the songs by Boris Grebenshchikov (e.g., "Nemoe kino" – Silent Movie), Maik Naumenko (e.g., "Oda k vannoi komnate" – Ode to the Bathroom) or Shevchuk's DDT (e.g., "Ne streliai" – Don't Shoot).

11 As explained in the previous chapter, even the 2012 Pussy Riot case, while slowly changing the musicians' and trendsetters' habits (and consequently their view on the function of art), did not lead, at least initially, to an upsurge in protest music. The separation between politics and music was one of the reasons why Pussy Riot did not receive much advocacy in the *nezavisimaia muzyka* community and did not start a trend of protest songs (*Afisha* 2012; Gavrilova 2012).

12 Another pretext for disruption was the article 282 of Russia's Criminal Code on the "incitement to hatred or enmity, as well as humiliation of human dignity". Its vague formulations allowed for broad interpretations (however, coincidentally, Putin had submitted a revision for partial decriminalisation of the article in early October 2018, approved by the Duma in December of the same year).

13 The band Pornofilmy (Porn Movies) saw some of its gigs in Russia disrupted in 2017, due not only to their name (which did raise concerns about uninformed parents), but mostly because of their protest songs (Zhelnov 2017). In particular, their album *V diapasone mezhdu otchaianiem i nadezhdoi* (In the Range Between Despair and Hope), which came out in 2017, featured highly political songs that achieved national resonance, including "Rossiia dlia grustnykh" (Russia for Sad People), in which the band sings: "Think right/Feel right/The heart is in the grave/The soul is in prison/This is Russia – Russia for sad people/No elections, no change!/You're hurting my feelings/ Why are you laughing like an asshole?/Russia is a temple of longing and sadness/See you at the courthouse!"

14 On the Soviet "black list", see Yurchak (2006, 214–15)

15 Curiously, Frendzona's singer Meibi Beibi became popular among Russian troops during the first months after the full-scale invasion, including among the Wagner group. The soldiers asked the singer to perform at the frontline to cheer their morale, but the singer did not reply to these requests (*Kholod* 2022).

16 https://www.youtube.com/watch?v=zKbozLYtWeM.

17 Katina and Volkova held each other's hands while singing their hit "Not Gonna Get Us" (Nas ne dogoniat'). The performance, organised by Channel One, showed how Russian state organs could use "rebellious" or "subversive" music to produce an international image that was in contrast with what occurred in its domestic politics. t.A.T.u.'s performance at the Sochi Olympics can be regarded as one of the earliest manifestations of "songwashing" after the authoritarian turn of 2012 (see later). It did not matter whether the Russian state believed in the values it hinted at internationally; what mattered was that the media event became an opportunity to songwash illiberal deeds into a liberal image of Russia. All of this, arguably, was done in an ironic, provocative and double-voiced key: on one layer, the state hijacked a message of sexual freedom in order to convince foreign audiences that Russia was not an anti-gay country; on another layer, as Vitaly Kazakov (2019, 107) argues, "they're not gonna get us" referred to the primacy of Russian athletes in the winter sport competition (see also Biasioli 2023, 686–87).

18 The video can be found here: https://www.youtube.com/watch?v=Gt3HauGnmEw.

19 As Goode (2018, 265) writes, SPPE budget went from a meagre 130 million rubles in 2001 to 1.67 billion rubles in 2016, despite the ongoing recession and the imposition of austerity measures in other sectors.

Patrioprotest 199

20 See, for example, the organisation Nashi (Ours), which was the pinnacle of this state-funded "NGO boom" in Russia (Hemment 2012, 234), and evidenced how Putin's idea of civil society was united with state sovereignty. At its peak in 2008, the movement boasted 300,000 members. Among the movement's tenets were antifascism, patriotism and the construction of a participatory civil society in Russia through youth-led and youth-targeted grassroots initiatives. Importantly, Nashi were hostile towards political opposition and pro-Western movements. Spin-offs of Nashi still in activity are: Stop-Kham (for responsible driving), Lev protiv (against smoking and drinking in public places), Khriushi protiv (for the display of good quality food products in supermarkets), Serdityi grazhdanin (Angry Citizen) for the collection and resolution of complaints, Advokat tela (Body Advocate) for a healthy lifestyle and so on.

21 https://www.youtube.com/watch?v=MBG3Gdt5OGs.

22 For example, Pornofilmy performed on June 12 in support of Ivan Golunov; Khadn dadn performed on September 29 in conjunction with the results of the Moscow Duma elections.

23 Khadn dadn are an electropop band with electronic influences, founded in Moscow in 2016.

24 Jars are a noise/post-hardcore group, founded in 2011 in Moscow.

25 https://www.youtube.com/watch?v=5epQ3i-TP4c.

26 https://www.youtube.com/watch?v=PVLt4tmbOkM&t=9s.

27 See, for example, Iurii Dud's (*Vdud'* 2020a, 2020b, 2019) interviews with Ic3peak, Monetochka and Pornofil'my.

28 Pechorin is the protagonist of Mikhail Lermontov's novel *A Hero of Our Time* (1841); Bazarov is the main character of Ivan Turgenev's *Fathers and Sons* (1862); Oblomov is the protagonist of Ivan Goncharov's novel of the same name (1859).

29 For example, riot grrrl's punk and feminist message feeding into Spice Girls' "girl power" (see Jones 2021).

30 The track, despite its direct reference to Putin as the rapist (as well as to sex, violence and drug use), was not banned, unlike others from Kuznetsov, such as "Iuda" in 2018, which was not near the same level of graphic depiction.

31 As Gorbachev (2017) described, Kuznetsov "reads songs against consumer society at the presentation of Esquire magazine which was paid for by luxury brands, or wears things from Adidas while speaking out against corporations". Kuznetsov's carefully honed contradictions, continued Gorbachev, were reminiscent of another complex and controversial figure such as Egor Letov, who went by the motto of "always being against".

32 See https://2019.rap-koktebel.ru/.

33 Of course, Khaski was not the first rapper to be arrested in Russia: Noize MC, for example, was incarcerated for ten days in 2010, and several of his gigs were disrupted because of his oppositional political stance (Ewell 2017).

34 See, for example, the administrative case against the rappers Morgenshtern and Eldzhei in 2021 (Ravin 2021), or a report commissioned by the Federal Service for Supervision of Communications, Information Technology and Mass Media (Roskomnadzor) on pop star Egor Krid, dated 27 September 2019 (Volkova et al. 2019). The report deemed Krid's songs capable of leading a minor to "emotional anxiety" and "stress", thus "blocking the development of the intellect". The 15-page document analysed not only Krid's music, but also Krid's tattoos: "Based on the singer's demonstrated affiliation with the New Age movement, which can be clearly discerned from his tattoos, we conclude that his ideological orientation is anti-Russian [*antirossiiskaia*]. This conclusion is supported by statements regarding rap as an ideological weapon of Satanism" (Volkova et al. 2019). Overall, the report was adamant that Krid's activity represented a danger for minors and advised the federal authorities to limit Krid's songs to a 18+ public. No further action ensued, but music journalists ridiculed the zeal with which the authorities filed the report on a kind of music that they perceived to be harmless at most (*The Flow* 2019).

200 *Independent Music in Russia*

35 The line of adequacy presents some similarities with Schimpfössl and Yablokov's (2017, 539) description of *adekvatnost* in relation to journalists in post-Soviet Russia: "the skills, sensitivity, and knowledge to navigate one's professional space", involving "sensing, accepting, and anticipating the (often unspoken) political line while trying not to cross the line into self-censorship". *Adekvatnost'* represented a way to retain some of the profession's creativity while relinquishing some of its creative freedom. Yablokov and Schimpfössl's arguments concerned media figures, often employed in state-loyal outlets. Musicians do not start from the same position in society, but at times their professional trajectories can resemble those of mainstream personalities; the larger the following, the more the attention from the authorities.

36 The song accumulated more than a million dislikes in a very short time – a record for a Russophone product on YouTube – and was eventually taken down (*RT* 2019).

37 Prilepin was also among the most vocal advocates for the rapper's immediate release. On 22 November, hours after the rapper's arrest, he wrote on his social media: "Husky is one of the most talented rap musicians in Russia, and a genuine patriot of our Motherland. What you are doing is a stupid mess. It disgusts me. [. . .] I wish my eyes could not see you, vampires" (Prilepin 2018). It is not clear whom Prilepin was addressing, whether local police authorities or Duma politicians, but it is clear how positions of support and contestation of power in Russia can switch suddenly.

38 The documentary, titled *ChVK Filarmoniia*, can be watched here: https://zen.yandex.ru/video/watch/6257fa4247ef2c3b4998512d.

39 Shortparis kept working in Russia after the start of the full-scale war.

40 In addition to the anti-gay propaganda law in 2013 and the absence of legal recognition or protection against discrimination of non-heteronormative people, in 2022 the international LGBTQ+ organisation was deemed as "extremist" and outlawed by the government. The Russian Orthodox Church, through the speeches of its patriarch, Kirill, framed LGBTQ+ activist groups as a product of the rotting West, echoing the official governmental line, which also linked LGBTQ+ values with the moral degradation of the West as part of its neo-traditionalist and nationalistic campaigns (see also Baer 2009, 6; Stella 2013, 478).

41 As the band recounted, they were called simultaneously "Nazis" and "Islamists" by worried passers-by, who also called the police, believing a terrorist attack was afoot (*Meduza* 2018c).

42 See *Radio Free Europe* (2007) and the documentary film *Beslan, Remember* (2019).

43 https://www.youtube.com/watch?v=FUdteCBRX9c.

44 Again, to continue the interpretative ping-pong: the fact that other, ethnically diverse people carry the pedestal as well may suggest that everyone is subjugated.

45 It is also worth noting that the band often made these statements for foreign media outlets and exclusively in Russian.

46 Even the totalitarian Soviet regime may at times differentiate strategies of distribution of the same cultural product depending on whether the target audience was internal or external: Loseff (1984, 223), for example, noted that "the films of Andrey Tarkovsky or certain of the works of [Vasily] Aksyonov were cleared by Soviet government agencies for distribution abroad while their domestic circulation remained an impossibility".

47 "Virtue signaling", Merriam-Webster Dictionary online, https://www.merriam-webster.com/dictionary/virtue%20signaling.

48 Of course, songwashing can be seen as a tool in the service of spin dictatorships in order to fashion an illusion of democracy. In Putin's fourth term, however, as factions of Russian society became more dissatisfied with governmental policies, overall life conditions, and state strategies of control, these sophisticated methods increasingly mixed with the deployment of "traditional" dictatorial ones, such as violent repression, instillation of fear and explicit censorship. Public awareness of this trick is, therefore, the primary obstacle to successful songwashing, which works effectively only if the subjects at which it is directed do not see it as such. Once exposed, songwashing has to evolve into different forms.

Patrioprotest 201

49 Manizha regularly gives interviews with Russian, Tajik and foreign media. To trace the trajectory of her career, see Golubeva (2018), Gaisina (2021), Zatari (2021), Barabanov (2017).

50 The video of the program is available at https://www.1tv.ru/shows/eurovision2021/o-proekte/evrovidenie-2021-nacionalnyy-otbor-chast-2.

51 I want to clarify that I do not wish to question the authenticity of Manizha's activism here; the question, rather, is how the state exploited the singer's activism to advance a different image of Russia internationally.

52 See: Sinelschikova (2021); *Sobaka* (2019b); *Asia Plus* (2020); Manizha, Instagram post, 26 June 2019 https://www.instagram.com/p/BzLlTadCES-/?utm_source=ig_embed.

53 Ambiguity is also embedded in the lyrics themselves: Lazarev sings "I'll swallow hard", for example, in the refrain of "Scream", Russia's 2016 entry.

54 The post can be found at https://www.instagram.com/p/CMKxX8KCosc/.

55 See Channel One's Instagram post at https://www.instagram.com/p/CMw4qunCzQP/; and see, for example, Alekseev (2021).

56 Moreover, selecting a Tajik-born artist as Russia's representative might appeal to Tajik and other Central Asian audiences, boosting Russia's soft power in the region, which Russia has increasingly had to share with China.

57 See the video of the night of the selection and Manizha's first interview with Kseniya Sobchak, at https://www.1tv.ru/shows/doctalk/vypuski/manizha-russkaya-zhenshina-dok-tok-vypusk-ot-15-03-2021. See also Manizha's interview with Katerina Gordeeva at https://www.youtube.com/watch?v=zCXkLrvoxSQ. For the reasons explained above, some commentators found the appellation *russkaia* problematic. See, for example, *Sygma* (2021).

58 Available at: https://www.instagram.com/thisisrussianwoman/?utm_source=ig_embed&ig_rid=e28a0970-f40c-4924-bd1c-0ec0ad50264f.

59 On women's rights and feminism in Russia, see, for example, Turbine (2015).

60 Peskov is referring to the Austrian singer and drag queen Conchita Wurst, who won the contest in 2014.

61 On gender and feminism in Russia see: Sperling (2015, 6–9).

62 https://www.youtube.com/watch?v=V-Di9A28e5E.

63 On the difficulty of tracking outcomes of sportswashing activities, see, for example, Kazakov (2023).

64 In an interview with Kseniya Sobchak a year later, Manizha explained the outcome of the quarrel: Taratuta had written the article so craftily that her lawyer advised against pursuing the case. See https://www.youtube.com/watch?v=k2skWVb-Z1Y&t=1622s.

65 Commodification is a typically capitalist move to preempt or defuse subversive potential. See, for example, Fisher (2009).

References

3voor12 extra. 2020. 'Shortparis: Dismantling Ideas about Russian Identity'. 7 March. URL: https://www.youtube.com/watch?v=Jr-u8bLJXG4&fbclid=IwAR096HAnDINaO j1T2uHQYI2kzEYtUomU1G4fBjqLSHBvtnFf9ySze769yUU (accessed 7 May 2020).

Afisha. 2012. 'Muzyka dolzhna oskorbit' chuvstva. Noize MC, Vasia Oblomov, Evgenii Gorbunov, i drugie obsuzhdaiut, pochemu molodye russkie gruppy ne poiut o politike'. *Afisha*, 11 September.

Alekseev, A. 2021. 'Stala i poshla: pochemu Manizha dostoina Evrovideniia-2021'. *Rossiiskaia gazeta*, 9 March. URL: https://rg.ru/2021/03/09/pochemu-manizha-dostojna-evrovideniia-2021.html (accessed 3 April 2021).

Amico, S. 2014. *Roll Over, Tchaikovsky! Russian Popular Music and Post-Soviet Homosexuality*. Urbana: University of Illinois Press.

Arnold, R.(ed.). 2021. *Russia and the 2018 FIFA World Cup*. New York: Routledge.

202 *Independent Music in Russia*

Asia Plus. 2020. 'UN Refugee Agency appoints 1st Goodwill Ambassador from Russia'. 14 December. URL: https://asiaplustj.info/en/news/tajikistan/society/20201214/un-refugee-agency-appoints-1st-goodwill-ambassador-from-russia (accessed 2 April 2021).

Baer, B.J. 2009. *Other Russias. Homosexuality and the Crisis of Post-Soviet Identity*. New York: Palgrave Macmillan.

Baliuk, O. 2018. 'Ego muzyka zvuchit v mashine chinovnikov'. *Znak*, 22 November. URL: https://www.znak.com/2018-11-22/kak_reper_haski_shel_k_arestu_cherez_druzhbu_s_prilepinym_donbass_adidas_i_otsylki_k_iisusu (accessed 6 July 2020).

Barabanov, B. 2017. 'Manuskript iz Instagram'. *Kommersant*, 22 May. URL: https://www.kommersant.ru/doc/3304314 (accessed 2 April 2021).

Barabanov, B. 2018. 'Nesanktstionirovannii patriotizm'. *Kommersant*, 14 December. URL: https://www.kommersant.ru/doc/3828618 (accessed 6 July 2020).

BBC. 2021. 'Russia's Tajik-Born Eurovision Star on the Abuse she's Received'. 24 March 24. URL: https://www.bbc.co.uk/news/av/world-europe-56501561 (accessed 4 April 2021).

BBC Russia. 2019. 'Nas koronovali - i eto zashkvar": gruppa Shortparis o populiarnosti, strakhe i tsenzure'. 21 June. URL: https://www.bbc.com/russian/av/media-48713910?fbclid=IwAR15dhoDMEF4ss5Qx6sPKxRYfeH1Jn12V0yA7YalMc6d60-Z6r_lfYTQIG8 (accessed 8 July 2019).

BBC Russia. 2020. 'Vse figuranty 'moskovskogo dela': kto oni i chto s nimi proiskhodit?'. 18 February. URL: https://www.bbc.com/russian/features-50055305 (accessed 28 May 2020).

Becker, H. 1982. *Art Worlds*. Berkeley, CA: University of California Press.

Bel'kova, L. 2018. "My prishli na konstruktivnyi dialog': repery obsudili s deputatami Gosdumy svobodu slova'. *RT na russkom*, 7 December. URL: https://russian.rt.com/russia/article/580320-reper-deputat-gosduma (accessed 9 November 2021).

Bennetts, M. 2021. 'Eurovision Singer Manizha Sangin 'Insult' for Russia, Say Far-Right nationalists'. *The Times*, 12 March 12. URL: https://www.thetimes.co.uk/article/eurovision-singer-manizha-sangin-insult-for-russia-say-far-right-nationalists-dhtg2gsrl (accessed 3 April 2021).

Beslan, Remember. 2019. '*Vdud*'. 2 September. URL: https://www.youtube.com/watch?v=vF1UGmi5m8s (accessed 6 July 2020)

Biasioli, M. 2023. 'Songwashing: Russian Popular Music, Distraction, and Putin's Fourth Term'. *The Russian Review*, 82, 4, pp. 682–704.

Blakkisrud, H. 2016. 'Blurring the Boundary between Civic and Ethnic: The Kremlin's New Approach to National Identity Under Putin's Third Term'. In Kolstø, P., Blakkisrud, H. (eds.) *The New Russian Nationalism. Imperialism, Ethnicity and Authoritarianism 2000–15*. Edinburgh: Edinburgh University Press, pp. 249–74.

Blinov, A. 2021. 'Narushenii v golosovanii na rossiiskom otbore na Evrovidenie ne nashli'. *360tv*, 11 March. URL: https://yandex.ru/turbo/360tv.ru/s/news/obschestvo/narushenij-v-golosovanii-na-rossijskom-otbore-na-evrovidenie-ne-nashli/?utm_source=turbo_turbo (accessed 4 April 2021).

Borealis, I. 2019. 'The Destruction of Text and Expectations. An Interview with Shortparis'. *Schmutz*, 10 September. URL: https://www.schmutzberlin.com/interview-with-shortparis/?fbclid=IwAR2z53IifZz8swOYdSMNybz0JHlbxWmDUqBreze41DijQhv18tjQvLfM-BRg (accessed 7 July 2020).

Boiarinov, D. 2021. '"Naruchniki eti nam – kak skrepy'. *Colta*, 23 April. URL: https://www.colta.ru/articles/music_modern/27196-pleylist-denis-boyarinov-protest-sovremennye-pesni-basta-antoha-mc-tarakany-haski-pussy-riot (accessed 17 March 2025).

Boutsko, A. 2021. 'Eurovision: Manizha from Tajikistan polarizes Russia'. *Deutsche Welle*, 19 May. URL: https://www.dw.com/en/eurovision-manizha-from-tajikistan-polarizes-russia/a-57577536 (accessed 1 June 2021).

Brock, M., Miazhevich, G. 2022. 'From High Camp to Post-Modern Camp: Queering Post-Soviet Pop Music'. *European Journal of Cultural Studies*, 25, 4, pp. 993–1009.

Patrioprotest 203

Bykov, D. 2012. *Sovetskaia Literatura. Kratkii Kurs*. Moskva: Prozaik.

Cassiday, J. 2014. 'Post-Soviet Pop Goes Gay: Russia's Trajectory to Eurovision Victory'. *Russian Review*, 73, 2, pp. 1–23.

Chatterje-Doody, P., Tolz, V. 2019. 'Regime Legitimation, Not Nation-Building: Media Commemoration of the 1917 Revolutions in Russia's Neo-Authoritarian State'. *European Journal of Cultural Studies*, 23, 2, pp. 1–19.

Churakova, O. 2018. 'Simonyan obiasnila osvobozhdenie Khaski vmeshatelstvom Kremlia. Istochnik Dozhdia eto podtverdil'. *Dozhd'*, 26 November. URL: https://tvrain.ru/news/ simonjan_objasnila_osvobozhdenie_haski_vmeshatelstvom_kremlja_istochnik_dozh-dja_eto_podtverdil-475852/ (accessed 6 July 2020).

Cloonan, M. 1999. 'Pop and the Nation-State: Towards a Theorization'. *Popular Music*, 18, 2, pp. 193–207.

Cushman, T. 1995. *Notes from the Underground: Rock Music Counterculture in Russia*. New York: State University of New York Press.

Denisova, A., Herasimenka, A. 2019 (April-June). 'How Russian Rap on YouTube Advances Alternative Political Deliberation: Hegemony, Counter-Hegemony, and Emerging Resistant Publics'. *Social Media + Society*, 5, 2, pp. 1–11.

Doak, C. 2020. 'Queer Transnational Encounters in Russian Literature: Gender, Sexuality, and National Identity'. In Byford, A., Doak, C., Hutchings, S. (eds.) *Transnational Russian Studies*. Liverpool: Liverpool University Press, pp. 213–31.

Dozhd'. 2014. 'Gitarist gruppy Kino Aleksei Rybin: Tsoi ne pel o peremenakh politich-eskogo stroia'. 23 October. URL: https://tvrain.tv/news/gitarist_gruppy_kino_aleksej_ rybin_tsoj_ne_pel_o_peremenah_politicheskogo_stroja-377042/ (accessed 19 December 2023).

Edelman, L. 2004. *No Future: Queer Theory and the Death Drive*. Durham, NC: Duke University Press.

Engström, M. 2018. 'Monetochka: the manifesto of metamodernism.' *Riddle*, 26 June. URL: https://ridl.io/monetochka-the-manifesto-of-metamodernism/ (accessed 1 July 2018).

Engström, M. 2021. 'Transgressing the Mainstream: Camp, Queer and Populism in Russian Visual Culture'. In Semenenko, A. (ed.) *Satire and Protest in Putin's Russia*. Cham: Palgrave Macmillan (e-book), pp. 97–120.

Esquire. 2019. 'Pevitsa Manizha zapustila prilozhenie dlia pomoshchi zhertvam domashnego nasiliia.' 28 February 28. URL: https://esquire.ru/articles/87072-pevica-manizha-zapus-tila-prilozhenie-dlya-pomoshchi-zhertvam-domashnego-nasiliya-i-snyala-klip-v-ego-podderzhku/#part0 (accessed 3 April 2021).

Ewell, P. 2017 'Russian Rap in the Era of Vladimir Putin'. In Helbig, A., Miszczynski, M. (eds) *Hip Hop at Europe's Edge: Music, Agency, and Social Change*. Bloomington: Indiana University Press, pp. 45–62.

Figes, O. 2002. *Natasha's Dance. A Cultural History of Russia*. London: Penguin.

Fisher, M. 2009 *Capitalist Realism: Is There No Alternative?* London: Verso.

Fontanka. 2018. 'Gruppa Ic3peak: Eta sistema mozhet s'est' vsyo. No my vsyo ravno budem delat' to, chto my khotim'. *Fontanka*, 30 December. URL: https://www.fontanka. ru/2018/11/29/146/?feed (accessed 7 May 2020).

France 24. 2021. 'Russia's Feminist Eurovision Singer Sparks Conservative Backlash'. 24 March. URL: https://www.france24.com/en/live-news/20210324-russia-s-feminist-euro-vision-singer-sparks-conservative-backlash (accessed 2 April 2021).

Frear, M. 2018. *Belarus Under Lukashenka: Adaptive Authoritarianism*. London: Routledge.

Friedman, J., Weiner, A. 1999. 'Between a Rock and a Hard Place: Holy Rus' and Its Alternatives in Russian Rock Music'. In Barker, A.M. (ed.) *Consuming Russia: Popular Culture, Sex and Society Since Gorbachev*. Durham, NC: Duke University Press, pp. 110–37.

Fruh, K., et al. 2022. 'Sportswashing: Complicity and Corruption'. *Sport, Ethics and Philosophy*, 17, 1, pp. 1–18.

Gabdulhakov, R. 2018. 'Citizen-Led Justice in Post-Communist Russia: From comrades' Courts to Dotcomrade Vigilantism'. *Surveillance & Society*, 16, 3, pp. 314–31.

204 Independent Music in Russia

Gaisina, I. 2021. "Sama sebe leibl': kak pevitsa Manizha boretsia so stereotipami i nasiliem i zarabatyvaet desiatki millionov rublei v god'. *Forbes*, 8 March 8. URL: https://www.forbes.ru/karera-i-svoy-biznes/410197-sama-sebe-leybl-kak-pevica-manizha-boretsya-so-stereotipami-i-nasiliem-i (accessed 2 April 2021).

Galeotti, M. 2017. 'Controlling Chaos: How Russia Manages Its Political War in Europe', *European Council on Foreign Relations*, pp. 1–18. https://ecfr.eu/archive/page/-/ECFR228_-_CONTROLLING_CHAOS1.pdf

Gavrilova, D. 2012. 'Russkie muzykanty o Pussy Riot'. *Afisha*, 6 August. URL: https://daily.afisha.ru/archive/gorod/archive/russkie-muzikanti-o-pussy-riot/ (last accessed 7 May 2020).

Gerasimenko, O. 2018. "Ia ideal'nyi chelovek-Rossiia': reper Feis ot 'Burgera' do Mandel'shtama'. *BBC Russia*, 6 September. URL: https://www.bbc.com/russian/features-45440153 (accessed 11 September 2020).

Gerschewski, J. 2013. 'The Three Pillars of Stability: Legitimation, Repression, and Co-Optation in Autocratic Regimes'. *Democratization*, 20, 1, pp. 13–38.

Giffney, N. 2009. 'Introduction: The 'q' Word'. In Giffney, N., O'Rourke, M. (eds.) *The Ashgate Research Companion to Queer Theory*. Farnham: Ashgate, pp. 1–13.

Gnatenko, A. 2018. 'Reperu Khaski dali 12 sutok za ulichnoe vystuplenie v Krasnodare'. *Komsomol'skaia Pravda*, 22 November. URL: https://www.kuban.kp.ru/daily/26911.4/3957061/ (accessed 15 June 2020).

Golubev, I. 2018. 'Gosduma ob'iavila o zapuske konkursa dlia nachinaiushchikh reperov'. *Afisha*, 13 December. URL: https://daily.afisha.ru/news/22490-gosduma-obyavila-o-zapuske-konkursa-dlya-nachinayuschih-reperov/?utm_source=facebook.com&utm_medium=social&utm_campaign=duma-fresh-blood.-&fbclid=IwAR2nPIuVB0G6UW85G58KpfkQiThwk9DnrXvIQwH6VO8TsNSX19mfG6InTQg (accessed 15 February 2019).

Golubeva, A. 2018. 'Manizha o proekte s Anei Chipovskoi, seksizme v professii i filosofii svoego tela'. *Hello!*, 4 December. URL: https://ru.hellomagazine.com/zvezdy/intervyu-i-video/28997-manizha-o-proekte-s-aney-chipovskoy-seksiszme-v-professii-i-filosofii-svoego-tela.html (accessed 4 April 2021).

Goode, P. 2018. 'Everyday Patriotism and Ethnicity in today's Russia'. In Kølsto, P., Blakkisrud, H. (eds.) *Russia Before and After Crimea: Nationalism and Identity 2010-2017*. Edinburgh: Edinburgh University Press, pp. 258–81.

Gorbachev, A. 2017. 'Pochemu Khaski – novaia bol'shaia zvezda rossiiskogo khip-khopa'. *Meduza*, 3 February. URL: https://meduza.io/feature/2017/02/03/pochemu-haski-novaya-bolshaya-zvezda-rossiyskogo-hip-hopa (accessed 24 December 2023).

Gorbachev, A. 2018. 'Avtor pesni "Mama, ia ne ziguiu" Monetochka zapisala luchshiirusskii pop-al.'bom goda. Ser'ëzno? (Da)'. *Meduza*, 25 May. URL: https://meduza.io/slides/avtor-pesni-mama-ya-ne-ziguyu-monetochka-zapisala-luchshiy-russkiy-pop-albom-goda-seriezno-da (accessed 3 November 2023).

Guriev, S., Treisman, D. 2022. *Spin Dictators: The Changing Face of Tyranny in the 21st Century*. Princeton and Oxford: Princeton University Press.

Hall, S. 2023. 'The End of Adaptive Authoritarianism in Belarus? *Europe-Asia Studies*, 17, 1, pp. 1–28.

Heller, D. 2007. 't.A.T.u. You! Russia, the Global Politics of Eurovision, and Lesbian Pop'. *Popular Music*, 26, 2, pp. 195–210.

Hemment, J. 2012. 'Nashi, Youth Voluntarism, and Potemkin NGOs: Making Sense of Civil Society in Post Soviet Russia'. *Slavic Review*, 71, 2, pp. 234–60.

Herzfeld, M. 2004. *Cultural Intimacy: Social Poetics in the Nation-State*. New York and London: Routledge.

Hollander, J.A., Einwohner, R.L. 2004. 'Conceptualizing Resistance'. *Sociological Forum*, 19, 4, pp. 533–54.

Human Rights Watch. 2017. 'Russia: Bill to Decriminalize Domestic Violence'. 23 January. URL: https://www.hrw.org/news/2017/01/23/russia-bill-decriminalize-domestic-violence (accessed 3 April 2021).

Patrioprotest 205

Hutchings, S. 2020. 'RT and the Digital Revolution Reframing Russia for a Mediatized World'. In Byford, A., Doak, C., Hutchings, S. (eds.) *Transnational Russian Studies*. Liverpool: Liverpool University Press, pp. 283–300.

Hutchings, S. 2022. *Projecting Russia in a Mediatized World: Recursive Nationhood*. London: Routledge.

Iaccarino, M. 2021. 'Il manifesto femminista di Manizha sconvolge la Russia: 'Delira, va bandita''. *Huffington Post*, 30 May. URL: https://www.huffingtonpost.it/entry/il-manifesto-femminista-di-manizha-sconvolge-la-russia-delira-va-bandita_it_60b346c8e4b0 6da8bd77a6f4 (accessed 1 June 2021).

Intermedia. 2018. 'Poklonniki poproshchalis's lezhashchim v grobu Khaski'. 16 September. URL: https://www.intermedia.ru/news/327284 (accessed 24 December 2023).

Izvestia. 2021. 'Repera Slava KPSS arestovali na sem' sutok'. *Izvestia*, 10 February. URL: https://iz.ru/1123083/2021-02-10/repera-slavu-kpss-arestovali-na-sem-sutok (accessed 25 February 2021).

Jagose, A. 1996. *Queer Theory*. Melbourne: University of Melbourne Press.

Johnson, E. 2014. 'A New Song for a New Motherland: Eurovision and the Rhetoric of Post-Soviet National Identity'. *Russian Review*, 73, 2, pp. 24–46.

Jones, E. 2021. 'DIY and Popular Music: Mapping an Ambivalent Relationship Across Three Historical Case Studies'. *Popular Music and Society*, 44, 1, pp. 60–78.

Jonson, L., Erofeev, A. (eds.). 2017. *Russia: Art Resistance and the Conservative-Authoritarian Zeitgeist*. London: Routledge.

Kaczmarska, K., Keating, V. 2019. 'Conservative Soft Power: Liberal Soft Power Bias and the 'Hidden' Attraction of Russia'. *Journal of International Relations and Development*, 22, pp. 1–27.

Kandelaki, T. 2021. 'Manizha na manezhe'. *RT na russkom*, 20 May 20. URL: https://russian.rt.com/opinion/863769-kandelaki-manizha-rossiya-evrovidenie (accessed 1 June 2021).

Karpitskaia, D. 2019. 'Kto i kak verbuet podrostkov dlia torgovli narkotikami'. *Komsomol'skaia Pravda*, 28 February. URL: https://www.kp.ru/daily/26948.1/4000283/ (accessed 11 July 2019).

Kazakov, V. 2019. *Representations of 'New Russia' through a 21st Century Mega-Event: The Political Aims, Informational Means, and Popular Reception of the Sochi 2014 Winter Olympic Games*. PhD thesis, University of Manchester.

Kazakov, V. 2023. 'Public Remembering of Sochi 2014 at a Time of War: The Kremlin's Soft Disempowerment Through Sport.' In Simon Chadwick et al. (eds.) *The Geopolitical Economy of Sport: Power, Politics, Money and the State*. London: Routledge, pp. 42–48.

Kazakov, V., Hutchings, S. 2019. 'Challenging the 'Information War' Paradigm: Russophones and Russophobes in Online Eurovision Communities'. In Wijermars, M., Lehtisaari, K. (eds.) *Freedom of Expression in Russia's New Mediasphere*. London: Routledge, pp. 137–58.

Kholod. 2022. 'Voitsy ChVK Vagner prosiat podrostkovuiu pevitsu Meibi Beibi vystupit' na fronte. Chego?!' 14 November. URL: https://holod.media/2022/11/14/maybelization/ (accessed 19 December 2023).

Kolstø, P. 2016. 'Introduction: Russian Nationalism Is Back – but Precisely What Does That Mean? In Kolstø, P., Blakkisrud, H. (eds.) *The New Russian Nationalism. Imperialism, Ethnicity and Authoritarianism 2000–15*. Edinburgh: Edinburgh University Press, pp. 1–18.

Kommersant. 2019. 'Khranit' nel'zya zhigat''. 23 September. URL: https://www.kommersant.ru/doc/4102444 (accessed 28 May 2020).

Kommersant. 2022. 'Glava VTB Kostin spel na VEF s Butusovym 'Gudbai, Amerika''. 6 September. URL: https://www.kommersant.ru/doc/5547995 (accessed 28 December 2023).

Komsomolskaia Pravda. 2012. 'Eks-gitarist grupy Kino Iurii Kasparian: 'Liudi, poiushchie na mitingakh pesni Tsoia, vyzyvaiut u muzykantov shutki i smekh'. 18 June. URL: https://www.spb.kp.ru/online/news/1177657/ (accessed 19 December 2023).

206 *Independent Music in Russia*

Kozyrev, M. 2020. 'Kozyrev – liubit' stranu i nenavidet' gosudarstvo'. *Vdud'*, 13 August. URL: https://www.youtube.com/watch?v=skFNJ3tB67M (accessed 10 September 2021).

Kozyrev, M. 2022. Public Post on Facebook, 24 March. URL: https://www.facebook.com/misha.kozyrev/posts/pfbid0BEW9REqUdwS1D3hM1y74fEEfZC3hfvwiTz4NtqJNwFP-PyPkHJhUYaqdxbJLxdAT6l (accessed 25 March 2022).

Kveberg, G. 2013. *Moscow by Night. Musical Subcultures, Identity Formation, and Cultural Evolution in Russia, 1977–2008*. PhD thesis, University of Illinois at Urbana-Champaign.

Laruelle, M. 2021. 'Russia's Niche Soft Power Sources, Targets and Channels of Influence'. *Notes De l'Ifri, Russia Nei Visions*, 122, pp. 5–27.

Lenta.ru. 2018. 'Putin predostereg ot zapretov rep-kontsertov'. 16 December. URL: https://lenta.ru/news/2018/12/15/putinrap/ (accessed 30 May 2020).

Levada Centre/Ebert Fund. 2020. 'Pokolenie Putina. Mezhdu loialnost'iu i protestom'. URL: http://library.fes.de/pdf-files/bueros/moskau/16134.pdf (accessed 9 June 2020).

Levchenko, G. 2018. 'Kreml' zaplatil GnoInomu za rolik s kritikoI videoblogera Soboleva. Bloger tozhe poluchaet den'gi ot vlastei'. *Meduza*, 7 September. URL: https://meduza.io/feature/2018/09/07/kreml-zaplatil-gnoynomu-za-rolik-s-kritikoy-videoblogera-soboleva-bloger-tozhe-poluchaet-dengi-ot-vlastey (accessed 31 July 2022).

Levchenko, L. 2019. 'V Rossii nakonets-to poyavilas' protestnaya muzyka. I ona ne protiv Putina'. *The Village*, 30 August. URL: https://www.the-village.ru/village/weekend/musika/360815-novye-pesni-protesta (accessed 29 May 2020).

Loseff, L. 1984. *On the Beneficence of Censorship: Aesopian Language in Modern Russian Literature*. München and Berlin: Verlag Otto Sagner.

Lotman, Y. 1990. *Universe of the Mind. A Semiotic Theory of Culture*. Bloomington: Indiana University Press.

Lusane, C. 1993. 'Rap, Race and Politics'. *Race and Class*, 35, 1, pp. 41–56.

MacFadyen, D. 2002. *Estrada?! Grand Narratives and the Philosophy of the Russian Popular Song Since Perestroika*. London: McGill-Queen's University Press.

MacFarquhar, N. 2018. 'Rapper Is Jailed for 12 Days in Russia as a Culture War Spreads'. *The New York Times*, 22 November. URL: https://www.nytimes.com/2018/11/23/world/europe/russia-rapper-husky-prison.html (accessed 20 May 2020).

Makarychev, A., Yatsyk, A. 2014. 'The Four Pillars of Russia's Power Narrative'. *The International Spectator*, 49, pp. 62–75.

McMichael, P. 2005. '"After All, You're a Rock Star (At Least, That's What They Say)': Roksi and the Creation of the Soviet Rock Musician'. *Slavonic and East European Review*, 83, 4, pp. 664–84.

McMichael, P. 2008. 'Translation, Authorship and Authenticity in Soviet Rock Songwriting'. *The Translator*, pp. 201–28.

McMichael, P. 2019. '"That's Ours. Don't Touch'. Nashe Radio and the Consolations of the Domestic Mainstream'. In Strukov, V., Hudspith, S. (eds.) *Russian Culture in the Age of Globalization*. London: Routledge, pp. 68–98.

Meduza. 2018a. 'V 2018 vlasti sorvali Bolshe 40 kontsertov. Posmotrite tablitsu'. 28 November (subsequently updated). URL: https://meduza.io/feature/2018/11/28/po-vsey-strane-vlasti-sryvayut-kontserty-posmotrite-tablitsu-tam-uzhe-bolshe-20-sluchaev (accessed 2 January 2019).

Meduza. 2018b. 'Pavel Chikov: 'chernyi spisok muzykantov sostavlen v tsentralnom apparate FSB''. 27 November. URL: https://meduza.io/news/2018/11/27/pavel-chikov-chernyy-spisok-muzykantov-sostavlen-v-tsentralnom-apparate-fsb?utm_source=facebook&utm_medium=main&fbclid=IwAR0uIJnaoHQ-CrldCvcGib2guipwVpaIKFEj8eDkrRKNsk3EOG32i-hhUfI (last accessed 30 May 2020).

Meduza. 2018c. '"Nas nazyvali islamistami i natsistami odnovremenno'. Gruppa Shortparis zakhvatyvaet shkolu: premera klipa 'Strashno". 19 December. URL: https://meduza.io/shapito/2018/12/19/nas-nazyvali-islamistami-i-natsistami-odnovremenno-gruppa-short-paris-zahvatyvaet-shkolu-premiera-klipa-strashno (last accessed 8 July 2019).

Meduza. 2019a. 'Mitingi na Sakharova i zaderzhaniya u administratsii prezidenta. Kak eto bylo'. 10 August. URL: https://meduza.io/live/2019/08/10/miting-vernem-sebe-pravo-na-vybory-hronika (accessed 28 May 2020).

Meduza. 2019b. 'Ne pro feminizm, a pro chelovechnost''. 28 February 28. URL: https://meduza.io/shapito/2019/02/28/ne-pro-feminizm-a-pro-chelovechnost (accessed 1 May 2021).

Meduza. 2021. 'Manizha sobralas' podat' v sud na Wonderzine iz-za kolonki glavnogo redaktora, nameknuvshei na ee sviazi s Kremlem'. 27 May. URL: https://meduza.io/news/2021/05/27/manizha-sobralas-podat-v-sud-na-wonderzine-iz-za-kolonki-glavnogo-redaktora-nameknuvshey-na-ee-svyazi-s-kremlem (accessed 1 June 2021).

Miazhevich, G. 2010. 'Sexual Excess in Russia's Eurovision Performances as a Nation Branding Tool'. *Russian Journal of Communication*, 3, 3/4, pp. 248–64.

Minaev, S., Yakovlev, S. 2019. 'Shortparis: 'kogda gruppa khochet vystupit' pered maksimal'nym chislom sovremennikov – eto plokho''. *Esquire*, 20 March. URL: https://www.pravilamag.ru/hero/90672-shortparis-kogda-gruppa-hochet-vystupit-pered-maksimalnym-chislom-sovremennikov-eto-ploho/#part3 (accessed 10 November 2024).

Morozov, V., Reshetnikov, A., and Gaufman, E. 2024. "'F*** tha Police!" à la Russe: Rancière and the Metamodernist Turn in Contemporary Russian Music'. *Nationalities Papers*, 52, 1, pp. 178–204.

Moskva 24. 2021. "Ia ne oplashchaiu': kakovy shansy u Manizha pobedit' na Evrovidenii-2021'. 9 March 9.URL: https://www.m24.ru/articles/kultura/09032021/157799 (accessed 3 April 2021).

Most.tv. 2015. 'Zakhar Prilepin: Tekh, kto govorit 'Pora valit'', nado valit' s p'edestala'. 27 May. URL: https://most.tv/most_projects/belaya-studiya/47143.html (accessed 17 November 2021).

Mouffe, C. 2001. "'Every Form of Art Has a Political Dimension": Chantal Mouffe, Interviewed by Rosalyn Deutsche, Branden W. Joseph, and Thomas Keenan'. *Grey Room*, 2, pp. 99–125.

MTV Russia. 2019. 'Shortparis – Netlenka/MTV (February 2019)'. URL: https://www.youtube.com/watch?v=0GAil4nanwM (accessed 14 March 2021).

Nechaev, I. 2021. 'Mezhdu Dostoevskim i psikhiatricheskoi klinikoi: kakim poluchilsia al.'bom Shortparis'. *RBK*, 29 June. URL: https://style.rbc.ru/impressions/60d9fb4c9a79472bb4208e08 (accessed 2 January 2024).

Nechepurenko, I. 2019. 'Russia's Youth Found Rap. The Kremlin Is Worried'. *The New York Times*, 21 May. URL: https://www.nytimes.com/2019/05/21/arts/music/russia-rap-hip-hop.html?fbclid=IwAR2RY-ajL3thFQFb2jtbumpLr73nswmRlYQ9FFdOrqr13KJWyR-_-IxnALk (accessed 10 May 2020).

Negus, K. 2019. 'Nation-states, Transnational Corporations and Cosmopolitans in the Global Popular Music Economy'. *Global Media and China*, 24, 4, pp. 403–18.

Nevanlinna, T. 2003. 'Avant-Garde and Politics'. *Eurozine*, 7 October. URL: https://www.eurozine.com/avant-garde-and-politics/ (accessed 2 January 2024).

Nezavisimaya Gazeta. 2019. 'Delo Ivana Golunova toksichno dlya vlasti'. 10 June. URL: http://www.ng.ru/editorial/2019-06-10/2_7595_red.html (accessed 6 July 2020).

Nezhnyi redaktor. 2018. 'Ugrozy, otmena kontsertov, dengi Khaski i Mikhalkov. Nastya iz Ic3peak'. 24 December. URL: https://www.youtube.com/watch?v=c9YAOzjixyo (accessed 21 May 2020).

Nooshin, L. 2017. 'Whose Liberation? Iranian Popular Music and the Fetishization of Resistance'. *Popular Communication*, 15, 3, pp. 163–91.

NTV. 2018a. 'Glava Sluzhby vneshnei razdelki prizval podderzhat' reperov dengami'. 29 November. URL: https://www.ntv.ru/novosti/2114360/ (accessed 6 July 2020).

NTV. 2018b. 'Minkul't prizval reperov 'bolee vydumchivo podhodit' k tekstam'. 29 November. URL: https://www.ntv.ru/novosti/2114520/ (accessed 6 July 2020).

Nye, J. 2013. 'What China and Russia Don't Get About Soft Power'. *Foreign Policy*, 29 April. URL: http://foreignpolicy.com/2013/04/29/what-china-and-russia-dont-get-about-soft-power/ (accessed 5 May 2021).

208   *Independent Music in Russia*

Open Media. 2019. "Surgutneftegaz', kokain I propekt Rotenberga. Reper Khaski opublikoval klip ko dniu rozhdeniia Putina'. 8 October. URL: https://openmedia.io/news/surgutneftegaz-kokain-i-prospekt-rotenberga-reper-xaski-opublikoval-klip-ko-dnyu-rozhdeniya-putina/ (accessed 24 December 2024).

Open Media. 2020. "Blagodat' na litsakh'. Reper Khaski vypustil trek o nasilii Putina nad nim i rossiianami'. 25 September. URL: https://openmedia.io/news/n1/blagodat-na-licax-reper-xaski-vypustil-trek-s-metaforoj-o-nasilii-putina-nad-narodom/ (accessed 24 December 2023).

Ovchinnikov, N. 2019. "Strashno'–eto saundtrek zhizni v Rossii 2019-go goda: interv'iu s gruppoi Shortparis'. *Afisha*, 23 May. URL: https://daily.afisha.ru/music/11980-strashno-eto-saundtrek-zhizni-v-rossii-2019-goda-intervyu-s-gruppoy-shortparis/ (accessed 10 March 2024).

OVD-Info. 2019a. 'Spisok zaderzhannykh na aktsii protiv sfabrikovannykh del v Moskve'. 16 June. URL: https://ovdinfo.org/news/2019/06/12/spiski-zaderzhannyh-na-akcii-protiv-•sfabrikovannyh-del-v-moskve (accessed 28 May 2020).

OVD-Info. 2019b. 'Spisok zaderzhannykh na aktsii protiv nedopuska kandidatov na vybory 27 iyulya 2019 goda'. 27 July. URL: https://ovdinfo.org/news/2019/07/27/spisok-zader-zhannyh-na-akcii-protiv-nedopuska-kandidatov-na-vybory-27-iyulya-2019 (accessed 28 May 2020).

Oxxxymiron. 2018. 'Oxxxymiron vstupilsia za Khaski'. 24 November. URL: https://www.youtube.com/watch?v=9uBSKX5ywWI (accessed 6 July 2020).

Pajala, M., Vuletic, D. 2022. 'Stagecraft in the Service of Statecraft? Russia in the Eurovision Song Contest'. In Tuomas, F. and Silke M. (eds.) *Russia's Cultural Statecraft*. New York: Routledge, pp. 162–83.

Pekacz, J. 1994. 'Did Rock Smash the Wall? The Role of Rock in Political Transition'. *Popular Music*, 13, 1, pp. 41–9.

Pervyi kanal. 2021. 'Na konkurse 'Evrovidenie' Rossiiu budet predstavliat' pevitsa Manizha'. 9 March. URL: https://www.youtube.com/watch?v=df9Novup7rg&t=63s (accessed 2 April 2021).

Petrova, P. 2022. "Potomu i strashno!' Analiz klipa gruppy Shortparis 'Strashno". *Nauchno-populiarnyi zhurnal 'Ikstati' (HSE)*, 5 May. URL: https://spb.hse.ru/ixtati/news/612149231.html (accessed 10 November 2024).

Piatin, A. 2019. "Miting na Sakharov stal krupneishim po chislu uchastnikov". *Forbes*, 10 August. URL: https://www.forbes.ru/obshchestvo/381623-miting-na-saharova-stal-krup-neyshim-po-chislu-uchastnikov (accessed 20 August 2019).

Pomerantsev, P. 2015. 'The Kremlin's Information War'. *Journal of Democracy*, 26, 4, pp. 40–50.

Prilepin, Z. 2018. Public Facebook Post. 22 November. URL: https://www.facebook.com/zaharprilepin/posts/2157809787596664 (accessed 6 July 2020).

Radio Free Europe. 2007. 'Relatives of Beslan Victims Apply to European Court'. 26 June. URL: https://www.rferl.org/a/1077334.html (accessed 6 July 2020).

Rancière, J. 2010. *Dissensus: On Politics and Aesthetics*. London: Bloomsbury.

Rauth, R. 1982. 'Back in the U.S.S.R.-Rock and Roll in the Soviet Union'. *Popular Music & Society*, 8, 3–4, pp. 3–12.

Ravin, S. 2021. 'Muzykalnyi leibl okazalsia pod ugrozoi shtrafa iz-za pesen Morgenshterna i Eldzheia'. *Lenta.ru*, 9 November 2021. URL: https://lenta.ru/news/2021/11/09/morgen_eldzhey/?utm_source=yxnews&utm_medium=desktop&nw=1636470162000 (accessed 9 November 2021).

REN TV. 2011. 'Noty protesta: spetsproekt'. 15 November. URL: https://www.youtube.com/watch?v=BU542UOZYtM (accessed 15 June 2020).

RIA Novosti. 2019. 'V Gosdumer v konkurse dlia reperov pobedil isskustvennyi intellekt'. 29 May. URL: https://ria.ru/20190529/1555081825.html (accessed 9 November 2021).

RIA Novosti. 2021. 'SK poprosili proverit' pesniu Manizhi dlia Evrovideniia'. 18 March. URL: https://ria.ru/20210318/manizha-1601791920.html (accessed 3 April 2021).

Rogatchevski, A., Steinholt, Y. 2016. 'Pussy Riot's Musical Precursors? The National Bolshevik Party Bands, 1994–2007'. *Popular Music and Society*, 39, 4, pp. 448–64.

Rondarev, A. 2020. 'Na kazhdogo iz nas legion mentov. Kak menialsia obraz politseiskogo v rossiiskoi muzyke – ot BG i Letova do Shortparis i Krovostoka'. *Meduza*, 22 March. URL: https://meduza.io/feature/2020/03/22/na-kazhdogo-iz-nas-legion-mentov (accessed 3 November 2021).

Rossiia 24. 2018. 'Aktivisty dobilis' zapreta v Krasnoiarske rok-gruppi 'Frendzona''. YouTube, 14 November. URL: https://www.youtube.com/watch?v=EUAJSsHghZs (accessed 30 December 2018).

Roth, A. 2018. '"Even a Half-Finished Show is a Victory': Russian Bands Fight New Crackdown'. *The Guardian*, 12 December. URL: https://www.theguardian.com/world/2018/dec/12/were-not-scared-bands-defy-russian-crackdown-on-political-music (accessed 20 June 2020).

Roth, A. 2021. '"I Won't Allow Myself to be Broken': Russia's Eurovision Candidate Manizha Takes on the Haters'. *The Guardian*, 9 April. URL: https://www.theguardian.com/tv-and-radio/2021/apr/09/russia-eurovision-candidate-manizha-takes-on-the-haters?fbclid=IwAR08YvUw0s_PyYkQukbvIWLcXAtwGCw0txwiUlltijJoL-PU4yE3qV_wnkzU (accessed 1 May 2021).

RT. 2018. '99 Problems but Gig Ain't One: Putin's Take on Rap'. 17 December. URL: https://www.youtube.com/watch?v=meObalAgf9g (accessed 20 January 2019).

RT. 2019. 'Russian Rappers Remove Ode to Moscow after Over 1 mn Dislikes on YouTube'. 10 September. URL: https://www.rt.com/russia/468460-russia-youtube-dislike-timati/ (accessed 21 June 2022).

RTVI. 2018. 'Atmosfera suitsida: pochemu Kreml' ustraivaet, chto muzykal'naIa tsenzura izbiratelna'. 1 November. URL: https://rtvi.com/stories/atmosfera-suitsida-kreml-ustraivaet-chto-muzykalnaya-tsenzura-izbiratelna/ (accessed 15 June 2020).

Rutland, P., Kazantsev, A. 2016. 'The Limits of Russia's Soft Power'. *Journal of Political Power*, 9, 3, pp. 395–413.

Ryback, T. 1990. *Rock Around the Bloc: A History of Rock Music in Eastern Europe and the Soviet Union, 1954–1988*. Oxford: Oxford University Press.

Schimpfössl, E., Yablokov, I. 2017. 'Power Lost and Freedom Relinquished: Russian Journalists Assessing the First Post-Soviet Decade'. *The Russian Review*, 76, 3, pp. 526–41.

Semenenko, A. (ed.). 2021. *Satire and Protest in Putin's Russia*. New York: Palgrave.

Sergunin, A., Karabeshkin, L. 2015. 'Understanding Russia's Soft Power Strategy'. *Politics*, 35, pp. 347–63.

Shanina, V. 2021. 'Repera Slavu KPSS zaderzhali iz-za lozungov vo vremia protesta 2 fevralia'. *Afisha*, 6 February. URL https://daily.afisha.ru/news/46979-repera-slavu-kpss-zaderzhali-izza-lozungov-vo-vremya-protesta-2-fevralya/ (accessed 10 February 2021).

Shenkman, I. 2021. '"Nam zadolzhali v etoi strane'. Novyi al'bom Shortparis: totalitarnaia isterika v kazhdoi note'. *Novaia gazeta*, 26 June. URL: https://novayagazeta.ru/articles/2021/06/26/nam-zadolzhali-v-etoi-strane (accessed 2 January 2024).

Shenkman, I. 2022. 'Prognis' i poi'. *Novaia gazeta*, 30 August. URL: https://novayagazeta.eu/articles/2022/08/30/prognis-i-poi (accessed 28 December 2023).

Simonyan, M. 2018. Public Post on Her Telegram Channel. 26 November. URL: https://t.me/margaritasimonyan/2018 (accessed 6 July 2020).

Sinelschikova, E. 2021. 'Meet Manizha, Russia's Choice for Eurovision 2021'. *Russia Beyond*, 11 March. URL: https://www.rbth.com/arts/333514-manizha-russian-eurovision-2021 (accessed 2 April 2021).

Skazhi Gordeevoi. 2021. 'Manizha: takikh, kak ia – vse!' 23 April. URL: https://www.youtube.com/watch?v=zCXkLrvoxSQ (accessed 2 May 2024).

Skey, M. 2022. 'Sportswashing: Media Headline or Analytic Concept?' *International Review for the Sociology of Sport*, 58, 5, pp. 1–16.

Snob. 2020. 'Glavnoe o dele 'Seti'. Za chto ego figuranty poluchili ot 6 do 18 let kolonii strogogo rezhima'. 10 February. URL: https://snob.ru/entry/188655/ (accessed 28 May 2020).

210   *Independent Music in Russia*

Sobaka. 2019a. 'Artemii Troitskii o Shortparis: 'eto samaya silnaya rok-gruppa vsekh vremyon". 5 November. URL: http://www.sobaka.ru/entertainment/music/98942 (accessed 7 July 2020).

Sobaka. 2019b. 'Manizha – o tom, kak podruzhit'sia s sobstvennym telom, i chto ne tak s bodipozitivom v rossiiskikh realiiakh'. 20 May. URL: https://www.sobaka.ru/health/health/90734 (accessed 1 April 2021).

Sobolev, O. 2019. 'Otvechai za slovo. Pochemu samaia ambitsioznaia russkaia rok-gruppa Shortparis – ne to chem kazhetsia'. *Lenta.ru*, 13 November. URL: https://lenta.ru/articles/2019/11/13/shortparis/ (accessed 10 November 2024).

Sokolov, D. 2021. 'Kakikh peremen zhdal Tsoi? Pochemu pesnia iz 'Assy' stala gimnom protestov v 2021-m'. *Sobesednik*, 19 March. URL: https://sobesednik.ru/kultura-i-tv/20210315-kakih-peremen-zhdal-coj (accessed 19 December 2023).

Sonevytsky, M. 2016. 'The Freak Cabaret on the Revolution Stage: On the Ambivalent Politics of Femininity, Rurality, and Nationalism in Ukrainian Popular Music'. *Journal of Popular Music Studies*, 28, 3, pp. 291–314.

Sperling, V. 2015. *Sex, Politics & Putin: Political Legitimacy in Russia*. Oxford: Oxford University Press.

Sprengel, D. 2020. 'Neoliberal Expansion and Aesthetic Innovation: The Egyptian Independent Music Scene Ten Years After'. *International Journal of Middle East Studies*, 52, 3, pp. 545–51.

Sputnik Tajikistan. 2021. 'Kreml' otsenil pesniu Manizhi dlia Evrovideniia 2021'. 11 April. URL:https://tj.sputniknews.ru/20210401/kremlin-pesnya-manizhi-eurovision-2021-1033114690.html (accessed 4 May 2021).

Starikova, M. 2019. 'Protiv Musora, za vrachei, shamana i vybory'. *Kommersant*, 25 November. URL: https://www.kommersant.ru/doc/4170706?from=main_6 (accessed 28 May 2020).

Steinholt, Y. 2005. *Rock in the Reservation: Songs from the Leningrad Rock Club 1981–1986*. Bergen – New York: The Mass Media Music Scholar's Press.

Steinholt, Y., Wickström, D.E. 2009. 'Visions of the (Holy) Motherland in Contemporary Russian Popular Music: Nostalgia, Patriotism and Ruskii Rok'. *Popular Music and Society*, 32, 3, pp. 313–30.

Stella, F. 2013. 'Queer Space, Pride, and Shame in Moscow'. *Slavic Review*, 72, 3, pp. 458–480.

Steward, T.P. 2013. *I am the Brave Hero and this Land is Mine: Popular Music and Youth Identity in Post-Revolutionary Iran*. Doctoral dissertation, University of Edinburgh, UK.

Strukov, V. 2016. 'Russian 'Manipulative Smart Power': Zviagintsev's Oscar Nomination, (non)government Agency and Contradictions of the globalize'. *New Cinemas: Journal of Contemporary Film*, 14, 1, pp. 31–49.

Studin, I. 2018. 'Introduction: Ten Theses on Russia in the Twenty-First Century'. In Studin, I. (ed.) *Russia: Strategy, Policy, Administration*. London: Palgrave Macmillan, pp. 1–14.

Sygma. 2021. 'O tom, kak Manizha na Evrovidenie ekhala, i o tom kak terzali ee, i kak v pole pravdu iskali'. 9 May. URL: https://syg.ma/@kollektiv-malyh-rek/o-tom-kak-manizha-na-ievrovidieniie-iekhala-i-o-tom-kak-tierzali-ieio-i-kak-v-polie-pravdu-iskali?fbclid=IwAR2Ii3kdDCjBI0WvpDc1cgJ6wVfT8Dv-6QGG4AVIv_DQUpl5n6ev6muqLJY (accessed 12 May 2021).

Taratuta, I. 2021. 'Pochemu vystuplenie Manizhi na 'Evrovidenii' ne raduet'. *Wonderzine*, 26 May. URL: https://www.wonderzine.com/wonderzine/life/life-opinion/256725-manizha?fbclid=IwAR3mTx8Q9sdT7YH_rSQiU7F7XqjqAR6BcTQyMk7772rO-aTA-H8iFezXvnBc (accessed 28 May 2021).

TASS. 2017. 'Viacheslav Butusov prokommentiroval vkliuchenie v chërnyi spisok saita Mirotvorets''. 3 June. URL: https://tass.ru/kultura/4311019 (accessed 28 December 2023).

TASS. 2019. 'Napisannyi neiroset'iu rep pobedil v konkurse, organizovannom komitetom Gosdumy'. 29 May. URL: https://tass.ru/kultura/6485687 (accessed 9 November 2021).

Patrioprotest 211

The Flow. 2018a. 'Timati voshel v spisok doverennykh lits Putina'. 1 February. URL: https://the-flow.ru/news/timati-i-putin-sila-druzhbi (accessed 21 June 2022).

The Flow. 2018b. 'Khaski vylozhil video, v kotorom udaliaet svoi novyi al'bom'. 10 September. URL: https://the-flow.ru/news/haski-delete-album (accessed 24 december 2023).

The Flow. 2019. 'Rep - agressivnaya totalitarnaya sekta: goseksperty razobrali tvorcehstvo Krida'. 25 October 25. URL: https://the-flow.ru/news/eksperty-razobrali-tvorchestvo-krida (accessed 15 June 2020).

The Flow. 2022. "Vynuzhdennaia mera, priniataia rukovodstvom Strany'. Timati ob. Operatsii v Ukraine'. 4 March. URL: https://the-flow.ru/news/vynuzhdennaya-mera-prinyat-aya-rukovodstvom-strany-timati-ob-operacii-v-ukraine (accessed 5 March 2022).

The Village. 2021. 'Moia kolonka – legitimnyi sposob vedeniia politicheskoi diskussii': Iuliia Taratuta – o tom, pochemu Manizhu vozmutil ee tekst'. 27 May. URL: https://www.the-village.ru/city/react/taratuta-pro-manizhy?utm_source=facebook. com&utm_medium=social&utm_campaign=strasti-po-manizhe-ne-utihayut-dazhe-posle&fbclid=IwAR20J5pFUX_JioiROoCt0zADS2Sui2mcTbIZFZqtshmUKxxexED-n6j43R-Q (accessed 1 June 2021).

Tolz, V., Teper, Y. 2018. 'Broadcasting Agitainment: A New media Strategy of Putin's Third Presidency'. *Post-Soviet Affairs*, 34, 4, pp. 213–227.

Troitsky, A. 1988. *Back in the USSR: The True Story of Rock in Russia*. London: Faber & Faber.

Trottier, D., Gabdulhakov, R., Huang, Q. 2020. *Introducing Vigilant Audiences*. Cambridge: Open Book Publishers (online).

Tukumbetov, R. 2016. "Est' narabotki, oni, suka, zhutkie': bol'shoe interv'iu Khaski, avtora klipa 'Chernym-cherno". *The Flow*, 17 March. URL: https://the-flow.ru/features/na-podeme-haski (accessed 17 November 2021).

Turbine, V. 2015. 'Women's Human Rights in Russia: Outmoded Battlegrounds, or New Sites of Contentious Politics? *East European Politics*, 31, 3, pp. 326–41.

Vasilyeva, N. 2021. 'Conservative Russia in Retreat as Tajik Refugee Raps her Way to Eurovision'. *The Telegraph*, March 13. URL: https://www.telegraph.co.uk/news/2021/03/13/conservative-russia-balks-tajik-refugee-raps-way-eurovision/ (accessed 1 June 2021).

Vdud'. 2019. 'Pornofil'my – pesni I segodniashnei Rossii'. YouTube, 15 October. URL: https://www.youtube.com/watch?v=WjqBS5TI2YE&t=1s (accessed 28 December 2023).

Vdud'. 2020a. 'Ic3peak – Music and Modern Art'. YouTube, 30 June. URL: https://www.youtube.com/watch?v=95ReakCrKX0 (accessed 28 December 2023).

Vdud'. 2020b. 'Monetochka – novaia zhizn', novyi dom, novyi al'bom'. YouTube, 20 October. URL: https://www.youtube.com/watch?v=SgV0-0puqWM&t=4145s (accessed 28 December 2023).

Vermeulen, T., Van den Akker, R. 2010. 'Notes on Metamodernism'. *Journal of Aesthetics & Culture*, 2, 1, pp. 1–14.

Vedomosti. 2019. 'OVD-Info utochnilo chislo zaderzhannykh na aktsii protesta v Moskve'. 4 August. URL: https://www.vedomosti.ru/politics/news/2019/08/04/808026-v (accessed 28 May 2020).

Volkova, A., Simonova, T., Shabalina, E. 2019. 'Kompleksnoe sotsiokulturnoe issledovanie mediasfery vystuplenii Egora Krida'. *Natsionalnyi sovet sotsialnoi informatsii*. Tyumen', 27 September. URL: https://www.nsk.kp.ru/share/i/13/4112586.pdf (accessed 15 June 2020).

Wickström, D.E. 2014. *Rocking St. Petersburg – Transcultural Flows and Identity Politics in Post-Soviet Popular Music*. Stuttgart: Ibidem.

Wolfe, S.V. 2020. 'For the Benefit of Our nation': Unstable Soft Power in the 2018 men's World Cup in Russia'. *International Journal of Sport and Politics*, 12, 4, pp. 545–61.

Wonderzine. 2019. 'Est' strakh sdelat' chto-to pervym: interviu Nasti Kreslinoi iz Ic3peak'. 17 June. URL: https://www.wonderzine.com/wonderzine/entertainment/interview/243901-ic3peak (accessed 15 June 2020).

212 *Independent Music in Russia*

Yurchak, A. 2006. *Everything Was Forever, Until It Was No More: The Last Soviet Generation*. Princeton, NJ: Princeton University Press.

Zagrutdinov, A. 2020. 'Oleg Likhachev darit rodine muzyku, nadezhdu i spermu'. *Batenka, da vy transformer*, 13 April. URL: https://batenka.ru/worship/oleg-likhachev/ (accessed 15 June 2020).

Zaitseva, L. 2018. 'Turmenedzher gruppy 'Frendzona' rasskazala podrobnosti otmena kontsertov kollektiva'. *Afisha*, 28 November. URL: https://daily.afisha.ru/news/22026-tur-menedzher-gruppy-frendzona-rasskazala-podrobnosti-otmeny-koncertov-kollektiva/ (accessed 15 June 2020).

Zatari, A. 2021. 'Za LGBT i protiv domashnego nasiliia: chem izvestna Manizha, vydvi-nutaia Rossiei na konkurs Evrovidenie'. *BBC Russia*, 9 March. URL: https://www.bbc.com/russian/features-56332260 (accessed 2 April 2021).

Zhelnov, A. 2017. 'Ne sovpali so skrepami: pochemu v Murome i Vykse zapreshchaiut kont-serty grupy Pornofil'my'. *Dozhd'*, 23 October. URL: https://tvrain.tv/teleshow/here_and_now/ne_sovpali_so_skrepami_pochemu-448379/ (accessed 20 December 2023).

Žižek, S. 1991. *The Ticklish Subject: The Absent Centre of Political Ontology*. London: Verso.

5 From the margins and back?

The transnational spread of
nezavisimaia muzyka

Introduction

"No Russian rock band has ever made a real career in the West", commented Interviewee 13 (the critic) during our interview in 2016, recognising also that "many have tried". While Interviewee 13's assessment might have been too harsh, it was also true that, on average, the export of Russian musicians to the West had almost always failed to leave a mark. In these terms, continued Interviewee 13, "Russia has been more the rule than the exception". Interviewee 13 referred to the fact that other independent bands from the global musical peripheries also rarely secured significant careers in the global market. Underpinning Interviewee 13's judgement was the idea that the political or economic peripherality of a country coincided with its musical peripherality. Russia, according to him, fell under this category. The critic's opinion tapped into enduring discourses of Russia's poly-peripherality (Martinez 2013, 54), whereby Russia is defined as a liminal empire consisting of a "conglomerate of marginalities, a centre and a periphery in itself" in its internal and international dimension.

There is more than a grain of truth in this assessment, especially when the lens of marginality is applied to Russian popular music on the global stage. While Russia has often contributed decisively to the development of European and global culture in terms of literature, classical music, film and visual art, the same cannot be said of its popular music. By following some of the main recent examples in the global spread of Russian independent music worldwide, this chapter argues that this musical liminality, interiorised and manifested in global dynamics, has influenced the ways in which musicians have tried to construct their image abroad.

In what follows, I first trace the recent evolution of the global music market, highlighting the disparity (not in number, but in impact) between the flows of products from the Anglo-American centre and the rest. I identify as "sonic capital" the sedimented political and economic power of a country as expressed in music during these flows. Together with this, and based on the analysis of the rather unexpected flow of Russian post-punk in Latin America, I coin the term "subflow" to denote a flow from one periphery to another, which, rather than subverting global hierarchies, reproduces them on a smaller scale. This sets the context for an analysis of the activities of the independent Russian agencies for musical export during the 2010s, and their struggles with internal infrastructure deficiencies and external disadvantages. I then

DOI: 10.4324/9781003248699-6

214   *Independent Music in Russia*

move to analyse two strategies that animated practitioners in their international promotional efforts: the first, which I call self-stereotyping, aimed to exploit global audiences' solidified condescending or negative expectations about Russia (e.g. vodka, criminality, squalor, backwardness, etc.) by offering an amplified textual and visual version of such expectations, which is recognisable as *stëb*. Interestingly, the Russian state joined in the reproduction of this *stëb* in the attempt to project liminality as a tool for nation-branding and a weapon for soft power. The second strategy, which I call "camouflage", aimed at masking these negatively perceived national traits in order to "fit in" the global, Anglo-American–dominated market. Both strategies had as objective the overcoming of a marginal starting point, but while the former embraced marginality and turned it into an entertaining commodity, the latter tried to hide it as a stigma and through metamorphosis into the dominant Other, not reckoning with the persistence of marginality associated with its carrier in the context of the "centre". Lastly, I return to the phenomenon of Russophone post-punk, framing it as the expression of an indeterminate and enduring condition of melancholy, existential angst and political resignation that is well-expressed by the Russian word *toska*. To this, I attach the examination of the remarkable global spread the genre has had since the 2010s. I do this by investigating its international fan communities online, on YouTube, where the genre became popular as "Russian Doomer", and where a certain feeling of longing for a lost future in the past (hauntology) can be observed.

Anglo-American conservatism, "sonic capital" and "transnational subflows"

Reflecting upon the transnational spread of popular music in the mid-2010s, ethnomusicologist Martin Stokes (2013, 826–42) suggested that, musically speaking, Europe was still divided into "Europe 1" and "Europe 2". Europe 1 was identified with Western Europe, while Europe 2, which included the former territories of the Ottoman Empire and the Warsaw Pact, remained secondary or invisible to the first. Europe 1, Stoke argued, continued to represent a "benchmark in the world's cultural hierarchies". Indeed, the possibility of reaching a transnational consumption in the Global North for East European music was still very limited (Mazierska and Győri 2019). East European music first had to compete with Anglophone products, then with West European ones, both of which traditionally owned more currency and prestige in the global market.

The hegemony of English-language products in European music leads to an assessment of taste and its hierarchies in the international context. As it "classifies the classifier" (Bourdieu 1984, 6) at a social and local level, taste also articulates, normalises and reproduces imbalances and inequalities among nations at a global level. Even with the global rise of decentralising music phenomena, such as K-Pop, global dominance across the 2010s still belonged to Anglophone, mostly Anglo-American products. As Lie (2015, 112) observed, "it would be misleading to equate global pop with American pop" but it would be equally wrong to deny the impact of Anglo-American music "in shaping a common soundscape around the world, especially among the youth of affluent countries", with English as the

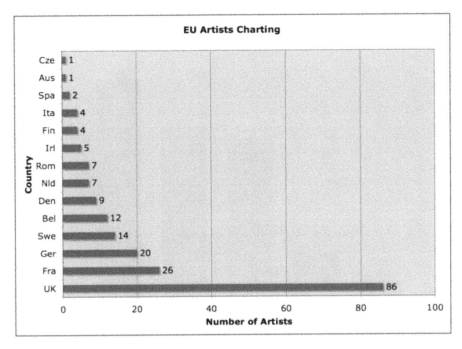

Figure 5.1 Graph showing the number of artists from EU countries crossing borders in airplay or digital in any of the six countries surveyed (Germany, France, Holland, Spain, Sweden, Poland) and in the pan-European charts in the early 2010s. Source: Legrand (2012).

lingua franca. Of course, Anglophone music has been locally adapted and transformed – hybridisation is a historically natural and inevitable process (Appiah 2006), yet to negate that the Anglophone West has fashioned the way in which fans around the world consume music – that is, their taste in general – would mean to gloss over uneven centre-periphery dynamics and one-way flows.

In 2012, a report jointly commissioned by the European Music Office and the festival Eurosonic Noorderslag demonstrated that Europe still struggled to keep the pace set by the US and, less so, by the UK (Figure 5.1). The other European countries showed a relative isolation of their local music markets, with only a few artists capable of trans-European reach. The report concluded that:

> [The] European repertoire fares quite well on a national level with local repertoire but the number of European artists capable of transforming a local success into a cross-border success is quite limited. […] The only music that crosses borders without limitations is US-based repertoire. […] In each European country, English-language repertoire heavily dominates the airwaves and digital downloads, with shares of local language music varying by country, but never over 25%.
>
> (Legrand 2012)

216 *Independent Music in Russia*

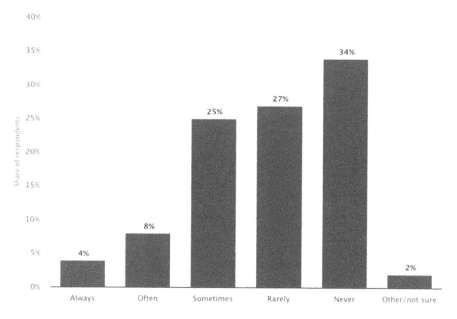

Figure 5.2 Graph illustrating the linguistic habits of American music listeners. Source: *Statista* (2015).

By evidencing Europe's fragility in exporting music, the report flagged the overwhelming strength of US products. At the same time, though, US music consumers' habits displayed a pronounced conservatism, with little consumption of non-Anglophone music. A 2015 survey (*Statista* 2015) indicated that only 12% of Americans regularly listened to music in a language they do not speak (Figure 5.2).

The situation did not change much in the second decade of the 2010s. Even though markets like South Korea and Japan were on the rise (IFPI 2017, 2018), the first music distributor, exporter and trendsetter remained the US, and the main language of pop, rock and indie songs remained English. For example, almost all the best-selling musicians of 2015–2017 were either American or British, and all the top ten artists, singles and albums of 2016–2017 were Anglophone (IFPI 2016, 2017, 2018).[1] According to Spotify data gathered by Demont-Heinrich (2019, 203), in 2017–2018, 71% of the service's top 10 tracks in Germany were in English. In Poland and Sweden, these figures were even higher (93% and 90%, respectively). Even in the Eurovision Song Contest, where the UK regularly dwelled at the bottom of the table, around half of the songs were performed in English.

Outside of Europe, the situation was complicated by the size of music markets in other languages: pop music in Spanish, Hindi, Chinese and Korean grew rapidly. As Ingham (2019) noted, the four top YouTube artists in 2018 performed their songs in languages other than English.[2] The upsurge in music from peripheral nations, however, did not affect the situation in the world's music foci – the US and

UK – where the percentage of English-language music on the charts neared 100%, and exceptions like the song "Gangnam Style" entered the charts as memes, subject to exclusively humorous reception. Moreover, according to IFPI (2014–2018), the vast majority of global music content was produced by English-speaking countries: America, Great Britain, Canada, Australia, Ireland and New Zealand.

Historically, the conservatism of the Anglo-American music market has been one of the by-products of its cultural hegemony. This hegemony implies the creation and reproduction of a system of coordinates that shapes the taste, imagination and dreams of the people who come under its influence (Schiller 1976). When Anglo-American popular music became a global commodity and a weapon of soft power for the countries producing it, many of its conventions, including English as a language, turned into fixed components of its form for audiences and aspiring practitioners abroad. English evolved, as Phillipson (2009, 148) observed, from lingua franca into "lingua emotiva", indissolubly entwined with the imaginary of Hollywood, popular music, consumerism and hedonism. Indeed, many musicians interviewed for this book claimed that English sounded "more musical" or "better" than Russian, yet this affective dimension was a long-term effect of the domination of Anglophone products: English sounds *better* because it sounds *the most* (Biasioli 2022).

Power, therefore, is one of the lenses through which we can analyse the global distribution, recognition and success of popular music: different political, economic and cultural capitals define and reproduce hierarchies in the perception of popular music during the process of its transnational promotion. As Connell and Gibson (2003, 270) wrote: "Popular music, like other popular media, has the ability to mediate social knowledge, reinforce (or challenge) ideological constructions of contemporary (or past) life and be an agent of hegemony".

It is in this international context that the concept of "sonic capital" may be proposed.[3] I understand "sonic capital" as the wealth of a country's popular music tradition, historically accumulated and internationally acknowledged. Like symbolic capital, which referred to performative speech and to the authority and prestige gained by a group of people through the repeated implementation of economic, political and cultural hegemony (Bourdieu 1991; Gramsci 1999), sonic capital is functional as a means to an end: the ability of one country to lead in the music market through attraction. In the international arena, this process of fashioning a country's attractive image – soft power – serves the purpose of achieving political ends (Nye 2013), and popular music obviously constitutes one of the choices in the toolkit (Cerqueira 2018). But while states can invest sonic capital in projections of the country's status in the global arena, sonic capital can also be shaped or mobilised by practitioners without any top-down support (e.g. grassroots practitioners, self-organised or organised around independent or major labels). The varying degrees of internationally acknowledged sonic capital will make a difference in the success of such projects. The reputation and authority of a country becomes a business card to its sound. Sonic capital is made of economic and political power integrated in the music.

Sonic capital, therefore, usually determines the international success of the popular musical products of a particular country. As a rule, a country with strong

218 *Independent Music in Russia*

sonic capital manages to spread its music rapidly and widely, thus replicating the same structures that favoured such spread in the first place; conversely, the music of a country with weak sonic capital will find barriers that are likely to impede or channel its transnational flow.

Despite Russian practitioners' attempts to enter the prestigious gates of Europe 1, attracted by the opportunities for international recognition, the export of Russian popular music has usually been circumscribed to the countries of the former Soviet Union and Europe 2 – that is, countries with less sonic capital in relation to Europe 1 and the Anglo-centric market. Over the 2010s, *nezavisimaia muzyka* bands increasingly performed across Eastern and Central Europe, while industry practitioners strove to develop ties in the area through participation in key initiatives like Tallinn Music Week and the Ljubljana MENT Festival. Russia, however, presented a dual character: on the one hand, it still constituted the main market for several bands from former Soviet countries (Galuszka 2021, 11); on the other, practitioners cultivated a desire to access the market of the Global North with its attractive sonic capital. In this, their hopes were often thwarted (see later in this chapter).

However, in the course of the 2010s, *nezavisimaia muzyka* reached other – more unexpected – peripheral domains, as illustrated by the case of the Rostov-on-Don–based band Motorama and the wave of Russophone post-punk in Latin America. Motorama achieved international popularity by entering the music markets of Mexico and South America: between 2012 and 2019 (with the exception of 2013), Motorama annually toured the continent, playing arenas of 3,000–4,000 people. Motorama became a significant global export product in Russian independent music, with more than 500 concerts on three continents, 125,000 followers on Facebook, 40,000 on Instagram and millions of views on YouTube (as of January 2022). Interviewee 32 explained this as a simple word-of-mouth effect:

> I think it [the spread of the band's music in Latin America] happened back when MySpace was in fashion, and we were putting a lot of music there. Somehow, some group of people in Mexico and Peru began to exchange it. And that's all, I can't explain it otherwise. Someone told someone else.

Motorama soon created Russian sonic capital in South America. After their success, and upon the band's recommendation, local promoters brought to South America Motorama's protégés, the Muscovite post-punk quartet Human Tetris, which was similar to Motorama in terms of sound, mood and aesthetics. Human Tetris toured Mexico and South America three times, sold out venues of 1,500 people, headlined festivals where American and English groups played before them (Contreras 2017) and were heralded by local journalists as "a reference for post-punk worldwide" (Vazquez 2018). Press coverage on Human Tetris presented a geographical paradox: scarce in Russia, where it consists of only a few articles (*Look At Me* 2009; *Indie Birdie* 2012), noticeable in Europe (*Ox* 2011; Berlin Beat 2012; Helbig 2012; Dimitriou 2017; Lusso 2017) and substantial in Latin America. In Peru, their EP *River Pt. 1* was defined "one of the best records of the year" (*Joinnus*, February 2017), while Mexican music zines dubbed their sound "timeless" (García 2018) and their live performances "an explosion of energy" (Gomez 2018). At the same time – unlike Motorama – Human Tetris never toured in Russia, and their solo concert attendance in their hometown of Moscow at the end of the 2010s was approximately 50 people (as personally observed). According to Interviewee 25, Human Tetris's largest fan base was located in Mexico, where three quarters of their Facebook subscribers – 75,000 in total – were from.[4] Comparing the ticket prices between their Muscovite and Mexican gigs also pointed at a disproportion,[5] and their artist fees in Moscow and Mexico also differed significantly, with Mexican organisers paying up to twenty-fold more (Interviewee 24). After Human Tetris, Belarusian Russophone darkwave band Molchat doma (The Houses Are Silent) were also invited to tour to Central and South America, but their gigs were postponed due to the coronavirus pandemic. When Molchat doma finally played there in 2022, they were met by tens of thousands of devoted fans.[6]

The success of Motorama, Human Tetris and Molchat doma – three bands with similar sonic qualities – in Central and South America testified to the spread of transnational flows outside of dominant cultural centres. In these flows, content is adapted and transformed locally before being sent around the world again. In our case, post-punk from 1980s post-industrial Britain journeyed to 2010s Russia, where local musicians converted it to their reality and fed it back into the global network, where it was taken again and consumed by Mexican fans. The traffic of cultural flows around the world thus leads to the creation of new cultural phenomena and endless stages of transformation, in which "hybridity and syncretism are inescapable" (Connell and Gibson 2003, 271) and the original may end up having a chronological primacy, but not a symbolic one (Marc 2015). Moreover, the flow of Russophone post-punk occurred between music cultures traditionally outside of the Anglo-American ruling highways, thus seemingly challenging dominant structures.

However, this challenge – as well as its implications – have limitations. Firstly, Motorama and Human Tetris sang in English, a testimony to the hegemony of Anglophone products in the global market, as well as of English as the language of popular music worldwide. Since national languages cannot but be entangled in transnational hierarchical relations of power (García 2009, 141), singing in English for a non-Anglophone band may incidentally reinforce unequal power relations even if the initial intentions may have been the opposite. Secondly, hierarchies may not be disrupted but instead transposed onto another plane and replicated. The musical relationship between the two peripheries (Russia and Mexico in our case) may present the similar hierarchical scheme that existed between the Anglo-American world (the centre) and Russia (the periphery), albeit on a smaller scale. For example, while Russophone artists toured with consistency in Central and South America in the 2010s, the same cannot be said of Central and South American artists touring Russia. Latin American popular music hardly found any space in Russia's youth magazines either. This perhaps suggests that, owing to the difference in sonic capital, peripheral flows may hit obstacles during their transnational

220 *Independent Music in Russia*

journey (powerful music industries, unequal access to opportunities, indifferent or biased audiences and so on), and these constraints channel the course of the flows: peripheral flows may continue to exist in parallel with the dominant flows, or re-emerge in other peripheral countries.

In this context, Thussu (2007) and Kavoori (2007) called for a reassessment of transculturation based on hard power (economics, politics) and soft power (cultural). Starting from the assumption that "our society is constructed around flows" (Castells 2000, 442), and that "such flows have shown extraordinary growth in direction, volume and velocity" (Thussu 2007, 10), these scholars pointed out the imbalance between the flows emanating from the core (princi-pally the US) and the rest of the world (see also Kayman 2004; Phillipson 2009). Following Nederveen-Pieterse (2004, 122), who termed the flows between two peripheral countries "South–South flows", Thussu (2007) differentiated between "dominant" flows – the ones originating in the core – and "subaltern" or "con-tra-flows" – the ones originating from the periphery. Contra-flows have increas-ingly challenged the dominant flows, reflecting the so-called "rise of the rest" (Thussu 2015). Lee (2014) observed that only the flows between peripheral or less central places, such as the spread of K-pop in East Asia, should be really called "transnational", because of their difference from the usual globalisation fluxes from centre to periphery. However, such subaltern or contra flows are still portrayed in scholarship as carriers of intrinsically anti-hegemonic value, and Anglo-American imperialism is often pitted against an idea of resistance that is not necessarily there.

The flows of post-punk from Russia to Latin America – and other similar occur-rences – may be better understood as subflows. The term "subflow" also describes the movement of cultural products across two (or more) "peripheral" countries, but, unlike contra-flows, subflows do not try to challenge or subvert the current macro-system; on the contrary, they may well reproduce the macro-system's hierarchies while emphasising their secondary character and initial common subordinate po-sition (in the case of the bands above, it is the [re]production and [re]adaptation of – as well as the cultural tribute to – 1980s British post-punk bands, sometimes filtered through the prism of Soviet new wave groups). Moreover, subflows are sub-products, since their production and consumption exist at the lower level of in-ternational cultural structures. In addition, subflows, in the sense of "underground" flows, may emerge to the surface and become internationally mainstream: the ac-cumulated accreditation in the periphery may give them dynamism to overflow to the global centre. Such rare occurrences, however, may indicate that subflows have been memeified or stereotyped in the centre, for example in the case of Molchat doma's TikTok boom (Biasioli 2024). Finally, crucial to the nature and direction of subflows is the role of sonic capital, which speeds up, slows down, enhances or re-duces the intensity with which subflows move; sonic capital increases or decreases the subflow's reach and the effect that it produces in foreign territories; unequal sonic capitals create barriers that channel subflows in one place rather than another. In our case, these barriers initially directed Russian post-punk in Mexico and South America, rather than North America or the Global North.

From the Margins and Back? 221

Russian agencies for music export

Structural inequalities at a global level were reflected in logistical difficulties for Russian independent musicians when it came to touring and also combined with domestic lack of investment and supporting infrastructure. In 2016, Interviewee 3, a musician with some experience playing at foreign showcases, stressed the DIY nature of *nezavisimaia muzyka* in relation to its promotion abroad:

> There are a lot of cool musicians in Russia who play not only here, but also around the world. This number is growing, and this speaks for itself. I think this is some kind of heroism: the musicians do everything themselves, no one helps them. [In Russia], unlike most European countries, there's no office for musical export that can sponsor musicians, pay for their tickets, and send them to festivals abroad. We do everything ourselves. And I think this is very cool – it tempers you.

Interviewee 3's arguments described a widely accepted situation in the Russian music industry in the mid-2010s. As confirmed by virtually all the practitioners interviewed during fieldwork, local music infrastructures capable of devising and sustaining export programs were traditionally deficient. The government promoted classical music and ballet almost exclusively, and piracy still hurdled practitioners from investing in touring. Promotion in the West for a Russian independent musician seemed both exceptional and difficult.

Together with internal infrastructural problems, international logistics played an important role in hindering the spread of *nezavisimaia muzyka* abroad. When the UK officially enforced Brexit at the end of January 2021, British musicians protested about the new musical policy, which may have required performers to apply for work visas in order to perform in Europe (Beaumont-Thomas 2021). On their social media, Russian indie musicians, while expressing solidarity, said something along the lines of "welcome to the club". Work visa issues were, unfortunately, integral to their touring practice. Motorama, for example, were denied entry at the UK border in 2016, when the border police claimed the band had the wrong type of visa. As a consequence, their gig was cancelled at the last minute, to the disappointment of fans and some financial loss for the venue, promoters and band.[7] These conditions render the whole international touring business unstable for *nezavisimaia muzyka* musicians, especially considering that they customarily played in small clubs that were unlikely to file a visa invitation for the artists. Receiving a work visa was a lengthy and complicated process. In the UK, for example, it cost £244 (as of 2019), and performers had to undergo bank checks (a minimum of £1270 in the bank was required to enter the UK – a sum that not everyone may have). On top of this, there was a significant degree of arbitrariness and no transparency on the end of bureaucracy – visas could be rejected without explanations, and musicians could be questioned and denied entry at the border. The situation was slightly easier in mainland Europe, but it still involved bank checks, visa applications and limitations on the performers' paid activity. For all these reasons,

222   *Independent Music in Russia*

nezavisimaia muzyka musicians sometimes ended up performing on tourist visas (which are simpler to obtain) and being paid cash.[8]

In the second half of the 2010s, however, thanks to the development of the domestic musical infrastructure, new independent organisations for the export of Russian music emerged. They set out to solve logistics problems and put independent Russian bands on the map of European and Western music markets. These agencies started promoting *nezavisimaia muzyka* with unprecedented consistency, providing a backbone for a potential increase in international demand for music from Russia (which, because of COVID-19 first and the war in Ukraine later, did not materialise).

More Zvukov (Sea of Sounds) – the first export agency focused on Russian and post-Soviet music – appeared in 2005 and, after a period in Rotterdam, resettled in Berlin. On its roster were Shortparis and Lucidvox.[9] Another agency for the development of Russian music abroad was RUSH, which appeared in 2017 thanks to the joint efforts of journalists and promoters. The agency's format was "temporary": each year, four acts entered the RUSH pool and spent twelve months under its supervision before the pool was updated. The project involved, for instance, Kate NV,[10] Glintshake, Shortparis and Maskeliade.[11] It was discontinued in 2020. The third export initiative was a spinoff of *Bol'*. In spring 2018, Stepan Kazarian and his team organised a tour that saw five groups from the festival – Shortparis, Glintshake, Kazuskoma,[12] Spasibo[13] and Elektroforez[14] – play in Warsaw, Poznan and Berlin. In September 2019, *Bol'* took part in the London International Festival Forum. Aigel,[15] Inturist and Pasosh were the bands chosen to represent Russia in the showcase. This project also ended in 2020. The fourth and last project was Moscow Music Week (MMW), also co-organised by Kazarian. MMW was an annual initiative that started in 2015 and consisted of performances by established and upcoming groups, as well as conferences attended by representatives of the Russian and European music industry. MMW, like Tallinn Music Week or the Ljubljana festival MENT, tried to connect Western and Eastern European industries. The scope of MMW grew over the years: in September 2019, the event took place simultaneously at 13 concert venues, where more than 100 musicians played over four days. That, however, was its last year.

Some of these agencies initially sought financial support from official institutions, soon realising that their energy could be better spent elsewhere: the Russian government did not seem interested in being involved in the promotion of *nezavisimaia muzyka* music abroad. Interviewee 38 – a journalist involved in one of the export projects – revealed that the agency turned to the Russian Ministry of Culture and was told that official support was considered only in the case of classical and, in some cases, folk music.[16] Similarly, another person involved, Interviewee 13, pointed out that "what the authorities are really interested in is the wider sphere, the mainstream, not the underground". State interest in popular music, including *nezavisimaia muzyka*, grew when music was placed in the context of large media events. It is in this arena that popular music could be exploited as a tool for soft power, as exemplified by Russia's recent Eurovision history (Heller 2007; Cassiday 2014; Kazakov and Hutchings 2019; Biasioli 2023). Mostly, however, independent music export organisations were self-financed and/or privately sponsored. On the one hand, the lack of official support problematised the development of the export of local music and made it unstable; on the other hand, promoters were free to choose whichever artists they pleased and maintained autonomy from the state. As Interviewee 37 –involved in one of the export projects – revealed: "The state is not interested in us at all. It doesn't support, and doesn't interfere either". Interviewee 30, part of another export project, discerned:

> We are afraid that if they [the state] begin to give money to us or to projects similar to ours, it will be in the context of an ideological struggle. I wouldn't want that. Otherwise, it will turn into politics, and we try avoiding it. It's hard for us financially, but in terms of reputation, in terms of business contacts, the fact that we don't have any relations with the Russian state helps us when we communicate with foreigners.

Even though the promotion of Russian independent music abroad turned out to be a financially risky and often unprofitable enterprise (Interview 11, 37, 44), the growth of the Russian export market in the second half of the 2010s was noticeable. Kate NV, Shortparis, Lucidvox, Glintshake toured Europe regularly between 2018 and 2020, which in turn generated an overall increase in demand for Russian music. According to Anton Repka, organiser of the Czech festival Pohoda, "in the 20 years that the festival has existed, Russian bands have regularly played our stage, but half of their total number have played in the last five years".[17] Reeperbahn in Hamburg, The Great Escape in Brighton, MENT in Ljubljana and many other European showcases increasingly accepted applications from Russian groups or agencies in the second half of the 2010s.

The professionals involved in these export projects denied the promotion of a specific type of *nezavisimaia muzyka*. Interviewee 37 argued that the only criterion was quality. Another promoter pointed out that the main principle was the credibility of the live performance: "we always review concert videos, that's the best way to understand whether the band is good, whether there is some special feature in it, some image that can be promoted".[18] Interviewee 39, another promoter, said that "the image of the band can never be fabricated", because this image is "formed before the musician becomes part of the export project". The agency's task, then, was not to create authenticity, but to help promote it, not to package a product, but to show it. Despite these claims, however, agencies seemed to regularly choose groups who sang in Russian and belonged to the New Russian Wave.

Out of these groups, export agencies all invested in Shortparis as "Russia's best live band" (Velichko 2018). These efforts were paired with the favourable reviews and encouraging opinions of several international experts. The pre-pandemic Western musical press consistently crowned Shortparis as the most promising group of the contemporary Russian scene (Doran 2018; Robb 2018a, 2018b; Foster 2019a, 2019b, 2019c; Trefor 2019). In 2018, *Louder Than War* editor and punk musician John Robb, who allegedly coined the term Britpop and introduced Nirvana to the British public, called Shortparis "today's band", making a case for their originality

224 *Independent Music in Russia*

and uniqueness (Robb 2018a). *The Quietus* editor John Doran (2018) described them as "full of revolutionary potential". Music journalist Richard Foster (2019d), deemed the group "sensational" and defined them as "a perfect marriage of the thoughtful and the visceral". *Gigwise* correspondent Cai Trefor (2019) was persuaded that "nothing will stop" Shortparis from becoming "huge". At Moscow Music Week 2019, participants shared the impression that the success of the New Russian Wave in Europe was nearing, and that Russian music could become the new K-pop.

Russian promoters bet on Shortparis as the initiators of a "Russian Wave" abroad, similarly to what happened when Bjork and Sigur Ros created a global trend of Icelandic music. Interviewee 37 argued: "If Shortparis succeed, Russian music will become a brand. To every sort of bullshit from Russia people will go 'oh my god, check it out!'" The Russian language in this sense can become part of a larger marketing system centred upon a specific idea of "Russian sound". The band, as discussed in the previous chapter, subverted expectations of Russian identity, not least because it refused to articulate dissent, while emphasising its Russianness and giving interviews with the foreign press only in Russian.[19] The fruits of the effort of Russian music agencies were yet to be fully seen when the halt imposed on live music activity by the coronavirus pandemic greatly slowed down the process of promotion and popularisation of *nezavisimaia muzyka* bands abroad. The start of the full-scale war in Ukraine also discontinued several of these initiatives. As for Shortparis, their rising career was certainly halted by the circumstances. While still based in Russia, the band has been touring less frequently than before 2020 and has not made much progress in the European market.

However, even before the COVID pandemic and the full-scale war in Ukraine, and despite the progressive appearance of Russian musicians on the European map in the 2010s, linguistic, cultural and economic barriers were always present. In particular, the sonic capital of the Anglophone market and its exclusionary cultural conservatism maintained the endeavour of exporting Russian music difficult. Interviewee 37, for example, noticed:

> The f…ing British booking agencies rule this continent. As soon as they decide to push someone, that someone becomes famous. I don't think that the point is nationalism; Australian and New Zealand groups are perfectly fine in the roster of all these agencies. This mainly depends on the desire not to work with non-Anglophone groups, and secondly, with groups that are non-native English speakers. For them, the world exists only as 'their world', and the rest of the world adjusts to them.

As Interviewee 37 maintained, the transnational spread of Russian popular music – including *nezavisimaia muzyka* – started with a disadvantage. Over the years, promoters and musicians devised various strategies to overcome the Anglo-American hierarchy and access the global market. Since Russian music export agencies were quite a novelty for Russia (and quite an extemporary one), musicians usually relied on their own personal initiatives to participate in the global conversation. To these initiatives and strategies we will now turn.

From the Margins and Back? 225

"The joke has gone out of control": Little Big and self-stereotyping

To acquire sonic capital and international recognition, Russian musicians adopted various strategies, the most common of which were self-stereotyping, camouflage and recycling of Soviet aesthetics. Self-stereotyping consists of the visual reproduction of widely assumed clichés about one's own country so that these could resonate with the expectations and biases of audiences around the world. That is how the band Little Big operated. Camouflage is the attempt to advance in the Global North by concealing one's national identity and/or swapping this identity with a new one in order to fit in the target environment. This is what Pompeya and Coockoo chose to do. The third strategy is to explore the Soviet past anew by reviving it in sound and visual atmospheres, which creates an enigmatic image: on the one hand, this can be viewed as tapping into transnationally widespread feelings of nostalgia or hauntology; on the other, it can be used to comment politically on the present. This is where Motorama situated themselves.

Let us start this analysis with the once-St. Petersburg-based rave band Little Big.[20] With more than 210,000 followers on Facebook, 670,000 subscribers on VKontakte, 2.5 billion views on YouTube,[21] tours in large arenas and festival participation, Little Big constituted the most globally successful Russian popular music act in the 2010s. Deemed "the Russian version of Die Antwoord" (*Sobaka.ru* 2015), Little Big rose to international fame thanks to self-othering images of uneducated Russian thugs and simultaneously bleak and ridiculous depictions of the Russian low life. Their visual representations of alcoholism, squalor and Russia's backwardness, mixed with tracksuits, Kalashnikovs and peasant costumes, immediately found an audience in the West. In the space of a few years from their founding in 2013, while they were still relatively unknown in Russia, Little Big became the most iconic Russian popular music export after t.A.T.u. Importantly, Little Big built most of their career being an independent project: the band scripted and released their music and videos through their own label Little Big Family (which became a subsidiary of Warner only in late 2018), and lived and worked in a mansion outside of St. Petersburg. Upholding the DIY ethos and artistic autonomy, the band has also experimented with different music genres, crossing from hip-hop through punk to hardcore. Lastly, their success was facilitated by the choice to sing in English, or better, in an intentionally simplified, broken English. Little Big's lyrics were peppered with conventional Slavic mistakes (lack of the verb "to be", lack of articles) and sung in a deliberately obvious Russian accent, which simultaneously emphasised difference, enhanced the humorous and stereotypical effect and made the band's message understandable at first listen by another non-native speaker. As Interviewee 35, a music critic and journalist, explained: "There are English words that are clear to everyone: 'come on', 'everybody', 'fuck you', etcetera. As far as I know, they invented that project counting on a foreign audience".

Indeed, by the band's own admission, Little Big was a project initially packaged for an international public and not aiming at domestic recognition (*Vdud'* 2017; *Ostorozhno, Sobchak* 2019). Even the titles of Little Big's songs of the period 2013–2015 were self-explanatory and described a specific type of Russia, targeted

226   *Independent Music in Russia*

at the amusement of a foreign audience: "Life in da Trash", "Russian Hooligans", "With Russia from Love" and so on. The same applied to the content of the videos and to the lyrics. For example, Little Big's first song, "Everyday I'm Drinking" (2013), which catapulted the band onto the international stage, presented a patriotically desperate image, defiant and self-deprecating at the same time. Indeed, together with a strong undercurrent of affect and belonging, the lyrics of the song depict Russia as a land lacking prospects and financial stability, in which there is nothing to do apart from boundless alcohol consumption and obscene acts as coping mechanisms, and in which perceived national symbols such as the matryoshka and the balalaika, devoid of any context, are mentioned only to enhance the crass cultural caricature.

In the song's video, the band members engage in squatting, vodka-binging and degraded versions of Barynya, a traditional Russian folk dance, while a hybrid flag, half Soviet and half Russian, stands behind them (see Figures 5.3 and 5.4). Towards the end of the video, the band leader, Ilya Prusikin, mimes coupling with a (fake) bear. Pussy Riot are also often referenced in the video through the presence of a woman in a balaclava – evidence of how the actionist group had transformed itself into another cliché in the Russian (and not only Russian) imaginary. As the magazine *Vice* pointed out, "Apart from dangerous driving, [the video for 'Everyday I'm Drinking'] has literally got every great stereotype that you could ever want from a Russian music video" (Wilkinson 2013).

Crucial in the international breakthrough of "Everyday I'm Drinking" was the foreign audiences' preparedness to recognise the band's visual aesthetics as typically Russian. According to the myth of exotic Russia, we, as Westerners, expect the Russians to be Russians, and, consequently, we tend to judge Russia's cultural production by how much it tallies with our presumptions (Figes 2002). Little Big, however, adopted and exaggerated these ways of seeing: instead of passive receivers of the Western gaze, they took on an active role in appropriating and reproducing Orientalist, belittling and reductive views about themselves and their country. Prusikin, who then called himself a "big patriot" (Gogov 2014), stated in a 2017 interview (*Vdud'* 2017) that the band "takes the mickey [*eto stëb*] out of Russian stereotypes, not out of Russia", and that he loved Russia "despite its many flaws" (as also stated in the lyrics for "Everyday I'm Drinking"). Because *stëb* contains a dualism of interpretations, Little Big's work could be also read as a genuine criticism of the criticism and, therefore, as a praise and a defence of Russia vis-à-vis the Western gaze. The multifaceted applicability of parody reveals its paradox between "conservative repetition and revolutionary difference" (Hutcheon 2000, 77), undermining and at the same time legitimising the object parodied. Eventually, laughter is sided by the undecidability of the author's intentions: who or what is the object of parody? It may well be the foreign viewer who is being tricked, together with their simplistic assumptions about Russia's backwardness. Self-Orientalism, as Kobayashi et al. (2019, 161) argue, refers to the wilful (re-)action of non-Western individuals and institutions to "play the Other" – that is, to use Western portrayals of the non-West – in order to strategically gain recognition and position themselves within the Western-dominated global economy, system and order". This, however,

From the Margins and Back? 227

Figure 5.3 and 5.4 Screenshots from Little Big's video for 'Everyday I'm Drinking (2013).
Source: YouTube.[22]

228   *Independent Music in Russia*

opens up new tools for subversion by exploiting the exploiter (Iwabuchi 1994). Little Big thus used self-Orientalism not only as a commercially viable strategy, but also as a way of empowerment against Anglo-American cultural dominance. Exploiting the multiform nature of parody and flipping Orientalism on its head, Little Big proudly turned the mirror to the West, saying something like: "Even if we were like this, so what"? Moreover, in their early works, Little Big paired hyperbolic representations of the subaltern with patriotism. For example, in "Kind Inside, Hard Outside", an anti-war video which centres on a hypothetical fight between Putin and Obama, Putin eventually floors Obama and compassionately helps him up, sealing the peace.[23] In the context of the increasing Russia-West political confrontation of the 2010s, this looked to be an affirmative projection of Russian nationhood that echoed the official one.

As Laruelle and Engström (2018, 12) have written about a very similar band to Little Big in terms of aesthetics – Leningrad – the characters of Little Big's videos are the poor provincial people still living in the "eternal 1990s" (a time of social chaos and lawlessness for Russia) who also represent Putin's "silent majority". These characters "act as tricksters and buffoons, stand-ins of cultural heroes, demonstrating the imaginary and conventionality of all social and cultural norms and restrictions" (Laruelle and Engström 2018, 12–13). Despite the often-gloomy plots of the clips and apparent transgression, *gopniki* (chavs) and *bydla* (thugs) "are perceived not as a negative reflection of a sad Russian reality, but as a recognisable and positive image of oneself" and – consequently – the nation (Laruelle and Engström 2018, 14), which can be pitted against the West in the international arena as a sign of "authenticity". Ultimately, as Rancière (2010, 144) suggests, "parody as critique" and "parody of critique" may well be equivalent.

It is for this reason that, despite the seemingly unflattering depiction of Russia that the band delivered, Little Big broke through in the domestic market as well, which evidenced the mutual appeal of Russian stereotypes both abroad and at home, as well as the different values attributed to them by foreign and local audiences. The band's 2019 "domestic" tour (nearly the length of the equator) saw them play stadiums and large arenas in 36 Russian cities, with Prusikin climbing to number 35 of the richest pop personalities in Russia (*Forbes* 2019). The band featured regularly on Channel 1 shows as well. Once fame was achieved (abroad and at home), the band moved from the projections of Russian specificities to a "universalist and therefore viral style that transcend[ed] national borders", switching from "hard *stëb*" to "soft *stëb*" (Patyk 2021, 227–30). At the same time, however, the Russian state took an interest: because *stëb* exposes, criticises but at the same minimises or even nullifies sociopolitical problems, it leaves room to be appropriated by official rhetoric as well. And so it did.

When, on 2 March 2020, Little Big were chosen to represent Russia at the year's Eurovision song contest (then cancelled due to the coronavirus pandemic), the news certified the endorsement of Russia's own stereotypical advertisement for an international audience at a state level. On *Vechernii Urgant*, Prusikin revealed he sent the song to the Russian Organising Committee (*Orgkomitet*), responsible for choosing

From the Margins and Back?   229

Russia's Eurovision entry, thinking the band would never make it. When they were told they had been selected, Prusikin commented: "now the joke has gone out of control", [*prikol vyshel iz-pod kontrolya*] alluding to the serious responsibility they had been invested with by the entire country (Prusikin in *Vechernii Urgant* 2020).

The choice of Little Big as 2020 Russia's Eurovision representatives had a massive resonance and was discussed among *nezavisimaia muzyka* export professionals. Natasha Padabed, the owner of the agency More Zvukov, for example, asked in conversation with Aleksandr Gorbachev: "Do you think there is something that unites the Russian bands that are currently most popular abroad, Little Big, Ic3peak, Shortparis? Maybe this is what's expected from Russia, this image of dangerous guys you'd better not mess with"? (Padabed in Gorbachev 2020). On the same post, journalist Denis Boiarinov observed: "Well, we must admit that Little Big – dangerous but funny idiots with dances and nuclear warheads – are the most adequate image of Russia for export now" (Boiarinov in Gorbachev 2020). Overall, Russia's cultural intermediaries reiterated that Little Big constituted a good fit for Russia not despite, but *because of* their stereotypical and backward depiction of Russia, which was seen as a reflection (for the better and for the worse) of the country's status in the international political context.

Indeed, the joke had "gone out of control" because the state had also adopted it in order to exploit it as a tool for soft power. Russia's choice to let Little Big represent the country in what is a contest with "both blatant and subtle political aspects" (Raykoff 2016, 3) was not only telling of the high degree to which stereotypes are endorsed by multiple actors (foreign audiences, domestic audiences, the Russian state), but also of the official strategy for the promotion of Russia's cultural image abroad. Little Big – and the investiture as Russia's musical representatives – embodied the point of juncture between the "transgressive consolidation" from the bottom up (Laruelle and Engström 2018) and authoritarian nation-building from the top down, masked as a show for the West.

Such an unlikely match was no surprise also because *stëb* had been previously used by official organs to challenge Western political assumptions about Russia. For example, one of RT's international branding campaigns, as Hutchings (2020, 297) reports, was conducted through posters affixed on the London Underground in 2017, whose titles included: "Beware! A 'propaganda bullhorn' is at work here", and "Missed a train? Lost a vote? Blame it on us!", with reference to the alleged Russian interference in the 2016 US presidential elections. As Laruelle (2021, 17) argued, the Russian regime was able to transfer the role of the "trickster" or "joker" in Soviet culture in the international political arena, and define itself as liminal and transgressive against the Western-dominated mainstream media ecology.

As in the case of Manizha a year later, Little Big offered the Russian state the opportunity to use grassroots cultural products as tools for soft power. This was done by exploiting the band's previous self-Orientalist projections: joking about Russia's criminalised and backward image may have trivialised this image further and eventually invalidated it. The result could have been a global reassuring laugh about Russia's social problems that turned these problems into a reason for patriotic pride internally, and aroused curiosity externally.

230   *Independent Music in Russia*

Little Big's participation at Eurovision, even if only scheduled and never realised, provided fresh material in the musical history of East–West relations. This is all the more significant since their national and international calibre compares to that of another massive export product of Russian music, t.A.T.u, who had competed as Russia's Eurovision entry in 2003. Yet, there are differences. t.A.T.u.'s hyperbolic image was based upon extra-national parameters, such as sexual liberation from traditional schemes of heteronormativity, and happened in a moment of openness to the West rather than confrontation with it. However cynical, it was progressive. In the case of Little Big, the hyperbole is constructed upon provincial and regressive national traits. While this simplified version of Russia works inasmuch as it is easy for audiences abroad (and domestic) to recognise and package it as Russia, the state officially supported the construction of such a reductive image of the nation as one of the strategies for its international advertising campaign. Once again, the geopolitical conditions were key factors: Little Big happened in a moment in which stereotypes of Russia's backwardness could be contrasted against the progressive liberalism of the West as a symbol of Russia's political ascendancy and cultural distinction.

Pompeya and camouflage

After the resonance acquired in the domestic music scene during the rise of the Anglophone Wave, Pompeya spent a few months every year between 2013 and 2018 in the United States. The Muscovite trio lived in Miami and Los Angeles on work visas provided by their US labels (first No Shame and then Moshi). Between 2013 and 2017, the group performed in the US more than 100 times, and their gigs took place in more than 30 cities, including New York, San Francisco, Chicago, Seattle and the Austin SXSW festival. Such concert activity led to a large number of reviews in American music publications, usually positive. *Noisey* saw Pompeya as the successful union between new wave music and a Caribbean beach (Hill 2014). In another issue of the same magazine (Bennett 2015), the group was proclaimed "an upbeat incarnation of The Cure (sans the white makeup and black hair dye) doing a dance with an updated Duran Duran (sans the mullets and penchant of popped collar pastel trenchcoats)". Across the American musical press, Pompeya were described as "no-nonsense" band with catchy music that revisited the best of the 1980s while leaving out its shenanigans.

Pompeya, like Shortparis a little later in the decade, defied audiences' expectations and subverted stereotypes around Russian identity. Unlike Shortparis, however, Pompeya did so through uplifting and bright soundscapes. US magazines emphasised the contrast between the geographical origin of Pompeya and their sound. The type of music proposed by the band, with its warm and relaxed atmospheres, was contrasted with fixed images of Russia's gloom and preconceptions around how music should sound there. Reviewing Pompeya's single "Slaver", *MTV* argued that it is "difficult to imagine the quartet's warm, ornate, '80s-inspired funk coming from the depths of an arctic tundra" (Silverstein 2013) (even if the band was from Moscow, not the arctic tundra). The zine *Dummy* (2013), talking about the single "Power", wrote: "You probably wouldn't realise it for all the funk

From the Margins and Back? 231

basslines, rollicking grooves, warm synths and perfect Americanised accents of 'Power', but Pompeya actually hail from Russia. It's a far cry from the cold portrayal of Eastern Europe that we're presented with over here". *Interview*, too, highlighted the divergence: "When you think of Moscow, words like 'sunny', 'bright', and 'breezy' probably aren't the first adjectives that come to mind" (Reese 2013).

The subversion of stereotypes about Russia was underlined in Pompeya's video clips, usually shot in summer weather, at the beach, along palm boulevards or in the desert. Above all, the videos are set in the US or the Dominican Republic, displaying no trace of Russia, and the musicians are portrayed inhabiting this space as *locals*. In the video for "Anyway" (2016), for instance, the band is filmed walking a dog in a residential street of Malibu (Figure 5.5). What better image to describe a sense of local belonging? What better strategy to transplant one of the pillar concepts of indie – locality – onto the visual ground?

These tactics of camouflage signalled a diachronic and synchronic variation in the traditional packaging and presentation of a Russian band for US audiences. One did not have to look far to notice, for example, the contrast between the famous cover of *Red Wave* in 1986 and the palm trees of Pompeya in the 2010s. Conceived of as a compilation of Soviet rock *magnitizdats* from four bands (Akvarium, Strannye Igry, Alisa and Kino), *Red Wave* was smuggled to America by musician and Kino guitarist's wife Joanna Stingray. The record was publicised with Cold-War overtones of danger, artist-state opposition and freedom-loving West vs. oppressive East, and eventually became another flop in the export of Soviet popular music in

Figure 5.5 Still frame from Pompeya's video for "Anyway" (2016). Source: YouTube.[24]

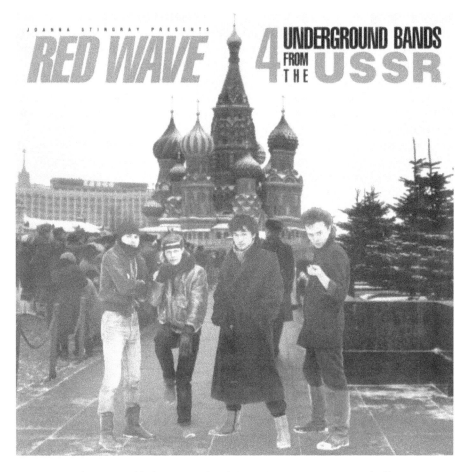

Figure 5.6 Still frame with the cover of *Red Wave* (1986). Source: YouTube.[25]

that period (see McMichael 2009, 338–42). On the cover of the compilation, in a disingenuously stereotypical fashion, the four band leaders were superimposed on the background of an unrealistic and snowy Red Square (see Figure 5.6). In Pompeya's work, everything was turned upside down: the cold gave way to the heat, the snow to the sun, the furry hats to hipster caps, the coats to flowery unbuttoned shirts, the gloom to light-heartedness. Russian stereotypes were used only as ironic corollary: "When people [Americans] find out that we are Russians, they sometimes come and touch us with their finger to confirm that we are real" (Interview 15). Furthermore, in contrast with other contemporary colleagues marketing their music abroad, for example, Little Big – who made an effort in the other direction by heightening their belonging to Russia through self-Orientalism – Pompeya deployed the strategy of camouflage: adaptation to the new setting and reconstruction of one's image in accordance with, and from within, the new context.

From the Margins and Back? 233

At the same time, the subversion of stereotypes in the native culture ran the risk of merging with the endorsement of stereotypes belonging to the target culture. For some Russian commentators, the absence of Russian markers and the overwhelming presence of US-based ones did not indicate the promotion of an internationalised Russian culture, but provincial imitation (see, for example, Gorbachev 2019). In other words, Pompeya's strategy, more than nation-branding, suggested nation-swapping. By adopting the language, style and visuals of the Other, as well as by physically being in the Other's territory, Pompeya thought to overcome the perceived gap between their peripheral origin and the Anglo-dominated global culture. The transnational transfer of their music was paired with the reinvention of themselves as identities, or, as one of the band members put it, the "guessing [of themselves] in a new time, context and language" (Interview 15).

However, despite the efforts at integrating in the dominant market and appropriating supposedly dominant identities, Pompeya's American adventure showed a declining trajectory. Between 2013 and 2020, Pompeya were indeed signed to a US label, toured, shot videos and gave interviews. From a 2013 gig in Dallas in which only one person showed up (Gorbachev 2015), the band slowly increased its fanbase. Between 2016 and 2018, the band played well-known indie venues, such as the Mercury Lounge in NY, The Echo in LA or Beat Kitchen in Chicago. However, the number of US gigs steadily dropped each year: 21 in 2015, 19 in 2016, 10 in 2017 and only 8 in 2018. Moreover, most of their income in this period still originated from concert activity in Russia, the large majority of YouTube views (and commentaries) on their videos were still Russian, and band members sporadically had to take on non-music-related part-time jobs while overseas (Interview 15, 22, 23). And while their 2018 album, *Dreamers* (released in the US in August), was indeed met with more positive reviews in America (Kalish 2018) than in Russia (Mezenov 2018), these commentaries were fewer than the ones on the band's previous works, and they failed to create a consistent resonance among the American public. The only articles that had come out in the US in relation to *Dreamers* – in *Earmilk* (Odutola 2018), *Vents* (Frometa 2018) and *Atwood Magazine* (Kalish 2018) – suggested that US press interest in the band had decreased. With COVID, the band moved back to Moscow on a permanent basis.

Nonetheless, it might be harsh to dismiss the band's US experience altogether. In late 2018, Pompeya boasted a monthly Spotify LA-based audience of 1,100 and a global one of 57,000 (excluding Russia, where Spotify had not arrived yet). In late 2023, the band's monthly listeners totalled 80,000. Although it was no longer possible to locate the audiences, this number excluded Russia, from which Spotify withdrew in 2022. Pompeya thus may have become a niche band in the US, just as the band members had foreseen in 2016 during our interview: "We want to be a part of the common musical arena, rather than the local one. And even if we are an insignificant particle in the common musical arena, it's worth it anyway" (Interview 15). Their consolidated status in Russia powered their efforts internationally, allowing for both potential expansion and the luxury of not quite making it on the global scale.

234   *Independent Music in Russia*

Coockoo and failure

If Pompeya's activities in the US between 2013 and 2018 did not lead to a significant breakthrough, the endeavours of the band Coockoo (later renamed February) in the UK between 2012 and 2015 were an overall flop. Let us start from the very end, with the words of one of the band members:

> We wanted to go to England, because a lot of things happen there and the industry is very advanced. If we could get inside that . . . how do they say: 'if you've conquered London, you've conquered the world'. Well, we wanted to do that but it didn't happen. Not this time.

> (Interview 16)

Coockoo formed in Moscow in 2009 as a five-piece band with female vocals. The group soon adopted an outward-looking marketing strategy by recording their first LP, *Cosmoventura*, in Rome in 2010, under the conviction that Russia was musically underprepared and undereducated. The Muscovite band had a negative and pessimistic view of Russia's music business: "industry people here suck the energy out of you" (Biasioli 2011). This affected their position as artists in Russia: "no one cares about us here" [*my zdes' nikomu ne nuzhni*] (Biasioli 2011). In 2012, the band relocated to London. Coockoo's move had been previously hinted at in their single (and video) "Groupies' Anthem (F.U.C.K.)", written and released in 2010, when the band was still based in Moscow:

> F-U-C-K I'm going to the UK
> F-U-C-K M-E I'll do it with you for free
> A-M-E-N now I know who is my man
> O-A-S-I-S Liam, kiss my little ass!
> F-U-C-K I'm going to the UK.
> F-U-C-K M-E I'll do it with you for free
> A-M-E-N now I know who is my man
> B-L-U-R Damon, take me in the car!
> F-U-C-K I'm going to the UK
> F-U-C-K M-E I'll do it with you for free
> A-M-E-N now I know who is my man
> P-U-L-P Jarvis, play your game with me!
> F-U-C-K I'm going to the UK
> F-U-C-K M-E I'll do it with you for free
> A-M-E-N now I know who is my man
> I don't need no sex at all
> If you don't play rock-n-roll!
> F-U-C-K I'm going to the UK
> I'm Going to the UK
> I'm going to the UK
> We are going to the UK!

From the Margins and Back?   235

The references in the song are clear: Liam Gallagher (Oasis), Damon Albarn (Blur) and Jarvis Cocker (Pulp). All three bands belonged to the genre of Britpop, which at the time exerted significant inspiration on the Moscow quintet. The lyrics interlaced the band's tribute to their influences with the humour of the groupie's fantasy, whose escapist tendencies were enhanced by the song's visual support. At the beginning of the video Maria Melnikova (Coockoo's singer) sits in her bedroom and reads *NME* (everything is in a cartoon style except herself and, later, the other band members). Words come from an old television, in a male voice: "Have you ever listened to rock music? Of course you have! 'Cause all cool people listen to rock music! You know that listening to rock music makes you 69% more awesome than any other average human being? [...] The ultimate secret to being awesome is listening to rock music!" (see Figure 5.7). The words run on the screen and in the last sentence they jump from the television into Melnikova's head (and here escapism is contaminated, arguably, with cultural imperialism). After the brainwashing, Melnikova starts singing, while her bandmates appear on TV playing the tune, with a British flag in the background. At this point, the UK storms in and, in a carnivalesque fashion, disrupts the routine of the post-Soviet bedroom: Melnikova starts packing her suitcase and psychologically travels to London, where she is surrounded by symbols of British culture: Big Ben, a double-decker bus, Queen Elizabeth, teapots, a telephone box, Tower Bridge, etc. (see Figure 5.8). In the last frame of the video, Melnikova joins the rest of the band inside the TV while exclaiming, "We are going to the UK!" She transforms herself from a groupie of her favourite bands into the actual leader of her own band.

The song (and the video) were simultaneously a hymn to fame, to escapism and to self-realisation abroad according to Anglo-American standards. Overall,) "Groupies' Anthem (F.U.C.K.)" articulated empowerment through identity changing, that is, through taking on the identity of the Imaginary West, the Other.

When they moved to London, Coockoo had been active in Russia for three years, toured the country twice, supported the US band Garbage during their Russian tour, opened for Western acts in prestigious Moscow concert halls and filled up mid-sized venues (up to 500 people) on their solo gigs. The band lacked this base in the UK and knew they had to start anew. Aged between 26 and 28 at the time they moved, the band underwent a radical change for what they perceived as a greater good – success in the country that they viewed at the centre of the music world:

> We had this plan from the start: move to London or to New York. Basically, where the centre of the music industry is. Because London was closer, we went there. This idea was born as soon as we founded the band [in 2009] and after that we did everything in our powers to go there. We were sure to go there, become worldwide famous and be understood everywhere.
>
> (Interview 16)

Forming a fanbase in London was perceived by the band to be the beginning of a knock-on effect – their efforts would then radiate out to other countries (including their own). In order to do this, the band settled in Kensal Green, north London,

236 *Independent Music in Russia*

Figure 5.7 and 5.8 Screenshots from Coockoo's video for "Groupies' Anthem (F.U.C.K.)" (2010). Source: YouTube.[26]

in a three-storey flat, converting the lounge into a studio. The band members quit their office jobs in Russia and set up a freelance advertising company within their group, with clients based in Russia, in order to be able to work remotely while playing music.

Coockoo borrowed 3 million rubles (around £50,000 at that time), which added to one million rubles (around £16,000) that they had raised through crowd-funding. They used this money not only for accommodation and subsistence, but also to hire Autonomous Music Group, a UK-based PR agency that helped with shooting video clips and promoting the band's new material. For the latter purpose they hired Jay Reynolds, a British producer who had worked with McFly and Paloma Faith.

Coockoo, who had already equated "sounding bad" to "sounding Russian" as a result of the supposedly poor training of the personnel in Russian studios, strived to achieve a British sound that would place them, in their view, on the same level of credibility as British bands. The result came out in October 2014, and was an EP called *Saviour*, three tracks ranging from indie pop to electronica through rock.[27] A few months before, Autonomous had suggested the band change their name to February – in their view a better-sounding name than Coockoo – advice that the band followed.

February's live activity intensified in connection with the promotion of the *Saviour* EP, with five London gigs in November 2014 alone. The venues were indie clubs such as Notting Hill Arts Club, Record Club Camden and Old Queen's Head, with a maximum capacity of 200 but an established reputation. After that good streak, however, the band did not play live again until March 2015 (Finsbury Pub, North London). Airplay on British radio stations included BBC 6 and Radio XFM, both in 2014. According to the band, no other significant airplay seems to have happened. At the same time, February were introduced in some British music webzines and blogs: *Louder Than War* (8 October 2014), *Record of the Day* (6 October 2014), *Crack* (29 September 2014), *It's All Indie* (17 October 2014) and *Right Chord Music* (8 August 2014). However, rather than articles that explored the band's activity or created hype around them, these were cursory mentions of the upcoming release of the *Saviour* EP without much content.

In late 2014 the ruble started a fall in conjunction with the Ukrainian crisis and the international sanctions, which led to the loss of half of its value in the following months. Since the band members received payment in that currency from their daily job, their income was halved, making them no longer able to sustain the cost of living in London. February eventually went back to Russia in March 2015. Their hopes of international success were frustrated by the absence of tangible validation, the solidity of the collective cracked and their creativity waned:

> In the last year and a half that we were there [in London] we did not write any new song. Perhaps because we were together all the time, perhaps because we couldn't see any evident progress, something that could push us forward like: 'we're gonna do this because of this big concert, or because of this radio airplay, or because of our video on TV'. Since there wasn't any evidence of this sort of success, we got demotivated and lost interest in creating together. It became clear that something was wrong. Something was broken.
>
> (Interview 16)

February split up soon after their return to Moscow. The band, who had moved to Britain at the top of their career as one of the leading collectives of the Anglophone Wave in Russia had failed to carve a niche for itself in the new context. The reasons for such a failure reside in several factors, both incidental and structural. It may have been due to an uncommitted PR agency, a tight budget that did not allow a larger promotional campaign, the relatively short time spent in the UK (less than three years), the commitment to a side job or simply bad luck. Or it may have

238 *Independent Music in Russia*

revolved around the conservatism of the British audience and the gap between the high expectations the band had (the "Imaginary West") and the toughness of the reality they actually encountered (the "Experienced West"). Whatever the reason, however, the outcome that February consigned to history was one of personal and professional disenchantment. The strategy of camouflage with its annulment of difference, no matter how duly played, did not lead to the desired result, evidencing, once again, the presence of barriers in the cultural flows between periphery and centre. Even if the periphery moves to the centre, it still brings its peripherality with it.

Of course, this peripherality can be flipped on its head and repackaged as positive difference: in the instance of Coockoo/February, this happened back home.[28] The "Experienced West" led the band's musicians to re-evaluate and revive the music traditions of their homeland upon their return to Russia. This reassessment originated according to a classic scheme of *ressentiment* and was directed towards the UK and its cultural codes. As Interviewee 16 discerns:

> The majority of our colleagues who sang in English did not get any world popularity either, and therefore we thought: 'well, maybe we can at least make some money here [in Russia], and decided to return to the roots, which is basically the right decision, because in Russia more people will listen to us, and here everyone knows each other, here it's clear how everything works. There's no need to leave for a foreign country, no need to talk with people who speak a different language and whom you don't understand. And not because you don't know the language. No. I speak English very well, but I'm sure that English people don't say what they really think. I think that English people have several layers of politeness, and they themselves don't know what they really think. I don't want to offend anyone now, but the truth is, I often had the feeling that people tell you some very good things and may even mean them, but actually, deep down, they don't, and they don't even know about it themselves. And it's very difficult to get through these difficulties in translation and constant miscommunication. But in Russia everything is clear. We were born here, we've lived here all our lives, and, in general, no matter how bad it is, how much we all whine every day, it's a million times clearer here than in any other country, because here we speak the same language.

"Speaking the same language", for Interviewee 16, encompasses not only the ability to understand the vernacular, but the ability to decode the entire array of social and cultural conventions, references and contexts that are attached to the vernacular. Interestingly, February's separation soon after their homecoming led to the formation of two distinct Russophone projects: some former February members founded Drug (Friend), an alternative-rock project with guest vocalists, while Melnikova started her solo career under the new name Masha Maria. Thus, the "Experienced West" altered the band members' perceptions and perspectives of themselves and their careers, from Anglo-centred dreams of global fame to cherishing Russia's cultural realities and downsizing audiences. Escapism was thwarted by the presence of unequal sonic capitals in the global industry, and Coockoo's failure in the

From the Margins and Back? 239

West marked a return to local cultural roots and the local language, networks, and music world. Of course, such trajectory from the Westernising to the national, and from inadequacy to empowerment, was a reiteration of Russia's intellectual discourse since the nineteenth century (see Chapter 1). This demonstrates, regardless of the many differences in time, context and scope, the persistence of the West as the main point of reference in patterns of sameness and rejection in Russian cultural identity-making.

Russophone post-punk, *toska* and hauntology

One of the most successful strands of Russian (and Russophone) independent music export is post-punk. In the case of the Rostov-on-Don band Motorama, subflows overspilled into Europe 1, including in the Anglophone centre, creating a fertile niche for the international consumption of similar music. Between 2019 and 2020, for example, the Belorussian Russophone post-punk band Molchat doma acquired transnational virality on YouTube and TikTok (Biasioli 2024). If Molchat doma were the most successful cognates of Motorama, other Russophone post-punk bands developed a degree of international resonance,[29] in connection with the mushrooming of curated playlists and dedicated channels, particularly on YouTube, of what was renamed "Russian Doomer Music". These compilations of Russophone post-punk usually displayed the meme of the "doomer" – a young, depressed person that has lost faith in the world and seeks respite in solitude – against the backdrop of snowy Soviet panelhouses. Quite astonishingly, "Doomer" playlists turned into a platform for audiences to share their sense of emotional displacement and offer each other support, creating transnational communities of ache that used post-Soviet post-punk as a cathartic soundtrack. As this section argues, post-Soviet post-punk centres, at production, on the feeling of *toska* (melancholy, spleen, existential angst), and, at (international) reception, on *hauntology* (the resurrection of lost futures in the past). Thus, the discussion below will analyse first production and then reception. But even if the meaning encoded by the author and attributed by fans differs, both acts start from the common ground of the past – the 1980s.

From the point of view of the author, working with the past implicitly recognises it as a source of inspiration (though not necessarily framed as positive), with the present seen as alienating, and the future as uncertain or negative. There is nothing unusual or specific to Russia in this. Each generation of creators, most likely everywhere in the world, constructs novelty by going back to the supermarket of bygone eras. What is culturally specific, however, is the historical moment that this past evokes. The 1980s in the USSR were not the same as in the West; stagnation, perestroika and disintegration were not the same as neoliberalism. What are the values that Russian musicians and transnational audiences attribute to these eras, and how are these contrasted with the present? Out of this temporal bridging, what are the messages that emerge? And is it really nostalgia what we see?

Of course, there is no single way in which contemporary Russophone musicians approach and deal with the task: studies of popular culture and beyond have identified contemporary uses of the past with various strategies and affective responses,

240   *Independent Music in Russia*

particularly nostalgia (longing for the past),[30] retrotopia (the past as the future),[31] retromania (the obsession with the past),[32] hauntology (the ghosts of lost futures in the past haunting the present),[33] recycling (Engström 2022, 2023), re-enactment (Agnew 2007) and so on. Among these, nostalgia is perhaps still the most popular frame of analysis, albeit perhaps no longer an adequate one in some cases.

It is indeed a widespread practice to inscribe music that deals with the past as nostalgic (Oushakine 2007; Platt 2013), but a closer look reveals that, at least in the recent period, something else may be at stake. As Svetlana Boym (2001) argued, the nostalgic condition is a "historical emotion", in which there is a *nostos* (a "returning home", a "homecoming") and an *algia* (a "longing", an "ache"). Nostalgia, particularly what she defines as "reflective nostalgia", is a strategy of survival to make sense of the impossibility of the *nostos*, the homecoming. No matter how imagined, imaginary or blurred this home is in the mind of the nostalgic, it is nonetheless a home. However, when we examine how Russophone post-punk looks back at the past, which periods in the past it engages in a conversation with and which values it assigns to these times, we begin to see that there is an *algia* with little *nostos*, a longing with no homecoming or home. In the case of 1980s revival, the ache concerns only style – the homecoming is strictly aesthetic. In an interview with the Russian media, for example, Belarusian post-punk trio Molchat doma was asked the question, "What else from the 1980s apart from music would you like to get back"? They replied, "Nothing really. We're ok with everything [*vsë ustraivaet*]" (*The Village* 2020).

Toska is exactly this: a longing without a definite object of longing, or, as Vladimir Nabokov (1990, 141) maintained, "a longing with nothing to long for". The subject desires something but does not know what and has no previous experience of it. *Toska* is not "wanting to return home and not being able to", but more "wanting something indefinite and not knowing what to do". It obviously does not mean that *toska* is a feeling unique to Russia (Salmon 2015, 18–22), or even at all untranslatable, like Nabokov (1990, 2012) argued, since near-synonyms are "yearning" (Fitzpatrick 2004), "melancholia", "spleen" and "angst" (Dickinson and Salmon 2015). But it is true that *toska*, as Dickinson (2015, 1) explains, is the feeling of the margin, what derives from meditation on one's own marginal condition. It stems from a reflection on the immutability of such a condition too, on the fact that past, present and future were, are and will be lived in liminality. *Toska* thus tends to be serious and pervaded by a sense of tragedy, and as such it is not the same as post-irony on "pain" and the metamodern treatment of the "Russian condition" discussed in Chapter 3.

When *toska* meets the re-enactment or recycling of the 1980s, we have post-Soviet post-punk. The ideas of recycling and re-enactment suggest an attempt at active creation and renovation, which counterbalances the contemplative element of *toska* and puts its restlessness into focus. In the case of the Soviet 1980s, the recycling concerns, again, only the genre; straight bass lines, dark atmospheres, drum machines and deep baritones are borrowed and repurposed with one eye on sound and one on commerce. Yet, recycling always involves a degree of re-enacting. In turn, re-enacting always involves fantasy, imagination, distortion: as Agnew (2007, 299)

From the Margins and Back? 241

writes, re-enactments are historical representations "characterized by conjectural interpretations of the past, the collapsing of temporalities and an emphasis on affect [...] rather than historical events, structures and processes". Recycling also involves transnational and multiple borrowings. Motorama, in fact, shared many features with 1980s British and Soviet post-punk, such as sonic underpinnings and a do-it-yourself approach to the production and distribution of music. Exclusively from their Soviet predecessors, they inherited a similar sociopolitical zeitgeist (e.g. the return of censorship, the authoritarian state, East–West divisions). All of these elements contributed to establish an overt emotional and cultural connection between the post-Soviet 2010s/2020s and the Soviet 1980s.

One of the most important features of post-Soviet post-punk's revivalism is the negative take it offers on the present and the future. This is a difference from British post-punk, which, as Reynolds (2005) argues, was busy putting together the fragments left by the failed revolution of punk in order to create a new space of possibilities that concerned not only aesthetics, but also politics and ethics (for instance, the possibility to circumvent the conventions of the capitalist system and create equitable market relationships and equal access to music production). Post-Soviet post-punk, on the contrary, seems to engage especially with the preservation of these glued-together fragments in a museum, in which we find exhibits that certify the absence of a positive future, then and now. Let us consider, for instance, Motorama's song "Heavy Wave" (2015), and particularly its video.[34]

The song opens with an ambivalent statement about a past that has been left behind for a future that is, nonetheless, uncertain and perhaps unpleasant. The hero waves goodbye to the past and welcomes a future that is, however, vague and sour. This future is also immediately undermined by references to some form of holistic defeat in the chorus. The second verse adds to this semantic reversal: the hero waves goodbye to the future and chooses to remain in their own recollections. The feeling of *toska* is enhanced and repeated obsessively at the end through a declaration of immutable solitude. Overall, "Heavy Wave" does not seem to offer any specific object of loss or longing, save the future and the past.

"Heavy Wave" connects to the late-Soviet era not only in terms of sound, but also because its video is a tribute to Vladimir Kobrin's short film *Present Continuous*, released in 1989. Kobrin (1942–1999) was an experimental and imaginative filmmaker, who was particularly attracted to philosophical questions: *Present Continuous*, for example, deals with the concept of time. The film displays a post-apocalyptic scenario, in which humans are nowhere to be seen and statues act as their stand-ins. The only entities that keep living are the objects humans created, which inhabit eerie places, and often consist of threatening assemblages. There is an idea of continuity between the pre-apocalyptic and the post-apocalyptic, which is reinforced not only in the title of the film itself, but also in the inscriptions that often feature in the film. For instance, when it is announced that all languages have disappeared, this is done through the use of language. The narrator of the film, Adam (as the first man), also makes clear that "there is no Time". Indeed, what we are left with is a present continuous, which is tellingly shown in its negative form in one of the opening scenes ("I'm not writing / You're not writing", etc.) (see Figure 5.9).

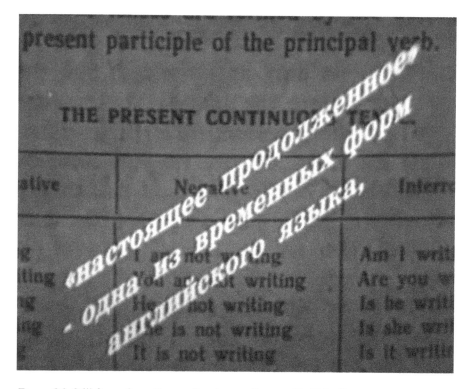

Figure 5.9 Still frame from *Present Continuous*. Source: YouTube.[35]

The connection between Motorama's song and Kobrin's film not only involves cultural recycling and trans-mediality, it also constitutes a social commentary, in line with Motorama's declared ethos to use the past to paint a vision of the present (Curtis-Horsfall 2021). *Present Continuous*, as a past cultural artefact itself dealing with the past, gives the band an enhanced opportunity to do so. And it is this negative present continuous which Motorama are returning to in order to comment on their own present. The past is a space of enquiry before a layer of losses, whatever these may be: the viewer is left wondering as to the nature and time of these losses across a blurred chronological continuum.

Ultimately, "Heavy Wave" does not articulate a form of nostalgia, as there is no *nostos*, no "homecoming" to long for. However, there is a parallel to be drawn: the impending collapse of the Soviet Union, the vanishing of a system and, together with it, of an ideology that was based on the idea of future, both featuring in Kobrin's film, serve to convey a sense of present desolation. The past Motorama are returning to had already been lost (and had already lost): bridging it with the present constructs a continuity of hopelessness and *toska*, a grand narrative of powerlessness and marginality (see Figure 5.10).

A different discussion concerns the international reception of Russophone post-punk. As the production of post-Soviet post-punk could be framed as an

Figure 5.10 Still frame from Motorama's video for "Heavy Wave" (2015). Source: YouTube.[36]

articulation of *toska*, its international reception and fandom have more to do with hauntology. This term, a portmanteau of the words "haunting" and "ontology", was originally coined by Derrida (1994) to encapsulate the timeless capacity of Marxism to haunt the West's current state of affairs, even after what Fukuyama (1992) had termed "the end of history" – that is, the end of ideological struggle between Soviet and Western blocs and the triumph of the capitalist system. As Jameson (2003, 76) famously argued, after the "end of history" it was easier to imagine the end of the world than the end of capitalism.

The concern that a "real alternative" to the system could not be imagined made utopias of the past infiltrate the present as ghosts. This temporal, historical and ontological disjunction regularly came back to trouble the present in regard to the present's lost futures, as an entity simultaneously not completely alive but not completely dead. Adapting the concept to culture, Fisher (2009, 2012) wrote that hauntology explains the stagnation of contemporary artistic production, stifled by capitalist appropriation, incapacitated to develop new ideas and caught up in endless loops of pastiches and revivalisms. These are products of the failure of different futures that became trapped in the past after the victory of neoliberalism and express an anxiety that no longer resembles a nostalgia for the past, but rather an agony about "what could have been" but never was. Applying the term to sound, Reynolds (2011, 355–61) argued that hauntological music contains an "ache of

244   *Independent Music in Russia*

longing for history itself" that has forced musicians to look backwards while attempting to go forwards, in a "precarious and paradoxical strategy". Confronted with "digital cul-de-sacs" (Fisher 2012, 16), Western musicians and audiences have attempted to revive past music mythologies, with particular focus on the 1980s. Thus, resurrecting the 1980s offers the possibility of remembrance of an alternative.

Hauntology informs the omnipresence of memes, tweets, posts and pictures about the 1980s on social media platforms. Let us quote one of them, published in 2019: "2000 was 20 years ago which is really weird because 1980 was also 20 years ago".[37] Moreover, in light of the global crises (climate, pandemics, wars), this distortion of time has gone even further: visualising in 2020 that the year 1980 was equidistant in time to 2060 was not so much frightening as it was questionable. Retreating into the last available pre-digital and pre-end-of-history era – the 1980s – becomes a declaration of non-involvement with the present and an evasion from thinking about a future which one feels no ownership of.

Recovering the past has been one of the primary aims of the Western music industry since 2000, and not only of niche genres such as vaporwave (Reynolds 2011); the list of pop and rock artists that have performed this strategy is endless, from The Strokes to Dua Lipa, from Arctic Monkeys to the Weeknd. This has paired with a huge upsurge in the production of content enabled by music digitalisation. If approximately 300,000 recordings were released in the year 2000, in the year 2020 the number of the tracks uploaded to streaming platforms reached approximately 21.9 million (Osborne 2021). This acceleration of cultural (re)production, however, does not seem to have led to an emergence of collectively recognised musics capable of exploring what Noys (2015) calls the possibilities of "friction" and tensions between past and future. Rather, this congestion of cultural artefacts appears to reflect the conflation of time, eventually spiralling back in the categorical refusal of the future. As Fisher (2014, 26–27) has it:

> Imagine any record released in the past couple of years being beamed back in time to, say, 1995 and played on the radio. It's hard to think that it will produce any jolt in the listeners. On the contrary, what would be likely to shock our 1995 audience would be the very recognisability of the sounds: would music really have changed so little in the next 17 years? Contrast this with the rapid turnover of styles between the 1960s and the 90s: play a jungle record from 1993 to someone in 1989 and it would have sounded like something so new that it would have challenged them to rethink what music was, or could be. While 20th-century experimental culture was seized by a recombinatorial delirium, which made it feel as if newness was infinitely available, the 21st century is oppressed by a crushing sense of finitude and exhaustion. It doesn't feel like the future. Or, alternatively, it doesn't feel as if the 21st century has started yet. We remain trapped in the 20th century.
>
> (Fisher 2014, 26–27)

International audiences seem to place post-Soviet post-punk before finitude and exhaustion. For them, these bands are able to convincingly re-enact an old world

From the Margins and Back? 245

afresh through the prism of an unkept promise for a better future that collapses onto history. This promise, as well as this history, are seen as worldly but also acutely belonging to the post-Soviet space. For audiences, this two-fold characteristic seems to have enhanced the significance of Russophone post-punk music on a global scale. The two "post" prefixes indicate two ghosts. The first – post-punk – refers to punk as a revolutionary space that became commodified; the second, post-Soviet, refers to the socialist bloc as an alternative to the capitalist West that also vanished. Indeed, for Russian (and Belarusian) performers, the fall of the Soviet Union has corresponded not only to the global triumph of neoliberalism and the "end of history", but also to the inability of Yeltsin to implement democracy, the emergence of an ideological vacuum and, above all, the rise to power of the autocrats Putin and Lukashenko, who have continued pre-empting the possibility of a different future.[38]

Therefore, the evocation of "mangled memories and distorted ideas about the eighties" (Reynolds 2011, 361) is facilitated by what audiences see as authentically belonging and culturally specific to the post-Soviet space. Post-Soviet post-punk is thus romanticised as the sonic embodiment of such hauntological authenticity, regardless of what the authors may have intended for it. As a result, independent post-punk turned into the flagship of Russia's sonic capital between the late 2010s and early 2020s.

Transnational listeners of the genre have not only elevated post-Soviet post-punk as the soundtrack of their perceived loss of future, but they have also played a crucial role in shaping global fan networks. These communities have appropriated, repurposed, and reinterpreted Russophone post-punk to generate new cultural texts—such as memes—and to foster shared experiences and social connections. This has been particularly evident on YouTube, where, at the end of 2021, I surveyed 40 compilations of "Russian Doomer Music" and "Russian post-punk" across ten channels dedicated to the genre. The most followed-channel was JustMyFavStrangeMusic (hereafter: JMFSM), which seems to have been also the first to rebrand the genre of post-Soviet post-punk as "Russian Doomer" and "memefied" it (turned it into a meme) among internet audiences. The "doomer" figure first appeared on 4chan in 2018,[39] as a variation on the "Wojack", another character that originated on 4chan in 2010.[40] The doomer is white, male, pale and in his early twenties. In his common representations, the doomer is portrayed with a black beanie, smoking and with an afflicted look on his face (Figure 5.11). He epitomises the youth's loss of faith in the future, emotional displacement, depression and loneliness. His outlook on life is bleak and hopeless, in contrast with the 'boomer',[41] the embodiment of the post-war generation animated by a blissful carelessness of world problems and a faith in progress. By feeling 'too acutely', the doomer is squashed by worries and eventually seeks shelter in contemplation and solitude.

The nihilism of the doomer has found a homey environment in post-Soviet post-punk YouTube playlists. Nearly all curators have placed the doomer meme as the opening image of their videos, while JMFSM has used it on each of their 48 "Russian Doomer" compilations (see Figure 5.12). The music, with its gloomy

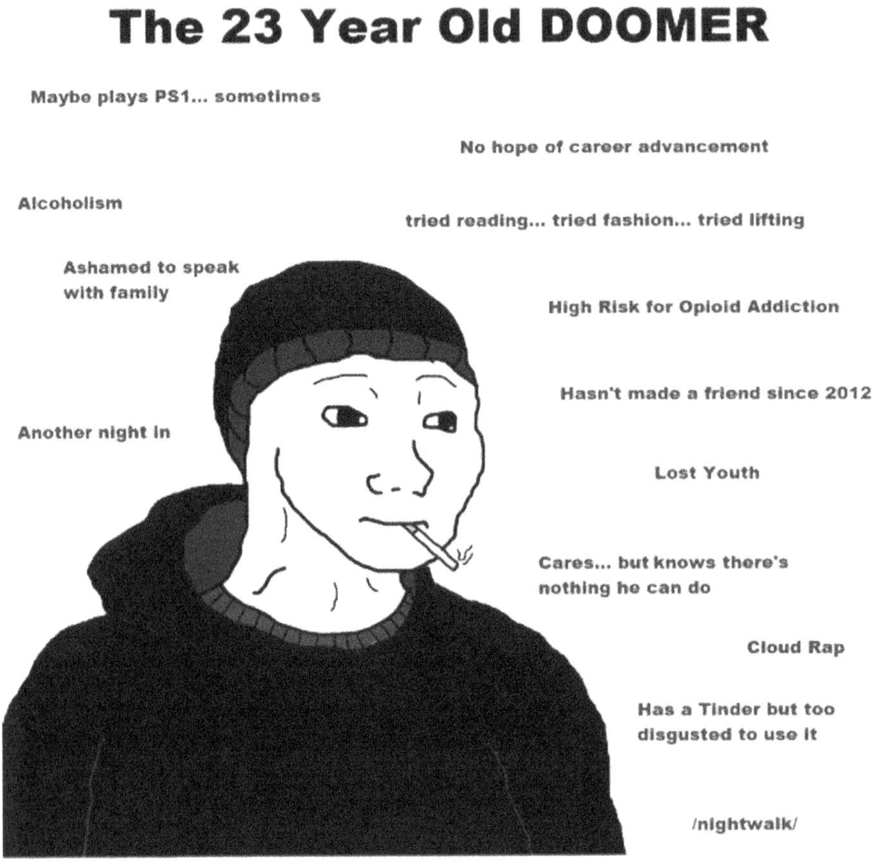

The 23 Year Old DOOMER

Maybe plays PS1... sometimes

No hope of career advancement

Alcoholism

tried reading... tried fashion... tried lifting

Ashamed to speak
with family

High Risk for Opioid Addiction

Hasn't made a friend since 2012

Another night in

Lost Youth

Cares... but knows there's
nothing he can do

Cloud Rap

Has a Tinder but too
disgusted to use it

/nightwalk/

Figure 5.11 A "doomer" meme. Source: *Know Your Meme.*[42]

atmospheres, icy soundscapes and low-reverbed vocals, provided a perfect match for this meme. As a rule, the doomer is framed against the background of Soviet *khrushchëvki*, concrete tall buildings and panelhouses, usually at night and in the winter to heighten the effect of introspection and sorrow.[43]

The doomer figure provided the point of departure for further memeification of post-Soviet post-punk. This mostly revolved around the emotion of sadness, and how this sad music may be interpreted differently in relation to different cultures (see Figure 5.13). Below are some memes found in the comment sections of JMFSM's compilations on YouTube.

Memes, as Shifman (2014, 3) argues, are bottom-up examples of intertextuality, as they are made in reference to each other. In the case of "Russian Doomer" music, this is joined with intermediality and interculturality too: here the primary text (the music) connects with long-standing imaginaries and constructs (upheld by both non-Russian readers and Russian cultural producers) of Russia as a land of

From the Margins and Back? 247

Figure 5.12 Screenshot from one of JMFSM's playlists. Source: YouTube.[44]

suffering, and gives birth to new texts that simultaneously reference the previous ones and add ironic intent.

Importantly, however, memes about Russian doomer music, together with the music they memeified, contributed to shape transnational (mostly male) communities in which people talked about experiences of pain and suggested ways

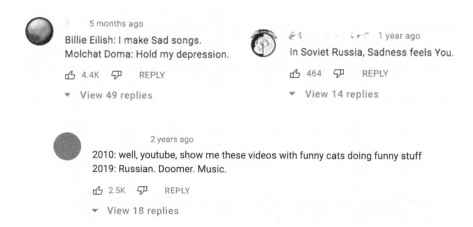

Figure 5.13 Comments on "Russian Doomer" compilations on YouTube. Source: YouTube.

248 *Independent Music in Russia*

to overcome or manage it. The practice starts with the fan's identification as a "doomer". Below are just some among the 32,000 comments from the "Russian Doomer Music vol.3 (Superior)" YouTube compilation [sic]:

> "with all due respect, may I join as a Serb doomer"; "As a hungarian doomer, I salute you, brother!"; "German Doomer in solidarity"; "Hey Eastern friends, French doomer here"; "Croatian doomer here"; "An Iraqi doomer wants to join in lads"; "Hello to everyone from an American doomer"; "Chinese doomer here"; "I'm a Bangladeshi doomer, [...] I understand shit, but I feel like it was written for me"; "Italian doomer i am."; "Brazilian doomer here"; "can i, as an indian doomer, join in?"; "doomer from algeria. life is overrated"; "Can i join as an icelandic doomer"; "I'm a mexican doomer and I feel the same".

Through the sharing of personal aches and low feelings, including when done in an ironic way, "Russian Doomer" fans constructed a sense of relief from the troubles of everyday life. Unlike many other cases across social media platforms, in which flaming and endless polemics are part and parcel of users' interactions, comments on "Russian Doomer" videos were surprisingly devoid of contentious attitudes and verbal skirmishes (not to take away from the moderator's abilities, of course). As one user remarked, "I've never seen friendlier people than on post-punk playlists' commentaries. Good on you".[45] Interactions seemed to often involve compassion and empathy, with many users finding the playlists' discussions cathartic and helpful for their mental health. As one user said in the comments of "Russian Doomer music playlist vol.1": "Finally, I found content that I like and people who are understanding. I never thought that this would happen thanks to memes".[46] On JMFSM's playlists, countless fans share stories about their difficulties in life and – surprisingly in the context of social media – find understanding and comfort. One user on "Russian Doomer vol. 4a", for instance, communicated: "Update: things are better, even between me and my parents things improved a bit. I appreciate everyone who commented, I'll still try to keep answering you guys because your stories and words helped me when I was feeling down and hopeless". Another user confessed: "Reading these comments whilst listening to this music makes me feel so happy. On the brink of crying, as, I know that I am not alone. I love you all, you're not alone. Love from Australia". Or, for example, another user admitted: "Guys, how emotional it is here, so much shit has poured out in 23 years that words cannot describe... The only place where it's nice to read comments and realise that I'm not alone". Below are some more examples from "Russian Doomer vol. 9 (new superior?)" (I have picked the shorter ones for brevity, but there are much longer comments and replies to comments). Among 7,800 comments, fans wrote [sic]:

> "Honestly all of these playlists have been getting me through these lonely nights. I can't thank you enough"; "Тепла вам, братья и сёстры. [Warmth to you, brothers and sisters (translation)]"; "My doomer friend- you're not alone. Love from Poland"; "Guys, everything will be fine, you will be happy,

From the Margins and Back? 249

you just need to be patient for a while. I love you, don't be sad"; "música doomer dá Rússia me faz sentir que nós brasileiros temos algo em comum com os russos. [Russian doomer music makes me feel that we Brazilians have something in common with Russians (translation from Portuguese)]"; "Люди в комментариях - самые добрые и сильные люди. Если у Вас случилось что-то страшное, прошу не опускайте руки. Вы справитесь, Вы сильные. Удачи [The people in the comments are the kindest and strongest people. If something terrible has happened to you, please do not give up. You can handle it, you're strong. Good luck (translation)]"; "Stay alive Kings. Lets be here for each other"; "This is the kind of experience that brings us all together and makes you remember we're just all the same everywhere. Cheers from Brazil"; "I keep returning to this specific volume over and over again. And the comments here are truly heartwarming. Greetings from Latvia, my doomer brothers"; "To all my doomer friends: you are not alone"; "hello friend, difficult day isn't it? sit back and enjoy these beautiful songs is not yet the end, the sun will still shine for us".

By establishing a dialogue based on similar experiences of life, fans enacted a transnational and public therapeutic session. Post-Soviet post-punk YouTube playlists provided them with a platform to express their hauntological condition, that is, to nurse their sense of displacement, voice their concerns about the world and share their thoughts about the broken promise of a better future that never materialised (see Figure 5.14).

Thus, whether as a soundtrack of depression, idealisation of Eastern Europe or romanticisation of the 1980s, Russophone post-punk enabled an important

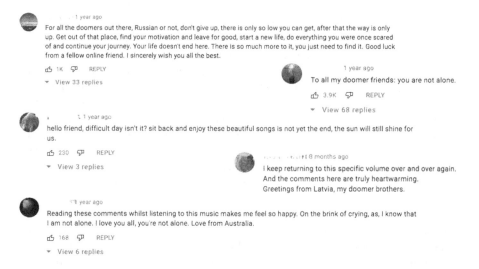

Figure 5.14 Comments on "Russian Doomer" compilations on YouTube. Source: YouTube.

250 *Independent Music in Russia*

cathartic escapism for fan communities worldwide. The reassuring retreat in the past contained in the music intersected with digital memes to create hauntological safe spaces. These provided fans with relief from the affliction of everyday life: taking into account the current global state of affairs, and the relevance of conversations around mental health, this practice was (and is) of high social value.

Conclusions

Towards the beginning of this chapter, I presented Interviewee 3's judgment on the shortcomings of the Russian music export sector in 2016. In the same interview, however, its potential was also highlighted:

> Sooner or later, the situation in my country will change, and people who are responsible for the cultural field will be interested not only in balalaikas and academic music – they will find the place and time for modern avant-garde, electronica, rock, and underground music. Because it is where all the juice, all the individuality, all our authenticity is located. Then they will begin to invest their attention and resources, and it will be so powerful that it will culturally blow up the whole world. I am absolutely convinced of this. It will happen in the next ten years. A hundred per cent.

Interviewee 3 believed that, by arriving "late" on the international music stage, *nezavisimaia muzyka* could renew it radically (in a similar way as nineteenth-century Russian writers advanced the genre of the novel). Russia, as a young country, could journey from the periphery to the centre of the global scene.

Three years later, in February 2019, I was sitting in The Temple, a trendy and loud Manchester bar that once was a public restroom. Next to me was an English young man in a sweater with the Cyrillic inscription "Gosha Rubchinskii" (one of today's most famous Russian fashion designers). I asked him if he knew what was written on his clothing item. "No, but I know it's Russian", he replied. "Why are you wearing it"? I said. "Well, it's cool" he responded. Previously, when conducting my research in Russia, I had numerous similar conversations on reversed terms: asking attendees at Anglophone bands' concerts whether they knew what the bands were singing about, I usually received a negative answer, counterpointed by appreciation of the music's energy. Now, Russian pop culture had become "cool" to the point that a Cyrillic inscription alone, no matter its meaning, was cherished. Such a form of interest in the "Imaginary East" was implausible ten years before, in late-2000s Britain. Maybe, positive perceptions between Russian and British cultures were transforming, along the lines of more balanced two-way flows.

The fascination Russia exerted on the imaginary of audiences abroad provided the basis for the appreciation of panelhouses, Soviet architecture, depictions of Russian thugs and other epitomes of "the new aesthetics of the second-world" (Laruelle and Engström 2018, 10–12). As Bartlett (2016, 284) notes, "the Soviet ugly is a new Western beautiful" (in post-Crimea *nezavisimaia muzyka*, the "Soviet ugly" became the new *Russian* beautiful). This international glamourisation of

From the Margins and Back? 251

Russia started to relate to its popular music too. Expressing Russianness in music was a tricky task: the Western foundations of Russian popular music challenged local musicians to find, often in extra-sonic domains, markers that could ground their music in a perceived national tradition. This was the reason why bands often resorted to "the visual" and the extra-musical in order to construct Russianness – interviews, clothing and videos, for example. However, the same extra-musical quest, albeit in the opposite direction, animated those musicians who adopted a strategy of appropriation of, and self-identification with, the Other's image. In these projections, Russian markers were concealed and the belonging to a transnational, Anglophone, cosmopolitan and somehow naively horizontal "imagined community" was promoted.

Not all musicians succeeded in sustaining a career abroad for long (Pompeya) or at all (Coockoo). Those who did, though, were stylistically diverse, employed various tactics and occupied different niches. Little Big's case showed that stereotypes about Russia were still topical and mutually upheld between Russia and the rest of the world. Importantly, Little Big's grassroots use of *stëb* as an international marketing tool was hijacked by the state, which sought to promote its own marginality as soft power against the media ecology dominated by the liberal Western world. "State *stëb*" shows how *stëb*'s constitutive open-endedness lends it to further inscriptions, that the joke goes both ways – not only from the bottom up, but also from the top down. This frames independent and state actors as caught up in struggles but also in synergies, each trying to inscribe their own narrative to cultural objects and global projections (Hutchings 2022). In this case, marginality was a coveted distinctive trait, both for internal nation-building and for external nation-branding.

Motorama's case, instead, showed that Russian post-punk could become an ambassador of the past, inspire a post-Soviet-based genre and generate a substantial transnational community of fans. As Isabelle Marc (2015) showed, when songs travel across space they often acquire different meanings among the receiving audiences. In the case in question, transnational fans actively translated post-Soviet post-punk into memes, injected hauntology into it and used it to build a collectively valuable space of conversation and relief. From the margins inhabited by *toska*, from an ache that cannot find a home to return to (because that home has never existed), Russophone post-punk travelled to the margins of hauntology, that is, to a liminal space where people constructed the loss of future as social bond.

When COVID hit, it remained to be seen how much the progress of *nezavisimaia muzyka* and Russian popular music into the transnational markets reflected an exotic, momentary fad or a durable cultural interest. A number of questions remained to be answered, about the possible changes in international barriers, Anglo-American biases, grassroots Russia-West cultural diplomacy, sonic capitals, centres-peripheries dynamics and whether or not Russia's musical subflows would turn into flows with consistency.

However, first COVID, but above all the full-scale war in Ukraine, have significantly downscaled the scope of Russian popular music export and complicated the activities of Russian independent musicians immensely. Receiving visas has

252   *Independent Music in Russia*

become more difficult. Interviewee 77, who relocated to Belgrade, had to cancel their band's international tour and renounced around £20,000 in honorary fees. Another migrant musician, Interviewee 75, who went to Belgium to play at a festival, was held in a prison cell in the local airport instead and eventually flown back with their visa annulled. Even Little Big, who relocated to Los Angeles in 2022 with the help of their major label, had to cancel their 2023 UK tour because their visas were not issued in time. Several bands are now scattered across the world: Interviewee 80, member of an alternative rock group, is now in Belgrade; another member lives in Tbilisi; a third is in Berlin; the fourth in New York.

For those independent musicians who did not leave Russia, touring in Central and Western Europe has almost ceased. On top of the exacerbation of bureaucratic indeterminacy, European booking agencies have not wanted to risk their reputation and money booking Russia-based artists: on the one hand, most Western audiences would not go to see a Russia-based artist who did not speak against the war; on the other, the Russia-based artist cannot speak against the war without incurring in likely draconian punishments for denouncing the regime's military actions.

Both migrant and non-migrant musicians have turned their gaze to Armenia, Georgia, Serbia and other territories with high concentration of Russian émigrés (e.g. the Central Asian states), due to favourable migration and travel policies towards Russians. This has no precedent in history (previous waves of Russian migration tended to be aimed at Western or Central Europe, or the United States, or China). Interviewees 64, 65 and 66, three local representatives of the Yerevan music scene, concurred that before 2022 Armenia was not even on the map of a Russian touring artist; now, a plethora of Russian musicians are coming, and their concerts at times even overlap. In Tbilisi, Yerevan and Belgrade, the three migratory hubs for Russians that I surveyed in summer 2023, the average was a mid-sized gig every two days, excluding the significant numbers of jam sessions and other informal live music gatherings happening on the side. This intense activity has of course changed the soundscape of the cities, considering also that other Russian émigrés, in the capacity of music managers, concert promoters and venue owners, started to open their own clubs and organise gigs for other Russian and international acts (also an unprecedented occurrence). All of this, on the one hand, has given a boost to the local scenes, especially in the Caucasian republics; on the other, it may have overloaded and destabilised them (not to mention the rise in house renting costs among the local population).

Paradoxically, it may well be that Russian independent music has now become truly transnational, with many of its key representatives living and working abroad in a self-imposed exile. This relocation, however, is mostly within Europe 2 and, as observed by several émigrés I interviewed in summer 2023, it has perpetuated, if not exacerbated, perceptions of liminality. Moreover, from what emerged during my participant observation, processes of integration between migrant and local music worlds had yet to decisively start, and the Russian independent music communities were, to a significant degree, still talking to themselves. Russian practitioners would often strive to get local musicians involved in their activities, but successful implementation was minimal, besides the punk context. This was due to

From the Margins and Back? 253

differences in language, financial resources and the locals' suspicion that a different kind of colonisation was afoot, particularly in Georgia, where Russian troops occupy 20 per cent of the territory. Only time will tell how long or effective these processes of integration, exchange and hybridisation will be.

Notes

1 The song "Despacito", occupying the second position in the 2017 singles chart, was bilingual.
2 Anuel AA (Puerto Rico), Neha Kakkar (India), Kumar Sanu (India), Alka Yagnik (India).
3 The expression "sonic capital" seems to have been introduced by Bürkner and Lange in 2017, in the article "Sonic capital and independent urban music production: Analysing value creation and 'trial and error' in the digital age". However, these scholars used the concept of sonic capital in a different way: for them, sonic capital is the skills that music professionals acquire in order to keep up with the evolution of the music market. For me, it is the power that the country's musical tradition owns in the international arena.
4 As of January 2022. As further proof of this fanbase "disbalance", the VK page of the band, which was likely to be visited by Russian or Russophone fans, had only 4,300 subscribers, almost 18 times fewer than the Facebook one, which was visited by a more global audience.
5 500 rubles and 400 rubles (£4.5 and £5.5) at 16 Tons in 2016 and Powerhouse in 2017, respectively, and 600 pesos (£25) at their gig at Indierocks Forum in Mexico City.
6 See, for example, a video of their gig in Chile: https://www.facebook.com/1816497732/videos/7237316319673254/. After Molchat doma, the Russian post-punk band Ploho (Bad) was also scheduled for a 2022 tour of Latin America, which was cancelled following the start of the war in Ukraine.
7 When, in 2018, I attended Motorama's gig at The Lexington in London, the UK-based promoters told me they were not sure Motorama would make it until show day, when they arrived on British soil. Their drummer was denied entry and remained in Calais, and Motorama had to perform as a duo with sampled drums. If they had been sure about visa policy, the organisers told me, they would have promoted the gig more widely and booked a larger venue, as they believed that Motorama would have filled it.
8 The politicised EU vaccination policy following the COVID-19 pandemic made matters worse for Russian musicians, as the EU did not recognise Sputnik, the vaccine developed and rolled out in Russia. Even for doubly vaccinated musicians, travelling was more difficult than ever.
9 Lucidvox are an all-female psychedelic post-punk band, formed in Moscow in 2013.
10 Kate NV is the solo project of Katia Shilonosova, vocalist of Glintshake. Her debut album came out in 2016. Her 2020 album *Room for the Moon* received international critical acclaim and was included in *Pitchfork*'s top 50 albums of the year (*Pitchfork* 2020).
11 Anton Maskeliade, stage name of Anton Sergeev, is an electronic music artist, active in Moscow since the early 2010s. Maskeliade also directs a popular school of music composition.
12 Kazuskoma are a stoner rock trio, active in Moscow since 2014.
13 Spasibo are a rock band and one of the primary representatives of the NRW, founded in Moscow in 2013.
14 Elektroforez are a synth-pop duo, established in St. Petersburg in 2012.
15 Aigel are an electronic-pop duo, established in 2016.
16 Veronika Belousova, speech at MMW, September 2019. Denis Boiarinov, personal interview, Moscow, November 2018.
17 Anton Repka, speech at MMW, September 2019

254 *Independent Music in Russia*

18 Veronika Belousova, speech at MMW conference, September 2019.

19 It is important to note, though, that Russian in the case of Shortparis is a verbal language as it is part of a broader body language. As Doran (2018) writes, the band's concerts are more performance art than music gigs. A similar point of view is held by music journalist Oleg Sobolev (2019), who identifies the stage presence of the band as fundamental in delivering their message. As Kazakov (2019, 101) reports, during the Sochi Olympics ceremony Diaghilev's Russian Ballet was described in similar terms, as "Russian language that is understood by the entire world". By subjecting to the theatrical dimension of the performance, Russian becomes a sound devoid of verbal meaning, an additional melodic instrument.

20 After the start of the full-scale war, Little Big moved to Los Angeles. The Russian Ministry of Justice added the band's frontman, Ilia Prusikin, to the list of foreign agents in January 2023.

21 As of January 2022.

22 https://www.youtube.com/watch?v=QrU1hZxSEXQ.

23 The video was removed in 2022 from the band's YouTube channel.

24 https://www.youtube.com/watch?v=-RGKoKWXQ9c.

25 https://www.youtube.com/watch?v=vzpXnLtf3GU&t=114s.

26 https://www.youtube.com/watch?v=3G23XDG3oJU.

27 *Saviour* was due to be followed by *Perfect Dependence*, a full-length 11-track album (the band recorded all the songs but eventually split up before releasing the record, which saw the light only in 2016).

28 In this regard, it is interesting to compare Coockoo's case with the Russian music export during perestroika, in particular with Boris Grebenshchikov, who, straight after the flop in the West of his Anglophone album *Radio Silence* in 1989, recorded *Russkii al'bom* (The Russian Album) in 1992, a Russophone record heavily influenced by traditional folk music. Both transnational adventures led to similar unsuccessful results and generated similar consequences, even if they started from different premises. While Grebenshchikov was heavily funded by his US major label and confident that his distinctly Russian poetics would represent innovation for the American public, Coockoo, as members of the Anglophone Wave and independent musicians were adamant that the (perceived) gap between Anglo-American and Russian music scenes had been filled and bands could now be judged on the basis of the quality of sounds and ideas. Both assumptions were disproven by the more complex reality of unequal sonic capitals.

29 For example, Ploho (Bad), Gde fantom? (Where Is the Phantom?), Chernikovskaya Hata (Chernihiv Hut), ssshhhiiittt.

30 See Boym (2001).

31 See Bauman (2017).

32 See Reynolds (2011).

33 See Fisher (2009; 2012).

34 https://www.youtube.com/watch?v=07FdNR6ikHI.

35 https://www.youtube.com/watch?v=FRqJqVnfJyI&t=620s.

36 https://www.youtube.com/watch?v=07FdNR6ikHI.

37 https://twitter.com/Quackity/status/1202688433619161097.

38 Even the challenge to the unipolar world which Putin set out as an objective of his rule did not correspond to a challenge to the neoliberal system (Strukov 2021).

39 https://knowyourmeme.com/memes/doomer.

40 https://knowyourmeme.com/memes/wojak.

41 https://knowyourmeme.com/memes/30-year-old-boomer.

42 https://knowyourmeme.com/memes/doomer/photos.

43 Notably, Russian Doomer compilations tend to host musicians from across the post-Soviet space, though they unite them under the "Russian" category (judging from the description of JMFSM's own account on Vkontakte, the user seemed to be based in Russia), thus problematically conflating all the post-Soviet space into Russia.

44 https://www.youtube.com/watch?v=wcaZcbain2s&t=24s.
45 https://www.youtube.com/watch?v=lgjguiFxtps&t=1851s.
46 https://www.youtube.com/watch?v=2WPIPlG_CvM&t=3s.

References

Agnew, V. 2007. 'History's Affective Turn: Historical Reenactment and Its Work in the Present'. *Rethinking History*, 11, 3, pp. 299–312.

Appiah, K.A. 2006. *Cosmopolitanism: Ethics in a World of Strangers*. London: Penguin.

Bartlett, D. 2016. 'The Socialist Sartorial Utopia: Then and Now'. *Brown Journal of World Affairs*, 23, 2, pp. 269–85.

Bauman, Z. 2017. *Retrotopia*. Cambridge: Polity.

Beaumont-Thomas, B. 2021. 'Elton John: Brexit Negotiators 'Screwed Up' Deal for British Musicians'. *The Guardian*, 7 February. URL: https://www.theguardian.com/music/2021/feb/07/elton-john-brexit-negotiators-screwed-up-deal-for-british-musicians (accessed 28 October 2021).

Bennett, K.T. 2015. 'Moscow's Pompeya Get Sax-y on New Tune 'Liar''. *Noisey* (*Vice*), 18 February. URL: https://noisey.vice.com/en_us/article/65zp4b/pompeya-liar-premiere (accessed 7 May 2020).

Berlin Beat. 2012. 'Interview: Human Tetris'. 4 February. URL: https://berlinbeat.org/2012/02/04/interview-human-tetris/ (accessed 7 May 2020).

Biasioli, M. 2011. *La musica a Mosca: suoni, voci, prospettive*. Masters Thesis (unpublished), La Sapienza University of Rome.

Biasioli, M. 2022. 'Between the Global and the Intimate: Language Choice in Russian Popular Music'. *Modern Language Review*, 117, 2, pp. 364–90.

Biasioli, M. 2023. 'Songwashing: Russian Popular Music, Distraction, and Putin's Fourth Term'. *The Russian Review*, 82, 4, pp. 682–704.

Biasioli, M. 2024. 'It Wasn't Our Song anymore': Molchat Doma, the Death of the Reader and the Birth of the TikToker'. *IASPM Journal*, 14, 1, pp. 151–71.

Bourdieu, P. 1984. *Distinction. A Social Critique of the Judgement of Taste*. London: Routledge.

Bourdieu, P. 1991. *Language and Symbolic Power*. Cambridge: Polity Press.

Boym, S. 2001. *The Future of Nostalgia*. New York: Basic Books.

Cassiday, J. 2014. 'Post-Soviet Pop Goes Gay: Russia's Trajectory to Eurovision Victory'. *Russian Review*, 73, 2, pp. 1–23.

Castells, M. 2000. *The Rise of the Network Society* (2nd ed.). Oxford: Blackwell Publishers.

Cerqueira, M. 2018. 'The Soft Power of the Music Industry—Where Does It Start and Where Does It End? Insights from the United States and Japan'. In Saxena Arora, A., Bacouel-Jentjens, S., Edmonds, J.J. (eds.) *Building Innovation Capabilities for Business Strategies*. Cham: Palgrave (e-book), pp. 87–100.

Connell, J., Gibson, C. 2003. *Sound Tracks: Popular Music, Identity and Place*. London: Routledge.

Contreras, P. 2017. 'Crónica: Human Tetris y The Kvb en Lima 2017'. *Conciertos Peru*. URL: http://conciertosperu.com.pe/coberturas/cronica-human-tetris-y-the-kvb-en-lima-2017/ (accessed 7 May 2020).

Crack. 2014. 'Exclusive: February –Saviour D/R/U/G/S Remix'. 29 September. URL: https://crackmagazine.net/article/news/exclusive-february-saviour-drugs-remix/ (accessed 7 May 2020).

Curtis-Horsfall, T. 2021. 'Motorama: "We Are Tired of the Global Political Media"'. *Giglist*, 15 February. URL: https://giglist.com/buzz/article/motorama-we-are-tired-global-political-media (accessed 30 March 2023).

Demont-Heinrich, C. 2019. 'New Global Music Distribution System, Same Old Linguistic Hegemony? Analysing English on Spotify'. In Boyd-Barrett, O., Mirrlees, T. (eds.) *Media Imperialism: Continuity and Change*. Lanham, MD: Rowman & Littlefield, pp. 199–212.

256 *Independent Music in Russia*

Derrida, J. 1994. *Specters of Marx: The State of the Debt, the Work of Mourning and the New International*. London: Routledge.

Dickinson, S. 2015. 'Preface'. In Dickinson, S., Salmon, L. (eds.) *Melancholic Identities, Toska and Reflective Nostalgia Case Studies from Russian and Russian-Jewish Culture*. Florence: Firenze University Press, pp. 7–10.

Dickinson, S., Salmon, L. (eds.). 2015. *Melancholic Identities, Toska and Reflective Nostalgia Case Studies from Russian and Russian-Jewish Culture*. Florence: Firenze University Press.

Dimitriou, M. 2017. 'Human Tetris'. *Last Day Deaf*, 25 January. URL: http://lastdaydeaf.com/human-tetris/ (accessed 7 May 2020).

Doran, J. 2018. 'Shortparis: Paskha'. *The Quietus*, 26 March. URL: https://thequietus.com/articles/24274-shortparis-easter-album-review (accessed 7 May 2020).

Dummy. 2013. 'Premiere: Pompeya – Power'. 17 October. URL: https://www.dummymag.com/videos/pompeya-power (accessed 7 May 2020).

Engström, M. 2022. 'Russian metamodernism: the neo rave and cultural recycling of the 1990s'. *Riddle*, 12 August. URL: https://ridl.io/russian-metamodernism-the-neo-rave-and-cultural-recycling-of-the-1990s/ (accessed 20 June 2024).

Engström, M. 2023. 'How the '90s Have become a source of inspiration for pop artists'. *Russia.Post*, 18 May. URL: https://russiapost.info/culture/pop_90s#:~:text=The%20phenomenon%20of%20the%20%E2%80%9CSoviet,grey%E2%80%9D%20zone%20of%20Soviet%20culture (accessed 20 June 2024).

Figes, O. 2002. *Natasha's Dance. A Cultural History of Russia*. London: Macmillan.

Fisher, M. 2009. *Capitalist Realism: Is There No Alternative?* London: Zero Books.

Fisher, M. 2012. 'What Is Hauntology?', *Film Quarterly*, 66, 1, pp. 16–24.

Fisher, M. 2014. *Ghosts of My Life. Writings on Depression, Hauntology and Lost Futures*. Winchester and Washington: Zero Books.

Fitzpatrick, S. 2004. 'Happiness and Toska: An Essay in the History of Emotions in Pre-War Soviet Russia'. *Australian Journal of Politics and History*, 50, 3, pp. 357–71.

Forbes. 2019. 'Little Big'. URL: https://www.forbes.ru/profile/380223-little-big-ilya-prusikin?from_rating=380099 (accessed 7 May 2020).

Foster, R. 2019a. 'New Weird Russia – Part One: Sampler'. *The Quietus*, 10 January. URL: https://thequietus.com/articles/25864-new-weird-russia-shortparis-glintshake-review (accessed 7 May 2020).

Foster, R. 2019b. 'New Weird Russia - #2 Moscow'. *The Quietus*, 12 February. URL: https://thequietus.com/articles/26019-buttechno-glintshake-new-weird-russia-review (accessed 7 May 2020).

Foster, R. 2019c. 'New Weird Russia - #3 St Petersburg'. *The Quietus*, 19 March. URL: https://thequietus.com/articles/26174-new-weird-russia-st-petersburg-shortparis (accessed 7 May 2020).

Foster, R. 2019d. 'Brutal Russian Truth: Shortparis Interviewed'. *The Quietus*, 17 April. URL: https://thequietus.com/articles/26337-shortparis-interview?fbclid=IwAR2_ytWb-FGYkK3ZZaVQmJUOgO8NZGrInkhBYCgyEKNh1XLnHu597W5UiSA (accessed 7 May 2020).

Frometa, R.J. 2018. 'Premiere: Pompeya Release New Single "Do"'. *Vents*, 10 August. URL: http://ventsmagazine.com/2018/08/10/premiere-pompeya-release-new-single-do/ (accessed 7 May 2020).

Fukuyama, F. 1992. *The End of History and the Last Man*. New York: Free Press.

Galuszka, P. 2021. 'Contextualising Research on the Eastern European Music Industry'. In Galuszka, P. (ed.) *Eastern European Music Industries and Policies after the Fall of Communism: From State Control to Free Market*. Abingdon and New York: Routledge, pp. 3–21.

García, J. 2018. 'Human Tetris esta de vuelta con su Memorabilia Tour Latin America 2018'. *La Cartelera MX*, 27 March. URL: http://lacarteleramx.com/noticias/human-tetris-esta-de-vuelta-con-su-memorabilia-tour-latin-america-2018/ (accessed 7 May 2020).

From the Margins and Back? 257

García, O. 2009. 'Education, Multilingualism and Translanguaging in the 21st Century'. In Mohanty, A., Panda, M., Phillipson, R., Skutnabb-Kangas, T. (eds.) *Multilingual Education for Social Justice: Globalising the Local.* New Delhi: Orient Blackswan, pp. 140–58.

Gogov, R. 2014. 'Il'ich i Gokk (LITTLE BIG) – Interv'iu (Tula 31.10.2014)'. 7 November. URL: https://www.youtube.com/watch?v=SAozC_hdj7Q (accessed 11 October 2021).

Gomez, C. 2018. 'Human Tetris: Desde Rusia con Post-Punk'. *Ka Volta*, 20 June. URL: http://www.kavolta.com/2018/06/human-tetris-desde-rusia-con-post-punk/ (accessed 7 May 2020).

Gorbachev, A. 2015. 'How to Make It in America, Russian Indie Band-Style'. *Newsweek*, 6 June. URL: http://europe.newsweek.com/russian-indie-bands-take-america-328349?rm=eu (accessed 30 May 2020).

Gorbachev, A. 2019. 'Epokha Zemfiry i mumiy troll zakonchilas. Teper' vsyo inache'. *Meduza*, 2 January. URL: https://meduza.io/feature/2019/01/02/epoha-zemfiry-i-mumiy-trollya-zakonchilas-teper-vse-inache (accessed 12 March 2019).

Gorbachev, A. 2020. Public Post on Facebook. URL: https://www.facebook.com/alexander.gorbachev/posts/10222224188221642 (accessed 11 October 2021).

Gramsci, A. 1999. *Selected Writings 1916–1935* (Edited by D. Forgacs). London: Lawrence and Wishart.

Helbig, R. 2012. 'Human Tetris – Happy Way in The Maze of Rebirth'. *NBHAP*, 11 February. URL: https://nbhap.com/sounds/album-of-the-week-human-tetris-happy-way-in-the-maze-of-rebirth (accessed 30 May 2020).

Heller, D. 2007. 't.A.T.u. You! Russia, the Global Politics of Eurovision, and Lesbian Pop'. *Popular Music*, 26, 2, pp. 195–210.

Hill, J. 2014. 'Firsties and Faves: Pompeya'. *Noisey (Vice)*, 17 June. URL: https://noisey.vice.com/en_us/article/rb4qqr/firsties-and-faves-pompeya (accessed 30 May 2020).

Hutcheon, L. 2000. *A Theory of Parody: The Teachings of Twentieth-Century Art Forms.* Urbana: University of Illinois Press.

Hutchings, S. 2020. 'RT and the Digital Revolution Reframing Russia for a Mediatized World'. In Byford, A., Doak, C., Hutchings, S. (eds.) *Transnational Russian Studies.* Liverpool: Liverpool University Press, pp. 283–300.

Hutchings, S. 2022. *Projecting Russia in a Mediatized World: Recursive Nationhood.* London: Routledge.

IFPI. 2014. Global Report. London: IFPI.

IFPI. 2015. Global Report. London: IFPI.

IFPI. 2016. Global Report. London: IFPI.

IFPI. 2017. Global Report. London: IFPI.

IFPI. 2018. Global Report. London: IFPI.

Indie Birdie. 2012. 'Human Tetris'. *Indie Birdie*, 5 January. URL: http://indiebirdie.ru/2012/01/human-tetris.html (accessed 10 May 2018).

Ingham, T. 2019. 'English-Speaking Artists are Losing Their Global Pop Dominance – and YouTube's Leading the Charge'. *Rolling Stone*, 1 February. URL: https://www.rollingstone.com/music/music-features/english-speaking-artists-are-losing-their-grip-on-global-pop-domination-and-youtubes-leading-the-charge-786815/ (accessed 30 May 2020).

It's All indie. 2014. 'D/R/U/G/S remixes February's 'Saviour''. 17 October. URL: http://www.itsallindie.com/2014/10/drugs-remixes-februarys-saviour.html (accessed 30 May 2020).

Iwabuchi, K. 1994. 'Complicit Exoticism: Japan and Its Other'. *Continuum: An Australian Journal of the Media*, 8, 2, pp. 49–82.

Jameson, F. 2003. 'Future City'. *New Left Review*, 21, pp. 65–79.

Joinnus. 2017. 'Human Tetris'. URL: https://www.joinnus.com/PE/entretenimiento/lima-human-tetris-the-kvb-8328 (accessed 30 May 2020).

Kalish, I. 2018. 'Embark on Neo New Wave Time Travel with Pompeya's Dreamers'. *Atwood Magazine*, 16 August. URL: http://atwoodmagazine.com/pompeya-dreamers-album-premiere/ (accessed 30 May 2020).

258 Independent Music in Russia

Kavoori, A.P. 2007. 'Thinking Through contra-Flows: Perspectives from Post-Colonial and Transnational Cultural Studies'. In Thussu, D.K. (ed.) *Media on the Move. Global Flow and Contra-Flow*. London: Routledge, pp. 44–58.

Kayman, M. 2004. 'The State of English as a Global Language: Communicating Culture'. *Textual Practice*, 18, 1, pp. 1–22.

Kazakov, V. 2019. *Representations of 'New Russia' through a 21st Century Mega-Event: The Political Aims, Informational Means, and Popular Reception of the Sochi 2014 Winter Olympic Games*. PhD thesis, University of Manchester.

Kazakov, V., Hutchings, S. 2019. 'Challenging the 'Information War' Paradigm: Russophones and Russophobes in Online Eurovision Communities'. In Wijermars, M., Lehtisaari, K. (eds.) *Freedom of Expression in Russia's New Mediasphere*. London: Routledge, pp. 137–58.

Kobayashi, K., Jackson, S., Sam, M. 2019. 'Globalization, Creative Alliance and Self-Orientalism: Negotiating Japanese Identity within Asics Global Advertising Production'. *International Journal of Cultural Studies*, 22, 1, pp. 157–74.

Laruelle, M. 2021. 'Russia's Niche Soft Power Sources, Targets and Channels of Influence'. *Notes De l'Ifri, Russia Nei Visions*, 122, pp. 5–27.

Laruelle, M., Engström, M. 2018. 'Vizualnaia Kultura i Ideologiia'. *Kontrapunkt*, 12, pp. 1–17.

Lee, H.K. 2014. 'Transnational Cultural Fandom'. In Zwaan, K. (ed.) *The Ashgate Research Companion to Fan Cultures*. Farnham: Ashgate, pp. 195–208.

Legrand, E. 2012. 'Europe's Music Scene – A Mosaic of Talent United by One Language'. *Legrand Network*, 10 January. URL: http://legrandnetwork.blogspot.com/2012/01/europes-music-scene-mosaic-of-talent.html and https://legrandnetwork.blogspot.com/2012/01/music-crossing-borders-part-2.html (accessed 1 May 2020).

Lie, J. 2015. *K-Pop. Popular Music, Cultural Amnesia, and Economic Innovation in South Korea*. Berkeley, CA: University of California Press.

Look At Me. 2009. 'Human Tetris'. *Look At Me*, 13 October. URL: http://www.lookatme.ru/flow/posts/music-radar/74789-human-tetris (accessed 10 May 2018).

Louder Than War. 2014. 'Free D/R/U/G/S Remix from Russian band February'. 8 October. URL: https://louderthanwar.com/free-drugs-remix-from-russian-band-february/ (accessed 8 August 2018).

Lusso, F. 2017. 'Human Tetris'. *Whitelight/Whiteheat*, 7 November. URL: https://whitelight-whiteheat.com/new-music/human-tetris-picturesruins-single/ (accessed 10 May 2018).

Marc, I. 2015. 'Travelling Songs: On Popular Music Transfer and Translation'. *IASPM Journal*, 5, 2, pp. 1–21.

Martinez, F. 2013. 'On the Peripheral Character of Russia'. *e-Cadernos CES*, 19, pp. 54–84.

Mazierska, E., Győri, Z. 2019. 'Introduction: Crossing National and Regional Borders in Eastern European Popular Music'. In Mazierska, E., Győri, Z. (eds.) *Eastern European Popular Music in a Transnational Context*. London: Palgrave Macmillan, pp. 1–25.

McMichael, P. 2009. 'Prehistories and afterlives: the packaging and re-packaging of Soviet Rock'. *Popular Music and Society*, 32, 3, pp. 331–350.

Mezenov, S. 2018. 'Chto slushat' v iiune'. *Colta* 13 June. URL: https://www.colta.ru/articles/music_modern/18318?page=9&part=2 (accessed 30 May 2020).

Nabokov, V. 1990. *Aleksandr Pushkin, Eugene Onegin, Trans. V. Nabokov*. Princeton: Princeton University Press.

Nabokov, V. 2012. 'Problems of Translation: Onegin in English'. In J. Biguenet, J., Schulte, R. (eds.) *Theories of Translation: An Anthology of Essays from Dryden to Derrida*. Chicago: University of Chicago Press, p. 127.

Nederveen-Pieterse, J. 2004. *Globalization or Empire?* London: Routledge.

Noys, B. 2015. 'Dance and Die: Obsolescence and Embedded Aesthetics of Acceleration'. In Martínez, F., Runnel, P. (eds.) *Hopeless Youth*. Tallinn: Estonian National Museum Press.

Nye, J. 2013. 'What China and Russia Don't Get About Soft Power'. *Foreign Policy*, 29 April. URL: http://foreignpolicy.com/2013/04/29/what-china-and-russia-dont-get-about-soft-power/ (accessed 10 March 2017).

Odutola, T. 2018. 'Pompeya deliver 80s rock heat on "Hot Summer July"'. *Earmilk*. URL: https://earmilk.com/2018/07/13/pompeya-deliver-80s-rock-heat-on-hot-summer-july-video/ (accessed 5 May 2020).

Osborne, R. 2021. 'Music by Numbers: A Conversation About Music Industry Data Archives'. Public Talk Hosted by the Center for Theory, UTA College of Liberal Arts and UT Arlington Sociology, 26 April.

Ostorozhno, Sobchak. 2019. 'LITTLE BIG – uspekh Skibidi, kollaba s Kirkorovym i rep-battl s Navalnym'. 26 June. URL: https://www.youtube.com/watch?v=9BAfdAuZrNc (accessed 7 May 2020).

Oushakine, S. 2007. '"We're Nosalgic but We're Not Crazy": Retrofitting the Past in Russia'. *The Russian Review*, 66, 3, pp. 451–82.

Ox. 2011. 'Human Tetris – Russia After Midnight'. August/September. URL: https://www.ox-fanzine.de/web/itv/4065/interviews.212.html (accessed 30 May 2020).

Patyk, L.E. 2021. 'Little Big and the Viral Gesamtkunstwerk'. *Studies in Russian and Soviet Cinema*, 15, 3, pp. 227–248.

Phillipson, R. 2009. *Linguistic Imperialism Continued.* Hyderabad: Orient Blackswan Private Limited.

Pitchfork. 2020. 'The 50 Best Albums of 2020'. 8 December. URL: https://pitchfork.com/features/lists-and-guides/best-albums-2020/ (accessed 2 April 2024).

Platt, K. 2013. 'Russian Empire of Pop: Post-Socialist Nostalgia and Soviet Retro at the "New Wave" Competition'. *The Russian Review*, 72, 3, pp. 447–69.

Rancière, J. 2010. *Dissensus: On Politics and Aesthetics.* London: Bloomsbury.

Raykoff, I. 2016. 'Camping on the Borders of Europe'. In Raykoff, I., Tobin, R.D. (eds.) *A Song for Europe: Popular Music and Politics in the Eurovision Song Contest.* Abingdon and New York: Routledge, pp. 1–12.

Record of the Day. 2014. 'Saviour (EP)'. 6 October. URL: https://www.recordoftheday.com/record-of-the-day/2014-10-06/saviour-ep2014 (accessed 5 May 2020).

Reese, N. 2013. 'Exclusive Album Premiere and Interview: 'Tropical'. Pompeya'. *Interview*, 30 October. URL: https://www.interviewmagazine.com/music/exclusive-album-premiere-and-interview-tropical-pompeya#_ (accessed 5 May 2020).

Reynolds, S. 2005. *Rip It Up and Start Again: Postpunk 1978–1984.* London: Faber & Faber.

Reynolds, S. 2011. *Retromania. Pop Addiction to Its Own Past.* London: Faber & Faber.

Right Chord Music. 2014. 'Coockoo – Saviour (The Daydream Club Remix)'. 12 August. URL: http://www.rightchordmusic.co.uk/coockoo-saviour-the-daydream-club-remix/ (accessed 5 May 2020).

Robb, J. 2018a. 'Shortparis: MENT Festival. Live Review: Brilliant Russian Band Combine Post Industrial with Stunning Vocals'. *Louder Than War*, 2 February. URL: https://louderthanwar.com/shortparis-ment-festival-live-review-brilliant-russian-band-combine-post-industrial-with-stunning-vocals/ (accessed 5 May 2020).

Robb, J. 2018b. '"Moscow Music Week: Live review of the New Russian Wave of Bands on Their Home Turf". *Louder Than War*, 5 September. URL: https://louderthanwar.com/moscow-music-week-live-review/ (accessed 5 May 2020).

Salmon, L. 2015. 'Chronotopes of Affectivity in Literature. On Melancholy, Estrangement, and Reflective Nostalgia'. In Dickinson, S., Salmon, L. (eds.) *Melancholic Identities, Toska and Reflective Nostalgia Case Studies from Russian and Russian-Jewish Culture.* Florence: Firenze University Press, pp. 11–30.

Schiller, H. 1976. 'Communication and Cultural Domination'. *International Journal of Politics*, 5, 4, pp. 1–127.

Shifman, L. 2014. *Memes in Digital Culture.* Cambridge: The MIT Press.

260   *Independent Music in Russia*

Silverstein, J. 2013. 'Moscow Band Pompeya Brings in the Funk with 'Slaver''. *MTV*, 9 November. URL: http://www.mtv.com/news/2699327/moscow-band-pompeya-brings-in-the-funk-with-slaver/ (accessed 5 May 2020).

Sobaka.ru. 2015. 'Batl: Die Antwoord vs Little Big'. 29 January. URL: http://www.sobaka. ru/entertainment/music/33035 (accessed 6 July 2020).

Sobolev, O. 2019. 'Otvechai za slova. Pochemu samaia ambitsioznaia russkaia rok-gruppa Shortparis – ne to, chem kazhetsia'. *Lenta.ru*, 13 November. URL: https://lenta.ru/articles/2019/11/13/shortparis/ (accessed 21 October 2019).

Statista. 2015. 'Do you Listen to Music with Lyrics in a Language You Don't Speak?' URL: https://www.statista.com/statistics/803372/listening-to-foreign-lyrics/ (accessed 5 May 2020).

Stokes, M. 2013. 'Afterword: a Worldly Musicology? In Bohlman, P. (ed.) *The Cambridge History of World Music*. Cambridge: Cambridge University Press, pp. 826–42.

Strukov, V. 2021. 'The Future State Russian Cinema and Neoliberal Cultural Statecraft'. In Forsberg, T., Makinen, S. (eds.) *Russia's Cultural Statecraft*. London: Routledge, pp. 120–40.

The Village. 2020. 'Molchat doma interv'iu'. 4 January, https://www.youtube.com/watch?v=AOTFzveuniQ (accessed 20 January 2024)

Thussu, D.K. 2007. 'Mapping Global media Flow and Contra-Flow'. In Thussu, D.K. (ed.) *Media on the Move. Global Flow and Contra-Flow*. London: Routledge, pp. 10–29.

Thussu, D.K. 2015. 'Reinventing 'Many Voices': MacBride and a Digital New World Information and Communication Order'. *Javnost – The Public*, 22, 3, pp. 252–63.

Trefor, C. 2019. '7 Things We Learned at Lithuania's Loftas Fest'. *Gigwise*, 3 September. URL: https://www.gigwise.com/features/3361403/7-things-we-learned-at-loftas-festival-review-2019?fbclid=IwAR2mtZT0OkOEgOVmzBwO7IN1exlVOvRMzsrW09JnDeo W_U-BKLROFvfctxk (accessed 5 May 2020).

Vazquez, H.F. 2018. 'Human Tetris, de Moscú con passion: La banda rusa regresa a la ciudad para promocionar su trabajo y presentar algo de su material más reciente' *Informador*, 31 March. URL: https://www.informador.mx/entretenimiento/Human-Tetris-de-Moscu-con-pasion-20180330-0117.html (accessed 5 May 2020).

Vdud'. 2017. 'll'ich (Little Big) – o Kirkorove i khudshem video v istorii'. 21 March. URL: https://www.youtube.com/watch?v=Ojh02PksAGY (accessed 7 May 2020).

Vechernii Urgant. 2020. 'Gruppa Little Big o podgotovke k konkursu 'Evrovidenie''. 13 March. URL: https://www.youtube.com/watch?v=9lwYrfE6FA0 (accessed 5 May 2020).

Velichko, N. 2018. 'Kak Shortparis stala luchshei kontsertnoi gruppy strany'. *The Village*, 25 May. URL: https://www.the-village.ru/village/weekend/music/312977-shortparis (accessed 5 May 2020).

Wilkinson, D. 2013. 'I Found the Russian Die Antwoord'. *Vice*, 5 December. URL: https://www.vice.com/en/article/r79y8y/i-found-the-russian-die-antwoord (accessed 22 October 2021).

Conclusions

Nezavisimaia muzyka is a cultural practice interwoven in the fabric of Russian society and the layers of Russian history. In the period studied, it constituted a community-based and stylistically fluid musical movement that displayed, reviewed and expressed, in miniature, the ambitions, conflicts and anxieties of Russia as a whole. *Nezavisimaia muzyka* practitioners' primary aim was the creation of a collective autonomous space that swayed between antagonism, compliance or indifference in regard to the state, but was also rooted in national identity quests that at times overlapped with it.

These identity quests changed over the years covered in this book. Between 2008 and 2012 the dominant identity in *nezavisimaia muzyka* revolved around the assimilation of the musical Other (the West) into Russia, together with the hope of the integration of Russia into the West-led global scene. Representatives of the Anglophone Wave aimed to solve the perceived inferiority complexes left by the adaptation of Western rock performed in the late-Soviet period by their predecessors – the *russkii rok* musicians – by focusing on the sound, rather than the lyrical aspect of music. From the *russkii rok* musicians, the Anglophone Wave inherited the deterritorialised yet local construct of the Imaginary West. Unlike their Soviet predecessors, however, late-2000s musicians could now make the Imaginary West real and avail themselves of technological and media advancements to join an apparently open and globally interconnected market. In this context, the choice of singing in English seemed to kill several birds with one stone. In their eyes, it was functional to innovating Russian popular music, to associating themselves with a worldwide community and to filling the gaps between their music and the Other's music.

However, the independent music *tusovka* was brusquely awakened by the authoritarian repression of protest in 2012, including the Pussy Riot affair, followed by Russia's occupation of Crimea in 2014 and the instauration of a climate of increasing confrontation with the West. In this new milieu rose the New Russian Wave, a movement in divergence with the Anglophone Wave, aimed at emphasising the difference between Russia and its Other. One of its characteristics was the engagement with Russianness: influenced by Soviet and British post-punk, marked by the use of the vernacular and presenting a darker mood and (post)ironic ambiguity, New Russian Wave musicians commented on the conservative turn taking place

DOI: 10.4324/9781003248699-7

262   *Conclusions*

in the country. Firstly, the increase in Russian-language products among musicians proceeded together with the gradual fall from fashion of domestic English-language songs among the youth and with the important activity of cultural intermediaries, gatekeepers and tastemakers, who undertook the task to promote a new version of *nezavisimaia muzyka* steeped in cultural intimacy. Secondly, the political directness of Pussy Riot left space for a metamodernist and unsynhtesised process of undulation between opposing poles, between political engagement and apolitical detachment, between the desire to reject and embrace the new reality, between seriousness and irony and between the instauration of a grand narrative about Russia and the impossibility, or wrongness, of such narrative, not least because of the looming presence of the state in the background. Out of this oscillation, national belonging was articulated in such an ambivalent way that fused together mockery and empowerment, embarrassment and pride, posture and sincerity. In other words, the government's line of cultural sovereignty was at once espoused and belittled.

Strictly connected to this metamodern murkiness and avoidance of clear statements, *nezavisimaia muzyka* at the turn of the 2020s conventionalised *patrioprotest* (the ambiguous and indecipherable amalgam of endorsement of the nation and contestation of the state and its system) as one of the possible forms of artistic protest and civil resistance. More than a binary, musicians picked apart both the nation and the state, filtered which elements to endorse and which to resist, which aspects to welcome and which to dismiss, and then put it all together again to fashion a form of nonconformism that could withstand the increasing authoritarian system. At the same time, the state, in its multiple, loose and often disconnected incarnations, also reacted in diverse, enigmatic and contradictory ways to *patrioprotest*, at times repressing, at times not caring, at times even sponsoring it, like in the case of Manizha. *Nezavisimaia muzyka* thus reacted to state propaganda in a way that was multifaceted and extremely distinctive, and which did not fit into common schemes of outright resistance to, connivance with or submission to power. Such dynamics invite us to move beyond binaries such as "musicians vs. the state" when interpreting alternative, underground and "independent" music worlds, especially in illiberal places, for the participants of these worlds always embody a more complex and multi-layered reality than just channelling dichotomies.

Parallel to this musical evolution within Russia's borders, the 2010s witnessed an increase in *nezavisimaia muzyka* bands on the international stage. An active role in the transnational spread of *nezavisimaia muzyka* was played by new, DIY and self-financed agencies for Russian music export, which packaged and displayed Russophone post-punk as their primary product in the hope of increasing *nezavisimaia muzyka*'s sonic capital. At the same time, in perceiving their position as marginal, and singing this marginality in different ways, musicians occupied a niche in the globalised arena through expressions of *toska* (Russian post-punk) or self-stereotyping of negative – but eventually empowering – national tropes (Little Big). However, the international market continued to be dominated by unequal sonic capitals which, when interacting in the global arena, constrained the transnational flows of Russian music culture, often re-routing them into subflows. Moreover, first COVID and then the full-scale war in Ukraine frustrated most of

Conclusions   263

the community efforts and relegated Russian popular music to its traditional marginal space in the global context once again.

Overall, the different aesthetic operations conducted by the Anglophone Wave and the New Russian Wave were both performed with the purpose of placing Russia on an equal footing with the West and filling a perceived gap in cultural authenticity. Likewise, both the Anglophone Wave and the New Russian Wave were fruits of the socio-political zeitgeist and its fluctuations. The affiliation of *nezavisimaia muzyka* participants to a particular imagined community (mainly either internationalised or localised) reflected the general sentiment of Russians as well as the cultural policy that the state tried to promote in that specific period, from apparent openness and integration of the Medvedev term to patriotism and exceptionalism during Putin's third and fourth term. Fundamental turning points, reflecting this change in policy and perceptions were the Pussy Riot affair in 2012 and the Russia-Ukraine conflict in 2014, followed by the sanctions and Russia's increasing political isolation from the West.

One of the main indicators of this shift in music was language. As Russia gradually changed its system of identification in the course of the 2010s, English in *nezavisimaia muzyka* songs increasingly made way for Russian, signalling the move from a music that sought deterritorialisation to one that could be recognisably local, and from an identity that could be cosmopolitan to one that could be primarily national. English and Russian corresponded to particular philosophies and missions, responded to particular external pressures and their turnovers revealed the power struggles within independent communities and networks. English, constructed by practitioners as the language of the soundtrack celebrating the tangible transfer of the Imaginary West into local settings and the perceived transfer of Russia in the global music arena, was no longer tenable after 2014. In an isolated and autocratic environment, the universal and deterritorialised songs of the Anglophone musicians no longer chimed with the priorities of the *nezavisimaia muzyka* community. Musicians from the New Russian Wave espoused this new societal anxiety and used Russian to comment – with various intents but in a language that all local audiences could comprehend – on the conditions of their country.

This book has hopefully advanced our understanding of a key aspect of Russian society – Russian independent music – whose contemporary manifestations had not until now received due attention in Western academic literature. This work has demonstrated that *nezavisimaia muzyka* was a vital and significant societal segment that participated in shaping Russia's discourses of nationhood, including language, imaginaries of Russianness, paths of development, attitudes to globalisation and relationship with the Other. Correspondingly, this study has hopefully complicated concepts of resistance, subversion, compliance and indifference within independent, non-state-funded music communities and art worlds (especially under autocracies or outside "the West"), revealing how these attitudes were all intertwined and at times simultaneous and undiscernible in the context of *nezavisimaia muzyka*.

The music world examined in this book disappeared in February 2022. Not only did the war in Ukraine scatter participants across Europe and Asia, but it also prompted a major reassessment of ethical and aesthetical priorities for those who

264   *Conclusions*

remained in the country. In the Telegram post with which the book opened, the same music journalist wrote that:

> The 2010s as we knew them ended on February 24. It was an amazing time, when we suddenly became interested in looking at ourselves and figuring out what there is in us Russians that others do not have. When we were having fun and it seemed that we could quickly come up with interesting and exciting things. The twenties have now begun: a time of fear, confusion and despair.

The events since February 2022 demonstrated that Russian independent music may be independent from commercial imperatives, but not from state ones. Of course, independence, more than an achievable fact, represents a drive, a movement towards something which never reaches its objective. It is exactly the lack of independence that fuels the idea of independence and prompts practitioners to seek it. In the UK, for example, independence was initially conceived of as the construction of alternatives to capitalistic, vertical and corporate market structures, embodied by the major labels. At that time and in that context, independent music movements, such as post-punk and indie, tried to turn their back to the system and projected a horizontal and intellectual alternative from the bottom up, whose priorities did not include frontal opposition to the political. Nevertheless, because practitioners refused to play the corporate game, imagined a different space of possibilities and created a substantial cultural movement, independent communities entered in a conversation within the public sphere, which was indeed political. But while in the UK independence was constructed primarily in relation to the market, in Russia the ethos of independence was (and, I believe, continues to be) constructed vis-à-vis the state, with all that this entails: ideological intervention, oppression, interference, unpredictability, randomness and so on. The main political theatre was not and is not the commercial, but the authoritarian system. It is in this precarious space that *nezavisimaia muzyka* repeatedly found itself, caught between the desire to disengage from the state and the drive to respond to it; between the practitioners' turning away from the authoritarian system and the impossibility of sealing themselves off from its presence and, perhaps paradoxically, its influence.

This is not, of course, the same as claiming that the state and the musicians are similar entities. In this sense, I have simply attempted to reject the conventional and unchangeable dichotomy between musicians and the authoritarian state, arguing instead that interactions between these two groups of actors are characterised by instability and fluidity. Furthermore, I do not imply that such interactions will be the same after February 2022. In fact, it is likely that the full-scale war has signalled the start of a new chapter in the relationship between power and popular music in Russia.

Clear contours of this phase, however, are yet to take shape, as the industry finds itself in a moment of huge transformation and transition. This was also evidenced by the variety of reactions among music professionals to Russia's war in Ukraine. In the immediate aftermath of the full-scale invasion, many musicians contested the decision of their government (*Colta* 2022a). Others decided to cancel or postpone their concerts.[1] Articulations of powerlessness, emptiness and shock ran across practitioners' social media. Music professionals in various capacities wrote open letters to Putin demanding the immediate cessation of the conflict.[2] When it became clearer that protest or grief yielded little result, and that a major line had been crossed with no return, several musicians chose silence, not only as a viable option, but also as a survival strategy to avoid institutional backlash. Others, in protest, gradually emigrated, particularly to Georgia, Armenia, Serbia and Kazakhstan, where they have attempted to join the ranks of local music scenes (Tikhonov 2022). Indeed, the trajectory of *nezavisimaia muzyka* in the period studied can be seen as proceeding from the escapist, psychological internal migration of the Anglophone Wave to the actual external fleeing of the community. This mass emigration of talent created a vacuum which other professionals have tried to fill, often in opportunistic ways or by showing unquestioning support for the government. For example, the singer Shaman, with his patriotic song "Ia russkii" (I Am Russian),[3] experienced a striking rise to fame, from near anonymity to performing next to Putin himself in just three months.[4] A similar inclination to profiteering regarded those musicians participating in the "Za Rossiiu" music marathons in support of the full-scale invasion of Ukraine: according to *BBC Russia*, musicians received millions of rubles from the state for their performances (Churmanova 2022). Structurally, however, the new packages of sanctions on Russia have seriously harmed a music industry that in recent years had developed national and international infrastructure, and growth has been halted and reversed by isolation (Biasioli 2022; Bychkova et al. 2022; Zav'ialov 2022).

The state, for its part, has raised its interference in musical matters to the highest levels in post-Soviet Russia. If in the period between the Pussy Riot affair (2012) and the full-scale invasion of Ukraine the state preferred accommodation and exploitation over repression, now the latter has significantly increased. This is evidenced, for example, by the number of musicians who have been recently labelled "foreign agents" (Face, Morgenshtern, Oxxxymiron, Noize MC, Zemfira, Monetochka and Grebenshchikov, to name a few), an unprecedented occurrence in Russian history, as well as by the number of concerts that have been cancelled since the start of the war, due to the status of "persona non grata" of the musicians performing (*RBK* 2022). Cultural censorship is now more consistent than sporadic. State-funded, state-approved or even grassroots associations of moral zealots, once reined in by the Kremlin if overstepping their line, are no longer restrained in their attacks on cultural producers. The digital vigilante group *Liga bezopasnogo interneta* (The League for Safe Internet), has regularly harassed musicians by demanding the censoring of their lyrics, performances and videos, and by acting as one of the state authorities' watchdogs in reporting trespassers, mainly authors of anti-war messages and alleged "propagandists" of drugs or LGBTQ+ values. Some musicians who came under the stormy eye of the *Liga* have had to publicly apologise to its head, Ekaterina Mizulina, rumoured in celebrity tabloids to be Putin's new lover (Moran 2024) (and later, confirmed to be in a relationship with Shaman). The performers had to take a selfie with her or delete tracks in order to continue working in Russia in relative peace (*Prodolzhenie sleduet* 2023). As music critic Nikolai Ovchinnikov (2023) wrote, Mizulina became the chief pop star of Spring 2023 in Russia.

266   *Conclusions*

The atmosphere certainly possesses undertones of a new "cultural revolution" (Fitzpatrick 1974), when the Stalinist state unleashed fanatical radicals on those cultural figures whose loyalty to the regime it questioned. In this new climate, the same performers may commit to acts of public support (like playing in occupied territories) while also seeing their concerts cancelled by authorities in Russia (*Meduza* 2024a; 2024b). Tacit consent, or even silence, may no longer suffice: public, verbal and unambiguous endorsement is now more actively encouraged, and even those performers who had not made any public statements have appeared on the radar of the authorities (Meduza 2024c). The various points of the state apparatus are now regularly intervening in, and more intensely dictating, what musicians should sing about, in attempts to prop up patriotic unity. However, the common denominator of national cultural distinctiveness, which for the past ten years had provided the porous zone of contact between independent musicians and power, may no longer exist either, because authorities are now demanding support for the state instead of the nation. By blatantly losing its mask in attempts at self-legitimation, power may have lost its capacity to attract or co-opt cultural producers, and the gap between the state and grassroots culture may no longer be bridgeable through patriotic discourses around the nation.

So, was it all in vain? Obviously not. No authoritarian or totalitarian system will ever be able to suppress nonconformist individual or collective creativity. Art worlds survive, mutate and evolve in direct relationship with their constraints, but in the case of *nezavisimaia muzyka*, this may happen without many of the key figures that built it in the 2010s. Possibly, the new *nezavisimaia muzyka*, just like in the late Soviet period, will flourish in the interstices of society and ideology. Perhaps, the new generation of practitioners will cherish, learn from and use the legacy of their predecessors. Or, perhaps, they may rip it all apart and start again. Or, as has often been the case in Russian independent music, something in between.

Notes

1 See, for example, Monetochka's public Facebook post from February 28, 2022: https://www.facebook.com/monetochkaliska/photos/a.1118765372273536/1201670323983040.
2 "Obrashenie rabotnikov koncertno-teatral′noi i muzykal′noi industrii", petition on Google Doc from 26 February 2022, https://docs.google.com/forms/d/e/1FAIpQLSe ML I3bhycHZ4m7m4EukzymR6o8q_TF-z3eMfncfJ43UyRRZg/viewform?fbclid=Iw AR0EfToFpaTCoJ7khIfnwQ6vxcxSaKgD5CsrWPfxo44-BzIB-oKlxLd-P5Q; see also: *Colta* (2022b).
3 The video of the song is available here: https://www.youtube.com/watch?v=FAPwIE WzqJE.
4 The video of the performance in question is available here: https://www.youtube.com/watch?v=ZA5L-Pg3BAw.

References

Biasioli, M. 2022. 'How Russia's Musicians Are Taking a Stand Against the War in Ukraine'. *The Conversation*, 28 March. URL: https://theconversation.com/how-russias-musicians-are-taking-a-stand-against-the-war-in-ukraine-179997 (accessed 28 March 2022).

Conclusions 267

Bychkova, K., Riabova, I., Il'ja Gar'kusha, I. 2022. 'Kak sobytiia v Ukraine vliiaiut na muzykal'nuiu industriiu'. *IMI*, 25 February. URL: https://i-m-i.ru/post/war-impact (accessed 28 February 2022).

Churmanova, K. 2022. 'Gastroli patriotov: Kak kremlevskie eksperty i shou-biznes zarabatyvaiut na koncertakh 'Za Rossiiu''. *BBC Russia*, 11 May. https://www.bbc.com/russian/features-61401033 (accessed 3 June 2022).

Colta. 2022a. 'Rossiiskie muzykanty vystupili protiv voiny'. 25 February. URL: https://www.colta.ru/news/29616-rossiyskie-muzykanty-vystupili-protiv-voyny (accessed 27 February 2022).

Colta. 2022b. 'Rossiiskie muzykal'nye zhurnalisty vystupili protiv voiny'. 27 February. URL: https://www.colta.ru/news/29643-rossiyskie-muzykalnye-zhurnalisty-vystupili-protiv-voyny?fbclid=IwAR0jzOr1c__siEa4RIRm11A72rXIlaMqh7ye3SdsoGash4kvhAK-0dhdgv8s (accessed 28 February 2022).

Meduza. 2024a. 'My svoi vybor sdelali i khotim zhit' v svoei strane: gruppa Komsomolsk, kotoraia była v spiske 'zapreshchënnykh artistov', vystrupila v okkupirovannom Melitopole'. 28 February. URL: https://meduza.io/feature/2024/02/28/my-svoy-vybor-sdelali-i-hotim-zhit-v-svoey-strane (accessed 2 April 2024).

Meduza. 2024b. 'U gruppy Komsomolsk otmenili tri kontserta v Rossii'. 13 March. URL: https://meduza.io/news/2024/03/13/u-gruppy-komsomolsk-otmenili-tri-kontserta-v-rossii-muzykanty-popali-v-spisok-zapreschennyh-artistov-a-posle-etogo-vystupili-v-anneksirovannom-melitopole (accessed 2 April 2024).

Meduza. 2024c. 'Meduza publikuet novyi spisok 'zapreshchënnykh rossiiskikh muzykantov'. 8 February. URL: https://meduza.io/feature/2024/02/08/meduza-publikuet-novyy-spisok-zapreschennyh-rossiyskih-muzykantov (accessed 2 April 2024).

Moran, C. 2024. 'Did Putin Invade Ukraine to Impress His New Girlfriend'? *The Times*, 24 February. URL: https://www.thetimes.co.uk/article/did-putin-invade-ukraine-to-impress-his-new-girlfriend-k7pqtb6nr (accessed 31 March 2024).

Ovchinnikov, N. 2023. 'Glavnaia pop-zvezda vesny: razbiraemsia, vyrastit li Ekaterina Mizulina novuiu patrioticheskuiu pop-kul'turu'. *Kholod*, 6 June. URL: https://holod.media/2023/06/06/glavnaya-pop-zvezda-vesny/# (accessed 2 April 2024).

Prodolzhenie sleduet. 2023. 'Top prisposoblentsev shou-biznesa: kak prodaiutsia I pokupaiutsia deiateli kul'tury'. 7 July. URL: https://prosleduet.media/details/2023-07-26-conformism-in-culture/ (accessed 2 April 2024).

RBK. 2022. 'V SMI opublikovan spisok 'nezhelatel'nykh' v Rossii muzykantov'. 8 July. URL: https://www.rbc.ru/spb_sz/08/07/2022/62c811f19a7947321a049390 (accessed 2 April 2024).

Tikhonov, R. 2022. "Muzyka v relokatsii: kak artisty i deiateli industrii perenesli svoe delo za rubezh". *IMI*, 21 October. URL: https://i-m-i.ru/post/relocation (accessed 10 November 2022).

Zav'ialov, V. 2022. 'Kak zhit' bez Spotify, Rammstein i Garri Stailza: problemy muzykal'noi industrii v 2022-m'. *Afisha*, 15 July. URL: https://daily.afisha.ru/music/23549-kak-zhit-bez-spotify-rammstein-i-garri-staylza-problemy-muzykalnoy-industrii-v-2022-m/ (accessed 1 August 2022).

Index

Note: *Italic* page numbers refer to *figures* and page numbers followed by 'n' refer to notes.

Abramovich, Roman 83
adaptive authoritarianism 185
Aesopian language 171, 173
Afisha magazine 12, 16, 70, 78–79, 84, 87–88, 90, 95, 107, 108, 110–111, 123
Afisha's Picnic 84, 127
Agnew, V. 240
Agutin, Leonid 56
Anderson, Benedict 28, 53
Anglo-American music conservatism 214–220
Anglo-American imperialism 220
Anglo-American music 34, 56, 73, 77, 108, 214
Anglophone bands 2, 61n26, 69, 70, 73, 74, 81, 82, 86, 89, 95, 108, 119–121, 123, 124, 250; devaluation of internal others 120–126
Anglophone collective 73
Anglophone groups 69, 73, 120
Anglophone music 121, 215
Anglophone performers 16
Anglophone Wave 3, 5, 14, 15, 46, 50, 52, 57, 69–98, 103, 107, 108, 110–112, 115, 126, 261, 263, 265; *russkii rok* 72–75
Antidiler movement 161
anxiety: of influence 72–75
artistic autonomy 106, 225
artistic creation 104, 171
Artplay 83
art world 2, 4, 9, 31, 49, 115, 171, 179, 180, 263, 266
authenticity 15, 32, 104
authoritarian state 27, 92, 106, 156, 164, 166, 184, 197, 241, 264
autonomy 31; *see also* creative autonomy

Bakhtin, M.M. 59n12, 92, 93, 138
Balabanov, Aleksei 10, 76
Bartlett, D. 250
BBC Russia 183, 265
Becker, Howard 49, 171
Bloch, Ernst 93
Bloom, Harold 72
Boiarinov, Denis 229
Bondarenko, Iurii 176
Borenstein, E. 110
Bosco Fresh Fest 70
Boym, Svetlana 240
Brat 76
Brat 2 76
Brod, Daniil 95, 111, 124
Brodsky, Joseph 10
Buerak 5; "Passion for Smoking" 134
Butusov, Viacheslav 157
Byford, A. 8
Bykov, Dmitry 170

Chaadayev, Petr 61n27
Cherepanov, Artem 130, 131
Chicherina, Tatiana 10
Chikov, Pavel 161
Chukhrov, Keti 134, 135
circumlocution 171
civic identity 7, 8
civilisational identity 8
civil society 130, 195
collective identity 9, 50–51
colonialism, colonial, coloniality 7, 10, 11, 13, 54, 104, 145n24, 156, 188
Colouring Books for Adults (Raskraski dlia vzroslykh) 138
communities of practice 9
concert crackdown 161–163

Connell, J. 32, 217
Coockoo (band) 234–239
copyright 39, 40
cosmopolitanism 14, 27, 29, 50, 52, 78, 136, 143, 170, 187, 193, 194
creative autonomy 31, 33
Crossley, Nick 28, 49, 59n6
cultural/culture 3–4, 6, 7, 10–12, 14, 16, 27, 38, 43, 44, 46–48, 50, 51, 71, 74, 92, 95, 104, 114, 117, 126, 171, 174, 176, 188; artefacts 76, 242, 244; autonomy 115, 142, 158; capitals 83, 217; entity 54, 155; figures 7, 28, 117, 172, 266; flows 51, 77, 219, 238; formations 27; forms 10, 44, 75, 84, 159; hegemony 217; heritage 103, 105, 141; history 94, 155, 156, 170; identity 47, 117; imperialism 12, 51, 235; intermediaries 49, 105, 119, 127, 229, 262; intimacy 47, 117, 118, 135, 143, 262; legitimacy 2, 5; movement 14, 27, 197, 264; nationalism 105; policy 263; practices 28, 40, 51, 261; producers 4, 44, 47, 85, 95, 104, 106, 246, 265, 266; products 53, 76, 93, 154, 171, 195, 196, 220, 229; recycling 117, 242; repression 161, 170; revolution 266; sovereignty 15, 126, 144n6, 262; space 5, 56, 85; transformations 2; trauma 57
Cushman, Thomas 16, 159

decolonial, decolonisation, decoloniality 3, 7, 11, 52, 142
defamiliarisation 137, 138, 140
Deleuze, G. 113
Demont-Heinrich, C. 216
Derrida, J. 243
DiMaggio, P. 115
discourse analysis 18
Doak, C. 179
do-it-yourself (DIY) principles 29, 35
domestic Anglophone groups 69, 122, 142
domestic violence 18
Don't Be Shy: A History of post-Soviet Pop Music in 169 Songs 13
Doran, John 224, 254n19
Dorn, Ivan 13
Dostoevsky, Fedor 10
Dozhd 69, 96n2, 155, 159, 176, 195
Dud', Iurii 128, 155, 156
Dugin, Aleksandr 117
Durov, Pavel 39
Dylan, Bob 72

Ebert Fund's survey 155
economic growth of Russia 81
Eddy, A. 87
Einwohner, R.L. 174
Ekho Moskvy 79
English Language 2, 11, 87
Engström, Maria 7, 15, 19n4, 20n8, 29, 37, 46, 578n3, 104, 106, 112, 117, 138, 140, 141, 144n4, 154, 180, 228, 229, 240, 250
Erofeev, A. 153
ethnic identity 8
ethnicities 7
Etkind, A. 130
Eurocentrism 59n4
European Project 57, 78, 118, 119, 124
Evdokimov, A. 87
exoticism 9

Fedorov, Evgenii 41
Fest, Sasha 178
financial crisis 113
Fisher, Mark 30, 31, 243, 244
foreign agents 43
foreign audiences 225, 226, 229
foreign language 56, 108
foreign politics 96, 142
Forma 83
Foster, Richard 224
Friedman, J. 156
Frith, Simon 94
Frolova-Walker, Marina 8
Fukuyama, F. 243

Gakkel, Vsevolod 41
Galeotti, Mark 6
Garage 83
Gaufman, E. 153
Gazmanov, Oleg 157
Gazprom-Media 79
Geneva Universal Copyright Convention 39
Gibson, C. 32, 217
Giffney, N. 179
Glintshake 145n11
global culture 20n10, 58, 213
Global North 54, 112–113, 218, 220, 225
Global South 51
Global Village 51
Goldenzwaig, Greg 79
Gololobov, I. 20n12, 145n24
Golos 96n4
Goode, P. 163, 198n19

270 *Index*

Gorbachёv, A. 12, 57, 58, 62n32, 74, 78, 90–91, 93, 107–109, 111, 118, 119, 124, 175, 199n31, 229
Gorbunov, Evgenii 111
Gorbushka 39
Gordienko, Anastasia 60n17
grassroots music practitioners 104, 120, 143
Grazhdanskaya Oborona 19n1, 58n1
Great North 51
Grebenshchikov, Boris 156
Greenfeld, Liah 55
Grisha Urgant 43
Gritskevich, Nadezhda 107
Groys, Boris 134
Guattari, F. 113
Guriev, S. 172
Gyrdymova, Elizaveta (*see also*: Monetochka) 127, 138, 140, 141

hauntology 239–250
Herzfeld, Michael 47, 117, 195
Hollander, J.A. 174
homemade culture 44
Human Tetris 69, 218–219
Hutchings, Stephen 6, 229
Huttunen, T. 126
hybridisation 52

Ic3peak 163–167
Ikra 87
Imaginary West 14, 75–76, 79, 92, 96, 235, 238, 261, 263
imagined communities 28, 53
imperialism 10
independence 5, 31, 32, 35, 41, 44–46, 58n1, 166, 186, 264
independent bands 157, 213
independent communities 14, 42, 47, 71, 111, 263, 264
independent creative activity 1
independent culture 27, 41, 85, 143
independent music culture 17, 18, 48, 154
independent music festival 83
independent practitioners 1, 3, 8, 14, 27, 33, 34, 142
Indi 58n1
indie bands 12, 30–33, 52, 88, 127, 160, 161
Indiuki 58n1
Indiushata 58n1
informal economy 35
Ingham, Tom 30, 216

interference (state) 45, 46, 161, 163, 264, 265
intermediaries 49, 50, 52, 53, 117, 120, 122
internal otherness 11, 105, 126
international audiences 177, 190, 191, 228, 244
international markets 89, 262
international popularity 95
international recognition 15, 108, 218, 225
international stage 190, 226, 262
Inturist 222
Iurchenko, Ekaterina 177
Ivanov, Kirill 107, 108
Izvestiia newspaper 79

Jameson, Fredric 93, 243
Johnson, Emily 187
Jones, Rhian 31, 40
Jonson, L. 153

Kapkov, Sergey 84
Karmunin, Oleg 120
Kavoori, A.P. 220
Kazakov, Vitaly 198n17, 254n19
Kazarian, Stepan 56, 114, 116, 127, 128, 222
Khaski case 5, 175–179
Kholodkov, Danila 183
Khrushchёva, N. 37, 95, 106
Kiselёv, Dmitri 177
Kiseleva, Maria 140
Klein, B. 31
Kobayashi, K. 226
Kobrin, Vladimir 241
Kolstø, P. 112
Komiagin, Nikolai 2, 122, 174
Kommersant newspaper 1, 45
Komsomolskaya Pravda 162
Kostylev, Nikolai 164
Kotelnikov, Leonid 130
Kozyrev, Mikhail 155, 156
Krasner, S.D. 144n6
Kremlin 106, 113
Kreslina, Nastia 164–166
Kretov, Kornei 88
Kruse, Holly 32
kuchkists' 8
Kuleva, Margarita 83
Kurёkhin, Sergei 37
Kushnir, Aleksandr 59n9
Kuznetsov, Dmitrii (Khaski) 175, 176, 178
kvartirnik 45

Lacan, J. 98n27
Laruelle, M. 104, 113, 228, 229
Lazarev, Sergey 187
Lebrun, Barbara 32
Lee, H.K. 220
Leningrad Rock Club 38
Leonov, Leonid 170
Letov, Egor 116, 117, 182
Levada Centre 82, 98n22, 113
Levchenko, Lev 168
LGBTQ+ rights 28, 161, 171, 173, 180, 184, 186, 187, 189, 265
liberalism 3
liberal multiculturalism 29
Lie, J. 214
Liga bezopasnogo interneta 265
Likhachëv, Oleg 157
Limonov, Eduard 117
linguistic identity 7
Lisichkin, Gleb 107
literariness 73
Little Big 225–230, 251, 252
local Anglophone bands 50, 69–71, 81, 105, 109, 123
logocentricity 38
Look At Me (Skolkov) 82, 88, 89
Loseff, L. 170
Loskutov, Artem 140
Lotman, Y. 196
Louder Than War (Robb) 223, 237
Luvaas, B. 31
Luzhkov, Yurii 84, 129

MacFadyen, David 60n18, 89
magnitizdats 35, 59n8, 231
Makarevich, Andrei 159
Mamut, Aleksandr 83
manipulative smart power 194
Manizha 184–195, 192, 262
Marc, Isabelle 251
Martin, Terry 19n7
Mashnov, Viacheslav (Slava KPSS) 157
Matvienko, Igor 158
Mayakovsky, Vladimir 177
McLaren, Malcolm 60n24
McLuhan, Marshall 51
McMichael, P. 35
Meduza 109, 118, 141, 145n18, 161, 173, 175, 182, 183, 190, 194, 195, 266
Medvedev, Dmitry 3, 6, 71, 81, 82, 112
metamodernism 46, 103–146, 144n7, 153, 171
migration (of Russian music practitioners) 93, 252, 265

Mikhailov, Stas 146n34
modernisation 14, 71, 81, 82, 85, 95, 96, 111, 129
Molchat doma 219, 220, 239
Monetochka 5, 141, 142, 146n31, 173
moral consciousness 28
Morozov, V. 11, 104, 153
Moscow Music Week (MMW) 83, 222, 224
Moskva 24 188
Moss, L. 60n16
Motorama 81, 97n16, 218, 219, 221, 239, 241, 242
Mouffe, Chantal 196
MTV Russia 78
Mudrik, Sergei 43
Mulligan, Mark 30
musical events 83, 177
musical movements 32, 33, 261
musical production 29, 36, 37, 77
music cultures 14, 55, 219
music export 250; Russian agencies 221–224
music festivals 17, 117, 122
music journalism 13, 30, 43
musicking concept 48
music markets 42, 216–218
music professionals 45, 264, 265
music world 18, 28, 48–51, 85, 116, 197, 235, 239, 263

Nabokov, Vladimir 240
Naryshkin, Sergei 176
Nashe Radio 57, 62n31, 104, 105
Nashestvie 104–105
National Bolshevik Party (NBP) 117, 145n17, 155, 156
national character 8, 11, 141, 142
national identity 3, 4, 7–8, 14, 108, 120, 122, 126, 135, 197, 225
nationalism 3, 103, 113, 170
nationalistic zeitgeist 114
national security 155
national values 196
neoliberalism 31
neotraditionalism 3
Neumann, I.B. 113
New Russian Wave 3, 5, 15, 18, 50, 52, 56, 95, 103–146, 167–170, 175, 223, 261, 263
nezavisimaia muzyka 2–6, 14–15, 17, 27–29, 31, 33, 35, 37, 39–53, 55–57, 79–81, 85–89, 95, 96, 103–105, 107–109, 111, 114, 119, 122–124, 142–143, 153, 158, 160, 169, 218, 221–224, 250, 251, 261–266; from

272 *Index*

1990s to mid-2010s 38–41; ambiguous resistance 153–201; in English, Anglophone-only label 87–89; historical account 33–45; history, structures and politics 27–62; imagined community 28, 51–53; "independent" creators 40; intermediaries 122; mid-2010s to full-scale war 42–45; as music world 48–51; networks 85–87, 96; politics of 45–48; protest and Pussy Riot 109–112; Soviet "independent" music 33–38; transformations 124; transnational spread 213–255; in West 29–33; *see also individual entries*
Nezavisimaya Gazeta 171
Nooshin, L. 174
Nosov, Dmitrii 161
nostalgia 106, 117, 156, 225, 239, 240, 242, 243
Noys, B. 244
Nye, Joseph 195

Oborona, Granzhdanskaia 116
Obrazina, Anton 168
On-The-Go 70, 81, 84, 85, 88
Orientalism 228
Oskolkov-Tsentsiper, Il'ya 78, 84
ostranenie 137, 138; *see also* defamiliarisation
Ostrovsky, Nikolai 19n1
Oushakine, S. 128
Ovchinnikov, Nikolai 265
Oxxxymiron 176

Padabed, Natasha 229
Pain Festival 9, 42, 44, 107, 114, 130
Pain Generation *(Bol')* 126–131, 135, 137, 138, 169
Paltrow, Gwyneth 78
Pasosh 5, 222
patrioprotest 15, 46, 58n2, 153–201, 262
patriotism 103, 104, 113, 126, 155–158, 170
Paulson, Andrew 78
Pervyi Kanal 5, 69, 96n1
Peskov, Dmitrii 189
Peter the Great 54
Phillipson, Robert 217
Philosophical Letters (Chaadayev) 61n27
Piknik Afishi 70, 79
Pilkington, H. 55, 77, 121
piracy 39, 40, 41, 221
Platonov, Rachel 36, 97n5

political/politics 2, 27, 29, 31–33, 35–37, 39, 41, 43, 45–49, 51, 110, 111, 114, 142, 143, 153–155, 158–161, 177; aesthetics 154; agendas 69, 119; ambivalence 4, 174; beliefs 111, 113; convictions 160, 174; developments 114, 124; disengagement 36; elites 7, 76, 113, 119, 128, 137, 163, 167, 174, 185; environment 34, 119, 178, 194; escapism 90–95; indifference and non-involvement 158–161; openness 81; opposition 103, 171, 194; orientation 113, 143; power 27, 217; strains 14; system 33, 76, 159, 166, 169, 179
poly-peripherality 213
Pompeya 2, 3, 5, 52, 55, 69–70, 73, 79–81, 84–86, 88, 90, *90*, 91, 93, 94, 108–109, 225, 230–233, 251; and camouflage 230–233
pop music 77, 216
popsa 60n19
popular culture 10, 80, 117, 239
popular music 4, 5, 10, 11, 32, 34, 35, 54, 55, 71, 72, 87, 104, 213, 214, 217–219, 222, 251, 263, 264
post-colonial/postcolonial 3, 7, 113, 119
post-irony 37, 106, 107, 126 -131, 133, 138, 140, 142, 143, 169, 240
post-punk 2, 15, 28, 34, 44, 49, 57, 73, 116, 118, 218, 219, 220, 239, 245, 264
powerlessness 1
Present Continuous 241, 242, *242*
Prilepin, Zakhar 175, 178
Primakov, Yevgeny 144n1
Prof-Media 79
protest 155–158; music 158, 175, 184, 196
proto-market 41
Prusikin, Ilya 226
Pushkin, Aleksandr 10, 155
Pussy Riot 3, 4, 6, 15, 46, 106–107, 109–112, 129, 139, 140, 176, 196, 261–263, 265; "Freedom to Pussy Riot" 140
Putin, Vladimir 3, 6, 7, 81, 82, 95, 103, 104, 109, 113, 114, 128, 129, 140, 158, 163, 166

Qu, S. 30
queer 173, 179, 180, 187, 189
The Quietus 224

racial identity 7
Radishchev, Alexander 8, 61n27

Rancière, J. 153, 154, 197n1
RAO (*Rossiiskoe avtorskoe obshchestvo* – Russian Author's Society) 40
reactive nationalism 113
Redkin, Kolia 44
Red Wave 231, *232*
Repka, Anton 223
Reshetnikov, A. 153
ressentiment 55, 238
Reynolds, Jay 236
Reynolds, S. 241, 243
Right Chord Music 237
Rilke, Rainer Maria 128
ritual classification 115
Robb, John 223
rock music 36, 73, 76, 235
Rodnoi Zvuk 115, 123
Rogatchevski, A. 156
'Rossiia' (song) 136, 138, 141
Rossiiskaia gazeta 188
Rubchinsky, Gosha 104
Runet 79
Russian Anglophone festival 123, 124
"Russian Ark" 138–142
Russian doomer music 239, 245, *246*, 247, *247*, 248, *249*
Russian identity 29, 103, 107, 170, 184, 224, 230
Russian language 89, 114, 118, 123, 224
Russian isolation 112–120
Russian protests 167–170
Russianness 3, 126, 134, 135, 158, 170, 251; and post-irony 126–131
Russia-West relations 3, 14, 71, 142, 251
russkii iazyk 7
"Russkii kovcheg" 138, 140–142
russkii rok 4, 19n5, 33–34, 41, 46, 47, 57, 59n7, 72–75, 78, 104, 105, 111, 156, 159, 160, 261
Russophobia 185
Russophone 73, 121; diasporas 39; post-punk 239–250
Russo-Ukrainian war 6, 11, 14, 15, 43, 45, 54, 117, 119, 140, 175, 224, 251
Ryazanova-Clarke, L. 126

Samoilova, Iuliia 193
Saprykin, Iurii 79, 110, 141
second-world aesthetics 104
self-identification 7, 15
self-orientalism 226, 228, 232
self-releasing artists 30
self-stereotyping 225–230

Semenenko, A. 154
semiotic dynamism 197
Sevidov, Anton 74
shamanism 160
Shapovalov, Ivan 80
Sharafutdinova, G. 110
Shenkman, I. 180
Shevchuk, Iurii 61n30, 72
Shifman, L. 246
Shklovsky, Viktor 137, 138
Shortparis 2, 5, 122, 173, 179–184, 223, 224
Siberia 145n24
Simonian, Margarita 176
Skolkov, S. 82
Slavic identity 7
Slavophiles 57
Slavophilia 56
Slavophilism 54
Small, Christopher 48
Smertach Daily 130
Smirnov, Ivan 107
Sobaka 78
Sobolev, Oleg 254n19
Sobyanin, S. 84, 129
socialism 76
social media 17, 124
soft power 76, 184, 185, 195, 214, 217, 220, 222, 229, 251
Sokurov, Aleksandr 138
Sologub, Viktor 159
Solyanka 87, 89
Solzhenitsyn, Aleksandr 155
Sonevytsky, M. 174
songwashing 184–195, 200n48
sonic capital 15, 213–220, 224, 225, 251, 253n3, 262
Soviet culture 56, 229
Soviet rock 34
spin dictatorship 6
Sprengel, D. 174
state actors 6
state politics 12, 36, 126, 159, 194
state power 8, 33
State Programme for Patriotic Education (SPPE) 163
stëb 36, 37, 159, 171, 214, 226, 228, 229, 251
Steinholt, Y. 36, 38, 110, 156
stereotypes 226, 228, 232, 233
Stites, Richard 16
Stokes, Martin 214
strangeness 9

274   *Index*

"Strashno" 182, 183
"Strast' k kureniiu" 133, 134, *135*
Stravinsky, Igor 8
Strelka 84
Strukov, V. 194
subflows 15, 16, 213–220
Surkov, V. 119
svoikh 45

"Tak Zakalialas Stal" 2
tangible West 75–80
Taratuta, Iuliia 186
t.A.T.u. 75, 79, 80, 162, 193, 198n17, 225, 230; "Not Gonna Get Us" 198n17
Tequilajazzz 41
Tesla Boy 55, 56, 69–70, 74, 79–81, 84–86, 88, 108, 115, 124
Thussu, D.K. 220
Timati 178
Time Out Moscow 78
Tolz, V. 3, 7, 11, 12, 19n3, 29, 55, 56, 113, 146n24, 172
Toomistu, T. 36
toska 239–250
Toynbee, J. 40
transgressive consolidation 104
transnational communities 239, 251
transnational flows 15, 52, 218, 219, 262
transnational listeners 245
transnational subflows 214–220
Trefor, Cai 224
Treisman, D. 172
Troitsky, Artemy 39, 40, 108, 179
Tropical album 2, 90, *90*, 91–93
Tropillo, Andrei 34, 59n9
Trotsenko, Roman 83
Tsentsiper 79
Tsoi, Viktor 116, 117
Turgenev, Ivan 20n11
Turino, Thomas 50, 125
tusovka 38, 44, 85, 87, 89, 92, 115, 261

Ukraine 1, 3, 6, 7, 10, 11, 13, 14, 15, 47, 112, 119, 120, 139, 140, 142, 156, 171, 172, 174, 175, 178, 185, 224, 264, 265
union identity 7
Urban, M. 87
urban culture 78, 84
Urgant, Ivan 43, 69
ustranenie 138

Van den Akker, R. 46, 106
Vechernii Urgant 13, 43, 69, 96n1, 228
Vermeulen, T. 46, 106
Viardot, Pauline 20n11
The Village 16, 84, 87, 123
virtue signalling 184–195
visual culture 134, 182
VKontakte 39, 60n15, 115, 122
vnye 36, 59n11
vokal'no-instrumental'nye ansambli (VIAs) 34
Vysotsky, Vladimir 72, 97n5

Walser, R. 94
Weiner, A. 156
Western audiences 89, 174, 193, 252
Western capitalism 76
Western civilisation 55, 58
Western culture 114, 155
Western Europe 3, 9, 13, 29, 40, 54, 214, 252
Western indie 33, 70
Westernised cosmopolitanism 29
Westernising Petrine reforms 54
Western radio channels 75
Western rock 72–75
Western scholarship 33
West-European "colonial" consciousness 11
Williams, Ralph Vaughan 48
Winzavod 83
Wonderzine 186, 193
Woolf, Virginia 128
World Bank 81

Yablokov, Ilya 200n35
Yandex Music 42
Yanukovich, Viktor 112
Yoffe, M. 37
Young Pioneers club 59n9
Youth Cultures 79, 177–179
Yurchak, A. 14, 36, 37, 59n8, 59n11, 75, 76, 92, 159, 197, 198n14

Zaitseva, L. 162
"Za Rossiiu" music 265
Žižek, Slavoj 196
Zorky, Vasily 108, 144n9